SAMUEL BECKETT

Poet and Critic

Samuel Beckett
Poet & Critic

BY LAWRENCE E. HARVEY

PRINCETON UNIVERSITY PRESS

PRINCETON, NEW JERSEY

1970

This book has been composed in Linotype Times Roman
Printed in the United States of America
by Princeton University Press, Princeton, New Jersey

CONTENTS

PREFACE

Beckett criticism has proliferated in the decade since the conception of this study. Unlike the "indigent proliferation" in *Watt*, generation by critics of means has produced healthy offspring and enrichment. We remain relatively impoverished, however, in our understanding of the literary beginnings of Samuel Beckett. The present work, which studies those beginnings, will not usher in the Lynch family millennium. May it prove free of the worst of their afflictions.

Everyone presumably aspires to a certain order and harmony in the structure of what he writes. I am no exception. Unfortunately, for my purpose, Beckett did not lay out his life and writing in neat categories, and the logic in the organization of this book may easily escape even the perceptive and well-disposed reader. Since structure follows and reflects aims, which in this case are several and diverse, it may be useful to make these explicit. This book began as a study of Beckett's poetry. It remains that, first and foremost, and the division of the book into two parts, the first devoted to poetry, attests this primary focus. By and large I accept and follow Beckett's evaluation and have included in Part 1 only those poems he has allowed to be republished.

Several factors led me to expand the scope of the book. First, I discovered that the early prose, the "jettisoned" poems, and *Watt* contain elaborations, variations, and extensions of attitudes and aesthetic materials utilized in the collected poetry. These writings are considered in Part 2, especially insofar as they add to our understanding of the poems of Part 1 and of Beckett the poet. For this reason *Murphy* and *More Pricks Than Kicks,* which in this perspective have less to offer than "Dream of Fair to Middling Women," receive relatively less attention.

Beckett's poetry turned out to be less "self-contained" than is some poetry. It has its aesthetic dimension and its antiaesthetic dimension. It points both to itself as art and to its maker as man, existing in the outer world of time and space and the inner world of the "Nothing, than which . . . naught is more real." The poems are difficult, if not hermetic, primarily because they are filled with allusions to worlds beyond the world of poetry—to literature and philosophy, to Ireland and France and especially the Dublin and Paris that Beckett knew as a young man, to events in the life of the poet. While my chief purpose in discussing the literary tradition, geographical setting, and biography is to illuminate the poetry, there is another reason too. This complex was the habitat of the young Beckett, the universe of his loves and antipathies. Perhaps there is something more deeply human than idle curiosity that leads us to look beyond even privileged works of art to the human realities from which they spring. In any case, there is no easy breaking point between the best of Beckett's poems and their existential ground. It is my hope, then, that readers will think of these adjuncts to the poems less as dry sources than as living extensions of the total being that was Beckett during those years.

As we move through the collected poetry an evolution becomes apparent, an evolution in thought, attitude, and style that transcends the poetry. The last two poems Beckett wrote, published in the Addenda to *Watt*, are at once the clearest expression of the reality he reached at the terminus of his poetic evolution and the manifesto of the prose and drama to come, which he envisioned as explorations and *approfondissements* of this essential reality. These two little poems form, as it were, the ideal bridge between the early Beckett and the mature artist possessed of and by his vision and fully in command of his artistic means. But to understand these two poems adequately, with some sense of their implications prior to their development in the prose and drama to come, an investigation of general themes in the early prose and poetry (Chapter VIII) and above all a somewhat detailed analysis of *Watt* (Chapter IX) proved necessary. Happily, Jacqueline Hoefer's study of *Watt* as satire and Ruby Cohn's chapter on the comic gamut in *Watt* allowed me to concentrate almost exclusively on those aspects of the novel that are most directly related to the poetry of Beckett.

Such considerations eventually brought me to realize that even though my major concern continued to be Beckett's republished poetry, any radical isolation of that poetry for the sake of generic purity or logically attractive organization of my own work would be false to its very nature and to the character of Beckett as creative artist. His later prose and dramatic writing are densely poetic in the sense that narration and dialogue expand at every moment beyond storytelling and communication to produce the distance of aesthetic contemplation through images that in the context become emblematic of man's condition and destiny. When he writes in a reflexive mode—as critic and theorist—about the novel, drama, poetry, painting, and criticism and theory themselves, we become aware that the practitioner of poetry was not long in developing a consistent view of art as making that can apply not only to poetry, not only to the various literary genres, but to all the arts. The relevance of this view of *poesis* to the collected poems accounts for the inclusion of Chapter X, a discussion of the criticism and aesthetics of Samuel Beckett. Hence also the title, *Samuel Beckett, Poet and Critic*, which might have been rephrased *Maker and Thinker*: for *Poet* is used here to mean both maker of lyric poems and maker in the broader Aristotelian sense that points to attributes held in common among poets, novelists, dramatists, and other makers in such fields as music and the visual arts, while *Critic* hopes to suggest the philosopher of art, one who thinks about the nature of making.

Beyond these aims but within this plan of organization, there were several subsidiary problems to face. *Whoroscope* calls for a relatively extensive account of the life of Descartes, upon which it is based, if the unusual aesthetic experience it offers is to be fully available. Such an account seemed justified for other reasons as well. *Whoroscope* is a representation in miniature of much that is to come. Beckett lived for a time in the world of Descartes, and the dualism of the French philosopher helped to inform his own divided world. He wrote *Whoroscope* with a three-inch-high sheaf of pages filled with notes on the life and works of Descartes at his side. Nonetheless, for the reader wishing to turn directly to the essay on *Whoroscope* (pages 33-66), an option is open. The index entry "Descartes" will refer him directly to any topic common to poem and philosopher, and the entry "*Whoroscope*" will locate Cartesian sources for each section of the poem (given in full on pages 8-12).

Readers will differ on the relative importance of description and evaluation in the study of poetry. I have tried first of all to clarify obscurities due in part to allusiveness and elliptical statement, in part to originality of imagery, style, structure, and thought. In accord with those who hold that overall aesthetic judgments are the result of a thousand judgments of detail, I believe that whenever a critic calls attention to such things as metaphoric coherence, structural unity, variety and complexity, vivid and apt imagery, and expressive use of patterned sound, he is making implicit value judgments, for these are positive values in poetry. Although not infrequently I also mention what seem to me flaws in the early writing,

I am principally interested in what the French call a "critique des beautés." While I cannot claim that the poetry, with its more limited purpose and scope, is comparable to the major achievement represented by the later novels and plays, it has many values that make it important per se. Moreover, in it the voice of the later Beckett can be heard again and again once one has learned to listen, and its worth as an aid to fuller understanding of the writing that follows is certain.

To the best of my knowledge there is no wholly effective way to deal adequately and unrepetitively with both what is unique to each individual poem and what is common to a number of poems. In the study of poetry, however, abandoning either aim is still less satisfactory. I have sought to combine topical and holistic criticism in a way that minimizes the shortcomings of each, while tracing at the same time a general evolution in the art and thought of the author. Since my central objective is the poetry, biographical, geographical, and literary sources have not been set apart in independent chapters, as was common in the older "life-and-works" approach, but have been brought to bear as closely as possible on individual poems or groups of poems. In the early writing, sources are still a considerable aid to understanding. Later, although Beckett belongs to the romantic tradition in that dramatizing the self takes precedence over the creation of "objective" characters, knowledge of the macrocosmic Beckett is of decreasing utility as the cleavage between big world and little world widens and he writes more and more exclusively from that inner realm to which only he has access. Like Murphy, he now seems to prefer those zones of the mind without parallel.

The last, but far from least, objective of this volume is to make available to students and readers of Beckett previously unpublished or out-of-print writings that throw light not only on his literary beginnings but also on the works of his artistic maturity. For permission to use these texts I am deeply indebted to Samuel Beckett; but my debt to him is far greater, for without his unfailing kindness and patience during a score of conversations in 1961-1962 and 1964-1965 that often lasted far into the night, without the generosity of his faithful replies to the queries in my letters when research had failed to turn up answers, the foundations of this volume could not have been laid. For the sins of omission and commission I have unwittingly perpetrated by less than satisfactory critical interpretations, may I be forgiven.

I should like to express my gratitude as well for support from many sources: to the John Simon Guggenheim Memorial Foundation for a Fellowship, to the American Council of Learned Societies for a Grant-in-Aid, and to Dartmouth College for research assistance, sabbatical leave, and a Faculty Fellowship; to many colleagues at Dartmouth and elsewhere, and in particular for their unfailing encouragement to Germaine Brée, Ruby Cohn, Hugh Davidson, Eugene Falk, Judd Hubert, Herbert Myron, Leonard Rieser, and Elias Rivers; for their cheerful and apparently inexhaustible resourcefulness to Virginia Close and her staff in the Reference Department of Dartmouth's Baker Library; to Jennie Wells and Barbara Wade for all but flawless typing and proofing; to the capable staff at Princeton University Press, especially to R. Miriam Brokaw for continuing enthusiasm and sympathetic understanding as the deadlines came and went, and to Linda Peterson for intelligent, tactful, and thorough editing; and finally to one most deserving of thanks and least willing to accept them, to my wise and patient wife, Sheila, to whom I dedicate this book.

L.E.H.

Hanover, New Hampshire
June 1969

Part 1 • Beckett the Poet

i. Cartesian Beginnings

The Biographical Poem and the Problem of Allusion

Whoroscope, the first important work of Samuel Beckett, appeared in 1930 in Paris. It was written in English by an Irishman about a Frenchman, René Descartes. It won a prize in a contest for the best poem on time and was published by Nancy Cunard at The Hours Press. For those who know the later Beckett, it will be hard not to make too much of these summary indications. The half-bitter comic touch in the play on words within the title; the profound commentary on time and the human condition that lies scarcely concealed beneath the sardonic humor; the nationalisms that dissolve into the universal, the aspatial and atemporal qualities of an art that is at once highly stylized and very concrete; and the ironic *préciosité* of the correspondence between subject, title, and press (carried out graphically on the cover, where the letters of The Hours Press form the circle and hands of a clock): all this and much more of what is to come seem to emerge from an initial dip into *Whoroscope*, as the past from Proust's cup of tea.

The allusion is not simply fortuitous, and it is perhaps well, before entering into a discussion of the poem itself, to mention the two authors whose names must be linked with the poem, not in terms of influence necessarily—this is not the focus of the present study—but rather because of artistic and intellectual affinity. Of somewhat less importance for *Whoroscope*, yet on the surface the more obvious candidate, is T. S. Eliot with *The Waste Land*. While the two poems share a number of characteristics (e.g., the use of discontinuous form), the most striking similarity and one that provides a ready way into the central problem of *Whoroscope* is the technique of allusiveness, and more specifically the apparatus of notes accompanying both poems. The basic question is whether the notes are to be considered part of the poem, products of the artist qua artist, or external elucidations of the poem's obscurities, that is, appendages affixed by the artist acting as scholar or critic.[1]

---

[1] Beckett's notes were not part of the original text. They were added at the request of Nancy Cunard. Nonetheless, since the author acceded to her judg-

3

W. K. Wimsatt, Jr., in "The Intentional Fallacy," argues in favor of the former position.[2] He quotes F. O. Matthiessen on internal allusion: "If one reads these lines with an attentive ear and is sensitive to their sudden shifts in movement, the contrast between the actual Thames and the idealized vision of it during an age before it flowed through a megalopolis is sharply conveyed by that movement itself, whether or not one recognizes the refrain to be from Spenser," and again, on the use of the notes: "Nearly everything of importance . . . that is apposite to an appreciation of *The Waste Land* has been incorporated into the structure of the poem itself, or into Eliot's notes." Wimsatt goes on to give several examples of the ironic use of notes that oppose to vulgar reality the idealization of poetry and myth and concludes that "Ultimately, the inquiry must focus on the integrity of such notes as parts of the poem. . . ."

In his effort to clarify the anachronistic but persistent confusion between the intention and the performance of the artist, between psychological or biographical studies and literary criticism, Wimsatt is led quite naturally in this discussion to make a rather sharp break between art and life, or at least to leave such a general impression with the reader. He is worried because "As a poetic practice allusiveness would appear to be in some recent poems an extreme corollary of the romantic intentionalist assumption . . . ," and he states firmly in closing: "critical inquiries are not settled by consulting the oracle," i.e., the author. I am not taking issue with Mr. Wimsatt and am well aware that he is very much concerned with the relationship between art and other forms of human activity, that he has, indeed, in his essay on the Chicago critics, written against a definition of poetry that is "strictly self-contained." Nonetheless, the logic of his argument on allusiveness and intentionalism leads him here to an either/or position: either notes must be a part of the work of art or else they must be the separate adjunct of a critic and aimed at clarifying that work. What I wish to do now is to explore

ment and has kept the notes in subsequent editions of *Whoroscope*, and since it would be difficult to rule out the influence, at some aesthetically operative level, of a creative as well as scholarly impulse in the author, the question subsists. It subsists all the more surely if we grant to poem and notes an autonomous, public existence.

[2] In *The Verbal Icon* (Lexington: University of Kentucky Press, 1954), pp. 3-18.

the possibility that there may be a third choice, a use of allusion that is at once poetic and antipoetic or vital.

Let us, first of all, admit two things: that the poem without Beckett's notes will hardly make much sense to the uninitiated reader and that, even with his assistance, much of the referential meaning of a number of passages remains obscure. For example, in lines 17 and 18 the narrator challenges: "Faulhaber, Beeckman and Peter the Red,/ come now in the cloudy avalanche. . . ." Without the help of the notes and unless the reader happens to be a Descartes specialist or at least remembers that Descartes was Seigneur du Perron or other bits of still more arcane information, he is unlikely to know even that Descartes is the narrator of the poem, let alone who Faulhaber and company are. The poet helps out by telling us that "He solved problems submitted by these mathematicians," but makes no effort to describe in any way the complex personal and intellectual relationships that existed between the three men and Descartes. As for the "cloudy avalanche," even the specialist may be excused for having forgotten about Descartes' interest in the avalanche effect in clouds, which he studied in the Alps and held responsible for the phenomenon of thunder; yet Beckett gives the reader no help on this point.

One purpose of the notes, then, is to provide some information for the reader. However, this is a secondary function, and it is essential to mark well the fact that Beckett provides considerably less than the minimum amount of information necessary to a full comprehension of all the allusions. The "cloudy avalanche" is one example among scores. For the four pages of richly allusive poetic language that comprise the work itself, there are only one and a half pages of dry, laconic, discursive notes. Instead of amplifying, the notes contract the text, squeeze out the juice of poetic life, and keep only a bare skeleton of biographical facts, a skeleton with a number of bones missing. The poem and the notes are in this sense sharply opposed, and the opposition reflects a prior contrast suggested by the discontinuous and freely associative structure of the poem—a contrast between the richness of a whole human lifetime and the paucity of the scattered recollections of a dying man that recapture so little of the past. And at this point we move from a first affinity, T. S. Eliot, to a second, Marcel Proust.

It is no accident that in the year following the publication of

Whoroscope Beckett brought out a monograph on Proust. In a sense *Whoroscope* attempts in poetic form what *A la recherche du temps perdu* effects in prose, a resuscitation of the past in all its integrity. In another and very important sense it is the *revers de la médaille*, for it expresses an experience of privation rather than gain, the tragic conviction that only a tiny fraction of lost time can be resurrected and, concomitantly, that present time is running out. The negative conclusion no doubt accounts for the extreme condensation of the work.[3] It also accounts, I believe, for the structure of receding planes, from the real life of Descartes to the narrator's brief recollections to the still briefer notes of the author. Such a telescoping effect—paralleled within the poem by reductive narrative shifts, in time from the fuller past to the more meager present and in space from the more southerly Europe of earlier days to the frigid climes of Sweden—creates a very poignant and powerful sense of vital contraction, of a life diminishing through time.

Eliot's notes function in several ways. For one thing, they help form a collection of poetic moments that can be set against the aridity of the modern waste land. "I sat upon the shore/Fishing, with the arid plain behind me," says the narrator, and again: "These fragments I have shored against my ruins." In *Whoroscope* the effect is the opposite. The notes are the arid remains, the dehumanized fragments, picked up by an outsider, of what was once living, and vital, and personal. This passage, for example:

> And Francine my precious fruit of a house-and-parlour foetus!
> What an exfoliation!
> Her little grey flayed epidermis and scarlet tonsils!
> My one child
> scourged by a fever to stagnant murky blood—

becomes in the notes, "His daughter died of scarlet fever at the age of six."

From the foregoing discussion it would seem perfectly possible to choose the first alternative suggested by Wimsatt and consider *Whoroscope* in its entirety as falling within the realm of fiction. The artistic materials are simply divided, according to a definite plan

---

[3] In purely practical terms, Beckett's brevity can be explained by the rules of the contest. The prize was for a poem of *not more* than one hundred lines. But the sonnet prospered for centuries in spite of—or perhaps because of—much more stringent restrictions. Art may thrive on obstacles.

6

and in order to achieve specific aesthetic ends, between the poem itself and the notes; the narrator is not the real but a fictionalized Descartes (plenty of evidence exists in the poem to support this view); and the annotator is not Samuel Beckett but one of the characters in the dramatic economy of the work. His is the role of the scholar, and his activity, as we have seen, is less to preserve the past from oblivion than to reduce it to desiccated fragments, certainly a role less worthy than that of the narrator-poet whose fragments are yet infused with life, even though they are no more than shadows on the cave wall.

If certain of the artistic effects of the poem are explained by such a view, others are not. Why the choice of a real—and famous— historical person, why the decision to employ notes, if not to break the fictional illusion again and again throughout the course of the poem? To adopt the first alternative exclusively would be to obscure a fundamental characteristic of Beckett's writing, the interplay between life and art. Even though the notes have an aesthetic function, *Whoroscope* is not self-contained art. It begins in reality with the life of René Descartes and ends in reality with the notes of Samuel Beckett; and within the poem, as well, the oscillation between past and present invites the reader to participate in a sequence of engagements and disengagements that links the life of the narrator to human existence in general. All art, of course, both engages the reader in its own world and implicates nonfictional reality, but the pure or self-contained tendency that is one of the two poles of art minimizes the art-life relationship, while Beckett shakes the reader mercilessly back and forth between fiction and reality. There is no place here for escapist aestheticism.

To the degree that the reader identifies with the narrator, he participates in the experience of Proustian recollection. The notes help to portray the concomitant experience of loss beyond recall of most of the past. No doubt the ideal reader would be one whose sense of both the vital reality of the gain and the enormity of the loss is keenest, Descartes himself perhaps, and after him a reader who had, some time before, immersed himself in the life and writings of Descartes, who would be dimly aware, although unable to bring it back into full consciousness, of the wealth of human existence hovering beyond and between the fragments of the poem. It is best, I think, at this point to face up to the fact that without some knowledge of the life of Descartes a full and satisfactory response to

7

Whoroscope is hardly possible. This is perhaps one reason Beckett abandoned the biographical poem and sought other literary forms to recreate what is essentially the same human experience inscribed here. And the notes, while their two principal functions are aesthetic, do provide some necessary elucidation of the text and, further, by their very inadequacy, invite the reader (and impel the scholar) to the life and writings of Descartes. If this be erudition, at least we can argue a direct aesthetic end as well as the goal of critical comprehension to justify it. In addition, then, to the following episodes, which are of major importance for *Whoroscope*, the reader is referred to the more extensive and detailed material in the original French and Latin.[4] In the translations I have sought to steer a course between essential accuracy and literalness and have felt free to omit parts of passages where desirable in order to achieve greater conciseness.

WHOROSCOPE

What's that?
An egg?
By the brothers Boot it stinks fresh.
Give it to Gillot.

Galileo how are you
and his consecutive thirds!
The vile old Copernican lead-swinging son of a sutler!
We're moving he said we're off—Porca Madonna!
the way a boatswain would be, or a sack-of-potatoey
    charging Pretender.
That's not moving, that's *moving*.   10

What's that?
A little green fry or a mushroomy one?
Two lashed ovaries with prostisciutto?
How long did she womb it, the feathery one?

---

[4] Two works are indispensable: *Oeuvres de Descartes*, ed. Charles Adam and Paul Tannery (Paris: Léopold Cerf, 1897-1910), Vols. I-XII, of which Vol. XII by Charles Adam is a historical study entitled *Vie & oeuvres de Descartes*; and Adrien Baillet, *La Vie de Monsieur Descartes* (Paris: Daniel Horthemels, 1691), Vols. I-II. Numbers preceded by AT or B and enclosed in parentheses refer to these two works, numbers in parentheses to the lines of *Whoroscope*, which is given in full above.

Three days and four nights?
Give it to Gillot.

Faulhaber, Beeckman and Peter the Red,
come now in the cloudy avalanche or Gassendi's sun-red
   crystally cloud
and I'll pebble you all your hen-and-a-half ones
or I'll pebble a lens under the quilt in the midst of day.
20

To think he was my own brother, Peter the Bruiser,
and not a syllogism out of him
no more than if Pa were still in it.
Hey! pass over those coppers,
sweet millèd sweat of my burning liver!
Them were the days I sat in the hot-cupboard throwing
   Jesuits out of the skylight.

Who's that? Hals?
Let him wait.

My squinty doaty!
I hid and you sook.
30
And Francine my precious fruit of a house-and-parlour
   foetus!
What an exfoliation!
Her little grey flayed epidermis and scarlet tonsils!
My one child
scourged by a fever to stagnant murky blood—
blood!
Oh Harvey belovèd
how shall the red and white, the many in the few,
(dear bloodswirling Harvey)
eddy through that cracked beater?
40
And the fourth Henry came to the crypt of the arrow.

What's that?
How long?
Sit on it.

A wind of evil flung my despair of ease
against the sharp spires of the one
lady:
not once or twice but . . . .

9

(Kip of Christ hatch it!)
in one sun's drowning   50
(Jesuitasters please copy).
So on with the silk hose over the knitted, and the morbid
    leather—
what am I saying! the gentle canvas—
and away to Ancona on the bright Adriatic,
and farewell for a space to the yellow key of the
    Rosicrucians.
They don't know what the master of them that do did,
that the nose is touched by the kiss of all foul and sweet
    air,
and the drums, and the throne of the faecal inlet,
and the eyes by its zig-zags.
So we drink Him and eat Him   60
and the watery Beaune and the stale cubes of Hovis
because He can jig
as near or as far from His Jigging Self
and as sad or lively as the chalice or the tray asks.
How's that, Antonio?

In the name of Bacon will you chicken me up that egg.
Shall I swallow cave-phantoms?

Anna Maria!
She reads Moses and says her love is crucified.
Leider! Leider! she bloomed and withered,   70
a pale abusive parakeet in a mainstreet window.

No I believe every word of it I assure you.
Fallor, ergo sum!
The coy old frôleur!
He tolle'd and legge'd
and he buttoned on his redemptorist waistcoat.
No matter, let it pass.
I'm a bold boy I know
so I'm not my son
(even if I were a concierge)   80
nor Joachim my father's
but the chip of a perfect block that's neither old nor new,
the lonely petal of a great high bright rose.

10

Are you ripe at last,
my slim pale double-breasted turd?
How rich she smells,
this abortion of a fledgling!
I will eat it with a fish fork.
White and yolk and feathers.
Then I will rise and move moving   90
toward Rahab of the snows,
the murdering matinal pope-confessed amazon,
Christina the ripper.
Oh Weulles spare the blood of a Frank
who has climbed the bitter steps,
(René du Perron . . . . !)
and grant me my second
starless inscrutable hour.

NOTES

René Descartes, Seigneur du Perron, liked his omelette made of
eggs hatched from eight to ten days; shorter or longer under the
hen and the result, he says, is disgusting.

He kept his own birthday to himself so that no astrologer could
cast his nativity.

The shuttle of a ripening egg combs the warp of his days.

Line

3   In 1640 the brothers Boot refuted Aristotle in Dublin.

4   Descartes passed on the easier problems in analytical
geometry to his valet Gillot.

5-10   Refer to his contempt for Galileo Jr. (whom he confused
with the more musical Galileo Sr.), and to his expedient
sophistry concerning the movement of the earth.

17   He solved problems submitted by these mathematicians.

21-26   The attempt at swindling on the part of his elder brother
Pierre de la Bretaillière—The money he received as a
soldier.

27   Franz Hals.

29-30   As a child he played with a little cross-eyed girl.

31-35   His daughter died of scarlet fever at the age of six.

37-40   Honoured Harvey for his discovery of the circulation of
the blood, but would not admit that he had explained the
motion of the heart.

11

The Basis in Reality

Even the title of Beckett's poem has its source in the events of Descartes' life. A letter to Mersenne dated January 29, 1640 speaks of one Hortensius who had his horoscope cast while in Italy. His death was foretold for 1639 and the deaths of the two young men with him for shortly thereafter. "Now when he did die this summer ...," writes Descartes, "these two young men were so shocked and filled with apprehension that one of them has already died and the other ... is so languishing and depressed that he seems to be doing his best to prove the accuracy of the astrologers. What a fine science that makes people die who might otherwise not have been even sick" (AT, III, 4). Almost ten years later Descartes has not forgotten his aversion for "astrology, chiromancy, and other such stupidities," for he writes on April 9, 1649 to ask Schooten to remove from his portrait the words "natus die ultimo martii 1596." He fears he might seem to be party to the errors of the horoscope-makers by furnishing the date of his birth (AT, V, 336).

While Descartes sometimes denied being opposed to scholasticism and, beyond the philosophy of the schools, to Aristotle, he had his anti-Aristotelian and antischolastic moments, so it is not surprising that the poem begins on such a note with a reference to the

Boot brothers (3), who attacked Aristotle in a book published in Dublin. Since Beckett was himself born in Dublin, the reference, if it cannot be considered a kind of signature attesting in itself the anti-Aristotelianism of the author, at least suggests that the boundaries between fiction and reality are not impassable. At the same time, the source in Descartes is indisputable, for Regius writes to Descartes in 1642 that every day "la Philosophie ancienne" or better the "manière ancienne de philosopher" becomes the object of new attacks by new philosophers. The Boot brothers, Dutch doctors in London, publish in Dublin in 1642 a book attacking Aristotle— and the internationalism is once again striking (B, II, 175).

The second section of *Whoroscope* (5-10) concerns another great figure taken from the real world, this time a contemporary of Descartes, Galileo Galilei. As in the case of Aristotle, Descartes' attitude toward the great Italian scientist seems ambivalent. There is, however, some basis in reality for the scornful tone of the passage. In 1638 Descartes wrote to Mersenne that he had never seen Galileo, had never had any communication with him, and therefore could not have borrowed any of his ideas. "In addition," writes Descartes, "I see nothing in his works that makes me envious and practically nothing that I would want to acknowledge as my own" (AT, II, 388-389). Earlier in the same letter, after praising Galileo, he adds, "But it seems to me that he is greatly at fault in that he digresses continually and never thoroughly explains any given subject; which shows that he has not organized his material nor considered the fundamental causal principles of nature but has sought out only the reasons for a few specific phenomena and has, therefore, built on sand" (AT, II, 380).

As Beckett points out in the notes, Descartes may have confused Galileo with his more musical father. He does indeed write on one occasion that the best of Galileo is to be found in his book on music and goes on to defend himself against charges of plagiarism.[5] "But those who know me could easily believe that he might have taken his ideas from me rather than the reverse. For I had written almost the same things nineteen years ago, and then I had not yet been in Italy." Baillet asserts that Descartes quite probably confused the scientist son with his father, Vincenzo Galilei of Florence, learned in mathematics and especially in music (B, I, 124-125). Given

---

[5] Descartes' *Compendium musicae*, written in 1618, was published in Holland in 1650 and in Paris (French translation) in 1664.

such a confusion between the two Galilei and given Descartes' pro-modern and antitradition bias (to the degree that it existed), it is not hard to understand his somewhat contemptuous attitude. Descartes uses the phrase "consecutive thirds" (6) in a passage from a letter to Mersenne dated May 15, 1634, where he argues against "musicians who refuse to recognize differences between half tones" (AT, I, 295-296).

Line 7 is richly suggestive of the Copernican-Ptolemaic disputes of the time, in which Galileo's brilliance, sarcasm, enthusiastic zeal, and potent dialectic played such a part. "Lead-swinging" no doubt refers to his work on the application of the pendulum to the regula-tion of clockwork, and it helps to evoke an atmosphere of vigorous and dangerous debate, but its primary meaning in this context—to translate an English idiom into its rough equivalent in American colloquial speech—is "bull-slinging." "Son of a sutler" achieves similar results by its reference to armies and warfare but also by its association with such expressions as "son of a bitch." The subtle effect of an alliteration that attenuates the harshness of the line and introduces a note that verges on the comic is characteristic of Beckett's manner. A very concrete, down-to-earth, and often brutal reality is stylized, comprehended, set at a distance by a small but potent dosage of wry humor. The allusion to Galileo's antecedents in this same expression echoes Baillet, who calls the house of Descartes one of the noblest and oldest in Touraine and adds that "those who profess to scorn such considerations will perhaps say that his birth, because it was a little too illustrious, kept him further from philosophy than it might have, had it been as undistinguished as Gassendi's or possessed the shortcomings of the birth of the famous Galileo" (B, I, 2).

The phrase "charging Pretender," while functioning primarily as an image relating to the Galilean discussions of relative motion, maintains at the same time the atmosphere of conflict and recalls a whole period of Descartes' early life during the Thirty Years' War (AT, XII, 40, 47, 60; B, I, 41-42). Both the image of the boatswain and the horseman in line 9 include the idea of simultaneous motion and immobility. The sailor moves away from the land but is motionless in relation to the ship that carries him. Like a sack of potatoes that limply follows each motion of the horse that carries it, the charging horseman can only pretend to be moving, for in rela-tion to the horse he is stationary. It is the horse that is moving.

Similar illustrations are used by Galileo in his *Dialogo dei massimi sistemi* and elsewhere in order to discredit the evidence of the senses and prove the rotation of the earth. The image of the moving ship and the stationary passenger or merchandise recurs often.

Descartes was similarly preoccupied with the concept of relative motion. Beckett's note links line 10, "That's not moving, that's *moving*," to "his expedient sophistry concerning the movement of the earth," which is clearly a reference to passages such as the following (AT, XII, 377-379):

> . . . Descartes is concerned with the movement of a solid in or with a liquid or fluid; let us frankly admit that he is concerned with the movement of the earth along with the matter enveloping it . . . around the sun, which he would like to make acceptable by showing that it moves and yet at the same time does not move. . . . He gives . . . examples of relative motion on several different occasions: the pilot, seated at the stern of a vessel, is motionless in relation to the vessel itself; he is in motion only in relation to the shore along which the vessel moves as it is carried along by the waves. And the watch in the pocket of the captain who walks on the bridge of this vessel, how many movements can we not distinguish in it? movement of its tiny wheels as long as it is running, movement of its owner who carries it on his person, movement of the ship, and of the sea, and of the earth itself . . . is this all? Descartes goes so far as to say that "we cannot find in all the universe a single point that is truly motionless. . . ." For those who would have none of this movement of the earth, he did his best to prove that in one sense it does not move. But, on the other hand, how could it be immobile, when nothing in this world is completely so? By such considerations he thinks he can gradually accustom people to admitting a system, which, presented in this way, may seem acceptable, and remove the scruples of the theologians.

The fourth section of the poem (17-20) is again filled with allusions opening out onto the life of René Descartes. The defiant tone of the passage is inspired by events such as the first meeting between Descartes and Faulhaber, a famous German mathematician who at first took his visitor for no more than a presumptuous young soldier who claimed he could solve the most difficult problems.

To make fun of him, he quoted several lines of Plautus to let him know that he took him for a Gascon braggart about as brave as the puffed-up swaggerer of the comedy. Monsieur Descartes, stung by such an unfair comparison and sensitive to this German's insult, challenged him to test him. Faulhaber . . . at first asked him some fairly standard questions. Seeing that he did not hesitate in his replies, he presented him with more difficult problems, which gave Monsieur Descartes no more trouble than the first. Faulhaber's attitude began to change. . . . He gave him the book in German that he had just written on algebra. This book contained nothing but bare problems, but of the most abstract kind, without explanations. . . . The rapidity and facility with which Monsieur Descartes solved those he happened on in leafing through the book, greatly astonished Faulhaber. But he was a good deal more surprised to hear him add at the same time the rules and general theorems to be used in arriving at true solutions for each kind of problem and all others of the same type.

(B, I, 68-69)

Baillet recounts a similar episode regarding a mathematical problem posted publicly as a challenge to mathematicians. A stranger, taking Descartes for nothing more than an overconfident young man, as did Faulhaber, translates the problem from Flemish into Latin for him—on condition that he bring him the solution. Descartes, the solution in hand, pays him a call the following day, which leads to conversation that amazes the stranger (who turns out to be Isaac Beeckman, rector of the College of the city of Dort). Beeckman is forced to recognize the superior genius of the young Frenchman, and they become, except for one short period of disharmony, lifetime friends and correspondents.

Peter the Red (Pierre Roten in Baillet) was a mathematician from Nuremberg who published answers to Faulhaber's problems, adding new problems of his own which Faulhaber found too difficult to solve alone. Descartes came to his rescue, and Baillet concludes: "The success with which he extricated him from this embarrassing situation finished convincing him that there was no problem that could stand before the powerful genius of this young man" (B, I, 69-70).

In all three episodes there exists the suggestion of youthful pride and self-confidence aroused by the irony or skepticism of less-gifted

16

men, and then the triumph that elicits unstinting admiration. Beckett captures and intensifies the mood when his narrator rises to the challenge and scornfully asserts his ability to solve the school-boy problems they propose: "come now . . . and I'll pebble you all your hen-and-a-half ones" (18-19).

The "cloudy avalanche" mentioned earlier has its function as an image, but it relates at the same time to the following passage describing a spring visit by Descartes to the Savoy Alps: "It was on this occasion that he thought he had discovered the cause of thunder and the reason there is less thunder in winter than in summer. He noticed that 'when the snows had been warmed and made heavy by the sun, the slightest movement of the air was enough to cause large masses to fall suddenly. In this region these were called *ava-lanches*, or rather *lavanches*. When they echoed through the valleys, they sounded very much like thunder.' From this observation he later conjectured that the phenomenon of thunder could be caused by a situation in which, with a relatively large number of clouds piled up, the higher ones, surrounded by warmer air, would fall suddenly [and come] crashing down with a great deal of noise on the clouds below" (B, I, 127). In its metaphorical implications the allusion sets up on the one hand an analogy between the intellectual qualities of the three Germans—Faulhaber, Beeckman, and Peter the Red—and cloudiness and heaviness. On the other hand it evokes an image of the sun (used so often during this century that culminated in the reign of the sun-king) and links it to the Cartesian clarity and penetration that bring low his three adversaries.

Baillet includes several long discussions about the relationship between Descartes and Gassendi and their common concern with the phenomenon referred to in Beckett's phrase "sun-red crystally cloud" (18). The story begins with an observation made in Rome on March 20, 1629 by the German Jesuit, Father Scheiner, who saw four "*parhélies* or false suns around the sun" (B, I, 188). Gassendi published a dissertation on the phenomenon, and later Descartes, writing his *Treatise on Meteors*, discussed it at length. "He examines in particular the way in which the clouds that cause several suns to appear are formed. He claims in this work that a large ring of ice forms around these clouds . . . which sometimes makes a large white circle appear in the sky. . . . It is possible to see as many as six suns within this white circle; the first directly; the next two by refraction; and the other three by reflection . . . those seen by refraction have red edges . . ." (B, I, 192). Echoes in "sun-red" of "Peter the Red" and in "crystally cloud" of "cloudy avalanche," as well as the later "lens," which recalls the idea of the solar crystal, knit the lines together poetically, while a passage like the following places Gassendi, along with the three Germans (and the earlier Galileo), in the camp of the adversaries: "I assure you," writes Descartes to Mersenne, "that there is not a single bit of reasoning in the . . . Latin dissertation that Monsieur Gassendi wrote . . . on this same phenomenon. But he is wrong to be offended that I tried to write the truth about something on which he had previously written nonsense; or to think I should cite him as a source when I got nothing at all from him . . . I should have thought it a greater disservice to him to inform my readers that he wrote on this subject than to remain silent" (B, II, 134).

The last line of this section of the poem, "or I'll pebble a lens under the quilt in the midst of day" (20), contains two specific allusions, the first to Descartes' interest in optics (AT, XII, 89-90) and the second to the privilege granted him by his spiritual adviser, Father Charlet, of staying in bed very late in the morning. "Descartes, who upon awakening found himself in full possession of all his mental powers and calm after the night's rest, would take advantage of this favorable combination of circumstances in order to meditate. This practice became a habit, so firmly established that he made it a way of studying for the rest of his life" (B, I, 28).

The fifth part of the poem, lines 21 through 26, introduces a change in tone. The triumphant aggressiveness gives way to a mixture of sadness and defiance. This time it is the world that wins in the person of an unjust brother, and Descartes suffers. Immediately, however, another shift occurs, and a note of indignation appears, to be followed as the passage ends by a return to something approaching the former tone of confident combativeness.

Pierre Descartes, Seigneur de la Bretaillière (Peter the Bruiser in the poem) was the eldest son of Joachim Descartes and Jeanne Brochard. Baillet writes that at the time of the family gathering called to settle the questions of inheritance after the death of Joachim, René "had difficulty in finding much equity and reasonableness in his elder brother," who was counselor in the Parliament of Brittany at the time (B, II, 218). In a letter written later in his life Descartes further clarifies his relationship with his older brother:

18

As for my brother's complaint, it seems to me very unjust. I did nothing except to send instructions to Poitou that I have given him no authority to act for me in my affairs; and that if he takes it upon himself to do something in my name, or as though counting on me to support him, he will be disavowed. When he complains that this is prejudicial to him, he is in effect admitting that he still desires to be my proxy in spite of me, as he was when my father's estate was divided and he used this as a way of depriving me of what was mine, knowing full well that I prefer to lose rather than go to court. Thus his accusation is like that of a wolf who would complain that the lamb harms him by running away when it fears it may be eaten up. (B, II, 349)

The expression "not a syllogism out of him," in which "syllogism" no doubt has something of the force of "time of day" in the current expression "He wouldn't give you the time of day," or of "hoot," "plugged nickel," and "red cent" in older expressions of negative value, is amply justified in its deprecatory implications by Descartes' quarrel with scholasticism and the Peripatetics. It links the first part of this section to the second, and in particular to the expression "throwing Jesuits out of the skylight." Baillet writes that "they [the Peripatetics] know that his low opinion of scholastic philosophy must put him on the side of their opponents" (B, II, 483). Earlier, Mersenne had written to Descartes urging him not to spare the scholastic philosophy taught in the Jesuit schools at the time, that the moment had come to sacrifice it on the altar of truth. Descartes replied "that he did not believe it would be hard to refute the school-men. . . . 'They agree on general principles, which can easily be disproved, and all their individual disputes seem inept because of this fundamental agreement' " (B, II, 86). More specifically, however, Beckett's lines refer to a still earlier period (1619) on the frontier of Bavaria, where Descartes sought solitude in the famous "poêle" (Beckett's "hot-cupboard"). This was a critical time for him, a time of visions and grandiose plans, of enthusiasm and concentrated intellectual and intuitive activity—one of those rare periods when the creative imagination is freest and most powerful. And it is during this time that he considers the destruction of the old systems, i.e., the Aristotelian scholasticism taught in the Jesuit schools, and particularly at La Flèche where he had been a student,

19

and the construction on new foundations of what will be the Cartesian philosophy. "Throwing Jesuits out of the skylight" is a poetic transposition of the destructive phase of this project.

During this same general period of his life Descartes spent a good deal of time in military service ("Them were the days"), and, as the poet implies (24-25), he did receive remuneration, although not under the usual circumstances. He served in the army of Prince Maurice of Nassau, but ". . . he became a soldier only in order to study the various ways of men as they really are, and to try to insure himself against all the misfortunes of life. So as not to be impeded by any superior force, he decided first of all to forgo all responsibility and support himself always at his own expense. But as a matter of form, he had to receive pay at least once, like a well-to-do pilgrim who feels obliged in starting off on his pilgrimage to ask for alms at least once, so that the custom of adopting the attitude of suppliant and beggar will not die out. He took care to keep this money for the rest of his life as evidence of his military service" (B, I, 41). It will be important to examine later the use that Beckett has made of this passage. For the moment it is perhaps enough to note that the last sentence accounts, at least in one way, for the avid desire expressed in the lines "Hey! pass over those coppers,/ sweet millèd sweat of my burning liver!" (24-25).[6]

The next lines that invite a modest expansion are 29 and 30, "My squinty doaty!/ I hid and you sook." Descartes uses this childhood affection as an illustration of one relationship between sense impressions, emotions, and intellect: "For example, when I was a child, I was very fond of a girl my age who was slightly cross-eyed. Because of this, the visual impression of her eyes askew was so firmly associated in my mind with impressions that gave rise to feelings of love that for a long time afterwards I was more strongly attracted to cross-eyed persons than to others, simply because they possessed this defect; and yet I was not aware of the reason for my feelings. On the contrary, since I have reflected on the matter and recognized this peculiarity as a defect, the attraction has ceased" (AT, V, 57).

The recollection of one beloved child brings another to mind, and the narrator's thoughts turn to the death of his daughter, Francine (31-35). Although the focus of interest shifts, Beckett's lines remain remarkably close to parts of the Baillet passages, not only

---

[6] For the "burning liver" see B, I, 41-42.

in the elegiac tone but in the presence of terms like "fruit" (B, I, ix), "scarlet" (cf. "pourpre" in Baillet), exfoliation and epidermis (which reflect indirectly Baillet's "corps tout couvert de pourpre"), and "house-and-parlour foetus" (which echoes, from a considerable distance, Baillet's moralistic discussion of Francine's legitimacy).

> Descartes was, it would seem, perfectly free to marry. Whatever reason he had for not appearing publicly to be what he may have been in private, he has given us reason to believe that he probably took advantage of this freedom, since he saw fit to declare himself publicly the father of a little girl whom he lost when she was still very young.
>
> Her name was Francine, and she was born in Deventer on July 19, 1635; and according to the remark of her father, she was conceived in Amsterdam on Sunday, October 15, 1634. . . . While everything seemed to be going according to plan [Francine was to go to France to be educated] and Madame du Tronchet was considering ways of furthering such praiseworthy intentions, Monsieur Descartes lost his beloved Francine, who died in Amersfort on September 7, 1640, which was the third day of her illness, her entire body a crimson color. He mourned her with a tenderness that made him realize that true philosophy does not stifle natural feelings. (B, II, 89-90)

Finally, the term "foetus," besides having a poetic function that will be discussed later, has Cartesian resonance because of the treatise *De la formation du foetus*, which, writes Baillet, "is no less daring, nor less ingenious than the other [*De l'homme*]. In it Monsieur Descartes considers the beginnings of man, and he explains the contribution of each of the sexes. He shows that the first organ formed is the heart, and he describes its movement in a way which helps to prove the circulation of the blood . . ." (B, II, 398).

And the word "blood" (36) forms a transition to the next part of the poem, where the narrator's thoughts turn to the circulation of the blood and its discoverer, William Harvey (37-40). Descartes goes into great detail in his explanation of the heating and expansion of the blood in the heart and the mechanism of the valves. "The red and white" of the poem echo the Latin terms he uses when he writes that the blood "becomes white [or lighter in color] in passing through the heart, as it becomes red in the liver . . . [and] no blood except white blood is contained in the arteries and none but red in the veins" (AT, IV, 4-6). In a letter recorded in Adam and Tannery, Descartes asks, "Have you not heard of a certain celebrated doctor in London by the name of Harvey, who wrote a book about the movement of the heart and the circulation of the blood? What sort of man is he? To be sure, he says nothing about the movement of the heart which has not already been said by others, nor do I agree with him completely.[7] But as far as the circulation of the blood is concerned, he has scored a triumph, and he should be recognized and honored as its discoverer" (AT, IV, 699-700).

The transition between this section of the poem and line 41 is hidden, because in neither part is the key word, "heart," mentioned. Yet only the "cracked beater" of Henri IV, and not his body, was transported for burial to the crypt at La Flèche while Descartes was a student there. Line 41 in its extreme understatement evokes a whole period in the past life of the narrator and goes beyond him to call up turbulent and picturesque times in the history of France (see especially B, I, 22-24). It illustrates particularly well the gulf that separates the modern reader from the Descartes of the poem. For the latter a myriad of memories and associations cluster about the unpretentious words, or so we must assume. For the former the line may, and in one sense should, mean very little. Words, as Beckett will suggest in the subtitle of *Echo's Bones*, are the paltry residue precipitated from the rich mixture of a human existence. "The Collège Henri IV could not forget its founder; and the king, for his part, did not forget the school he had founded. He decided that his heart would rest later in the chapel there; and, in effect, after the assassination of May 14, 1610 by Ravaillac, the royal heart was transported from Paris to La Flèche. It was received with great pomp on the fourth day of June. Descartes was present at the ceremony, which must have made a great impression on him; he even took part in it as one of the young noblemen chosen to march in the procession" (AT, XII, 28).

The next part of the poem (45-55) refers a second time to the critical period during October 1619 in the "hot-cupboard," but this time more specifically to the quasi-mystical nature of Descartes'

---

[7] Descartes believed in the existence in the heart of heat analogous to the heat caused by fermentation. This heat, he felt, rather than Harvey's "vertu pulsifique" (AT, XII, 493), which he rejected, caused the blood to move from one side of the heart to the other or, as the poem puts it, to "eddy through that cracked beater."

22

experience there. In September he had been at the coronation of the emperor Ferdinand II in Frankfort. From there he went into winter quarters on the frontier of Bavaria during the month of October. "He found himself in an out-of-the-way place so little frequented by people whose conversation might have interested him that he was able to find the sort of intellectual solitude possible for someone leading an itinerant existence. Thus insured against intrusions from the outside and fortunate enough to have the interior tranquillity that goes with freedom from cares and strong emotions, he remained all day long shut up alone in a heated room, where he had nothing to do but think and meditate" (B, I, 78). It was during this time that the germ of his great enterprise began to develop: to demolish the edifice of traditional knowledge acquired at La Flèche and construct a new system on new foundations. The search for ways to accomplish the first step in the enterprise, however, "caused him violent mental agitation, which increased more and more because of his intense intellectual concentration unbroken by strolls or company. He became so mentally fatigued that, his brain on fire, he fell into a kind of rapture, which prepared his already exhausted mind for dream images and visions [the "visions" of Beckett's note]. He informs us that on November 10, 1619, having gone to bed *filled with this rapture*, and completely preoccupied with the thought that he had *discovered on that day the foundations of a wonderful knowledge*, he had three consecutive dreams in a single night, which he imagined could only have come from above" (B, I, 81). During the course of these dreams he feels the effects of "an impetuous wind," which he later interprets as evil: "The wind that impelled him toward the school church, when his right side was causing him pain, was nothing else but an evil spirit trying to fling him into a place to which he intended to go voluntarily" (B, I, 81, 85). It is not difficult to retrieve here and above the essential elements of the corresponding lines in Beckett's poem (45-51):

> A wind of evil flung my despair of ease
> against the sharp spires of the one
> lady:
> not once or twice but . . .
> (Kip of Christ hatch it!)
> in one sun's drowning
> (Jesuitasters please copy).

While the "despair of ease" probably refers directly to the difficulty he experienced in walking during the first dream because of the pain in his right side, it also suggests his general fatigue and difficulty in finding sleep. Similarly, "not once or twice but . . ." alludes no doubt to the "several times" (B, I, 82) that the wind almost knocked him over, but it recalls at the same time the three dreams, or visions, of that fateful night, described in the phrase "one sun's drowning." The Ptolemaic overtones of the phrase might reassure those Jesuits opposed to the Copernican theories, but the pejorative suffix would be quick to undeceive them about the narrator's real sympathies.

Toward the end of Baillet's six-page-long description and interpretation of the dreams, it becomes more explicitly a question of "the one lady," linked by Beckett to the church spires. The following excerpt elucidates the reason for the double layer of hose and the walking shoes ("So on with the silk hose over the knitted, and the morbid [soft, pliable] leather—" or the still softer "canvas" [53]). Loretto (in the notes and in Baillet) cedes for poetic reasons to Ancona, the nearest large city, just to the north ("and away to Ancona on the bright Adriatic" [54]). "He then called upon the Holy Virgin for her help at this juncture [in deciding on the future direction of his existence], which he judged the most important in his life. And in order to try more urgently to win the intercession of the Blessed Mother of God, he seized upon the trip to Italy he had been planning to begin shortly as an opportunity to take the vow of making a pilgrimage to Our Lady of Loretto. His zeal went still further and induced him to promise that once in Venice he would take the land route and make the pilgrimage to Loretto on foot; that if this effort turned out to be too much for his strength, he would at least adopt the most devoted and humble means possible to him in order to acquit himself of his obligation" (B, I, 85-86).

The final line in this section of the poem (55) brings in the "yellow key," or gold cross, "of the Rosicrucians." "The Rosy Cross of the Rosicrucians is always a gold cross with the distinctive looped ends. . . . There is always ONE red rose in the center of the Cross. . . . The most ancient of all pictures of the Rosicrucian symbol, and all references to it in the most ancient manuscripts, describe it as a gold cross with a '*ruby red rose*.' "[8]

The Rosicrucian reference occurs at this point in the poem first

[8] *Rosicrucian Manual*, ed. H. Spencer Lewis, 7th edn. (San Jose, California: Rosicrucian Press, 1938), p. 88.

of all for chronological reasons. Descartes became interested in their society during the winter of 1619 in the *poêle*. More important, however, was their claim to esoteric scientific knowledge, which interested Descartes at this time because of his own search for truth and his new resolve, following upon the visions, to rebuild his own knowledge on entirely new foundations. Beckett replaces the word "cross" with the term "key" because the latter, while suggesting the Rosicrucian cross, at the same time calls up the idea of *clue*. With this key he hopes to open the door that will lead to truth and knowledge (B, I, 87). Descartes' curiosity, however—at least according to Baillet—was never satisfied. He did, nevertheless, hear about the society several years later, which accounts for the temporary nature of the narrator's farewell to the Rosicrucians ("farewell for a space") (B, I, 90-91). Baillet goes on to discuss in detail (B, I, 107-110) the events following Descartes' return to Paris: the rumors that he was a member of the society, whose adherents were now derisively called "les invisibles," and the attack on their doctrines (as promulgated by the Englishman Robert Fludd) by Descartes' close friend, Father Mersenne. Adam and Tannery, however, question the objectivity of Baillet's attempt to absolve his subject of such dubious connections. Descartes was a friend of Faulhaber, who was affiliated with the Rosicrucians; "his seal, with the two interwoven initials R and C (René des Cartes), happened to be exactly the seal of the Rosicrucian Brotherhood"; and he shared with them, among other things, an interest in magic, alchemy, and astrology (AT, XII, 48). In a poem called *Whoroscope* an allusion to the Rosicrucians, then, becomes doubly significant.

The twelfth part of the poem (56-65) refers, as the notes inform us, to "His Eucharistic sophistry, in reply to the Jansenist Antoine Arnauld, who challenged him to reconcile his doctrine of matter with the doctrine of transubstantiation."

> They don't know what the master of them that do did,
> that the nose is touched by the kiss of all foul and sweet air,
> and the drums, and the throne of the faecal inlet,
> and the eyes by its zig-zags.
> So we drink Him and eat Him
> and the watery Beaune and the stale cubes of Hovis
> because He can jig
> as near or as far from His Jigging Self
> and as sad or lively as the chalice or the tray asks.
> How's that, Antonio?

25

Arnauld, who was only twenty-eight years old at the time, had accepted Mersenne's general request for criticism directed to the faculty of theology at the Sorbonne. Descartes was delighted with the brilliance and kindness of his remarks and especially with the comparison between his own philosophy and that of St. Augustine. To the third group of Arnauld's criticisms Descartes acceded wholeheartedly, with one exception: the arguments concerning transubstantiation, to which he replied in considerable detail and, according to Baillet, with great subtlety and persuasiveness: "So that, as long as the Schoolmen discuss the manner in which the Body of Jesus Christ exists in the Blessed Sacrament and wish to explain it in terms of the natural laws of physics, there will be reason to hope for much from the successful efforts of Cartesians to elucidate this question on the basis of their master's principles. Therefore Monsieur Descartes did not despair of seeing the time come when the view of the Scholastics who admit *substantial accidents* would be rejected as *dubious as an article of faith, contrary to reason*, and *completely incomprehensible*: and that his view would be accepted as *certain* and *indubitable*" (B, II, 127).

In his reply to Arnauld, Descartes aligns himself with Aristotle and against those scholastic theologians who believe in "accidents réels" that can supposedly continue to exist without the substance to which they are normally attached. This would simply mean for him that they are themselves substances, in fact if not in name. He proposes instead his concept of surfaces (*superficies*) which are responsible for all our sense impressions and which are extension only. The *superficie* of the bread and wine can remain the same while their substance is changed into the body and blood of Jesus Christ. Descartes uses two analogies. The river that flows between two shores is constantly changing, since its waters are never the same, yet it is always the same river, since the outline of its shores, its *superficie*, is relatively unchanging. Similarly, through "natural transubstantiation," or digestion, the human body is continually renewing its substance while preserving the same *superficie*. Foreign substances, once they are united to a human soul, become part of the human body. Yet for our senses, impressed by surfaces, no change has occurred. Similarly, but without the process of digestion, the bread and wine, once united to the soul of Jesus Christ, become His body and blood, although no apparent change takes place because their extension remains unaltered. Descartes defines extension in the following way: "by the surface of the bread or wine or any other body, I do not mean any part of the substance, nor even of the quantity of this same body, nor any part of the surrounding bodies, but only this limit that we conceive as intermediate between each of the particles of this body and the bodies surrounding it, and which has no other entity save modal entity" (AT, IX, 193).

In the light of this background, it becomes quite probable that "They" in line 56 of *Whoroscope* does not refer, as we might assume, to the Rosicrucians of line 55, but rather to the scholastic theologians who argued in favor of "accidents réels." The "master" is Aristotle and "them that do [know]" are the "numerous other philosophers" in the following excerpt: "For contact is made only with surfaces, and contact is so necessary for sensation that without it, I believe, not a single one of our senses could be stirred; and I am not the only one to hold this opinion. Aristotle himself and numerous other philosophers before me agreed on this point. So that, for example, bread and wine are not perceived by the senses, except in so far as their surfaces are touched by the sense organ, either directly, or indirectly through the medium of air or other bodies . . ." (AT, IX, 192). Descartes reiterates his conviction that all the senses are in reality forms of the sense of touch: "and Aristotle himself admits that not only this sense that has the special privilege of being called the sense of touch, but also all the other senses function solely through contact" (AT, IX, 194). The narrator of the poem expresses this basic idea in lines 57 through 59, where he says in effect that the nose and ears and tongue and eyes are all "touched" by the air, which serves as means of contact. And, for obvious reasons, the sense of touch itself is omitted.

The wine, mixed with water during the Mass, and the bread, which are the occasion of the whole discussion, enter the picture in line 61 as the "watery Beaune" and the "stale cubes of Hovis." The idea of movement is first introduced with the "zig-zags" of the air (59) and is amplified in lines 62 to 64 through the metaphor of the dance ("jig"), which expresses first the removal of the bread and wine from one place to another ("as near or as far"), and second the movement of the particles within the two substances, which depends on the type and condition of the bread and wine used ("and as sad or lively as the chalice or the tray [metonymy for wine and bread] asks"). While these lines are too richly evocative to be limited narrowly to such a reading, the following passage gives it considerable plausibility as a primary interpretation: "We must also take note that this surface is not only moved in its entirety, when the bread as a whole is carried from one place to another, but that it is also moved in part, when some of its particles are agitated by the air or other bodies that enter its pores; so that, if there are bodies of such a nature that some or all of their particles are in a constant state of motion (which I think is true for some particles of the bread and all those of the wine), we shall also have to conceive of their surfaces as being in a state of perpetual movement" (AT, IX, 193).

The eighth section of *Whoroscope* adds the name of another great contemporary of Descartes: Francis Bacon, Baron Verulam, chancellor of England under James I. Beckett's Descartes swears by him, as he did by the brothers Boot, because of Bacon's attack on the deductive method of the scholastics and their practice of subordinating scientific research to religious and theological authority. At the same time, as the author of the *Novum organum*, Bacon shared with Descartes the dream of creating a new method. In 1596, the year of Descartes' birth, writes Baillet, "Ancient philosophy, and particularly that of Aristotle was coming under sharp attack . . . and Chancellor Bacon was already laying the foundations of the new philosophy" (B, I, 10). This same movement of destruction followed by creation reappears in a number of other passages associating the names of Descartes and Bacon, notably B, I, 147-149.

Section fourteen of *Whoroscope* shows once again how Beckett condenses into a few powerful and poetic lines a lengthy, picturesque, and no doubt memorable event in the life of Descartes. According to Baillet, Voetius was doing everything in his power to ruin Descartes' reputation at the University of Utrecht. In 1640 he decided to attack the philosopher through Monsieur Regius, professor of medicine at the university, a friend of Descartes, and, like him and Harvey, an exponent of the new theories concerning the circulation of the blood. Regius, in order to defend himself and sound out opinion at the university, chose to put his book into the form of theses before publishing it and asked Descartes to revise the theses for him before the public debate at the university. Descartes did so and even expressed his willingness to come to Utrecht and watch the debates, provided he could remain hidden in the tribune of Anne Marie de Schurmans. It is at this point that the description of Beckett's Anna Maria takes place. In the following passage all italics are mine except in the case of the saying of St. Ignatius. They point up phrases that serve as direct sources for lines 68 through 72 of the poem.

We can judge by the proposal, which Monsieur Descartes made to Monsieur Regius, that he use the tribune of *Mademoiselle de Schurmans* [cf. 68], that this marvel of a girl was not unknown to him. *At that time she was still only twenty-eight years old, but she had out-distanced most old men in her knowledge of the arts and sciences* [cf. 70]. She had both a spoken and written command of a very great number of languages. . . . She not only knew the theory of all the fine arts, but had acquired as well an exquisite refinement in their practice. . . . She had gone no less deeply into the sciences, even those that seem the most abstract and the most thorny. Besides mathematics, she knew scholastic philosophy and sophistry. She would dispute and reply better than the old university professors and better than the Irish. Finally, she had studied scholastic theology thoroughly and *had a complete mastery of Holy Scripture* [cf. 69] and Saint Thomas, not to mention the Greek and Roman Fathers. All this considerable and excellent learning was buttressed by an incomparable modesty and by an unusual love for seclusion, study, and prayer. She had not limited herself to the commandments of the gospel only; *she had embraced its most severe counsels. She had denied herself the most innocent pleasures; she practiced extraordinary abstinence* [cf. 71], having taken for her motto the beautiful saying of the martyr, Saint Ignatius, *Amor meus crucifixus est* [cf. 69]; . . . When Monsieur J. Labadie came to preach a new reformation among the protestants, she submitted to his discipline with a view to greater perfection, and lost in the eyes of the Calvinists, who took Labadie for a schismatic or false prophet, the fruit of all her good works.

Monsieur Descartes, while not a prophet, had had some premonition of what was to happen to this poor girl [cf. 72]. *He felt that an unbridled curiosity to know too much and to pierce the most inaccessible mysteries of theology, for those of her sex, could well carry her too far and degenerate into a presumption that would bring upon her the fate of the foolish and imprudent virgins of the gospel* [cf. 70]. [Later, Descartes reports that, dominated by Voetius, Mademoiselle de Schurmans] *no longer does anything but engage in theological disputes* [cf. 71]—*so that she*

29

is losing social contact with all sensible and cultivated people
[cf. 70]."   B, II, 60-62)

An unusually rich human life, summed up by Baillet and abridged above, is further condensed into a few fleeting memories by the narrator. Beckett's brief note gives us her story in capsule form. It is the epitome of the condensation of an abridgment of a summary: "Schurmann, the Dutch blue-stocking, a pious pupil of Voët, the adversary of Descartes."[9]

Lines 72 through 76 of *Whoroscope* refer to the conversion of St. Augustine. They will be especially useful in trying to assess the part of the poet, which comes to light in his departure from the source materials. For the time being, we can note simply the fusion of Augustine's "Si fallor, sum," used to refute the skeptics of his day (*De libero arbitrio* II, iii, 7), and Descartes' "Cogito, ergo sum." Beckett's version, "Fallor, ergo sum," changes the hypothetical form, leaving no doubt that "I am deceived." The irony of his metamorphosis leaves Augustine's existence intact but undercuts the basis of his conversion. Baillet gives an account of the views of Antoine Arnauld on the relationship between Descartes and Augustine (II, 126) and of Descartes' own opinion of the different uses made of the *cogito* by himself and by his illustrious predecessor (II, 535-536).

The *Whoroscope* passage contains several indirect references to Augustine's dissolute life before his conversion: "coy," which is perhaps an allusion to his desire to have the Lord and his pleasure too; and "frôleur," primarily calling up the garden setting but not without its sensuous overtones. "Tolle'd and legge'd" is a direct transposition of the Latin phrase cited in the *Confessions*, while line 76, "and he buttoned on his redemptorist waistcoat," refers to his conversion.[10] In this passage the narrator recalls a critical episode in the life of Augustine. One day, when he had left his friend and gone to meditate alone in a grove of trees in his garden, he thought he heard a voice that said, "Take and read; take and read" ("Tolle, lege; tolle, lege"). Strongly moved by the call, he rejoined his

[9] For the protracted history of the machinations of Voetius against Descartes, see Baillet, II, 24, 28-32, 57-59, 92-93, 142-158, 175-197, 204-205, 249-263, 467-470.

[10] Since the Redemptorist Order was not founded by St. Alfonsus Liguori until 1732, it is unlikely that the term, uncapitalized in the poem, is more than a general reference to Augustine's conversion.

friend, where he took up a book of the Epistles of St. Paul and opened it at random. The passage he came upon ended his vacillations: "Do not spend your life in banqueting and the pleasures of the table . . . but put on your lord Jesus Christ, and beware of satisfying the immoderate desires of the flesh." From this moment forward he abandoned the life of dissipation he had led until then.[11]

The sixteenth section of the poem, lines 77 through 83, is a poetic metamorphosis of part of Descartes' proof of God from our idea of perfection (AT, IX, 38-40). He considers exhaustively (Beckett, not without irony, says in the notes, "He proves God by exhaustion") the possible sources of a being with such an idea and eliminates himself as his own creator ("so I'm not my son" [79]). If he had been able to create himself, he would also have been able —and would certainly have acted ("I'm a bold boy I know" [78]) —to provide himself with all the perfections he lacks and is conscious of lacking. He also eliminates his parents as source of his thinking being ("nor Joachim my father's [son]" [81]), and settles on God as his only possible cause ("a perfect block that's neither old nor new,/. . . a great high bright rose" [82-83]). The "perfect block" of line 82 is probably a recollection of a related passage, in which Descartes describes all perfections as being "joined and assembled in the single perfection that is God. The unity, simplicity, or inseparability of all the things that are in God," he continues, "is one of the principal perfections that I conceive to be in Him" (AT, IX, 40). At the same time, it is very likely that this same line, which describes the "perfect block" as "neither old nor new," includes an allusion to the line of Augustine, "Late have I loved Thee, O Beauty so ancient and so new"—especially since the latter occurs in the same book and chapter of the *Confessions* (X, 27) as the episode of the conversion in the garden, to which Beckett has just referred (75). Similarly, the "great high bright rose" with its "lonely petal" (83) recalls, in a different key, the size, height, and brilliance of Dante's mystical "rosa sempiterna" in Canto 30 of the *Paradiso*, where, incidentally, petals are also mentioned. A later allusion to Dante in *Whoroscope* is further evidence of the important place the great Italian poet holds among "Beckett's authors."

The last part of the poem, and of Descartes' life, takes place in Stockholm.[12] Rahab (91), whom we shall meet again in the early

[11] See the *Confessions* of St. Augustine, Bk. X, Chap. 27.
[12] See especially B, II, 369-370, 386, 411, 417-418.

poem "From the Only Poet to a Shining Whore," is the Biblical harlot (Joshua 2:6) who finds her way into Dante's third heaven. Rahab sheltered the Israelite spies in the town of Jericho, and Queen Christina invited the Catholic Descartes into Protestant Stockholm. However, although she did eventually defect to Rome, Christina betrayed Descartes as much as her capital by her invitation, for it brought about the destruction not of the city but of the philosopher. More directly murderous, she later ordered the assassination of her favorite, Gian Rinaldo Monaldeschi. The extreme cold of the Stockholm winter, the 5:00 A.M. meetings with the dangerous queen, her virility, and her conversion to Roman Catholicism all figure in these lines:

> Then I will rise and move moving
> toward Rahab of the snows,
> the murdering matinal pope-confessed amazon,
> Christina the ripper.

The final lines of the poem evoke the closing episode in the life of René Descartes, Seigneur du Perron, as he was known to the end of his days among the members of his family.

> Oh Weulles spare the blood of a Frank
> who has climbed the bitter steps,
> (René du Perron . . . . !)
> and grant me my second
> starless inscrutable hour.

Weulles, appointed by the queen to care for Descartes during a serious illness, was his "sworn enemy" on philosophical, religious, and scientific grounds and had sought to "do him disservice" ever since his arrival in Sweden. During the first days of his illness Descartes had refused all medical attention for fear of falling into the hands of charlatans or incompetents. Finally, however, out of respect for the queen and to please his friend, Chanut, he consented to see Weulles. After consultation, the verdict was for a bloodletting, which Descartes firmly rejected as the quickest way to aggravate his condition and shorten his life. As his fever increased, however, so did the insistence of physicans and friends, but Descartes continued to reply *Gentlemen, spare the blood of a Frank* (Baillet's italics). Finally, by now past help, he did agree to the bloodletting and not long afterward succumbed (B, II, 417-418).

32

The final allusion of the poem, "who has climbed the bitter steps" (95), reinforces the sense of loneliness and suffering in a foreign land by its reference to Dante's moving lines on the hard way and the bitter bread of exile.

> Tu proverai sì come sa di sale
> Lo pane altrui, e come è duro calle
> Lo scendere e 'l salir per l'altrui scale.
> (*Par.* XVII, 58-60)

The Part of the Poet

The question now arises, since he is present in every line of the poem: Why Descartes? What did the great seventeenth-century philosopher mean to the avant-garde twentieth-century poet? Which of the many possible Descartes did Samuel Beckett choose—or did he invent a new Descartes? Before attempting to answer these questions, it is perhaps only fair to tell the story of the genesis of *Whoroscope*, if only to reject as superficial the reductive kind of answers it may suggest.

Beckett was at the Ecole Normale in the fall of 1929 and had been working on Descartes for some time. He was intent upon an academic career and had no thought then of becoming a writer. One afternoon around four o'clock a friend stopped by and told him of a prize offered by Nancy Cunard and Richard Aldington at The Hours Press for the best poem on time. No outstanding manuscripts had been received and the deadline was midnight. At his friend's suggestion, he decided to have a try at it and worked from then until three o'clock in the morning, with a break for dinner. Since it was too late to mail the manuscript, he carried it personally to The Hours Press. When the decision was announced, Beckett, who had written his poem almost as one who accepts a dare, was very surprised to learn that he had won the competition.

Given these circumstances, it is only too easy to dismiss the poem as the inconsequential occasional verse of a student of letters. I think this would be a mistake. The circumstances and the superficial motive may have been relatively frivolous but, as Beckett admits, the writing itself was quite serious. Often the external pretext of an incipient poet masks a more profound reason and need. As for the short time of composition, the nine hours must be considered as the culmination of a long and close association with

Descartes. As he wrote the poem Beckett had before him a thick notebook filled with quotations he had copied from Descartes and Baillet, a notebook which unfortunately has since been lost. Finally, it is well to stress the value of the relatively spontaneous writing of the young poet for the study of his later work.

In France, more than abroad, Descartes is felt to divide the old from the new, and it has taken an Etienne Gilson with his work on the medieval origins of Cartesian philosophy to relax a little the rigidity of the division and reestablish to some degree the continuity between past and present. However, when we examine the Descartes of Beckett's poem, it is this image of the destroyer of the outworn and the architect of the future—which still has a great deal to be said for it historically—that first emerges. Many passages from the life of Descartes could be brought forward in support of such an image. One incident, which paints in miniature what history will spread out as a vast fresco, occurs in the presence of Cardinal Bérulle:

> One Monsieur de Chandoux . . . set forth his unorthodox views and made an impression on his audience, except however on one of them, who was precisely Descartes. Bérulle noticed it and invited our philosopher to speak: he accepted and, with an ease that surprised everyone, completely demolished his adversary. . . . Cardinal Bérulle realized immediately that he had before him, not merely an innovator, but a veritable reformer; he therefore engaged him in discussion and made it a matter of conscience that he devote his life henceforth to the reform of philosophy. . . . Descartes followed the advice of Bérulle, which agreed only too well with his personal inclinations and what his friends expected of him. Did they not consider him the champion of the new philosophy, the only one capable of feats of prowess against the giants of scholasticism?   (AT, XII, 95-97)

With its very title, *Whoroscope* is under the sign of destruction, for Beckett has chosen the Descartes who rejected the medieval heritage of astrology, chiromancy, and magic. As a man with a tormenting itch might call it a b-itch, so Beckett attacks the idea of horoscopes by the addition of a *w*. Later, in *En attendant Godot*, he will ridicule the Academy in a similar way by the addition of stuttering syllables that introduce the infantile word in French for excrement, *Acacacacadémie*. The technique is made explicit in an often-quoted passage of *Molloy*:

"Moi je l'appelais Mag, quand je devais lui donner un nom. Et si je l'appelais Mag c'était qu'à mon idée, sans que j'eusse su dire pourquoi, la lettre g abolissait la syllabe ma, et pour ainsi dire crachait dessus, mieux que toute autre lettre ne l'aurait fait."[13]

There is no doubt some analogy between the late-scholastic speculations on the life to come, which represented a tendency opposed to the empirical and scientific side of Descartes' mind, and on another plane the divination of the future by means of horoscopes. At any rate, a generally antimetaphysical or antiabstractive bias coupled with a disposition favoring the present and the concrete is what Beckett found in Descartes—and, though more poet than scientist, in himself as well. It may seem strange to find the author of the *Metaphysical Meditations* opposed to metaphysics, but Descartes in his *Principles of Philosophy* drastically reduced the part traditionally assigned to metaphysics and gave it an ancillary position in the order of presentation, which amounted to "nothing less than a revolution." Metaphysics is no longer the servant of theology; "it is oriented almost solely and exclusively toward natural science, and its chief aim is to furnish the principles needed by natural science" (AT, XII, 369-370). *Whoroscope* opens with the oath "By the brothers Boot." With this the narrator aligns himself with the physicians who refuted the Aristotle of primal matter and substantial forms—and beyond him the contemporary Peripatetics—in a book published in Dublin, as Beckett (for once proud of his native city) points out in the note.[14] Soon we find the narrator making disparaging remarks about syllogisms and Jesuitasters and throwing these practitioners of the scholastic method "out of the skylight." "[Descartes] took alarm and from then on considered the Society as a formidable army coming at him. He was not at all disconcerted, but calling up all his courage, he resolved to march out alone against them all . . ." (B, II, 74). Later, in another tone, he deplores the downfall of Anne Marie de Schurmans, become through scholastic disputations "a pale abusive parakeet." But most important

---

[13] (Paris: Les Editions de Minuit, 1951), p. 23.

[14] As Beckett once mentioned, this is an event of which even Joyce was unaware.

35

are the two references to the critical period Descartes spent in the "hot-cupboard" (26, 45-56), where the great plans for destruction and re-creation germinated. "He spent the rest of the winter and Lent on the Bavarian frontier in a state of indecision, thinking himself well rid of the prejudices of his education and his reading, and continuing to meditate upon his plan to rebuild everything from the bottom up" (B, I, 91). And elsewhere, "The following nine years were spent by Descartes in an attempt to rid himself of his prejudices. . . . But at the same time as this work of destruction, he pursued another task, with a view to reconstructing a truly scientific doctrine" (AT, XII, 59).

In the poem, Beckett suggests this more creative urge by linking Descartes to others associated in one way or another with the new science, or with innovations in mathematics and philosophy: Galileo, Bacon, Harvey, Faulhaber, Beeckman, Roten, Gassendi, and even the Rosicrucians. "In the name of Bacon," swears the narrator, who also invokes as a cherished colleague the discoverer of the circulation of the blood. At the same time, the fictional Descartes is no more a believer in "creation by committee" than his real prototype, who tells us at some length in the second part of the *Discours de la méthode* of his preference for individual achievement. Hence, the above relationships are generally critical and even on occasion contemptuous: "if he was of one mind with the innovators in the design of toppling Aristotle, he hardly agreed with them on a new doctrine to replace the old one" (AT, XII, 83). Descartes' confidence in his own ability to erect the city of the future is great—and the narrator's is even greater in the first part of the poem. Beckett conveys the latter's proud self-assurance through excessive abuse of Galileo, which, significantly, is based on an error in identification, and through the arrogance of such expressions as "I'll pebble you all your hen-and-a-half ones."

If Beckett chooses an antischolastic and proscientific Descartes, it is a choice perhaps even more of the concrete as opposed to the abstract than of science as opposed to scholasticism, but its repercussions are undoubtedly no less substantive than formal. It is also, and centrally, a declaration against the outworn commonplace that has become superficial and hollow and in favor of personal insight; against erudition and for the wisdom of experience; against logic, for intuition. The chief reason Samuel Beckett left an academic career that was well underway was the distasteful necessity he felt as a professor of pretending to know what he really did not. On the most profound level, the affinity between the mind of Descartes and the mind of Beckett, so different in other ways, may lie in this need to know through the personal experience of meditation. The following passage describing the seventeenth-century philosopher might well apply in this sense to the twentieth-century poet. Baillet writes that Descartes read little, had few books, and had "decided to study nature directly and seek truth independently of what had been written before him. . . . [He] felt there was a great difference between erudition and knowledge. He easily understood how reading commonplaces, tables, collections, and other catalogues can stock the mind and make a man superficially learned in a short time. But he did not think this the way to become wiser nor better. . . . True knowledge depends . . . on interior meditation . . ." (B, II, 467-470). The strong sense, which emerges from all of Beckett's work, that most of human existence takes place "on the surface," as a disconnected series of automatic responses cut off from deeper reality, probably derives from such a turn of mind. So does his rejection of conventional literary form and his personal preference for the novel over the theater. Conventional form, like abstract knowledge, seems to appear to him, whether in life or in art, as less real than the apparent formlessness of an inner monologue that follows the rhythms of being.

When Beckett, like Descartes, attacks abstract speculation, he chooses a different way, the way of the poet. (Paradoxically, several times it is the abstract speculation of Descartes himself that he attacks. If not a scholastic, Descartes was, after all, a philosopher and not immune to the temptations of theological debate.) One example among many of the poetizing of the abstract occurs in the passage on the Eucharist (56-65). The technical, philosophical atmosphere disappears. Aristotle, for example, becomes "the master," and the movement of air and molecules the specific and humanized movements of the zigzag and the jig, both at the same time onomatopoetic and unifying on the level of sound. Similarly, contact becomes "kiss." The role of the senses and sense impressions is greatly increased and made much more concrete. The "olfactory sense," for example, becomes simply "nose," while bread and wine are specified as "the watery Beaune and the stale cubes of Hovis." The conventional formulas of language are broken, and Beckett attempts, as every poet must, to revitalize his instrument.

37

We no longer "partake of the bread and wine, which is the body and blood of Christ" but, in a reversal of order that cracks the cliché "breadandwine" and a telescoping that strips dogma of its linguistic veils, we "drink Him and eat Him." Perhaps even more striking, however, is the shift from the engaged, serious, confident tone of someone convinced he has made a discovery that will lead a step further on the road to truth, to the half-amused, half-nostalgic skepticism of the disengaged poet, who would perhaps like to share such a commitment but cannot, for whom all this is a game, a "sophistry"[15] that at best furnishes material for poetry. There is no revolt here and hardly any bitterness, only a gentle and suffering irony that hovers between sympathy and satire. In "what the master of them that do did" the deliberate use of incorrect English and the comical alliterative juxtaposition of *th*'s and *d*'s are, basically, reductive. "Watery" and "stale" and "How's that, Antonio?" undermine in a similar way the seriousness of the Cartesian enterprise, the first two by stressing the imperfection of things human, the last by the flippant familiarity of the question and the implication that the whole demonstration is no more than clever casuistry.

While in this passage Beckett has drawn a Descartes who in comparison with his model is considerably less sanguine, the tone of the passage remains quite ambivalent, although tending certainly toward the pessimistic. The association of "throne" and "faecal," "foul and sweet," and "sad or lively" is indicative of the survival in the narrator of positive attachments. In the final analysis, nevertheless, this is a case in which the fictional Descartes, who occupies a kind of middle ground between the real philosopher, René Descartes, and the poet, Samuel Beckett—shifting now closer to the one, now to the other—moves decidedly in the direction of the poet-author and away from the philosopher-source. The language becomes poetic—concrete, imaged, emotive. The tone, more subjective, suggests in its ambivalence both human idealism and human misery. While abandoning the abstractness of philosophical language, Beckett keeps the universal implications of Descartes' discussion, so that each detail, woven into the sensuous fabric of a particular human existence, at the same time opens out onto a perspective of the condition and fate of man. It is this expansive force of Beckett's writing, perceptible as occasional flashes in *Whoroscope* and in his later work gaining in intensity and especially

---

[15] See Beckett's note on lines 56-65.

in the power to sustain itself unbroken almost indefinitely, that makes him one of the most poetic and moving of modern writers.

Descartes and the narrator diverge (or Beckett and the narrator converge) again in the phrase "in one sun's drowning," which permits another glimpse of the part of the poet. In the context, "(Jesuit-asters please copy)," the implications for Descartes are scientific, and the phrase suggests the Ptolemaic view that the sun moves around the earth. For Beckett, the somewhat timeworn image has the triple advantage of referring to the astronomical debates that involved Descartes, of evoking the night of visions in the *poêle*, and of serving his own purpose as a poet by reinforcing the poem's general movement from life to death. It is not a Cartesian expression. In its fidelity to a real world of the senses that maintains itself and its value as sensuous experience, while at the same time, and with discreet persistence, speaking of man's fate—in its love and its sorrow—it is typical of Beckett. In its lack of originality and in the relative weakness of the message that comes through, it is not yet the mature Beckett.

More suggestive of what is to come, more original, and especially important in that they show a characteristic tension between romantic nostalgia and tough realism are the lines "Leider! Leider! she bloomed and withered,/ a pale abusive parakeet in a mainstreet window" (70-71). Later the part of romanticism will dwindle until, in a recent work like *Comment c'est*, it survives only as occasional memory-images of "the blue" in the world above. The nostalgia never disappears completely, however, and in the play *Happy Days* neither irony nor suffering can mask it completely.

The lines are important for two other reasons. Descartes had attributed the downfall of Anna Maria Schurmans to her "excessive curiosity in wanting to know too much," to the desire "for someone of her sex to penetrate the most inaccessible mysteries of theology" (B, II, 61). What she should have done, according to him, was to develop her artistic and social talents. Beckett's criticism is much more radical. The whole poem is dedicated to the proposition that not only women but men also, philosophers also—Descartes himself—are doomed to failure if they try to penetrate the mystery of the "starless inscrutable hour" (98). And here we come to one of the themes that lies at the heart of Beckett's thought: man's utter inability to know—God, the world, others, himself. The very existence of all four is called into question (but never triumphantly reaffirmed, as by Descartes). For Beckett, again unlike Descartes, what is sacrificed in such an attempt is not so much artistic talent and social life as elemental existence, a loss which is suggested in this particular passage by the words "bloomed," "withered," and "pale"; elsewhere, for example, by the contrast between unsubstantial "cave-phantoms" (67) and the solid nourishment of bacon and eggs (66) (with the pun on the chancellor's name reinforcing the contrast through an opposition between unsubstantial metaphysics and solid experimental science).[16]

Besides representing poetically the sacrifice of concrete being to abstract speculation on the unknowable, the lines are significant because they are a second reflection or résumé of the central structure of the poem, which portrays, after its initial ascent, the downward trajectory of human existence. And in this focus on man's inevitable ending, sometimes too lightly—as though it were not inevitable—called pessimistic, we find another profound difference from Descartes with his robust "optimism," his concentration on the constructive possibilities of the individual and the race. It is true that Descartes is aware of limitation and writes, "I believe that this [astronomy] is a science which is beyond the grasp of the human mind," but he adds, "yet I have so little wisdom that I cannot keep myself from pondering over it" (B, I, 235). Baillet writes that Bacon's "motto, or rather the prophecy of this magistrate, *Multi pertransibunt et augebitur scientia*, helped a great deal to encourage him [Descartes] in the hope that others who come after him will be able to continue what he has begun" (B, I, 149). Beckett the poet, who is concerned not with furthering scientific knowledge but with suffering, in its original sense, and with portraying all that is deepest and truest in his own human experience, is no stranger to the predicament that deadlocks aspiration and impossibility. The struggle is everywhere implicit in his work and often explicit, but the balance of persuasive power lies clearly on the negative side. What seems essential is man's profound ignorance, his aloneness, his suffering, and his death. The Descartes of progress and achievement is undone in *Whoroscope* as the Voltaire of progress and achievement is demolished in *En attendant Godot*. Man's stature is not increasing; it is diminishing.

[16] With his profound sense of the vanity of human knowledge already evident, it is hardly surprising that Beckett abandoned the academic profession a few years later.

A final non-Cartesian theme is the revolt against this human plight, against a destiny that keeps us, like the embryonic chick of the poem, in darkness and then kills us before we have really begun to live. Beckett's characters can be situated at different points on a scale ranging from revolt to apathetic acceptance, as his art can be said to vary in the proportion of satire and poetry it contains. He is always to some degree the ironist who criticizes, even if only implicitly, as well as the poet who recreates experience. The obscene puns in *Whoroscope* and elsewhere, which have been too often criticized as hollow preciosity or "Irishism," in reality function, often quite effectively, as an expression of that revolt.

If the part of the poet is to be found in the selection of particular Cartesian characteristics, as well as in the choice of components that can hardly be ascribed to the seventeenth-century philosopher, it is also evident in the exaggeration or distortion of other traits, and, finally, in the absence of certain qualities one might expect to find present. Descartes defended himself against the implication that he had said nothing with his "cogito, ergo sum" that Augustine had not said before him. While we can see here the germ of the narrator's derisive remarks about the "coy old frôleur" (74), the poet has turned self-defense into aggression, a happy circumstance for those in search of Beckett behind the mask of Descartes. As Baillet writes, "Of all the instances in which Descartes' thought coincided with that of the ancients, none surprised him more agreeably than his meeting of minds with Saint Augustine. . . . It was not only that this saint rejected the judgment of the senses, and that he admitted still other opinions which they seemed to hold in common with the disciples of Plato. It was principally in the matter of the distinction between mind and body, and his great principle of *thought*, from which he concluded in favor of our existence" (B, II, 535-536).

In *Whoroscope* the Cartesian "cogito, ergo sum" fuses with the Augustinian "si fallor, sum" to become "Fallor, ergo sum!" (73), and, typically, thinking becomes erring. Although he admitted the fallibility of human reason, Augustine claimed knowledge of man's condition and destiny. The poem denies the possibility of such knowledge. At the time of his conversion, Augustine left a life that in some ways—in its submersion in elemental physical existence, in its chaos and meaninglessness, but also in its suffering and anguished need to know—makes contact with the existence of Beckett's characters. The narrator, when he rejects the *cogito* but

41

keeps the *sum*, refuses to renounce such elemental existence. In the scorn implicit in the Anglicizing of the Latin ("He tolle'd and legge'd" [75]) and in the reduction of spiritual conversion to a superficial change of clothes ("he buttoned on his redemptorist waistcoat" [76]), we can see Beckett's attack on such "escapism" in the face of the disagreeable, but for him real, human condition of ignorance and abandonment.

More often, instead of molding the real Descartes (or the Baillet Descartes) to fit his own image of man by reshaping an attitude or increasing the vehemence of an antagonism, the poet simply omits a qualifying statement, a complementary position, or a tactical motivation. Descartes was not wholly committed, for example, to "throwing Jesuits out of the skylight" (26). "He never failed to show his gratitude to his teachers at La Flèche, and missed no opportunity to praise them.[17] In this he was without a doubt sincere; but self-interest was certainly involved also. Author of a new philosophy, he would have liked the Jesuits to adopt it in place of Aristotelianism in their schools" (AT, XII, 32). Thus, he sent *Le Monde* to the Jesuits at La Flèche in 1637, as soon as it was published, "not only as the grateful homage of a student to his former teachers, but especially in the hope that they will become interested in his new ideas, receive them with favor, and in some way adopt them . . ." (AT, XII, 168). As for the scholastic method of syllogistic reasoning, despite his criticisms Descartes employed it himself and on occasion called others to task not so much for using it as for violating the rules governing its use. "All the same, he recognized in logic many precepts that are very true and very good . . ." (B, I, 24).

The narrator's diatribe against Galileo is very much less Cartesian, all things considered, than his attack on the scholastics: "the telescope, with the marvels that it immediately revealed in the sky, was perhaps the great event of Descartes' childhood. His whole philosophy would later be affected by this early enthusiasm" (AT, XII, 29-30). Baillet writes that although Descartes was only partly aware of the merit of Galileo, "he nevertheless considered him one of the leading figures of the century" (B, II, 176); and Descartes himself writes, "I find that in general he [Galileo] is a much better than average philosopher in that he abandons whenever he can the errors of scholasticism and tries to apply mathematical reasoning

[17] See also Baillet, II, 70-72, 483, 489-490.

to the study of physics. In this I am in complete agreement with him, and I hold that there is no other way to find truth" (AT, II, 380). It seems strange at first that Beckett failed to take advantage of this common antischolastic and proscientific position of Descartes and Galileo. Instead he sets Descartes in violent, and mistaken, opposition to the great Italian scientist. As always, such apparent anomalies are revealing. If the narrator attacks Galileo, he also attacks the historic Descartes, for the latter was equally serious in his interest in relative motion. This is obviously one of those times when the narrator is less Descartes than Beckett. As Beckett, he is consistent, since he attacks a kind of abstract reasoning that the poet rejects, in conformity with his typical—and very un-Cartesian—view that sees a radical divorce between thinking and being. If Descartes can be antischolastic and a rationalist at the same time, Beckett, a more thoroughgoing critic of human reason, cannot.

As implied already, there are other explanations as well. Descartes' motives in his discussion of relative motion were at least as much strategic as scientific.[18] If such debates seem inherently arbitrary and unreal to the poet, when they become political maneuvers also they risk appearing insincere, dishonest. Both the gratuity of the game and the equivocal motive are blamed in Beckett's note with the word "sophistry."

More important for *Whoroscope* are the structural reasons for the narrator's divergence from his model. The blustering self-assurance of the beginning contrasts sharply with the suppliant's plea at the end. These are the two terminal points of the axis of decline to which the various episodes in the poem must be referred. It would be too much to call this a tragic pattern; for one thing, no possibility of transcendence is present. At the same time, the passage from pride to humility, from error (not only the confusion between the two Galilei, but especially the hybristic illusion of re-creation) to a better realization of man's place in the universe, is analogous to a truncated version of the fall, a fall without redemption. We need not go that far afield, however; no doubt the simple parallel with the basic pattern of any human existence, the archetype of descent to the grave, is enough to explain much of the effect of *Whoroscope*.

Beckett's portrayal of the relationship between Descartes and Bacon is limited to an oath that binds the two together in common

---

[18] See above, pp. 14-15.

opposition to systematic philosophy (66-67). After admitting that Descartes approved of Bacon's plan to "shake off the yoke of scholasticism," Baillet writes that the French philosopher disagreed on the manner of accomplishing this task. Descartes' "aim was to build his system, without stopping to try to destroy that of others: while . . . Bacon, Telesius, Campanella, and the other modern innovators have had more success in destroying traditional dogmas than in establishing those for which they had undertaken to gain acceptance" (B, II, 539-540). This picture of Descartes as more creator than destroyer is in clear contrast to Beckett's vision, which places the emphasis on attack and destruction. It is easy to understand the desire of Baillet, the religious apologist, to stress the positive, and it is equally understandable, given the central human experience evoked by *Whoroscope*, that Beckett should accentuate the negative. He omits all reference to the constructive side of Bacon's thought, and his radical epistemological skepticism stands in sharp contrast to the Englishman's optimistic vision of possible scientific progress. In the poem, very little remains of Descartes' philosophical and scientific achievements. What seems important for the narrator at the end of his life is reliving moments of being that have somehow survived the passage of the great destroyer, time.

Baillet indicates some of the many similarities between the thought of Descartes and Plato, and Socrates' quarrel with the Sophists has points in common with the Cartesian objections to scholasticism. However, the Descartes who, as Plato did before him, calls into question the validity of the world of the senses is not the Descartes of Beckett's poem. "Cave-phantoms" (67) are opposed to the sensuous reality of bacon and eggs and are not, as we might hastily conclude, an allusion to the Platonic devaluation of the material world. In a context including the name of Francis Bacon, they refer specifically to the English philosopher's "idola."[19] The historical Descartes lost confidence in the truth of what was taught him at La Flèche, and he used physics to bring metaphysics down to earth when he attempted a natural explanation of the super-

[19] In the destructive or critical part of the *Novum Organum*, Bacon distinguishes four classes of illusions ("phantoms") that lead men into error: 1. "idola tribus," those attributable to social organization; 2. "idola specus [cave]," to individual formation and character; 3. "idola fori," to the inadequacy of language; 4. "idola theatri," to fallacious intellectual constructs like closed philosophical systems.

natural in his discourse on transubstantiation. The fictional Descartes goes him one better in the warm-blooded reality of poetic statement on the same subject (56-65). Bacon attacked closed systems ("idola theatri") and promoted direct observation of discrete natural phenomena. Beckett follows him in spirit by undermining formal artistic coherence. He seeks the authenticity of individual impression and insight. Direct, if momentary, contact between subject and object takes priority over tight verbal or semantic correspondence. In this early impulse to slacken the reins of cerebral control and loosen the unity of the poem we can see the revolt of Beckett the young poet against Beckett the young intellectual. Hardly more than two years later (in January 1932) he resigned his academic post at Trinity and shortly thereafter in a poem called "Gnome" delivered his brief indictment of the scholarly life.

When René Descartes recalls his affection for his cross-eyed childhood playmate, it is solely in order to illustrate from the data conveniently provided by his own experience certain general physiological and psychological theories. In later life he felt an unreasonable attraction to cross-eyed persons, he tells us, because of this childhood attachment. "For the objects which affect our senses move, by way of the nerves, certain parts of our brain, creating, as it were, folds which disappear when the object ceases to act on the senses; but the part of the brain affected retains the disposition to be folded again in the same manner by another object resembling the first in some particular, even though not similar in every way" (AT, V, 57). He goes on to assert that such an inclination can be overcome once reason becomes aware of its true nature and cause[20] (an idea which, even taking into consideration important differences, suggests Freud's cathartic psychotherapy). What is important for our purpose, however, is the typically scientific attitude (whether in its inductive or deductive phase) that tends to subordinate the particular to the general, to see in individual experiences no more than data to be used either to formulate broad hypotheses or to illustrate and confirm them. In eliminating the psychological and physiological context and in adding his own particularizing detail, the game of hide-and-seek, Beckett reveals once again the poet's concern with ungeneralized experience for its own sake. What counts for the narrator is the moment of concrete existence, not the scientific or philosophical implications it may contain.

[20] See above, p. 20.

Every good poem has its own internal laws, its own secret coherence, which betray the hand of its maker. Beckett's Descartes may begin by resembling the fiery innovator who, "animated, like all reformers (I was about to say apostles), by an ardent spirit of propaganda . . . desired above all that . . . [his ideas] be accepted everywhere" (AT, XII, 168), but the prudent Descartes who changes his plan to publish *Le Monde* when Galileo is condemned by the Inquisition in 1633 has little in common with the narrator of the poem. One of the voices of the seventeenth-century philosopher states, "I am not of those who wish their opinions to appear original: on the contrary, I adjust mine to those of others as far as truth permits" (B, II, 536), and again, "As for me, I seek only peace and tranquillity of mind, which are goods that cannot be possessed by those who harbor animosity or ambition" (AT, I, 282). Reasonableness, detachment, serenity seem quite foreign to the Descartes that is the creation of Samuel Beckett, poet. This fictional being is violent and exuberant; punning, swearing, obscene; skeptical and sarcastic; sorrowing, anguished, and suppliant. Even such tumultuous vitality and apparently chaotic disorder have, nevertheless, unity and direction. If Beckett is a translator of the diary of existence, he is also (even though to some degree unwillingly and in spite of himself) an artist, a maker of form, which is order. In the last part of this essay, I shall abandon for the most part the effort to confront the poet with the philosopher and seek this order more directly and exclusively in the outcome of their encounter, in the work of art itself.

The Illusion and Its Destruction; The Reality and Its Expression

When Samuel Beckett wrote *Whoroscope* in the fall of 1929, the prosperity of the United States was crumbling under the effects of the great Depression. The world of the twenty-three-year-old Paris student had been and was the world of letters, however, and his vision of human bankruptcy was literary and existential, not economic. It came to him in part through his professor at Trinity, Thomas B. Rudmose-Brown, who exercised a profound influence on him and who preferred the poets of darkness: Racine, Baudelaire. Beckett found elements of this vision, too, in the inferno of Dante. When this maturing vision came up against the Cartesian

46

dream in *Whoroscope*, the dream took on the colors of illusion against a somber background that seemed more real. As Descartes, sensing the unreality of the world his education had erected around him, had tried to rebuild from the ground up, so Beckett, faced with the world of Descartes, rejected it in favor of a reality his nature and experience told him was deeper, truer—at least for him.

The structure of the poem reveals the salient features of Beckett's landscape and replaces at the same time the Cartesian architecture we might have expected to find present. The image of a loom, on which the fabric of a human existence is woven, recalls Clotho and her spinning wheel. "The shuttle of a ripening egg combs the warp of his days," writes Beckett in the notes. The image gives an accurate account of the basic design of the poem, essentially like the grid formed on the loom by the shuttle that comes and goes and, like the succession of the days that ripen the egg, little by little creates a horizontal dimension across the strands of the warp until the pattern of the cloth—or a man's life—is consummated. The image is significant also because the subject of the composition and the weaver are not the same. Descartes' fate is in hands other than his own, a power symbolized again at the end of the poem by a murdering queen and a powerful, antagonistic physician who is petitioned in vain. The choice of such a key metaphor shows a radical difference in point of view between Beckett and Descartes. The images chosen by the philosopher are equally revealing and recur with a persistence that guarantees they are much more than arbitrary rhetorical decorations. Descartes is forever speaking of roads that lead toward coveted goals. Images of increase, ascent, and harvest appear; he writes of the pilot that guides the ship and of piercing the walls of a dark cave to let in light; but the fundamental figure, without a doubt, is the construction of buildings and cities, with emphasis upon the importance of the foundation and its relation to the solidity and height of the structure. All this Beckett abandons. *Homo faber*, the humanist and idealist, the architect of his own destiny, vanishes, for progress is either a myth or occurs on the periphery. Every individual moves downward along a dead-end road, and this is what counts.

Stasis and disintegration, two experiences of living that Beckett considers primordial, will be conveyed in *En attendant Godot* and elsewhere principally by circular and linear movement. Both are already present, although in more rudimentary form, in *Whoro-*

scope. Since the remembered events of the poem do not follow a chronological development, he relies here on a repeatedly inter-rupted recollection of the past. The back-and-forth movement between present and past in the end creates the impression of the passage of time in much the same way that a series of flashbacks in a film does. Different moments in the past are illuminated one after another until a sense of the span of years reaching from child-hood to maturity is produced. As we have seen, Beckett portrays the experience of decline (a prefiguring of the disintegration depicted in the novels and plays) primarily through a progressive shift in tone. Since Descartes died at the relatively young age of fifty-three, he can foreshadow only in a very remote way the future development of the Beckett protagonist, who experiences the physi-cal and mental deterioration of the very old. At the same time, this theme is vividly suggested in the image of the ripening egg, which reflects, in a complex blend of the comic with derision and pity, the maturing of the philosopher.

The experience of immobility, of standing still while the days come and go in monotonous succession, clashes directly with the images of travel, of building, and, to the degree that it exists, of progress in the writing of Descartes. It is this profound intuition of the static nature of existence and the superficiality of progress that makes Beckett lash out against Voltaire in *Godot.* Motionless, man is carried along in gray obscurity toward the night. He does not march triumphantly upward in ever-increasing enlightenment. The figure of the clock on the cover of *Whoroscope* suggests the circular aspect of time, its essentially repetitive nature. The very title of the poem suggests an immobile spectator who watches the hours go by, and we could hardly ask for a more appropriately named press or a more fitting subject for the competition. (Even if things did start out the other way around, all is grist for an ingenious author's mill!) The poem itself describes a metaphorical circle, since it begins with the title *Whoroscope* and ends on the key word "hour."[21] Lines 7

---

[21] The use of circularity to express stasis, through repeated returns to the same point, will be much more fully developed in other works, from "Ding-Dong" to *Come and Go.* In its incipient form in *Whoroscope,* however, it already represents a tendency, one quite opposed to the direction of Cartesian thought. "The scholastics maintained, since Aristotle, that circular move-ment, of which we have the finest example constantly before our eyes in the movement of the heavens, is the perfect movement. This was a prejudice to be destroyed, and Descartes invokes divine immutability a second time:

through 10 are especially significant because they have to do with relative motion: "That's not moving, that's *moving*." Here, as in the poem and in human existence, immobility and movement are inseparably united. It is hardly less than extraordinary that Beckett should have discovered and placed at the beginning of his first published work a figure that so perfectly incarnates the two central intuitions that he was to develop in his writing over the succeeding thirty or more years. "That's not moving, that's *moving*" figures in a context of science and space. Beckett will shift the context to art and broaden it to include human time. In *En attendant Godot* especially he will make brilliant use of motion and stasis not only to represent man's environment but also to symbolize the temporal aspect of his existence. This space-time art, so expressive of a modern sensibility that has come to feel instinctively the interpenetration and fundamental identity of the two dimensions, was no doubt encouraged in its development by the contact with Cartesian and Galilean discussions both of relative motion and of the Copernican theory (7). We have already seen how for Descartes the figure of the stationary man on the moving boat suggested the earth, motionless with regard to the ether carrying it along but at the same time moving with reference to the sun.[22] Such spatial considerations, of course, contain within them a temporal dimension, and the revolution of the earth around the sun suggests already in its circularity the repetition of the days suggested by the shuttle that moves

---

circular movement supposes a change in direction at every moment and therefore does nothing itself but change" (AT, XII, 375). This revelation of the linear within the circular might be seen as a figure of seventeenth-century scientific progress breaking out of what seemed to be the immobile perfection of medieval tradition. Beckett, in *Godot*, reverses the process. The myth of scientific progress is absorbed into the eternal repetitions of human existence: the straight line is subsumed under the circle.

[22] The occasionalist philosopher Arnold Geulincx inspires a number of variants in Beckett's trilogy. See for example pages 101, 104, 106, and 216 in *L'Innommable* (Paris: Les Editions de Minuit, 1953), or the beautiful passage on page 76 of *Molloy* that links the metaphor of the voyage toward the west with the theme of man's very restricted freedom: "Moi j'avais aimé l'image de ce vieux Geulincx, mort jeune, qui m'accordait la liberté sur le noir navire d'Ulysse, de me couler vers le levant, sur le pont. C'est une grande liberté pour qui n'a pas l'âme des pionniers. Et sur la poupe, penché sur le flot, esclave tristement hilaire, je regarde l'orgueilleux et inutile sillon. Qui, ne m'éloignant de nulle patrie, ne m'emporte vers nul naufrage."

rhythmically across the warp of man's life. In line 15 of *Whoroscope* "three days and four nights" have gone by, and in *Godot* Pozzo's speech links the cosmic movements to the passage of man's life.[23] At the same time, the theme of waiting, closely associated with varying degrees of immobility in *Godot*, is already central in the narrator's long wait for the ripening egg in *Whoroscope*, and present as well in the lines, "Who's that? Hals?/ Let him wait" (27-28). Structurally, however, it is the five passages and several allusions forming the horizontal axis of the poem that, apart from the specific nature of their content, recreate the sense of the static by their refrain-like character.

In effect, and appearances notwithstanding, *Whoroscope* is not unlike an ancient ballad in its form. A series of stanzas carry the story forward, while a recurrent motif is maintained in the burden of the poem. Besides combining the fundamental movements of variation and repetition, such a pattern is profoundly poetic in that the refrain, like the chorus in a Greek tragedy, may reveal a universal meaning or archetypal experience that lies half-hidden in the concrete particularity of the narrative. In *Whoroscope* we witness the beginning of a disintegration of form that is typically modern and that Beckett, in a novel like *Comment c'est*, will carry further and use more effectively than perhaps any other twentieth-century writer. Nevertheless, the traditional structure is still quite visible. A more significant departure from literary convention and no small achievement on the part of the young poet is the use of the refrain for its own sake, as refrain. In *Whoroscope* it is recurrence as a modality of being, the static as an elemental component of human existence, that Beckett expresses in the repeated return of the motif, in "the shuttle of a ripening egg."

If this "poem on time," in the central meaning that emerges from its basic structure, is concerned both with man's existential immobility in the midst of the ephemeral agitations that disturb the surface of life (the tumult of episodes from Descartes' past) and with his gradual downward course toward the grave, it also implies a particular awareness of time itself. In the third of the metaphysical meditations, and precisely in that part Beckett used as a source in his rendering of the proof of God "by exhaustion," Descartes expressed a view of time that has several points in common with the temporal consciousness of Beckett's later characters. This view

[23] (Paris: Les Editions de Minuit, 1952), pp. 60-61.

is probably closely related, as well, to the general organization of *Whoroscope* and later works. "For the entire duration of my life can be divided into an infinity of parts, none of which depends in any way on the others; and thus, from the fact that a little earlier I was, it does not follow that I must now be, unless it so happens that at this moment some cause produces and creates me, as it were, a second time, that is to say, preserves me. . . . Natural reason shows us clearly that preservation and creation differ only by reference to our mode of thinking, and not at all in fact. All that is necessary here then is that I question myself, in order to determine whether I possess some power and ability that will enable me to act in such a way that I, who am now, shall still be in the future . . ." (AT, IX, 39). Such a view stresses the discontinuity of time, the absence of any causal connection between the discrete moments of existence. In *Whoroscope* we find a similar string of isolated moments recalled by the narrator from his own past. They are not arranged in any strictly chronological or logical order. One thing leads to another through a process of association that suggests the freedom of the dream state, or of involuntary memory—or simply the relaxing of conceptual control that may characterize the process of poetic creation. The "squinty doaty" of Descartes' childhood calls up his own child of later years, perhaps because of the infirmity of each or because he loved them both, perhaps because both were little girls, but probably for all of these reasons together, and others. One could multiply the examples: "blood" is a link between Francine's illness and the research of Harvey, and the heart or "cracked beater" between the English scientist and Henri IV, king of France. A question of justice and of money leads from his brother, Peter, to his army service; "syllogism" brings the Jesuits to mind; the combination of pseudo-science and mysticism in the Rosicrucian writings perhaps makes him (or Beckett) think of his "sophistical" natural explanation of the supernatural in his debate with Arnauld over transubstantiation.

In the case of Descartes, the notion of discontinuity is much less apparent in other areas of his thought and in his mode of thinking than we might expect. In the *Metaphysical Meditations*, for example, where he has a certain number of topics to treat, we might have anticipated a relatively exhaustive treatment of each topic in its place and a comparatively loose relationship between topics. On the contrary, in order to strengthen the logical connections, he allows himself, as he admits in the résumé that precedes the work, to treat a single subject in several different places: "But because it may happen that some will expect me to adduce proofs of the immortality of the soul at that point, I feel that I must advise them now that, having tried to write nothing in this treatise for which I did not have very exact evidence, I found myself obliged to follow an order similar to that used by geometricians, that is, to include all the steps on which the proposition to be proved depends before coming to any conclusions." An analysis of Descartes' style discloses the same preoccupation with logical interconnections, and the *Discourse on Method* outlines a procedure in which everything is strictly dependent on what precedes. This is the way of the architect and builder, revealed in the images he chooses. It is as though, faced with a chaos of information learned at school or acquired through sense perception from the world about him; realizing that the jumble contains truths, half-truths, and error; and conscious above all of the disparate, unrelated nature of the components of this "world," in space and in time, Descartes were driven to seek continuity, hierarchy, order. As a philosopher dealing discursively in concepts, he had no obligation to describe in and through his style the ideal structure he created (at least partly as a reaction to the reality he saw). To some degree—as poet and visionary—he did so, but primarily he remains the abstract idealist for whom language is essentially no more than communication.

To Beckett, artist in search of reality, ideal visions resemble escapist utopias, concepts are at best by-products, and words are music, color, and clay. The starting point, the initial vision of reality, seems to have been similar for the two men. Certainly, the modern world Samuel Beckett grew up in and came to know as an adult was at least as chaotic as that of his seventeenth-century model. Beckett, however, did not follow the path of the idealist in an attempt to create order out of chaos. He took the road of realism instead. He chose, as had other modern writers before him, to create in art a mirror of reality. For those to whom the multiform natural and social patterns, like the inner orderings of the mind, appear hardly more real than those momentary designs traced by shifting currents on the surface of a stream, no other serious artistic alternative is possible.

We have only to consider the way in which Descartes integrates the idea of discontinuous time into a structure of logical argumentation, where it serves as a building block in the erection of a metaphysical system, in order to realize that Beckett's Descartes is more Beckett than Descartes. Far from absorbing discontinuity into a larger continuity, the poet disregards logical and chronological sequence in the episodic recollections of the narrator, expressing in this way a discontinuity that will become much more radical in later works. The past in *En attendant Godot* is still further fragmented. The link between past and present becomes tenuous as memory fails. In *Comment c'est* the very existence of this phantom reality that once may have been is called into question. The uncertainty about the future, about whether Godot will come or not, for example, is already present as well in *Whoroscope*. No one can foresee what is to come, as the title indicates. Only death can be forecast with certainty. The skies are "starless, inscrutable," like the shell of the egg that reveals nothing to the occupant within.

When the past and future have no necessary relationship to the present, when doubt begins to eat away their substance until they seem like "cave-phantoms," present time may become a last refuge of being. The concrete reality of the moment, which the refrain brings back again and again, and the undeniable physical presence of the egg foreshadow the preoccupation with the physiological details of living in the here and now, of eating and sleeping, moving the parts of the body, suffering and inflicting pain, which play such a prominent part in Beckett's later works. The routine of everyday living, monotonous and meaningless though it be, can serve as a last stronghold against the terrible sense of unreality that may pervade both past and future.

Even the present, however, is not immune. A man builds his knowledge of himself and his sense of personal being on patterns that emerge from a past made up of moments bound one to the other. Or else he finds his identity in an ideal built on faith in the future, in plans projected into a familiar world linked to the present in a thousand ways. When continuity between past, present, and future dissolves, the foundations of ontological certainty are shaken, and the feeling of estrangement from self can only be parried, not exorcised, by the sense of physical existence in the present. The uncertainty about time's two other dimensions invades the third. In this respect, Beckett's narrator differs profoundly from René Descartes, whose own being, we suspect, was never seriously questioned, whose religious faith was at most held in abeyance for a

53

short period, and whose confidence in the existence of the natural world soon became unshakeable. Purpose, plan, and progression mark his thought. In *Whoroscope*, on the contrary, random recollections and an enigmatic future cast their shadow over the present. While the existence of the egg is literally assured, the embryonic state of the chick inside clearly parallels the undeveloped nature of true being in man. The life of the chick will be cut short before it has its "second starless inscrutable hour." Being, shadowy and uncertain in the past and future, is stunted in the present.

In later works, a dichotomy develops between what Beckett calls "existence by proxy" and this more real but rudimentary being, between life on the surface—conventional, habitual, automatic—and a deeper, truer, but inchoate reality. The split is present already in the horizontal and vertical axes of *Whoroscope*, in the narrator's memories and final prayer that contrast with the recurrent motif of the egg, but it has not yet found anything like a full or adequate artistic expression. Later it will be the keystone of Beckett's dramatic and novelistic structures. Here it is implicit; in *All That Fall* it becomes almost explicit. Mrs. Rooney speaks:

> I remember once attending a lecture by one of these new mind doctors. . . . I remember his telling us the story of a little girl, very strange and unhappy in her ways, and how he treated her unsuccessfully over a period of years and was finally obliged to give up the case. He could find nothing wrong with her, he said. The only thing wrong with her as far as he could see was that she was dying. And she did in fact die, shortly after he washed his hands of her. . . . When he had done with the little girl he stood there motionless for some time, quite two minutes I should say, looking down at his table. Then he suddenly raised his head and exclaimed, as if he had had a revelation, The trouble with her was she had never been really born![24]

In a poem that is under the sign of destiny's loom, in which both the refrain and the thread of narrative tell of lives snipped off too soon, we might expect to find other untimely ends, and indeed we do. In fact, three moments, elegiac and symbolic, contrast with passages expressing the aggressive, vital urge to conquer and create —in a word, to live. Two lament the end, real or figurative, of young girls, Francine and Anna Maria Schurmans; the third recalls

[24] (New York: Grove Press, 1957), pp. 50-52.

the unexpected demise of Henri IV, exemplary in his kingship, under an assassin's blade. All three figure the unfulfilled nature of man's essential being.

Baillet wrote that Bacon wished to reconcile the human mind with nature or natural things and to reestablish communication between them. Beckett shows a similar concern for concrete reality, an equal distrust of abstract knowledge, and less confidence in the human mind. How can a dwarf, incapable of the plenitude of being, know much of anything? As an artist, nevertheless, Beckett is concerned not only with tangible things but with their "meaning." Some critics have objected, with some justification, to the use of the term symbol in connection with his writing.[25] It is unquestionably wise to stress the presence of things for their own sake in the works of this realist. It is nonetheless true that, although he avoids self-conscious or artificial symbols, the poetic quality of his writing comes above all from the expansive power of a reality that points beyond itself. Natural and contingent symbols are everywhere in his work. In a poem where line 10, "That's not moving, that's *moving*," is echoed by line 90, "Then I will rise and move moving," a poem that incorporates movement and stasis into its very structure, the phrase "stagnant murky blood" in line 35 leaps into meaningful juxtaposition with "dear bloodswirling Harvey" in line 39. Why shy away from the term symbol under such circumstances, especially since blood, which appears once again in line 94 ("Oh Weulles spare the blood of a Frank") is both a natural and traditional symbol of life?

Examples of words and phrases that assume sudden significance because of their context are numerous in *Whoroscope*. Closely related to blood and the theme of incomplete being is the image of the heart, linked in the poem to the death of Henri IV and to the research of Harvey. The case of the "cracked beater" provides an excellent example of the manner in which Beckett creates symbols. Heart, both inherently and conventionally a symbol of life, retains its extraliteral significance when it becomes "cracked beater." At the same time, the expression is more concrete and specific, since the heart is, of course, made up of two distinct parts, suggesting a cracked organ, and its function is to beat. The new term, in replacing the cliché, represents a definite gain in vividness. On the other

[25] Encouraged no doubt by the final line of the Addenda to *Watt*: "no symbols where none intended."

hand, the symbolic sense is particularized to fit the experience expressed in the poem. The heart no longer stands for life in general but for defective life. In effect, Beckett has succeeded both in anchoring his symbol solidly in physical reality and in heightening its emblematic value.

Within the context established by the primary episodes and structure, a series of details that might otherwise be heterogenous and neutral cluster into meaningful relationship. The "foetus" (31) repeats the central theme of embryonic being, and, as we have seen, is immediately associated with the heart in Baillet's description of Descartes' study, *The Formation of the Foetus*. The variant theme of infirmity occurs again in the impaired vision of the "squinty doaty." Like the narrator in the starless darkness, despairing of his attempt to scrutinize the inscrutable, she is the handicapped seeker in the hide-and-seek of life. Later we sense the imperfection of the chip from the "perfect block" (82) and the insufficiency of the "lonely petal" fallen from the "great high bright rose" (83). In these images we verge upon the theme of exile, which, in fact, appears in a matching position toward the end of the next and final part of the poem. Through an allusion to Dante, the exile, the poet not only recalls again Descartes, the Frenchman in Holland, but also Beckett, the Irishman in France (at the Ecole Normale), as well as man, the chronic exile. We begin to perceive how alienation, even voluntary, is intimately linked to the experience of unfulfilled being. The psychic sense of plenitude develops in part at least as a concomitant of social development and integration. We are all aliens, to some extent, even in our native habitats, but the sense of estrangement—ontological and, for many, metaphysical—is intensified by literal expatriation. However successful the adaptation to a new environment, the ghost of another self, abandoned before maturity, remains to haunt the consciousness of someone "living by proxy."[26]

In the perspective provided by such a constellation of interdependent symbolic values, the essential significance of the poem's title becomes apparent. "Whoroscope" as a word is much more than an attack on the horoscopes of the astrologers through an obscene

---

[26] When we consider recent Irish history and Beckett's personal experience of censorship in the Emerald Isle, we may postulate here too a vision of interrupted development. Ireland, like Anna Maria Schurmans, promised so much, but "the harp that once through Tara's halls. . . ."

pun. It implies a judgment on human existence. Beckett the poet, after all, is the one who is "seeing the hours" of Descartes' (and every man's) life. He finds the time short. The ancient image of the ephemeral flower, which sums up the *vita brevis* of man in "bloomed and withered," reinforces the ending of the poem. After having had the hour of his birth, the hour of the horoscope, the narrator asks for his "second . . . hour," which will not be granted him. Life, then, must be counted in minutes, for the hour of birth is also the hour of death. Life is truncated for the narrator but even more explicitly for the two young men with Hortensius in Italy when the latter had his horoscope cast. In taking his title from this episode in the life of Descartes—which shows the philosopher protesting angrily against premature and unnecessary death—as in choosing to stress the untimely end of Descartes, Beckett reveals the central concern of the poem.

If the title, in this way, sums up the movement along the vertical axis of the poem, it also gives its ultimate meaning to the motif of the egg. Why should the précis of life in the horoscope reading have anything to do with a prostitute, as the title implies? First of all, there is the explicit connection between the whore and the egg in lines 12 and 13. In the narrator's enumeration of egg dishes, he proceeds from two kinds of omelet to that Anglo-Saxon standby, ham and eggs, "two lashed ovaries with prostisciutto." The play on the Italian word for ham, *prosciutto* (which, incidentally, puts the pig in the same boat with the chick, victims each of a system that destines them for other ends than living), and the substitution of ovaries for eggs suggests not only the whore of the title but her symbolic value. Through a deliberate ambiguity, the word "lashed" suggests both scrambled and tied off, at the same time the destruction of embryonic life in the egg and the sterility of the prostitute. In both cases life is cut short and the creative possibilities of the female are frustrated. It is hard not to see an analogy here with Beckett's manipulation of his source material, since the creative urge and achievements of the historic Descartes are thwarted and destructive tendencies dominate in *Whoroscope*. Other details of the poem are illuminated in turn once the import of the title is fully apparent: the connotation of incompleteness in "hen-and-a-half" as applied to the childish problems of Faulhaber, Beeckman, and Peter the Red; the relation of the lens (20) to the scope in *Whoroscope*; the ambiguous activity "under the quilt"; the suggestion of sterility in the hermaphrodite "concierge"; and the reference to a brothel in the oath "Kip of Christ hatch it!" (49).[27]

Descartes' curious preference for eight- to ten-day-old eggs becomes comprehensible in the poem when we realize that his relation to the embryo parallels the relation of destiny to man. If the occupant of the egg were capable of speech, it would perhaps echo the narrator's plea to Weulles, and the plea would no doubt fall on ears equally deaf. There is something cruel, not to say ghoulish, in the closing lines on the egg theme (84-89) and, all sentimentality aside, the reader is likely to feel a twinge of sympathy for the baby chick:

> Are you ripe at last,
> my slim pale double-breasted turd?
> How rich she smells,
> this abortion of a fledgling!
> I will eat it with a fish fork.
> White and yolk and feathers.

Half-egg, half-chicken, not yet a fledgling, this abortive being is represented as the excrement of creation. And the ambivalence of "double-breasted" makes it clear that we are talking about man as well as chicken! Besides, the sections of the poem given over to the song of the egg are separate from those describing the ripening of the narrator until the very end of the poem, when they merge, removing any doubt that might have persisted. The fate of the egg is the fate of man. What is most significant about this parallel is its dampening effect on the fires of metaphysical revolt. Beckett modifies the romantic oversimplification that makes man the wholly innocent victim of an unjust executioner. If fate is cruel, so is man. Beckett is wise enough and realistic enough and humble enough to recognize the ambiguity of a mechanism in which man is somehow implicated and thus to some degree guilty and responsible. And he is consistent. Thoroughgoing revolt by an abortive being in the darkness and ignorance of an egglike universe is hardly imaginable. Hence the tone of sardonic semiresignation that begins here and permeates the works of the author's maturity.

[27] It is not without skepticism that the reader may wonder whether Beckett chose Faulhaber in part for the *faul* that describes an overripe egg in German and Beeckman for the relation implied between chick and man. Still, anything is possible with a poet who is also a polyglot punster deeply conscious of the artistic potential present in the interplay of sound and meaning.

As an artist, who must express his experience and his vision in language, Beckett is in command of a complex instrument that can perform several kinds of work in a number of different ways. Like the sculptor, he has two basic tasks: to chip away the inert matter on the surface and to give form and life to the half-perceived figure beginning to emerge. This double operation of destruction and creation, carried out on seventeenth-century French history, is reflected in miniature in the transformation of clichés into meaningful poetic expression. As we have noted, ham and eggs become "ovaries and prostisciutto," and "the chalice and the tray" or "the watery Beaune and the stale cubes of Hovis" replace the usual "bread and wine." Similarly, proper names in new contexts or in translation, which often discloses etymological meaning, acquire new reality or regain long-lost sense. Jack the Ripper becomes "Christina the Ripper"; Pierre Roten, "Peter the Red"; Pierre de la Bretaillière, "Peter the Bruiser"; Anne Marie (in Baillet), "Anna Maria"; Frenchman, "Frank"; La Flèche, "arrow"; Antoine Arnauld, "Antonio." To the same end, common nouns like heart and chicken are made specific as "cracked beater" and "the feathery one," while Henri IV becomes "the fourth Henry" in a reversal that heightens our sense of the passage of time by emphasizing numerical succession.

Someone once wrote that a great poet must have three attributes: wisdom gained through experience, a way of understanding through and by means of concrete things, and a love of words for themselves. Until now we have been concerned more with the first two than with the last. But Beckett is also a master of verbal expression, and his use of polyvalent language, which includes the puns to which some critics have taken exception, is a sure sign of this. We have mentioned the double connotation of "lashed ovaries," but lashed may easily allude, as well, in the sense of whipped, to the sexual beating undergone by the prostitute. Similarly, the "arrow" is not only the name of the Jesuit school. It also suggests the arrow of fate, which kills. This in turn influences and enriches the already ambivalent "cracked beater." "It stinks" has the colloquial sense, "it's no good," and at the same time points up the paradox of the egg that smells bad when fresh and "rich" when eight to ten days old. In its context, to "pebble," from the Latin *calculus*, has the literal meaning "to calculate," but it also suggests the surface of a lens as well as attack by stoning; while "morbid" carries both the Romance meaning, soft or supple, and the connotation of deadly.

We have already discussed puns like "concierge" and "René du Perron," but it may be well to reiterate the fact that they are rarely if ever simply gratuitous in Beckett's work. The neologism (to the best of my knowledge) in the line "In the name of Bacon will you chicken me up that egg" (66) does indeed create a pun, but it has multiple reverberations that break the surface of verbal humor at the same time. It brings Bacon and Descartes together, with all that such a juxtaposition implies; it unites the chicken and the egg verbally, as they are in fact united in the central symbol of the poem; it echoes in "bacon and eggs" the "ham and eggs" of an earlier pun that was far from gratuitous itself, thereby recalling the themes of sterility and abortive being and at the same time helping to unify formally the disparate parts of the poem through its symbolism; and finally it points back into history to the irony implicit in the death of Francis Bacon, who succumbed to an attack of bronchitis after a chill brought on when he stuffed a chicken with snow to determine whether or not the cold would delay the process of putrefaction.

On the level of sound patterns also, and in spite of the absence of a regular structure of rhythm and rhyme, the concern with words is striking. Beckett changes, for example, the destination of Descartes the pilgrim—Loretto, on the Adriatic coast—to the nearby city of Ancona (54). The passage becomes:

> what am I saying! the gentle canvas—
> and away to Ancona on the bright Adriatic.

The harmonic gain is evident. The key expression, for its semantic value, is "gentle canvas," which implies a need to ease as best one can the hard pilgrimage of life. Its primary character, harmonically, is the apophony *en-an*, which Loretto would have done nothing to support. Ancona, on the other hand, adds its *an-on* to the *an* of the preceding "and" and the "on" that follows. It also brings two *a*'s—in the critical beginning and ending positions—to the two *a*'s in "canvas" and the five other *a*'s in line 54. Finally, its *c* echoes the *c* in "canvas." Not only would "Loretto" have failed to contribute to this imitative pattern, it would have supported the system of *t*'s, *d*'s, *th*'s, and *r*'s that suggests the difficulty of the journey in the phrase that immediately precedes: "over the knitted, and the morbid leather." The effect of contrast carried out on both semantic and harmonic levels would have been, in a word, spoiled.

60

Many other examples of the expressive use of sound exist in the poem. A particularly interesting one occurs in lines 29 and 30. In order to create the atmosphere of childhood in this resuscitation of a very early episode in the life of the narrator, Beckett employs the suffix of infantile language and its characteristic reduplication (cf. mommy, mama):

> My squinty doaty!
> I hid and you sook.

"My" adds a visual variation to the two y's and a note of affection. For the childhood game, the author invents, as children are constantly doing, a spurious preterite. "Doaty," a common form in Ireland, carries not only a connotation of endearment, but secondarily a nuance of foolishness and senility (cf. dotage, dotard). Besides expressing defective vision by purposefully defective language, the author suggests subtly the return of old people to the underdeveloped and handicapped state of infancy. The lines are important both in their relationship to the central theme of the poem and as an early foreshadowing, as we know in retrospect, of Beckett's later procession of ancient protagonists.[28]

Alliterative combinations flower in profusion in *Whoroscope*. Homophonous pairs are separated often by one or more words, and like sounds may appear in the initial position or elsewhere. In the absence of rhyme, assonance and apophony are frequent. Without being exhaustive, the following examples will give some idea of the density of vocalic and consonantal interplay in the poem: by-brothers-Boot; egg-give-Gillot-Galileo; consecutive-Copernican-porca; vile-old-lead; swinging-son-sutler; potatoey-Pretender; come-cloudy-crystally; I'll-pebble-all-lens-quilt; hen-and-a-half; brother-Peter-Bruiser; pa-pass-coppers; sweet-sweat; fruit-foetus-exfoliation-flayed; blood-belovèd; came-crypt; evil-ease; sharp-spires; Kip-Christ; don't-do-did; them-that; shall-swallow; pale-parakeet; parakeet-mainstreet; coy-old-frôleur; tolle'd-legge'd; bold-boy; so-son; chip-perfect-block; neither-new; lonely-petal; great-bright; high-bright; great-bright-rose; slim-pale-double; breasted-turd-rich; she smells; fish fork; abortion-fork; fledgling-fork-feathers; fork-yolk; murdering-matinal-amazon; Christina-Ripper; Weulles-blood; and finally, and significantly, second-starless-inscrutable-hour. It is a tribute to the subtlety of Beckett's art that such sound patterns,

---

[28] Cf. especially the egglike form of the narrator in *L'Innommable*.

in spite of their density, are not obtrusive in the poem itself. The author, typically, avoids brutal alliterative combinations by inter-spacing and in general prefers the sophisticated shadings of apophony. He uses sound associations with varying frequency to point up important passages and create semantic groupings. At the same time, in a poem that shatters traditional forms of stanzaic arrangement and the regular patterns of rhythm, rhyme, and line length, he weaves a new and more refined and complex unity. The figure of the loom is far from an arbitrary image. Not only in *Whoroscope* but in all his works Beckett rejects formal rigidity (preferring, for example, the novel to the theater, because the latter imposes greater formal restrictions) in favor of a less obvious and more supple organization that better approximates the relative chaos of brute existence. In Beckett we find the paradox of a writer extremely conscious of form and strongly opposed to stylization. Faithful to his experience of inchoate being, feeling existence as a purposeless, shapeless jumble, he nonetheless writes as an artist, compelled in the direction of order, sensing correspondences every-where. Perhaps no other work better illustrates the result of this apparently insoluble conflict than the recent *Comment c'est*, an intricate masterpiece translating the struggle of incipient form emerging briefly out of existential formlessness.

Rhythm is as important as harmony in the modern music of Beckett's poetry. For its sake, he does not shy away from an archaic accent in "sweet millèd sweat of my burning liver" (25), since it enables him to avoid a succession of three stressed syllables. At the same time, the rhythmical, rhetorical quasi-apostrophe stands out in ironic contrast to the prosy colloquialism of the preceding and following lines: "Hey! pass over those coppers" and "Them were the days." The irony—directed as much against the form itself as against the content—is also perceptible in the contrast between the declamatory rhythm and words like "sweat," which reduces and undermines "sweet" in like fashion. Again, a galloping combination of iambs and anapests suggests vividly the movement urged by Galileo: "The vile old Copernican lead-swinging son of a sutler!/ We're moving he said we're off—"(7-8). Here the gallop comes to an abrupt halt with an oath reinforced by a rhythm. The wall of dactyls and trochees is like a dike against the rising rhythmic tide. "Porca Madonna!" exclaims the narrator and soon explains, "That's not moving, that's *moving*." In effect, Beckett has employed expressive rhythm that incarnates, as it were, what the words say. Movement that is also stasis impinges on our sensibility through rapid pulsations followed by two hammer blows.

The rhythms in *Whoroscope* are not always so directly and specifically imitative. However, examples of dactyls or trochees that interrupt a more or less regular flow of iambs and anapests are common: "(Kip of Christ hatch it!)" (49); "what am I saying!" (53); "How's that, Antonio?" (65). Such sharp breaks in the memory-stream are, nonetheless, much less frequent than the numerous splinterings within the lines themselves, which give the rhythm an appropriate limping, hesitating quality that accords with the irregular line length. All such small-scale ruptures reflect the general structure of the poem, in which the present breaks in repeatedly on the past in the recurrent theme of the egg. In a still more general way, rhythmic irregularity constitutes still another manifestation of the controlled destruction of traditional forms and literary conventions. Later on, Beckett will write two-act plays, abandon normal syntax, invent organic subdivisions to replace the logic of paragraphs. The revolt against form in Beckett does not, however, imply a radical rejection of all form as such nor a belief in surrealistic automatism. It masks a more positive search for new forms to express being that, when all is said and done, stops short of total formlessness. In *Whoroscope*, rhythm is fractured, not annihilated. As we read through the poem attentive to its cadence, we are aware again and again of beginnings that never develop, of metric feet that fail to stretch out into metric lines. The strands of rhythm are severed just as the pattern begins to emerge. Here again the poet expresses being that remains *in ovo*.

Throughout Beckett's writing, real life tends to intrude into the world of fiction. We have discussed the historical source of the poem and the author's notes. Less obviously, both irony and the comic, which often imply judgment of the fiction by its creator, lead us from art to life, sometimes to the apparent detriment of art. An idealist, finding life incomplete, may put his trust in the formal perfection of art. A realist in the same predicament must renounce such "escapism." If he is Beckett, he will find ways of assaulting the fortress he himself builds in obedience to other laws. It is the author, more knowing than the narrator, who speaks in the ironic juxtaposition of Descartes the egg-eater and Descartes the suppliant. He is also discreetly present in the gentle humor that tempers the mortal seriousness of the subject. In the following lines (42-44), as often in his writing, humor is at once a form of courage that defies desperation and a *divertissement* that turns the mind momentarily away from the specters of human existence.

> What's that?
> How long?
> Sit on it.

Like a man awakened suddenly from a dream and not recognizing his surroundings, the narrator emerges from his own past bewildered at first; then, slightly annoyed, he gives a clipped retort that conjures up the droll image of a human being replacing the brooding hen. A similar exchange of roles had already been suggested subtly in the immediately preceding break in the narrative thread, when Descartes had asked, "Who's that? Hals?" and ordered, "Let him wait" (28). Franz Hals, who was to fix Descartes' features forever just before his death in a famous portrait, waits here like a figure of the grim reaper, or like the hen sitting on the egg until it is ripe—for destruction in the frying pan. The variation in a humorous key on the same motif, which associates the fate of man and chicken, provides a moment of respite from the sorrow that precedes and the anguish that follows. At the same time, the poet, who is quite aware of the comic extravagance of his implied metaphor, pokes gentle fun at himself. Art is not only a way of probing human experience. It is also play, and the game often consists of breaking the rules by destroying the illusion that art has created and then, like a clever magician, building it up again. Estragon and Vladimir in *En attendant Godot* will play this game, and Winnie in *Happy Days* knows the uses to which a song can be put, or a line of poetry, "One loses one's classics. Oh not all. A part. A part remains. That is what I find so wonderful, a part remains of one's classics, to help one through the day."[29]

[29] *Happy Days* (New York: Grove Press, 1961), pp. 57-58. Elsewhere in the same play it is a question of eggs, jokes, life, and literature. Winnie watches an emmet through a magnifying glass. It is carrying a tiny white ball that turns out to be an egg. Willie remarks, "Formication." They both laugh. Then Winnie says, "How can one better magnify the Almighty than by sniggering with him at his little jokes, particularly the poorer ones? I think you would back me up there, Willie. Or were we perhaps diverted by two quite different things? Oh well, what does it matter, that is what I always say, so long as one . . . you know . . . what is that wonderful line . . . laugh-

64

The mind of the narrator, as death approaches, tries to hold together the fragments of his life, soon to be scattered forever; against it is pitted another force, working toward dissolution. The author, as though divided against himself, plays both roles, that of man striving to survive and that of a disjoining destiny. On the plane of his art, he executes the latter imperative whenever he dissolves the cohesive elements joining the parts of his poem: by his notes, by interrupting the narrative with the egg motif, by destroying logical connectives in style and structure, by questioning the fiction itself through irony or the comic. The same effect is created through the kaleidoscope of emotional tones that, on the one hand, reflects the checkered wealth of attitude and feeling of a whole lifetime and draws a multitude of moments together and, on the other hand, by the very association of colors that contrast too sharply, suggests discontinuity and divergence. When joy and anguish; exultation and despair; the lyric, the rhetorical, the familiar; gentleness and brutality; prayer and blasphemy; the comic, the satirical, and the tragic become close neighbors, the result may be more explosive than harmonious. When the centrifugal force of personality begins to fail, the little worlds of a human lifetime are in danger of whirling off into the void.

The point of view of a man not far from his end reappears again and again in Beckett's works. Baillet writes of the dying Descartes, "During all the time of his delirium, those who approached him noticed a rather singular circumstance in a man whose mind, as some believed, had been filled all his life with nothing but philosophy and mathematics. All his ravings tended toward piety and were wholly concerned with the greatness of God and the misery of man" (B, II, 419). The *rêveries* of the sick or the old, which relax the bonds of reason, may at the same time bring a man closer to the essential. The trappings are sloughed off at such moments. Beckett keeps the mode, but the content has changed. The theocentric cedes to the humanistic, the future to the past, the abstract to the concrete. Of Descartes' two preoccupations only the "misery of man" remains, and in *Whoroscope* this misery assumes the related forms of abortive development and discontinuous existence, translated by formal disintegration. It is quite possible, especially with the specific allusion to Dante near the end of the poem, that the ninety-eight

ing wild . . . something something laughing wild amid severest woe" (pp. 30-31).

lines of *Whoroscope* are set in deliberate contrast to the one hundred cantos of the *Commedia*. The unstated denouement of the poem is not a vision of God but the end of man, and the symbolically truncated form reflects both the loss and the unavowed need.[30]

The particular point of view chosen also makes possible the numerous shifts in tense as a human mind moves back and forth, like an eccentric water beetle, over the stream of time. From lines 21 to 28, we look back ("he was my own brother"), move back (a subtle use of the imperfect for the pluperfect marks the progression into the past: "no more than if Pa *were* still in it"), are back ("Hey, pass over those coppers"). We retrace our path with "Them were the days" to end again in the present with "Who's that? Hals?" Throughout the poem the successive upstream and downstream movements are like so many escapes and returns on the part of the narrator, illusory freedom of a being carried ineluctably on toward nonbeing. "That's not moving, that's *moving*." Like the fluctuating aesthetic distance of the author (and the reader), such oscillations in time and space contribute to the painting of intermittency. The egg "stinks fresh" (3), but smells rich when old. Just before death the wealth of a whole lifetime is available; yet then, precisely, one understands that nothing has been or ever will be completed. Apparent continuity dissolves, and life appears as broken fragments that do not fit together, form no recognizable design.

In *Whoroscope*, lines 48 to 50 may well be symbolic in their ambivalent reference both to egg and to the line of verse—and beyond this to the poem—that the artist would like to complete:

> Not once or twice but . . .
> (Kip of Christ hatch it!)
> in one sun's drowning

Harmony, symmetry, wholeness are denied to the realist who would paint fragmentary existence. His task is to break up the illusory patterns that give life an apparent order. If being is undeveloped, he must strip away the layers of habit and custom that lend it a semblance of completeness. At the same time, a diminished reality implies a narrowed scope for the writer. The result is an ascetic art. The poet becomes a perfectionist haunted by the specter of creative sterility.

[30] More prosaically, the prize given by The Hours Press was for a poem of fewer than one hundred lines.

ii. Echo's Bones

Echo's Bones and Other Precipitates is a collection of thirteen poems ranging in length from four to seventy-six lines.[1] They span the period from 1931 to 1935, when Beckett set out on the professorial path at Trinity College in Dublin; resigned his post there while on vacation in Germany; left for Paris, where he eked out an existence doing translations; and moved on to London for two months of impoverished misery before returning, "tail between legs," to Ireland. As another latter-day prodigal son, Beckett fitted neither the Biblical nor the Gidian version. Squandering only the long years of preparation for an academic career and a bright future at Trinity in his decision to resign, he was lured away neither by frivolity nor by the call of freedom. Caught between the two impossibilities of domestication and exile and unfailing in filial devotion, he found return and departure almost equally painful—and equally desirable—alternatives.[2]

He had been home less than a year when the critical event of this period occurred. In June of 1933 his father died. The only real information on the young man's reaction to this event and on the two unhappy years that followed in London—where he endlessly walked the streets of the labyrinth trying to find his lost way, and where his reading and writing were part of the same search—comes to us in *Echo's Bones* and in his first novel, *Murphy*, both completed during this period. Perhaps the capital development of these critical years, both biographically and literarily, is the shift toward "life" in the art-life balance. *Whoroscope*, for all its significance and its promise, is still a "literary" work. Real events lend a new poignancy to many of the poems in *Echo's Bones*. Nevertheless, the literary sources are still numerous and important. It would indeed

[1] (Paris: Europa Press, 1935). Beckett's collection of poems has been republished in English and German in *Samuel Beckett, Gedichte* (Wiesbaden: Limes Verlag, 1959); and in *Poems in English* (New York: Grove Press, 1961).

[2] See especially the poem entitled "Sanies I," in which the following lines occur: "tired now hair ebbing gums ebbing ebbing home / good as gold now in the prime after a brief prodigality" (33-34). The poem "Gnome" (published in 1934), which testifies to the ambiguity of the prodigal's feelings, is discussed at the beginning of Chap. V.

have been surprising had the young intellectual abandoned the very real life of the intellect in the face of onslaughts from another quarter of reality, and in fact these poems are most easily accessible, up to a certain point at least, through an examination of their relation to the literary tradition.

Beckett and the Literary Heritage: Affinities and Metamorphoses

The allusions sprinkled liberally through most of Samuel Beckett's writing are rarely, even in the early works, mere name-dropping. He either espouses a point of view from the tradition because it has become part of his personal world (in which case his choice among innumerable possibilities can be very revealing) or else he transmutes the unacceptable past, creating through the destruction of the comfortable cliché—be it a worn phrase from Shakespeare himself—the gold of renewed poetic expression in a flash that shocks the reader into active response. And the shock is never senseless. The direction of his transformations is consistent, and his rejections disclose as much as his espousals.

1. Ovid

Echo's Bones was born under the sign of Ovid and of metamorphosis. If there is a single literary and philosophical insight that can be called central in these poems, it is surely the perception of flux and the change it brings in the lives and loves of men and women. Spurned by Narcissus, Echo, writes Ovid,

> . . . frets and pines, becomes all gaunt and haggard,
> Her body dries and shrivels till voice only
> And bones remain, and then she is voice only
> For the bones are turned to stone. She hides in woods
> And no one sees her now along the mountains,
> But all may hear her, for her voice is living.[3]

Three elements from these lines find counterparts in the poems in *Echo's Bones*. The first is the loss of the beloved. In the introduction to his translation of the *Metamorphoses*, Rolfe Humphries writes: "Ovid's great work, whatever the official and ostensible

---

[3] *Ovid's Metamorphoses*, trans. Rolfe Humphries (Bloomington: Indiana University Press, 1955), p. 69.

theme, is really one long love poem, or series of love poems: not only the love of young man for young woman, and vice versa, but also the love of father for son, of daughter for father, of brother for sister, god for mortal, mortal for goddess, two old people for each other and the gods, even the love of the self."[4] Man's need to possess what is *other*, or to give himself to the other, the whole question of his complex relationships to the other, along with the alternative of solitude, remain crucial throughout Beckett's writing, and the very suggestive story of Echo and Narcissus might serve as prologue to the study of almost any one of the author's works. In Ovid's account, possession is impossible and at the same time necessary for survival. For the Roman poet, evidently, things might have gone otherwise with Narcissus had it not been for his pride; for Beckett the dilemma is built into the human condition and becomes a metaphysical concern rather than the ethical problem it was for Ovid. In this sense the frustration of Echo is reflected and reiterated in the even greater frustration of Narcissus. At the same time the need is not merely physical. The beauty of Narcissus is so great, attracting everyone, of both sexes, that it tends to become ideal and exemplary. Its transformation from real, as desired by Echo, to illusory, in the reflection pursued by Narcissus, comes to suggest the idea that perfection is unattainable. Such a motif gains strength toward the end of the tale in the lines, "And even in Hell, he found a pool to gaze in, / Watching his image in the Stygian water."[5] The doubly unsubstantial reflection of a reflection, the shade's image, recalls the Platonic overtones of "shadows on the cave wall" in *Whoroscope*.

Most of the poems in *Echo's Bones* are concerned with the need and impossibility of love's fulfillment, and a whole series of themes from absence to sterility suggest this unresolved tension. The sick "darling" in "Enueg I" and the Biblical Veronica in "Enueg II"; Dante and Beatrice in "Alba"; the "spoilt love" and the "dauntless nautch girl" in "Sanies I"; and the "quarried lovers" of "Serena I" all point clearly not only to love but to the obstacles that confront it. In "Serena III" the phrase "she is paradise" is immediately preceded by the words "leave her"; the whole poem "Malacoda" centers on the loss of a beloved father; and in "Da Tagte Es" all the "surrogate goodbyes" of life are a preparation for the final separation.

The metamorphosis of the lover through suffering caused by frus-

---

[4] *Ibid.*, p. vii.　　　　　[5] *Ibid.*, p. 73.

tration of desire (the wasting away of Echo and later of Narcissus) is central in Ovid. In the poems of *Echo's Bones* the emphasis changes, and the lover is thwarted in his love through life's cruelty toward the beloved. Sickness, aging, death are the real culprits. Hence the lover's partial withdrawal, his reluctance to engage himself further and invite further suffering. From concern with the other, then, the focus shifts to the self, and the second element in Ovid's story—narcissism—comes into the foreground. The plight of the original Narcissus represents ironic justice called down upon him by one rejected youth: " 'May Narcissus / Love one day, so himself, and not win over / The creature whom he loves!' Nemesis heard him, / Goddess of Vengeance, and judged the plea was righteous."[6] No doubt, the inward-turning of a Beckett is more a quest for understanding, for the bases of being, than a yearning for ideal beauty. Desire that refuses to die and satisfaction that eludes the seeker, however, are present in both cases. Many a passage in later works by the Irish writer betrays the survival of a need so tenacious that it finally assumes ontological status. I need, therefore I am. One can only speculate about the legitimacy of the quest. Is it ultimately courage or pride or inability to do otherwise or some of each of these that leads man to plumb the inner depths? Can Ovid's words apply to the twentieth-century seeker: "he saw / An image in the pool, and fell in love / With that unbodied hope, and found a substance / In what was only shadow"?[7] The transformation of Narcissus into a flower (a toxic flower at that), and the root meaning of *narkê* (torpor), in any case, sound a warning and prophesy a human trajectory. The unquiet waiting in *Godot* and the metamorphoses of forms tried on like clothes to fit a formless but sensed identity in *L'Innommable* perhaps have their distant origin in this crucial story from Ovid. And in *Echo's Bones*, as well, Beckett is preoccupied with human change. The stones of a cairn in the Dublin mountains become a mother's knees for a child's evening prayers, and the image reaches deep into the phenomenon of death's transforming power:

> the fairy tales of Meath ended
> so say your prayers now and go to bed

[6] *Ibid.*, p. 70.   [7] *Ibid.*

> your prayers before the lamps start to
>   sing behind the larches
> here at these knees of stone
> then to bye-bye on the bones.
>   ("Serena II," 49-53)

Similarly, the narrator in "Malacoda" refers to the father's body as a stage in the metamorphosis of an insect: "mind the imago it is he." Behind such lines work a mind and heart filled with a deep sense of the unreality of the human wrapping and a strong faith in the presence—veiled, elusive, abortive even—of a being somehow independent, at least in part, of its surface covering.

The third essential element that Beckett draws from Ovid, art as theme of art, exists in the story of Echo and Narcissus only symbolically, or at best by implication. The modern poet, so often introspective and self-conscious, naturally tends to write poems on poetry, and Beckett is no exception. Besides, it is a short step from the metamorphoses of Ovidian mythology to the metamorphosis of reality effected by the artist. However aware or unaware of his role as poet-magician Ovid may have been, Beckett, by the very title *Echo's Bones and Other Precipitates*, points with sardonic humor and something less than unshakable faith in the glory of poetry to the negative transformation that ends in bones and other chemical deposits. Only slightly more sanguine is the possibility of flower as poem—especially since Baudelaire, of course—but even more to the point, because of the antecedent self-destruction of the narcissistic poet. The forlorn Echo, too, offers herself as figure of the latter-day singer of songs, but creation has become imitation and fragmentary imitation at that.

In *Echo's Bones* poetry itself becomes, then, a kind of inferior substitute for life. Life eventually destroys a person, and the poet salvages what he can. Like the flower that was Narcissus, the bones, which achieve a kind of immortality through metamorphosis into rock,[8] and the diminished voice that lives on are figures of the poet's poor achievements. This idea is clearly expressed in the opening poem of the collection. Here the poet appears as vulture, able to feed only on the dead. "Stooping to the prone," who are only sleep-

---

[8] Cf. the fine painting by Poussin in the Louvre, where Echo's tragic end is suggested by the rock she leans on as she contemplates the beauty of the sleeping Narcissus.

71

ing, he is "mocked by a tissue that may not serve / till hunger earth
and sky be offal." Given this view of art, which we shall return to
later, it is not hard to understand that the literary tradition too—
living in the mind of the poet, yet definitively a part of the dead
past—may well serve as material available to the "poet-scavenger."
By this route, then, we return to Beckett's literary affinities and proceed from Ovid to Rimbaud.

2. Rimbaud

The *Illuminations* of Rimbaud have been interpreted as mystic
visions, as social rebellion, as dreams produced by drugs, as pure
escapism, as hermetic poetry to be unlocked only by a knowledge
of esoteric literary or pseudo-scientific sources or of biography, and,
more aesthetically, as verbal play that creates a virginal world of
imagination. For Wallace Fowlie, "Barbare," the poem from the
Illuminations that interests us now, is an apocalyptic vision of
destruction and an "apocryphal message, after the extinction of the
city," in other words, a purification after which a "new world will
begin."[9] Beckett's "Enueg I" presents a vision of a dying world, and
it has this in common with "Barbare." Rimbaud's violence and the
disintegration of syntax in the poem are missing, however, and a
greater realism fuses with a tone of anguish and suffering. The poet
no longer wills destruction; he laments its inevitability. Even the
title "Barbare" connotes something quite different from the funeral
chant indicated by "Enueg I."

We are concerned more specifically with the quasi-refrain "Le
pavillon en viande saignante sur la soie des mers et des fleurs
arctiques; (elles n'existent pas.)," which Beckett translates "Ah the
banner / the banner of meat bleeding / on the silk of the seas and
the arctic flowers / that do not exist." Charles Chadwick believes
that the phrase "symbolizes 'the ineffable torture' Rimbaud suffered
in pursuing . . . his painful way toward a paradise where he hopes
finally to attain peace and happiness." "The objective on which his
eyes are fixed," he continues, "is no doubt bloody and repulsive,
but this objective is no more than the landmark that guides the
crusader toward a sweet, fresh, and flowered land." Perhaps the

---

[9] *Rimbaud's "Illuminations," A Study in Angelism* (New York: Grove
Press, 1953), pp. 108-109.

goal is illusory, but in spite of his anguish he continues on his way.[10] For Beckett, less optimistic, the ambiguity dissolves. There is no new, purified world. The "sweet, fresh, and flowered land" is clearly a mirage. Both idealism and art that can imagine and depict seas of silk and flowers in the arctic wastes are utopian—precisely because what is real is bloody, "pressed down and bleeding," as he writes in "Serena I." Human suffering overwhelms us and destroys the reality of beauty. Beckett's affinity for Rimbaud, as for Ovid, is only partial. His vision is darker, and he rejects the triumphant metamorphosis of cruel reality into transcendent art. The flowers do not exist, because the demands of the real are too imperious.

3. Schopenhauer and Habbakuk

The fifth poem in *Echo's Bones*, "Dortmunder," tells us a good deal about the intellectual and affective affinities of Samuel Beckett during those early years when he began writing. His spiritual kinship with two writers named in the poem, Schopenhauer and Habbakuk, is undeniable and explains a number of tendencies in his later work. In *Proust* (1931), Beckett had already put to use the well-known lines of Calderón, much appreciated by the German philosopher: "El mayor delito del hombre, / Es haber nacido."

DORTMUNDER

In the magic the Homer dusk
past the red spire of sanctuary
I null she royal hulk
hasten to the violet lamp to the thin K'in music of the
    bawd.
She stands before me in the bright stall
sustaining the jade splinters
the scarred signaculum of purity quiet
the eyes the eyes black till the plagal east
shall resolve the long night phrase.
Then, as a scroll, folded,
and the glory of her dissolution enlarged
in me, Habbakuk, mard of all sinners.
Schopenhauer is dead, the bawd
puts her lute away.

[10] *Etudes sur Rimbaud* (Paris: Nizet, 1960), p. 113. (The translation is mine.)

A conflict between two modes of existence underlies the poem. Life during the day, by implication, is rejected in favor of the night. From the poem itself we learn little of the ordinary world except by suggested contrast to the world described in the poem, but that is enough to allow several important conclusions. Dusk is a magic time, a time when the mauve light that Homer writes of fills the evening like a liquid, and a time when the beings of literature come to life. Night ushers in the realm of music. "Thin K'in" melodies, the Oriental nature of which the poet ingeniously evokes by his almost onomatopoetic use of sound, suggest an exotic world far removed from diurnal possibility. The church is relegated to the daytime and replaced by the haunt of the bawd. Again, with singular ingenuity, Beckett achieves a poetic metamorphosis (suggested by real German church spires, literally red), when he associates that color with religion and trades the red light of the brothel for a "violet lamp" that adds to the nobility suggested by the mention of Homer and by the phrase "royal hulk." "Bright stall," more appropriate to a religious setting, reinforces the transposition of value from church to house of prostitution. This same denigration of the day and exaltation of the night is produced by another musical reference. Dawn becomes the "plagal east" that resolves "the long night phrase." As a technical musical term, "plagal" suggests a break in the harmonic cadence (of the "authentic" mode), but also, by its etymology, a wound. The "rosy-fingered dawn," then, becomes the bloody east that delivers a fatal blow to the nocturnal contemplation that produces music and literature. This mood of contemplative ataraxy, which contrasts with daytime activity, is strengthened by the coolness associated with jade. Erotic pursuits have ceased and quietude, filled only with musical splinters from the bawd's lute, prevails.

The destruction of passion and activity—brought about symbolically by the coming of dusk, refusal of religious commitment (probably meant to suggest the rejection of moral striving), stress on music and the Orient, cessation of amorous endeavor with resulting quiescence, the very contrast of "hasten" to what follows, and indeed the simple departure from an everyday world and entry into a different realm—is further evident in the choice of "characters." The narrator describes himself as "null." He is the passive observer and listener, and later the scribe who, like Habbakuk, records what he sees and hears. (At the same time, in the use of the Old Testament prophet, we see of course the continuation of the religious metaphor discussed above.) The theme of passivity is apparent also in the choice of the bawd. Appropriately, she is termed a "hulk," a word about which clusters a whole group of connotations: the ship that has carried many, the voyage of life, something dismantled, worn out, hollow. Beckett stresses, however, the notion of passivity, and in so doing links the poet and the bawd. Life writes on both as on a scroll, and neither escapes unscarred. Her "dissolution" is matched by his own as "mard of all sinners."

The significance of "Dortmunder" becomes fully evident, however, only upon consideration of the words "Schopenhauer is dead" in line 13.[11] No doubt the German philosopher's view of woman as a creature to be kept in subjection, unmoral rather than immoral, incapable of assuming any responsibility, has something to do with the portrait of the bawd, who is more a sufferer than an actor. More important, however, is his vision of the world as dual—as composed of a fundamental and primary substratum ("nisus," or will) and a secondary outgrowth of will, which is intelligence and which provides us with a representation of the world constructed on a "principle of sufficient reason." It is not this representation, built by intellect from the sense data provided by the phenomenal world, that is ultimately real. The nisus that permeates the universe, that can be arrived at by direct intuition, that is not phenomenal and is quite apart from the intellect—this nisus is the *Ding-an-sich*, the irreducible reality. In this vision of a world divided into the more real and the less real, we have an obvious link to the dualism of Descartes—and in "Dortmunder" an offspring of *Whoroscope*. This is not to say, of course, that ultimate reality is the same for the two philosophers. They share, rather, an intuition of the relative unreality of the phenomenal world, with the important difference that the German philosopher's system fails to provide a God to guarantee, finally, the otherwise uncertain data of the senses. And here Beckett joins Schopenhauer. From the schizophrenic, who, Murphy suggests, has chosen the inner world and dissociated himself from the macrocosm outside, to the *Innommable* in search of ultimate being

---

[11] The number thirteen is often important in Beckett's works, no doubt because he is fully conscious of the ironic possibilities inherent in the accident of his birth, which took place on Good Friday, April 13, 1906. Man, for Beckett, is destined to be "crucified" from the moment of his birth, but the dawn of Easter Sunday holds no certainty of resurrection.

in a world of dissolving forms, the path of the poet is undeviating. It is not the day but the night, figure of this inner world, that is more real.

Schopenhauer's view of both ethics and poetry helped to affirm central tendencies in Beckett's thought. The philosopher came to regard life "as one continual struggle between diverging principles all endeavouring to assert themselves whilst only one could ultimately prevail. Hence came that constant consciousness of defeat to be overcome only by giving up the struggle as useless that associates Schopenhauer's name more than almost any other with the doctrine of pessimism. He longed for relief such as the ascetic succeeds in reaching, although it meant mere withdrawal into negativity." In "The Two Fundamental Problems of Ethics" (Frankfort, 1841), "he formulates his scheme of morality, morality signifying the inevitable consequences which are realized when man reaches self-consciousness. Man has to become aware that life is self-delusion, and morality becomes inward self-abnegation and renunciation of the world as it has hitherto been known to us."[12] Influenced by Buddhism, Schopenhauer came to believe in the possibility of attaining to a "condition of *nirvāna*—a state of non-being where the will has vanished and knowledge only is left." Giving up the struggle meant also "realizing our identity with other beings," and the motif of compassion that runs through the works of Beckett suggests similar conclusions on the part of the poet. Finally, for Schopenhauer, "artistic contemplation such as we experience in music" helps make possible the escape from the misery of the world that we accomplish by our renunciation of will. Sometimes regarded as poet-philosopher, he himself called his philosophy "philosophy as art."[13]

"Dortmunder" ends with the coming of dawn. Music stops as "the bawd puts her lute away"; the scroll is folded, and the contemplation of the poet—"null," without individual will, a scribe only—must cease. "Schopenhauer is dead" because the nightlike nirvana that he believed possible, the aesthetic ataraxy achievable (music aiding) once desire is spent, eventually has to give way as dawn intrudes and day ushers in the struggles of will. In like manner Murphy is plagued by intrusions from the macrocosm.

[12] *Encyclopedia of Religion and Ethics*, ed. James Hastings (New York: C. Scribner's Sons, 1921), XI, 250-251.

[13] *Ibid.*, pp. 251-252.

As it turns out, the enigmatic title "Dortmunder," which Beckett claims has no connection with the poem, is not wholly without significance. The poem was written in Kassel, Germany, "under the influence of Dortmunder beer." It is perhaps foolhardy to attempt an explication of a poem that the author insists he does not understand and to propose a meaning for a title he declares meaningless in terms of the poem. Beckett pleads failing memory, but perhaps an understandable and wholly justifiable unwillingness to become the critic of his own work, and in a larger sense a reluctance to abandon, even momentarily, a creative for an analytical role are more pertinent reasons. One can surely argue, as Beckett has on other occasions, the inhibiting effects of the conceptual intellect on poetic creation. In any case, there would seem to be a real relationship between the effect of alcohol—as imbibed in Dortmunder beer—on the mind and will of the poet and the effect of darkness, music, locale, quiescence on the mind and will of the scribe-narrator in the poem. Once again, as in "The Vulture," we come to poetic creation as theme of poetry—and to the beginning of a breakdown in the distinction between life and art. The poet becomes the protagonist of his poem, and the protagonist finds himself drinking Dortmunder beer and writing a poem under its liberating influence. And this poet-protagonist feels himself a scribe who simply records, for the active will has been nullified.

Who or what is this twentieth-century muse that dictates to the listening poet? In the poem we find Habbakuk, one of the twelve minor Jewish prophets, who wrote under the dictation of Jehovah. But the choice of Habbakuk is important for a different reason. It is he who brings a new note to the body of prophetic writing. "He dares to ask God to account for his administration of the world. Yes, Judah has sinned, but why does God, who is holy, who has eyes too pure to look upon evil, choose the barbarian Chaldeans as instruments of His vengeance, why does He have the wicked man punished by a man more wicked than he, why does He seem to contribute to the triumph of the unjust? Habbakuk brings up the problem of evil, on a national scale, and his scandal is that of many moderns."[14] A sufferer himself from the suffering around him,

[14] *La Sainte Bible*, traduite en français sous la direction de L'Ecole Biblique de Jérusalem (Paris: Les Editions du Cerf, 1956), p. 986; the translation is mine. Hereafter referred to as the *Jerusalem Bible*. (Unless otherwise identified, as here, all Biblical quotations are from the King James version.)

Beckett, "mard of all sinners," is tempted by the great sin of ingratitude, revolt, desertion. After all, has he not, in resigning his post at Trinity in the middle of the year, broken symbolically with family, society, and even God?[15] Through the coming years, in all his writings, the opposed temptations of the philosopher and the prophet will be his own. The half-resigned, half-rebellious tone in many lines of *Echo's Bones* betrays a position somewhere between Schopenhauer's nihilistic passivity and Habbakuk's metaphysical quasi-revolt, the two poles of attraction for this particular Irish expatriate.

4. The Tradition of the Troubadours

Withdrawal and revolt can be extreme and often sterile reactions to suffering. Artistic creation, viewed as psychologically and socially therapeutic, has been considered a preferable alternative, but as critics of the early Freud have pointed out, the artist may for several reasons prefer the "neurosis" to the cure that does away with the source of his art. In any event life often has a way of renewing inspiration by providing new sufferings, with or without the writer's consent. Poets who are lovers are peculiarly vulnerable, or masochistic. Such strands of love and suffering and art are woven into the poetry of the troubadours, and there Beckett found further elements of spiritual affinity.

The troubadours were sometimes themselves jongleurs, wanderers from court to court, and often exiles even when they were able to lead a more sedentary existence. Some were adventurers and some pilgrims and crusaders. While this is not the whole explanation of a body of literature that is often quite frankly conventional in content, it is nevertheless to be expected that reflections of such experience should appear in the troubadours' poems; and the themes of *amour lointain*, of the desire and pain aroused by separation and absence, of the suffering caused by an idealism forever doomed to unfulfillment certainly do have an important if not preeminent place in their writing. Denis de Rougemont linked the poetry of the troubadours to the Cathar heresy and its Manichean background,[16] and there is little doubt that the hypersensitivity to suffering so characteristic of Beckett the man and the poet is psychologically congenial to a philosophy like the Manichean, which deifies the principle of

---

[15] The poem was written in January 1932, just after his decision to resign, while he was staying at the home of relatives.

[16] *L'Amour et l'Occident*, 2nd edn. (Paris: Plon, 1956).

evil. One is even tempted to associate with the Cathar cult of sterility Beckett's avowed sympathy toward those who, either for similar
philosophical reasons or simply because they are unwilling to add
to the potential suffering in the world, refuse procreation.

If we move to individual poems, it is possible to see not only these
general analogies of idea and theme but also how they are worked
out and varied on the level of form. The most striking fact, to begin
with, is that this modern minstrel chooses titles for seven of his thirteen poems directly out of the troubadour tradition (and "Dortmunder" is an *alba* in disguise). After the short poem that serves
as prologue come two long poems entitled "Enueg I" and "Enueg
II." Here a curious and revealing fusion has occurred, for Beckett's
enuegs combine characteristics of two medieval genres, the *enueg*
and the *planh*. Guillaume Molinier describes the latter as a poem
expressing the great displeasure and sorrow one feels at a loss or
misfortune, whether of a loved person or of an object, for example
a city destroyed by war. The planh includes praise of the person or
object as well as an expression of grief at the loss.[17] Still more
important, often, is another element: satire of an evil world and
destiny. The following lines are particularly close in tone and view
to Beckett's "Enueg I":

> If love quits this place of suffering and sorrow,
> The reason is that joys are vain and false.
> The world gets worse, all turns to pain:
> Each day is worth less than yesterday.[18]

The planh, then, and the similar Latin *planctus* have two sides—
reflected in the ambiguity of the modern French *plaindre* and in the
related English words "plaintive" and "complain": on the one hand
there is the suggestion of suffering inflicted on a subject by an event

---

[17] *Las Leys d'amors*, in *Monumens de la litterature romane*, 1st edn.
(Paris: Gatien-Arnoult, 1824), Vol. I, Part 2, pp. 347, 349.

[18] The oldest planh that has come down to us is a work by Cercamon on
the death of Guillaume X in 1137. Gaucelm Faidit wrote a planh on the
death of Richard the Lion Heart, and one of the most beautiful of these
funeral elegies is that of Bertran de Born on the death of young Prince
Henry of England in 1183. The above lines come from this last poem, which
can be found in André Berry, *Florilège des troubadours* (Paris: Firmin-
Didot, 1930), p. 145. (English translations from Berry are mine.) For further discussion of the planh see Alfred Jeanroy, *La Poésie lyrique des troubadours* (Paris: Didier, 1934), II, 237-246.

in the world about him, and on the other the reaction of the subject, who may lash out against that world in retaliation. We are not far from the passive and active responses touched on above in the discussion of Schopenhauer and Habbakuk.

Of the second genre, the enueg, R. T. Hill writes:

> Among the many forms of poetic composition cultivated by the troubadours of Provence during the twelfth and thirteenth centuries, one of the most distinctive is that listed in the *Leys d'Amors* under the name *enueg*. This word, a Provençal form of the Latin *inodium*, means literally "vexation" or "that which is vexing"; and technically it designates a poem which treats the annoyances of life from mere trifles to serious insults, from improprieties at the table to serious misdemeanors. . . .
>
> The most striking feature of the *enueg* is the great lack, or one might almost say the entire absence, of continuity of thought; for each line or group of lines is absolutely without relation to those which precede or follow. The only link is the poet's dislike which is applied indiscriminately. . . . In outward form, i.e., in the rhyme scheme and structure of stanzas, the *enueg* presents only one especial characteristic: the repetition at regular or irregular but frequent intervals of a word or phrase which indicates the attitude of the poet. This is usually some form of the word *enueg*, but it may be a different word of similar meaning. . . .
>
> . . . the individuality of the *enueg* has always consisted in its disconnected structure, which distinguishes it from a satire, to which in other respects it often bears a resemblance.[19]

The following stanza, one of nine in an enueg ("Fort m'enoia, so auzes dire . . .") written by the "Rabelaisian" Monk of Montaudon toward the end of the twelfth century, will give a more direct idea of the nature of the genre.

> Enoia·m longa tempradura
> E carns quant es mal coit' e dura,
> E prestre que men ni·s perjura,
> E veilla puta que trop dura.
> Et enoia · m, per saint Dalmatz,
> Avols hom en trop gran solatz,

[19] "The Enueg," *PMLA*, XXVII, No. 1 (1912), 265-266, 294.

E corre quan per vi'a glatz,
E fugir ab caval armatz
M'enoia, e maldir de datz.[20]

Although there may be considerable variation in the gravity of the vexations listed in the enueg, the genre tends toward the witty and amusing and in some cases toward the epigrammatic. We must turn to the planh for the funereal atmosphere as well as the bitterness based in suffering that characterizes Beckett's enuegs. "Enueg I" begins as the narrator comes out of a nursing home where his "darling" is dying. In "Enueg II" the failing narrator, one of the "morituris" he pleads for, is the subject of his own funeral lament. Suffering and a sense of helplessness before a cruel destiny pervade both poems, but on occasion a more active response takes the form of direct revolt or bitter irony: "my skull sullenly / clot of anger / skewered aloft strangled in the cang of the wind / bites like a dog against its chastisement" ("Enueg I," 12-15). Later in the same poem a similar tone dominates the description of Democritus, the laughing philosopher, "a little wearish man / . . . scuttling along between a crutch and a stick, / his stump caught up horribly, like a claw, under his breech, / smoking" (30-34). And finally, of course, like the troubadours (and whatever the therapeutic value) Beckett chose to make poems of his love, his suffering, his resignation, and his revolt.

The question we are forced to ask at this point is "Why are these planh-like poems called enuegs?" The answer seems to lie in the realm of form. Like their Provençal prototypes, Beckett's enuegs are made up of a string of disparate observations. He draws on the landscape about him during the course of two walks in the environs of Dublin. These apparently disconnected and objective notations,

[20] It annoys me to wait too long to be served at table,
And to have meat that is tough and badly cooked.
I dislike a priest who lies and perjures himself;
And an old whore who won't die.
I hate, by Saint Delmas!
An imbecile who is too happy;
I don't like to run when the road is icy,
Nor gallop along when I'm fully armed.
The oaths of dice players offend me.
(Berry, *op.cit.*, p. 361)

sometimes connected by words like "now," "then," "next," "so on" and sometimes merely juxtaposed, are in reality linked by a subjective interpretation, by an attitude on the part of the viewer. This attitude is not the annoyance of the Monk of Montaudon, but a morbid grief that infuses every scene with the signs of death, from the clouds that are "throttled" ("Enueg I," 9) and the skull that is "strangled" (14) to the tulips "shining . . . like an anthrax" ("Enueg II," 25).[21]

The use of discontinuous form may not seem especially significant, but like the sprout of the Biblical mustard seed it will come to loom disproportionately large in Beckett's later literary development, and many a tiny subject will rest in its branches. In "Enueg I" in particular, even the typographical arrangement on the page serves to stress the seriatim nature of the poem. The lines devoted to each observation are separated from what precedes and follows and set off by the spacing. And the discontinuous nature of the sections further emphasizes the blank spaces between. As we read the poem and imagine the walker trudging along, from time to time aroused from his thoughts by some sight or sound or other sensation reaching him from the world outside, our sense of the presence of a man and of a mysterious inner life, to which the words between the spaces point suggestively, increases until his love and pain and anger and despair impress themselves more powerfully on our awareness than would seem possible through the mediation of words alone. Like the brilliance of the stars as town lights go out or the noises of nature when a village becomes quiet, the emotions of a man can be more clearly perceived in the pauses, where meaning is still. And the spaces become real pauses only when the causal bridges of language have been torn down.

The poem following "Enueg II" is entitled "Alba." The dawn songs of the troubadours appeared toward the end of the twelfth century, and the genre became well established in France and in Germany, where the *Wächterlieder* or sentinel songs of the *Minnesänger* were eventually to inspire Wagner's treatment of the entire second act of his *Tristan und Isolde* as a vast alba. An anonymous dawn song sums up the genre: "While the nightingale sings day and night beside his mate, I am with my beloved beneath the flowers until the sentinel from the height of his tower cries out: 'Lovers, rise

---

[21] The macabre medieval theme of death in life was current during the Romantic period; Gautier's "La Comédie de la mort" is one example.

up! Dawn is coming and the bright day.' " Often, however, early examples of the genre were in the form of dramatic dialogues between the lovers or between lover and sentinel. In the alba the poet sings of the sorrow and anguish of the lovers at the approach of dawn, which means their separation. Therefore, the natural symbolism of dawn as a new beginning, a rebirth after the terrors of the night, is reversed. The nighttime becomes the longed-for utopia that, ironically, is destroyed with the coming of dawn. The pattern is consistent with the one discussed above in connection with the poem "Dortmunder." In "Alba," a further dimension exists and can best be understood by contrast with the religious alba of Folquet de Marseille:

My God, Your name and holy Mary's are on my lips
as I awake today! For the day star rises over
Sion and bids me say:
    Up, up, rise up
    Men who love God!
    For the day is here,
    Night follows its course;
    Let us praise the Lord God,
    And adore Him!
    Let us pray that he grant us peace
    During our whole lives.

The shadows flee, the day breaks
On a calm and pure sky;
Dawn hesitates no longer
But comes, in beauty and perfection.[22]

In the religious context, dawn is associated with resurrection and redemption, which helps to explain the following lines in the somber dawn song of Beckett:

    So that there is no sun and no unveiling
    and no host
    only I and then the sheet
    and bulk dead   ("Alba," 14-17)

The Irish poet has taken the metaphysical preoccupation of the religious alba—implicit perhaps in some of its profane counter-

---

[22] First stanza and refrain of a five-stanza alba. Berry, op.cit., p. 337.

parts—but only in order to reject transcendence, thereby ranging himself on the side of those troubadours whose values stood in ambiguous relationship to the social and religious norms of the day.

The next to last poem in *Echo's Bones* introduces a dark vision of a dawn that brings only death. Its title, "Da Tagte Es" ("Then Came the Dawn") is taken from a poem by the medieval German poet Walther von der Vogelweide. After a vision of idyllic love that occupies thirty-one of the forty lines in the poem, the illusion dissolves: "dô taget ez und muos ich wachen." The last stanza, however, optimistically sets forth the narrator's attempt to make reality correspond to the dream.[23] Typically, Beckett chooses the moment of disillusion and leaves the rest. In the alba, dawn is the critical moment of transition in the lover's future. This it has in common with death, and it is of the moment of death that Beckett writes in "Da Tagte Es." The tight four-line poem presents a vision of ultimate separation that is a masterpiece of epigrammatic statement, suggesting a good deal more than it makes explicit.

> redeem the surrogate goodbyes
> the sheet astream in your hand
> who have no more for the land
> and the glass unmisted above your eyes

As in "Malacoda," the voyage archetype lends its universal appeal and power to the poem. There, it was "all aboard all souls" (27). Here, the shipboard call, "Any more for the land" ("all ashore that's going ashore"), is reflected in line 3. Like pledges of the definitive departure, the surrogate separations of one's life are redeemed at last. He who has seen others off must now take the trip himself. Traditionally, it is interesting to note, the poet uses the image of dying to portray his sense of his own diminished existence in the absence of the beloved. Moving from poet of love to poet of dying, Beckett reverses the tradition. The partings of life become vehicles in an image whose tenor is death. By shifting the focus to the ultimate separation, he reduces all earlier absences to the status of prophetic sign or symbol. Through striking images that link the deathbed and the departing ship, the poet suggests a comparison

---

[23] The poem, which begins " 'Nemt, frowe, disen kranz,' " can be found, together with a modern English translation, in *Poems of Walther von der Vogelweide*, intro. Edwin G. Zeydel and Bayard Quincy Morgan (Ithaca, N.Y.: Thrift Press, 1952), pp. 32-35.

between a handkerchief waved in farewell and the bed sheet (appropriately "astream") clenched in the dead man's hand. In an even more subtle image, he points to a contrast between glasses misted by tears and the mirror held over the face to verify—"unmisted"—the end of breath and life. At the same time, "glass" (as in "Malacoda") and "astream" suggest respectively the ship's barometer and sails. By such means the poet achieves a fusion of disparate experiences that reveals their hidden unity and profound significance. On the surface, the association of a corpse in a bed with a man waving good-bye from a pier would seem to have little to recommend it. But the compelling suggestion, worked out with consummate skill through the imagery, that the two are one and the same, that there is no essential difference between the lessening of life through the loss of those we love and the final decrease that comes with our own end, discloses upon meditation over this little poem, which at first appears so enigmatic, that the choice is far from arbitrary. Unlikely as it may seem, "Da Tagte Es" is not unrelated to the experience Ovid dealt with when he described the mortal deprivations of Echo and Narcissus. If Beckett, as is so often claimed, is a gloomy author, he is also a man who has known the pain of loving one's brother as oneself.

Echo's Bones includes, besides two enuegs and three dawn poems, three examples of another troubadour genre, the *serena*. Similar to the alba, which laments the coming of the light that will separate the lovers, the evening song expresses the lover's unhappiness during the daytime and his longing for the night that will reunite him with his beloved. Guiraut Riquier has left us one example of the serena in his poem beginning "Ad un fin aman fon datz . . ." and ending with the following stanza:

> Quels tourments sont destinés à l'amoureux sans soutien! Voyez dans quelle langueur le jour tenait cet amant accablé de chagrin! Et il disait, soupirant: "Jour, vous croissez à mon dam. Du soir la longue attente me tue."[24]

A refrain, similar to the one in the last lines above, is common to alba and serena and occurs in Beckett's poem too. In "Serena I," even though it is repeated only once and then in truncated form, it sounds the keynote.

[24] Modern French translation by André Berry, *op.cit.*, pp. 422-424.

> hence in Ken Wood who shall find me
> my breath held in the midst of thickets
> none but the most quarried lovers
>
> . . . .
>
> but in Ken Wood
> who shall find me.
>
> (24-26, 44-45)

Here the sense of the world's hostility increases. "Quarried" like animals in the forest, the lovers become the object of a murderous hunt. And throughout the poem the world is indeed the villain. Even though the narrator is not himself the lover in this image or even explicitly in this poem, he too would escape from this alien world if he could. The poem is built on this conflict, not between world and love as in the Provençal mode but between world and the self that finds its peace only in solitude. Besides the longed-for but threatened refuge provided by Ken Wood in the northern section of London (with its reminiscence of the German *kennen* that suggests retreat into a mental haven,[25] especially for the author, so recently back from some six months in Germany), there is also the "grand old British Museum," the starting point of his walk through the city and both a sanctum and a gateway into other worlds of the mind ("Thales and the Aretino . . . Defoe"). Unfortunately, the British Museum closes and ejects its occupants into the macrocosm. It is true that the phlox in Regent's Park is "scarlet beauty," but it crackles under the assault of the thunder and exists in a world likened to a "dead fish adrift."[26] The narrator finds himself taking London's "Crystal Palace for the Blessed Isles from Primrose Hill" and ruefully admits, "Alas, I must be that kind of person."[27] "That kind of person" is no doubt the inveterate idealist, sensitive to beauty, desiring, needing, demanding more of perfection than earth has to offer. The consequent disillusionment and pain find such

[25] Cf. *Murphy.*

[26] Cf. Thales' image of the earth as a flat floating disk superimposed on water (Aristotle's *Metaphysics* I, 2, 983b19-984a4).

[27] In Greek mythology the Hesperides (daughters of the western land) were the nymphs, daughters of Hesperus, who were fabled to guard with the aid of a dragon the garden in which the golden apples grew in the Isles of the Blest, at the western extremity of the earth. Hence the name came to mean the garden itself. The Hesperides are also the "Fortunate Islands" or "Isles of the Blest" where the garden was situated—and most probably too the western "islands of glory" to which Beckett refers in "Serena II."

86

ironic contrasts as those suggested above: between the promise of language (Crystal Palace, Primrose Hill) and the inadequacy of the corresponding London realities, between those realities and the imagined beauty and desirability of the sunset islands of mythology.

For the most part, "Serena I" envisions the world as a cruel and painful place. The narrator's walk through London is less an imaginative escape into literary utopias such as the Blessed Isles than a series of physical flights from one spectacle of suffering after another. Regent's Park Zoo is a prison filled with cells in which the birds and animals are confined (like the lovers in their thicket, at once a refuge and an enclosure into which society has forced them). The birds too gaze toward the west and their former freedom in the mountains and forests of South America:

> . . . the harpy is past caring
> the condor likewise in his mangy boa
> they stare out across monkey-hill the elephants
> Ireland
> the light creeps down their old home canyon
>
> (8-12)

The arrangement of the lines, with Ireland standing alone, is eloquent, and we begin to understand something more of the significance of the Hesperides for this lonely, unhappy expatriate of the westernmost reach of Europe. Two lines later a homely detail adds a comic touch, corrective to nostalgia: "That old reliable / the burning btm of George the drill" evokes the puritanism of his childhood nurse, who used the letters as a euphemistic substitute for the objectionable term "bottom." The word "aloof" is another indication of the narrator's attempt to disengage himself from his sorrow at the plight of the birds, which is also his own. Immediately, however, he is transfixed with horror at the sight of an adder (imprisoned, too, in its well-heated, well-lighted glass case) in the process of swallowing a white rat. There is no doubt about the fact that the lot of prisoner is shared by all, for later in the poem the narrator finds himself "caged panting on the platform" of the tower erected to commemorate the great fire of London. The image is broadened further by the vision of the sick sealed "in the grey hold of the ambulance / throbbing on the brink ebb of sighs." The city itself becomes a kind of enormous prison.

In order to get along one must pay homage, and the poet sees the stack of a boat lower as though in slavish compliance: "a funnel hinged / for the obeissance to Tower Bridge / the viper's curtsy to and from the city." The viper recalls the adder, and the association of images suggests the base estate that must be accepted if one is to survive in society. The price of food, lodging, and very circumscribed movement is servility, loss of freedom, and willingness to inflict suffering or worse on one's fellow. Other images of prison, fire, blood, and cruelty found in the real landscape and chosen by the poet further help to unify the poem ("Bloody Tower," "burning btm," "flaring urn," "Wren's giant bully"), and the following curious incident suggests the narrator's frustration at the importunities inflicted by society upon the asocial. It may serve also as a warning against an oversimplified interpretation of the poem as social satire. The narrator, like other men, is capable of scorn and rage toward his fellow, for cruelty is metaphysically built in and not to be exorcized by social nostrums:

> then I hug me below among the canaille
> until a guttersnipe blast his cernèd eyes
> demanding 'ave I done with the mirror
> I stump off in a fearful rage. . . .
>
> (35-38)

Briefly, alternative adjustments of the solitary self to society are considered and found unacceptable or impossible. Dominion over the city is a hybristic illusion:

> . . . in the dusk a lighter
> blind with pride
> tosses aside the scarf of the bascules
> (30-32)

Perhaps only the writer can achieve a kind of *modus vivendi* that gives him the kind of freedom he seeks, and Beckett did make a short-lived attempt at journalistic writing during this period. In the poem the narrator envies Defoe, who, far from succumbing to the city, turned it into mere material for his craft. The narrator, having climbed to the top of the monument erected to commemorate the great fire of London, stands "caged . . . on the platform," and recalls the writer who described that same fire, creating out of the city's destruction: "I . . . curse the day . . . I was not born Defoe."

Other elements of the poem's unity come at the beginning, about a third of the way through, and at the end. These are moments of relative detachment during which the narrator turns from the vision of the city to an effort at understanding. The reference to Thales and the related image of the world as a "dead fish adrift" are followed by the lines "all things full of gods / pressed down and bleeding," the first part of which is attributed to Thales by Aristotle, who goes on to remark, "Certain thinkers say that the soul is intermingled in the whole universe, and it is perhaps for that reason Thales came to the opinion that all things are full of gods."[28] "Pressed down and bleeding" belongs to Beckett. This vaguely pantheistic sense of fellowship with all living things, reinforced by animistic imagery, is very often evidenced in his writing by compassion, suffering with the suffering around him. The source of the pain is subtly suggested in the lines immediately preceding: "on the bosom of the Regent's Park the phlox / crackles under the thunder." The ruler who hurls his thunderbolts at the personified park over which he presides can hardly be anyone but Zeus, especially given the introduction of the definite article before "Regent's." A single line, set off from the lines preceding and following, picks up the theme in a more urgent way. The sight of the adder swallowing her white rat, "strom of peristalsis," wrenches from the spectator a prayer that is at once a question and a reproach, a prayer that stops short as though to exclude purposely the lines of acceptance that follow: "ah father father that art in heaven." But it is only in the final stanza of the poem, written months later at Cooldrinagh, the

---

[28] *De Anima* I, 2, 405a19; I, 5, 411a7. The following brief excerpts from Diogenes Laertius, *Lives of Eminent Philosophers* (trans. R. D. Hicks, Loeb Classical Library [Cambridge, Mass. and London, 1925], I, 23-45) will give some hint of the affinity Beckett must have felt with the Greek philosophers: "Heraclides makes Thales himself say that he had always lived in solitude as a private individual and kept aloof from State affairs"; "When he was asked why he had no children of his own he replied, 'because he loved children.' " "To him belongs the proverb, 'know thyself,' which Antisthenes in his *Successions of Philosophers* attributes to Phemonoë, though admitting that it was appropriated by Chilon."

The narrator's reference to the Aretino at the beginning of the poem (Beckett had been reading his work at the British Museum before beginning a walk similar to that taken by the narrator) is appropriate because of the Italian's journalistic *Lettere volanti* but more especially because of his violent satire of the world of his times based on direct observation. Beckett admired the concrete language of both the Aretino and Defoe.

family home near Dublin, that the metaphysical indictment is spelled out, embedded in the image but clear nonetheless:

> my brother the fly
> the common housefly
> sidling out of darkness into light
> fastens on his place in the sun[29]
> whets his six legs
> revels in his planes his poisers
> it is the autumn of his life
> he could not serve typhoid and mammon
>
> (46-53)

The common destiny extends even to the humble housefly. In his metamorphosis of the Biblical lines on serving two masters,[30] Beckett maintains the opposition between God and the world, but by substituting typhoid for the Divinity he specifies his view of the relationship. Since God at best permits the existence of evil and suffering, it is unimaginable that someone who loves his fellow man can also love and serve God. The revolt of the fly, who has turned to his particular form of self-enjoyment, abandoning his servile role as a carrier of disease to man, has in so doing doomed himself ("it is the autumn of his life"), for the price of rebellion, as Lucifer learned, is death. At the same time, the fly's choice is indeed a service to man, if only in a negative way. The cultivation of the self, then, may be something more than selfish. In this passage Beckett links God and the evils of the city (most obviously, the disease recalls the ambulance) and places in opposition to these the cultivation of the self, as the least harmful of human pursuits.[31]

[29] "Place in the sun" is an echo of Pascal, who wrote: "Mien. Tien. —Ce chien est à moi, disaient ces pauvres enfants, c'est là ma place au soleil. Voilà le commencement et l'image de l'usurpation de toute la terre" (*Pensées*, No. 295).

[30] Matt. 6:24 and Luke 16:13.

[31] In a related passage from *Watt* (New York: Grove Press, 1959), pp. 236-237, we find another miniature portrait of the hero as an old fly. The sorry state of the creature—emaciated, imprisoned in an alien environment, pitifully in need of the brief and meager pleasure available to it—explains the narrator's weary indictment of creation in the antidawn motif: "The flies, of skeleton thinness, excited to new efforts by yet another dawn, left the walls, and the ceiling, and even the floor, and hastened in great numbers to the window. Here, pressed against the impenetrable panes, they would enjoy

In its structure the poem moves *grosso modo* from the "metaphysical" to a vision of the city and, after a brief recall of the metaphysical, to the utopian sentiments of the refrain (the first twenty-six lines). In the last twenty-seven lines the same elements—descriptive, emotive, intellectual—recur in that order. Thus the poem begins and ends (with a brief echo at line 20) in thought, while its heart is an alternation of concrete observation and affective response. This is not to say that the three elements do not to some degree interpenetrate. They do, of course. The purpose of these brief remarks on structure is rather to call attention to the characteristic richness of this poetry that neglects neither thought, emotion, nor senses, and to point out once again Beckett's strong sense of order and arrangement. If he is in one sense an *anti-poète,* he has at the same time a strong constructive bent. The maker accompanies the destroyer, the artist the man.

Turning as briefly to language, we discover in this poem a distinctive and significant stylistic trait: the substitution of the nonreflexive "me," as direct object of the verb, for the reflexive "myself": "I find me taking the Crystal Palace / for the Blessed Isles from Primrose Hill";[32] "I surprise me moved by the many"; "then I hug me below among the canaille." The choice of the archaic form, displaced by the reflexive in current usage, strengthens the object and gives it as much relief and autonomy, so to speak, as the subject, with the result that the reader has the impression that two selves coexist. The dualism is reinforced by such phrases as "alas I must be that kind of person," which suggests that one self is half a stranger to the other, and "the light . . . sucks me aloof to that old reliable," which portrays one self moved along independent of the will of the other. This separation reflects the conflict between the city and the individual (and hence contributes to the aesthetic unity of the poem); it is as though one of the two selves, the exterior one, belonged to the city, while an inner self somehow remained alien and solitary.

The foregoing discussion has taken us some distance from the

---

the light, and warmth, of the long summer's day." See also Beckett's poem "La Mouche," discussed below in Chap. IV.

[32] This section continues with a play on words ("hence in Ken Wood who shall find me") that brings out sharply the distinction between the "me" that is found in each case. The play on words supports the point of the succeeding discussion.

troubadours and the type of poem called a serena. And yet the germ of self-division is present in the minstrel's lover, whose daytime existence seems unreal and alien by comparison with the fulfillment of the night. In Beckett's poem the evils of the day have metaphysical roots and the day, we soon perceive, comes to represent life itself. By contrast, darkness and the approach of darkness (the evening when the walk takes place, the autumn of lessening light, Ireland and the western lands where the sun sets, the shadows of thickets in Ken Wood) suggest possibilities of relief or release. Diurnal exposure and vulnerability are countered by the various images of enclosure and protected places: the British Museum, the Crystal Palace, the Blessed Isles, the Ken Wood thickets again— but not of course by the independent pattern of prison images associated with suffering. One exception to the symbolism of day and night comes at the end of the poem, when the fly sidles out of darkness into light, fastens on his place in the sun, and revels in his physical existence. The fly is a rebel and metaphysical deserter and has found his place. Perhaps, then, under certain conditions, existence in the light (though it be the fading autumn light) is conceivable. A second exception comes in the lines that describe the movement of the light that "creeps down their old home canyon / sucks me aloof to that old reliable." The narrator, even if not completely of his own volition, follows after the waning light. At the same time the revealing syntax that splits "and curse the day" so drastically from the related adjectival clause, "I was not born Defoe," and tends to give it terminal value, at least temporarily, sounds a strongly contrasting note:

> and curse the day caged panting on the platform
> under the flaring urn
> I was not born Defoe   (41-43)

The ambivalent imagery and language correspond no doubt to a deep ambiguity in the poet's mind and heart. Life is as difficult to abandon as it is to accept.

The symbolism of day and night, light and darkness, plays a still greater role in "Serena II." The first line, separated typographically from the rest of the poem, sets the tone, determines the principal pattern of imagery, and provides a cosmic setting that guarantees expansion from these deeply personal incidents and emotions to more general human significance. In fact, the terse phrase "this clonic earth" fairly well sums things up. The earth is a spasmic planet that alternates violently between the contractions of the day and the relaxations of the night. Man, caught "in the claws of the Pins"[33] like the dog dreaming fitfully beside him, is an earthbound creature taking his own nature from the clonic mother that bore him and keeps him prisoner. Everything in this tightly unified poem reflects and reinforces this central core of meaning. The time of narration is dusk, and in the dog's dream it is dusk—the moment of transition in the convulsive rhythm. The first main section of the poem opens with a related image: "see-saw she is blurred in sleep / she is fat half-dead the rest is free-wheeling." Besides contributing the appropriate image of the seesaw, the lines make the link to sleep and the nighttime and express the self-division we noted in "Serena I." The bitch, too fat for long hikes in the mountains, is physically exhausted, but sleep releases her psyche from the limitations of the half-dead body. At the same time, "free-wheeling" recalls the earth's movement through space and "half-dead" brings together the ideas of sleep and death—and by extension the analogy between waking-sleep and life-death. But the packed lines do more, for "fat" pre-pares the way for the images of pregnancy and birth that come in the next section. The general alternating movement that informs the poem finds its next expression in figures that associate illicit love with the birth-death motif:

> hound the harlots out of the ferns
> this damfool twilight threshing in the brake
> bleating to be bloodied
> this crapulent hush
> tear its heart out   (7-11)

The injunction, inspired by the restless movement and abortive growls of the sleeping animal, urges the interruption of activities that might terminate in conception and eventuate in new life ("har-lots" not because socially unsanctioned but because all procreation in a diseased world is illegitimate) as well as a quick end to the dying day that would foolishly and in suffering perpetuate itself.

The dog trembles, matching the nervous agitation of the narra-tor, and in her dream is no longer in the Wicklow mountains but back in the place that gives its name to Kerry Blue Terriers ("part

---

[33] The Twelve Bens (or Pins), a series of mountain peaks six miles in diameter in the Connemara district of Galway in western Ireland.

the black shag the pelt / is ashen woad"), the western part of the western land. The minor spasms of her trembling suggest the contractions of labor, and she is in parturition. "Panting" and the image of swans, like sailors pulling together repeatedly on a rope, "yo-heave-hoing" the islands in Clew Bay out to sea at once repeat the clonic alternation and reflect the dog's labor. The "doomed land" is already in darkness, suggesting again the equation between death and night. The "islands of glory" are still in the light, but the whales are dancing in Blacksod Bay, a name hardly calculated to inspire confidence. In this context it evokes the grave more than fertility. The real bay is geographically farther west, but it cannot long remain free of the lengthening shadows. "The asphodels come running the flags after" in a vain attempt to flee the land. To the imagery of declining day the poet adds the waning of the season with the early-blooming daffodils (a variety of narcissus!) followed by the later iris—all hurrying to their end. The "garlands" too, vestiges of the Sabbath festivities of the pilgrims, must go the way of Croagh Patrick, the pilgrims' destination, which has "waned Hindu," i.e., become part of the east as the light moves west. The night will swallow up the land and all that are of the land, religion notwithstanding. Yet escape to the west is escape into death, with seaweed suggesting the "tresses" of the engulfed. And even the islands of glory, like yellow flowers in the fading light over Clew Bay, must share the common fate;[34] the poet's phrase is "Clew Bay vat of xanthic flowers," which calls up not only a color and a chemist's cauldron but also disease and death. The birth of the puppies, dropped in an ominously suggestive bog hole, takes place amidst an inauspicious celebration, to say the least. Even the mother "thinks she is dying" and "is ashamed." While this may stem from the traditional belief that animals go off to hide in solitude when they sense the approach of death, it also suggests the shame that should accompany giving birth in such a world.

The next division of the poem takes us back to the Wicklow mountains and the plight of the narrator. That he too would like to leave the land is implied in the line, "a rout of tracks and streams

[34] There may be a reminiscence here of Shelley's lines (*Hellas* I, 1050-1052):

Through the sunset of hope,
Like the shapes of a dream,
What Paradise islands of glory gleam!

94

fleeing to the sea." The inner vision projects itself upon the land-scape, and the poet recreates the world in his own image. But flight is difficult. The "posses of larches there is no going back on," memo-ries of the cherished grove of trees beside his Foxrock home, follow after him. From the watershed he can see County Meath to the west "like the rubrics of a childhood / . . . shining through a chink in the hills." The spires of Dun Laoghaire below seem like "kinder-gartens of steeples," and the curved arms of the harbor, "like a woman making to cover her breasts," suggest maternal surprise, shock, or perhaps reproach. The early years and the early loves are so many ties, bonds and also fetters, to his Dublin home. The long walks through the mountains he once tramped with his father hardly succeed in easing his anguish. It is rather the countryside that takes on the color of his fear and suffering, as he eventually realizes: "there shall be no loss of panic between a man and his dog / bitch though he be." "He" may refer to the generalized masculine "dog," but it sounds a strange note after the succession of feminine pro-nouns referring to the bitch. The ambiguity is no doubt intentional, and the primary meaning seems to be that even if the narrator were callous enough to leave his recently widowed mother and the land that has become a constant source of pain to him, this would not guarantee his peace: "Post equitem sedet atra cura."

The final section of the poem picks up the main theme: "the light randy slut can't be easy / this clonic earth" and adds the visual image of "phantoms shuddering out of focus" as well as the auditory image (since "it is useless to close the eyes") of "the chords of the earth broken like a woman pianist's."[35] The narrator comes upon a cairn (thought to be an ancient burial mound) that reinforces the theme of death. Waking reality is "worse than dream." Reassured by the sight of a sodden cigarette package among the stones of the cairn, prosaic and familiar antidote to the awesome solitude of the wild, ghost-ridden mountains at nightfall, he prepares for sleep. The poet ends his poem in a moving reenactment of a childhood bedtime ritual, fusing with the beautiful but impossible utopia of the past the hard destiny that makes sleep a forerunner of death. He accepts in this final gesture—because there is nothing else to

[35] The idea that women are more often guilty than men of the annoying practice of bringing out the melody in Romantic music by playing certain notes in a chord after the others, instead of bringing all the fingers down on the keyboard simultaneously.

do—the coming death of his mother and his oneness with her and with all the generations stretching back to Celtic times: with mankind, doomed issue of the clonic earth.

> the toads abroad again on their rounds
> sidling up to their snares
> the fairy-tales of Meath ended
> so say your prayers now and go to bed
> your prayers before the lamps start to sing
>   behind the larches
> here at these knees of stone
> then to bye-bye on the bones   (47-53)

"Serena I" and "Serena II" share many of the same themes. Both portray suffering, the first in the city (London), the second in the wild nature of the Wicklow mountains south of Dublin and in western Ireland (Kerry, Galway, and Mayo). Both to different degrees make use of the images of light and darkness and their correlatives. In each are implicit a metaphysical concern and religious imputations. The desirability and the difficulty or impossibility of flight, however, are perhaps central in both poems—as well as in "Serena III": flight from the suffering and cruelties of the day to the protection of the night (or some utopian equivalent) in "Serena I"; flight from childhood, Ireland, mother (or earth-mother), from nameless anxiety and unhappiness in "Serena II." But in the latter poem especially, the poet's images tell a tale of quasi-resignation to the futility of flight and at the same time to the inevitable and only half-wanted future release. Even escape in sleep is a doubtful remedy, for dreams are nearly as bad as waking reality (a persistent motif in Beckett's poetry, novels, and plays). The terrier imagines as it gives birth that it is dying, while the travail of the straining sailors in the accompanying image seems aimed at salvaging from the moribund land its island offspring and bringing them into the light of day. Similarly, the day of the clonic earth-mother must die into night before her issue, the new day, can be born. And for the individual man the cycle is the same. Each night is a premonition of the night from which, for him, there will be no rising. And what will the painful labor of his days bring forth into the light of that day he will not see?

This is, in essence, the question the narrator asks himself in "Serena III," the first of the three poems that deals specifically with

the theme of love as the troubadour poet understood it. There are
several alternatives to flight, several adjustments to society that
might make life in Ireland possible. The first is art (1-2), which
seems to be linked to love (3-4), and the objection is that happiness
may mean loss of vision, without which art is impossible. Innocent
love in paradise was also the blindness of unknowing.

> fix this pothook of beauty on this palette[36]
> you never know it might be final
>
> or leave her she is paradise and then
> plush hymens on your eyeballs   (1-4)

The solitary life of the bachelor in Ireland, where there were and
are so many bachelors, is a possibility that has little to recommend
it. The first two lines of the next section of the poem, "or on Butt
Bridge blush for shame / the mixed declension of those mammae"
(5-6), probably express primarily the fear of arrested sexual development. The rest of the stanza is a poignant evocation—in frank,
realistic, and very modern terms—of the separation of the lovers,
sung in a wholly different key by the troubadour poet. Images of
eternal separation include bold phallic symbols as well as figures
of feminine chastity and virginity: separation of the crescent moon
from Venus, the evening star; forlorn isolation of the exaggerated
cylinder of the gasometer, newly painted red; separation of Mary
and Joseph; and finally, the unbridgeable gulf between the two
lighthouses marking the channel entrance in Dublin Bay.

> cock up thy moon thine and thine only
> up up up to the star of evening
> swoon upon the arch-gasometer
> on Misery Hill brand-new carnation
> swoon upon the little purple
> house of prayer
> something heart of Mary[37]
> the Bull and Pool beg that will never meet
> not in this world   (7-15)

[36] "Pothook" (as in the expression "pothooks and hangers") here refers to
William Hogarth's eulogy of the sigmoid line in his *Analysis of Beauty*
(1753). Cf. also his self-portrait holding a palette inscribed with a sigma.

[37] The omission of "immaculate" has the paradoxical effect of laying stress
on this key word that suggests the virginal purity of Mary. At the same time
the offhand, belittling substitution sets the stage for the denial of the ascetic
vision in the final section of the poem.

In the last lines of the poem the narrator rejects this solution, paints a libertine landscape that belies his portrait of abstinence, and castigates the puritanically hypocritical Ireland, land of the modern-day pharisee, with a contemptuous pun. He resists the temptation to take refuge either in love or religion and turns once again to aimless solitary flight: "keep on the move / keep on the move." The ancient tradition of the *serena* has been drastically altered, but deprivation remains.[38]

5. Dante, Goethe, and the Poems on Poetry

The great Italian poet is implicated in an important way in four of the poems in *Echo's Bones*. Curiously enough, he does not appear as exile and wanderer. As might be expected, on the other hand, he represents the artist, the lover, the religious and metaphysical thinker, and one who painted an imperishable portrait of eternal woe. We first meet him in a relatively obscure allusion at the beginning of "Enueg I":

> Exeo in a spasm
> tired of my darling's red sputum
> from the Portobello Private Nursing Home
> its secret things
>
> (1-4)

The Portobello House is a very real building that still exists, facing the Grand Canal in south Dublin. Beckett simply takes advantage of the unconscious irony in the name "Portobello Private Nursing Home," by which, as he recalls, it was known. The "beautiful harbor," with its connotations of refuge, longed-for peace and security, final destination, contrasts sharply with the realism of the first two lines. The verb *exeo*, left in Latin for the sake of the ambiguity, denotes not only departure (after a visit to the sick) but also the final departure of death; and from a nursing home one is perhaps as frequent as the other. As though the patient's illness were contagious (spasms are a symptom of the disease called life, as we learn from "Serena II"), the narrator comes out of the building caught up in the coughing of his beloved. Even if we grant that *porto* might conceivably suggest Dante's *porta*, or gate of hell, the

---

[38] For further discussion of this poem, especially the last section, see below, pp. 151-153.

phrase that follows, "its secret things" ("le segrete cose," *Inf.* III, 21), is clearly a strict minimum if the allusion to Dante is to be poetically functional. Behind the façade of the nursing home, then, one may expect to find what Dante found when Virgil led him through the gate inscribed "Lasciate ogni speranza, voi ch'entrate!"[39]

Quivi sospiri, pianti e alti guai
　　Risonavan per l'aere sanza stelle,
　　Per ch'io al cominciar ne lagrimai.
Diverse lingue, orribili favelle,
　　Parole di dolore, accenti d'ira,
　　Voci alte e fioche, e suon di man con elle,
Facevano un tumulto, il qual s'aggira
　　Sempre in quell' aura sanza tempo tinta,
　　Come la rena quando turbo spira.
　　　　　　　　　　　　　　(*Inf.* III, 22-30)

For Dante the greatest torment of hell's inhabitants was loss of the vision of God ("il ben de l'intelletto," III, 18). For Beckett, present physical pain is a sufficient disaster: he had not forgotten the epigrammatic reply given during his youth to a frightened maid who had just heard a fire-and-brimstone sermon: "Hell is now." The rest of "Enueg I" is a hallucinatory vision of a dying world populated by putrid flora, verminous fauna, and miserable, moribund human beings.

Beckett still remembers a saying impressed upon him when he was young ("When it's morning wish for evening; when it's evening wish for morning"—the first part of which irresistibly evokes Winnie in *Happy Days*) as a way of limiting a horizon of unbroken misery. The serenas in *Echo's Bones* follow tradition in describing the daytime as a time of suffering, and both "Dortmunder" and "Alba" accept the proposition of the troubadour dawn song that happiness is linked to love, music, and the night. Woe is not yet total.

[39] Another echo of this aspect of Dante's thought occurs in *Watt* when the narrator remarks that "little by little Watt abandoned all hope, all fear, of ever seeing Mr Knott face to face . . ." (p. 146).

ALBA

Before morning you shall be here
and Dante and the Logos and all strata and mysteries
and the branded moon
beyond the white plane of music
that you shall establish here before morning

    grave suave singing silk
    stoop to the black firmament of areca
    rain on the bamboos flower of smoke alley of willows

who though you stoop with fingers of compassion
to endorse the dust
shall not add to your bounty
whose beauty shall be a sheet before me
a statement of itself drawn across the tempest of emblems
so that there is no sun and no unveiling
and no host
only I and then the sheet
and bulk dead

"Alba" is divided typographically and structurally into three parts. Sections one (lines 1-5) and three (lines 9-17) set up a parallel, and a contrast, between the couple in the poem and Dante and Beatrice. Even though the name of Beatrice is never mentioned, her relationship with Dante serves as prototype and point of reference for the situation in the poem. As Beatrice was in one sense responsible for both the religious and artistic salvation of Dante, so the Alba (as the girl in question is named in "Dream of Fair to Middling Women") is at once the open sesame to the narrator's inner paradise and the source of his artistic inspiration. To understand part one, the reader must take account of a grammatical ellipsis and supply "shall be" after "branded moon." (A comma at the end of the first line also helps.) The girl does not with her coming usher in Dante's otherworldly world of art, as one might be tempted to suppose. On the contrary, she dispels the fumes of cerebration when she enters the room, and Italian scholarship gives way to the magic of music. Dante and company retreat to their literary heavens. The transcendent is banished to its transcendental abode, and horizontal barriers are set against vertical impulsions.

The first line limits the focus of the poem in time and space to "Before morning" and "here." Line 5 closes the earthly circle (at variance with Dante's metaphysical circles) by repeating "here before morning" in a reversed order that returns us to the starting point. Lines 2 through 4 begin at the top with the highest of poets (in another poem Beckett calls him "the only poet") and "the Logos and all strata and mysteries," descend to the lower level of "the branded moon,"[40] and come to rest in terrestrial art with "the white plane of music." Semantically, all this is relegated to a "beyond" (4), while structurally the reader follows the narrator's return to earth. The pattern of descent continues in section two with "stoop to the black firmament of areca" and the image of falling rain. "Stoop" is repeated in section three in a Biblical allusion[41] that brings the trinitarian Logos of section one down to earth as a humanly forgiving Christ and at the same time compares and contrasts His gift with the girl's bounty.

Section two is a remarkable, melodious incantation that in the harmonically restrained context of the rest of the poem stands (set off and indented) as a passage of verbal music that not only describes but in some measure imitates the music of the lute played by the girl. The song of the *s*'s, *v*'s, and *i*'s, as much as the images recalled from oriental paintings (translucent rain on the thin verticals of

[40] "Branded" because it falls within the shadow of the earth. The spirits inhabiting the circle of the moon in the *Commedia* were more "worldly" than those in higher spheres. In Italian folklore the moon spots are Cain carrying a bundle of thorns (*Inf.* XX, 126), suggestive of both guilt and suffering.

[41] "And the scribes and Pharisees brought unto him a woman taken in adultery; and when they had set her in the midst, They say unto him, Master, this woman was taken in adultery, in the very act. Now Moses in the law commanded us, that such should be stoned: but what sayest thou? This they said, tempting him, that they might have to accuse him. But Jesus stooped down, and with *his* finger wrote on the ground, *as though he heard them not*. So when they continued asking him, he lifted up himself, and said unto them, He that is without sin among you, let him first cast a stone at her. And again he stooped down, and wrote on the ground. And they which heard *it*, being convicted by *their own* conscience, went out one by one, beginning at the eldest, *even* unto the last: and Jesus was left alone, and the woman standing in the midst. When Jesus had lifted up himself, and saw none but the woman, he said unto her, Woman, where are those thine accusers? hath no man condemned thee? She said, No man, Lord. And Jesus said unto her, Neither do I condemn thee: go, and sin no more" (John 8:3-11).

bamboo,[42] a flower as delicate as smoke, the wispy tracery of sad, graceful willows) conjure up an inner world remote from both the surface reality of student life at Trinity College and the abstract complications of Ptolemaic and scholastic metaphysics as elaborated in the upper reaches of the *Paradiso*—a world linked to love and art and the nighttime and compelling in its beauty and experiential reality.[43]

"Alba" implies and works in relation to a background that includes ascent as well as descent. Resurrection and ascension follow the incarnation. Dante makes his way up the mountain of purgatory and on through the spheres of paradise after his descent into the inferno. Beatrice herself descends from the empyrean to serve as guide during most of Dante's way up through the successive heavens. And the sun, after its setting and its nether journey, rises out of the dawn. Beckett achieves his particular effect in section three by denying all such resurrections.[44] The key word "stoop" in the second line of section two (7) is repeated in the first line of sec-

[42] Cf. Watt's fondness for the sound of Mr. Knott's voice when he talked to himself, even though "it came, a wild dim chatter, meaningless to Watt's ailing ears . . . [like] rain on the bamboos, or even rushes . . . [like] the land against the waves, doomed to cease, doomed to come again" (p. 209).

[43] Questioned, Beckett was kind enough to reveal the *raison d'être* of the troublesome black areca. It refers to the wood of a Chinese lute. The silk that stoops, on the literal level, is the string of the musical instrument that under the pressure of the player's finger bends and approaches the soundboard. While this helpful information, like the source for "its secret things," reinforced an interpretation worked out beforehand, the fact that most readers are likely to miss more than a few such "hermetic" references does pose something of an aesthetic problem. Many first-rate authors require special exegesis, of course, and in defense of this particular poem one can argue that the essential musicality of the passage, the quality of its images, and its general sense within the context of the whole poem are available either immediately or upon reflection without "inside information." What knowledge of the source does add, for example, is greater specificity to the link between Dante's spheres, the "white plane," and the "black firmament." The firmament-shaped resonance chamber of the lute gives concrete form to the microcosm of art—and suggests an analogy with the microcosm of the mind and images that relate to it in "The Vulture," "Enueg I," *Murphy*, and elsewhere.

[44] It may be worthwhile recalling the fact that Dante's trip through the inferno, the only way to a new life, began on a Good Friday, as did Beckett's existence. Christ died on Good Friday and thereafter made a similar descent that preceded resurrection.

102

tion three (9) and two analogous but distinct actions are brought together for comparison by the repetition. The girl's fingers first press upon the silk strings of the lute, bringing them down to the "black firmament" that suggests the poet's dark world. Her gift is music that fills and soothes the mind. Then in lines 9 through 11 she is imagined in a hypothetical situation: Christlike, she brings compassion and forgiveness. In devaluating this second gift, the poet rejects the moral and spiritual in favor of the earthbound realm of the aesthetic. The juxtaposition of bounty and beauty in lines 11 and 12, suggesting concepts of the good and the beautiful and the areas of religion and art, reinforces this preference.

Other key words combine to deny transcendence. "White plane" in line 4 relates to "sheet" in lines 12 and 16. Whiteness comes with the Latin etymology of "alba," and here, besides describing the pre-dawn lightening of the night sky, refers both to the literary genre and, as the title of this specific poem, to the girl herself. "Sheet," in addition to its erotic and funereal overtones, continues the motif of whiteness and reinforces the idea of a horizontal barrier, first suggested by "plane." In the final lines of the poem, space is limited, transcendence is explicitly denied, and time is stopped.[45] Unlike Dante's emblematic *Commedia* with its levels of meaning that link earth and heaven, man and God, the narrator's poem (perhaps suggested in the ambiguity of "sheet" and "statement" in lines 12 and 13) will point nowhere, since the beauty of the Alba, unlike that of Beatrice, confers only earthly beatitude.[46] The cloak of night

[45] The tradition of the alba finds one of its most beautiful echoes in the closing lines of Petrarch's first sestina (*Le rime*, XXII) where the poet wishes that time might stop and the dawn never come:

> Con lei foss'io da che si parte il sole,
> e non ci vedess' altri che le stelle,
> sol una notte, e mai non fosse l'alba,
> e non se ne transformasse in verde selva
> per uscirmi di braccia, come il giorno
> ch' Apollo la seguia qua giù per terra!
> Ma io sarò sottera in secca selva,
> e 'il giorno andrà pien di minute stelle,
> prima ch'a sì dolce alba arrivi il sole.

[46] Cf. Beckett's description of Joyce's "purgatorial" world contrasted to Dante's transcendental universe in his early essay "Dante. . . Bruno. Vico. . Joyce," which appeared in a collection of essays by Beckett and others entitled *Our Exagmination round his Factification for Incamination of Work in Progress* (Paris: Shakespeare and Co., 1929), pp. 3-22. See esp. pp. 21-22.

will be lifted by no sunrise, and no unveiling will disclose a sun-shaped monstrance and a God. "Bulk dead" (or "bulk banished," as Beckett writes elsewhere) refers to the "miraculous" sense of physical absence occasioned by the experience of the microcosm. For the achievement of this substitute salvation, a bounty so great it can hardly be increased (11), the girl, music, the night are requisite intermediaries. It is nonetheless the solitary paradise of a latter-day Narcissus.[47]

In "Alba" Beckett defines himself by comparison and contrast with Dante, both in matters of religion and art. In "Sanies II," which at first seems no more than a frivolous exercise in linguistic virtuosity, a picture of Dante and Beatrice on the wall of a brothel provides the ludicrous contrast that sets the tone for this farcical, rollicking portrait of a world in which literature and life merge. It is almost as though the poet were trying to win a wager that art can transform and make palatable the most recalcitrant materials: unappetizing disease, prostitution, masochism—in other words, that art can make the nasty business of living (which is also dying) possible. "Sanies," the title of two poems in the collection, is defined by Webster 3 as a "blood-tinged seropurulent discharge from ulcers or infected wounds," which is not too far from an older meaning: "a watery vital body fluid; *esp*: one comparable to blood." Poetry, then, as we have seen on other occasions, is the product of dying (or of the partial deaths that are disease, wounds, suffering); but not the product only. If it can hardly be called the cure, at least it may serve as occasional anaesthetic and continuing palliative. "Sanies" also recalls the word "sucus" ("sève" in the French translation), used by Ovid in describing the lingering death of Echo: "in aera sucus / corporis omnis abit" (III, 397).[48]

The poem opens with the establishment of a kind of international "utopia":

> there was a happy land
> the American Bar
> in Rue Mouffetard
>
> (1-3)

---

[47] For further remarks on both "Dortmunder" and "Alba," and for a discussion of the expanded significance of such terms as "null," "bounty," and "bulk," see below, Chap. VI, esp. pp. 258-262.

[48] Literally: "all the vital fluids of her body evaporated."

By the end of the poem this "land" includes by reference or use of foreign words not only the Americans and the French but Scandinavians, Germans, Irish, Italians, Latins, Chinese, and Greeks. The flagellation scene is the prime example of Beckett's multilingual verbal pyrotechnics:

> quick quick the cavaletto supplejacks for mumbo-jumbo
> vivas puellas mortui incurrrrrrsant boves
> oh subito subito ere she recover the cang bamboo for bastinado
> a bitter moon fessade à la mode
>
> (34-37)

Here consonants and vowels echo and cluster, rhythms and words become onomatopoetic, and the whip and crack of the lashes come through in the choice and arrangement of sound sooner than at the level of meaning. The flagellation scene had been prepared earlier in the poem by the portrait of the old man ("skinnymalinks") fresh from a steam bath and a glass of sherbet,[49] happy under his dirty rags in the thought of his spotless body. He "sails" up the "gauntlet of tulips," his loose old suit easily suggestive of flapping canvas, and glides then through the "fjord" of shops selling Easter eggs and flowers (appropriately called "thongbells"). Everywhere in the poem, imagination's associative powers are given free reign and one thing leads to many others in the good-humored game of metamorphosis. In two lines on autoeroticism, reality is softened by the use of a dialect form, ballad-like repetition, redundant pronoun, and the refrain from an Irish song, "Molly Malone": "lash lash me with yaller tulips . . . / my love she sewed up the pockets alive the live-oh. . . ." An allusion to Puvis (de Chavannes) and his frescos in the Panthéon not only makes explicit the poet's conscious concern with the possibilities of art but also adds, in the context, a vaguely erotic note. Besides, "frescos" furnishes material for fancy's lighthearted play of *f*'s that seems to imitate a breeze blowing against sails: "frescoward free up the fjord." Such sound combinations are everywhere in the poem: *b*'s, *m*'s, and *t*'s combine in a vivid image of the Barfrau. (Barmaid in a bordello? Hardly.) The amusing hesitation between figurative and literal meanings continues the comic tone: "the Barfrau makes a big impression with her mighty bottom." A few lines later she has become "Madame de

---

[49] A cooling Turkish drink served in the *mosquée* where the bath was taken.

la Motte" (a famous poisoner but introduced here mainly for the sake of the alliteration) and soon after "Becky" (recalling the celebrated Irish madam). Rhythms, ballad allusions, and further consonant clusters (*n*'s, *sh*'s, *l*'s, *m*'s, *c*'s) complete the caricature:

> upon the saloon a terrible hush
> a shiver convulses Madame de la Motte
> it courses it peals down her collops
> the great bottom foams into stillness
>
> (30-33)

The picture of Dante and Beatrice (on the brothel wall) inspires amused irony; the contrast with their real counterparts is so great that the art-reality fusion comes close to splitting apart in irrepressible laughter: "Dante and blissful Beatrice[50] are there / prior to Vita Nuova." A few lines later that is just what happens: "lo Alighiero has got off au revoir to all that / I break down quite in a titter of despite." Between the two allusions to Dante, the poet calls on characters from Perrault's enchanted world, along with none other than Shakespeare himself:

> Gracieuse is there Belle-Belle down the drain
> booted Percinet with his cobalt jowl
> they are necking gobble-gobble
> suck is not suck that alters[51]   (23-26)

Besides describing the run-down state of Belle-Belle, the phrase

---

[50] The use of the redundant adjective is one of many examples that show how etymology-conscious a poet Beckett is.

[51] "Love is not love / Which alters when it alteration finds" (Sonnet 116). That "Sanies II" is one of Beckett's Anteros poems (see below, Chapter VII), a satire of Eros, is clear from the following interplay between Belacqua and the Smeraldina in "Dream of Fair to Middling Women":

He felt her exasperation behind him and heard her drumming on the table with her nails. She had polished off her little feast of cream and chocolate. Very well then: why wouldn't he come to her? He continued to look out the window with his back turned to her, he ignored the drumming. He felt queasy from all the rubbing and pawing and petting and nuzzling, all the rutty gobble-gobble and manipulation. Suck is not suck that alters. . . . All of a sudden he felt clammy, he felt a great desire to hurry out and lie down in the snow. He pressed his face against the rimy pane. That was lovely, like a glass of water to drink in prison.

In a paroxysm of pruritus she stamped, she set up a nasty caterwauling.

(p. 96)

"down the drain," which continues the pervasive water imagery that can be traced back beyond "fjord" and "sailing" to the steam bath, is suggested most immediately perhaps by the preceding line in which billiard balls "splash," a verb inspired no doubt by the double meaning of "mackerel," at once fish and the billiard-playing pimps. The pattern continues with "suck" and concludes with "foam." Archaic literary terminology ("lo," "hark," "thee," "thine") is another device used to effect the transmutation of brute reality. Verbal free association and dissociation and punning are others: "a bitter moon" suggests honeymoon under flagellation conditions; caviar becomes red eggs (which turn up anon as the "dyed eggs" of Easter) and then the gruesomely descriptive "henorrhoids" ("there were red eggs there / I have a dirty I say henorrhoids").[52]

What happens at the end of "Sanies II" is symptomatic in Beckett's writing. However ingenious the artistic camouflage, the danger of reality showing through is always close at hand. There comes a moment when the game suddenly seems hollow pretense and the mask of play falls. Signs of pain usually precede such a moment. Suffering is not funny. And so the poem draws to a close:

> oh Becky spare me I have done thee no wrong spare
>   me damn thee
> spare me good Becky
> call off thine adders Becky I will compensate
>   thee in full   (38-40)

The anaesthetic is wearing off, the clown's makeup begins to run. Between these and the last three lines a curious shift occurs, as though the poet himself had replaced the fictional character, and the poem ends in a universalizing kyrie eleison. The narrator's suffering, after a meaningful hesitation, becomes the suffering of all mankind. And after an equally meaningful pause, the supplication becomes the conclusion to the entire poem.

> Lord have mercy upon
> Christ have mercy upon us
> Lord have mercy upon us
>   (41-43)

[52] The hemorrhoid was also a serpent whose bite was fabled to cause unstanchable bleeding. In this meaning it relates to the flagellation scene, where thongs are called adders. As in "Serena I," the snake is linked to suffering.

In the poem "Malacoda" Dante is once again implicated, and once again we find the attempt to exorcize suffering by transmuting it into art. Not only does the poem contain specific allusions to the *Inferno* but, less obviously, homage is paid to the master by the use of his hallmark, the number three. The poem is divided into three clearly distinguishable parts or phases, each beginning in the same way ("to measure," "to coffin," "to cover"), and the three-line introduction begins with the word "thrice." In addition, each part ends with a line that tells of the son's repeated attempts, each less successful than the last, to shield his bereaved mother during the painful moments preceding the burial of her husband: "hear she may see she need not," "hear she must see she need not," "hear she must see she must." Finally, the poem ends with a three-line conclusion.

At the beginning of "Malacoda" we are in the real world, but already—in the masklike visage of the undertaker's aide and his hat that acts as a shield to protect him from the world of suffering and sorrow into which he enters as he crosses the threshold of the home—the artist has begun his poetic metamorphosis:[53]

> thrice he came
> the undertaker's man
> impassible behind his scutal bowler
>
> (1-3)

Despite these safeguards (the motif of the shield is repeated in line 21 with the term "targe"), which reflect the psychological protection of the son's self-control, each act of the aide is a blow that calls for bracing. Words help, and one resorts to reason; but still, the shock is perceptible: "he came . . . / to measure / is he not paid to measure," and later: "to cover / to be sure cover cover all over."

The primary means of metamorphosis, the surest shield, however, is the burlesque fiction the poet finds in Cantos XXI and XXII of the *Inferno*. Into the fifth *bolgia* or trench of the eighth circle a "diavol nero" carries each sinner guilty of graft, slung upside down over his back. They are submerged in a river of boiling pitch and can surface for momentary respite only when they manage to foil the ferocious surveillance of clawed demons or *malebranche* bearing such individual names as Alichino, Farfarello, Barbariccia,

---

[53] Cf. the symbolic value of the many other hats in the works of Beckett. A tilt of the head and the brim becomes a screen.

Cagnazzo, Graffiacane, Rubicante, Scarmiglione, and led by Mala-coda. The last two are utilized by Beckett, who keeps the grossly comic incident described by Dante at the end of Canto XXI and the beginning of Canto XXII but adopts language that is, appropriately, more circumspect. Dante maintains farce and fear in precarious equilibrium; Beckett must balance heartbreak. Dante's Malacoda gives his signal to the demons escorting the wayfarer and his guide to the nearby ridge by a resounding blast from his rump ("Ed elli avea del cul fatto trombetta"). With mock seriousness Dante sol-emnly describes all the departures, musters, retreats, scouting and foraging expeditions, tournaments and jousts he has seen, along with the various means of signaling, from bugles and bells through drums, fires, and flags. Never yet, however, by land or sea, had he seen anyone or anything respond to signal from such a pipe.[54]

Beckett's Malacoda is assistant to the undertaker (a suitably expressive title), which speaks volumes about the author's views. With the studied decorum befitting his profession, he puts his "tail" to good—but not wholly effective—use. Despite all efforts, demonic nature will have its way. The "tail" is "bad" literally, because it does not suppress the indiscreet signal for departure. At the same time, the name suggests the "evil end" to which all must come whatever their virtues or vices during life. "Hell is now," we recall, and the inferno to which the soul now descends is a purely literary one:

> Malacoda knee-deep in the lilies
> Malacoda for all the expert awe
> that felts his perineum mutes his signal
> sighing up through the heavy air
> must it be it must be it must be
>
> (8-12)

[54] Io vidi già cavalier muover campo,
    E cominciare stormo, e far lor mostra,
    E tal volta partir per loro scampo;
   Corridor vidi per la terra vostra,
    O Aretini, e vidi gir gualdane,
    Fedir torneamenti, e correr giostra,
  Quando con trombe, e quando con campane,
    Con tamburi e con cenni di castella,
    E con cose nostrali e con istrane:
Nè già con si diversa cennamella
    Cavalier vidi muover, nè pedoni,
    Nè nave a segno di terra o di stella.
        (*Inf.* XXII, 1-12)

109

On several occasions Dante makes reference to the heavier atmosphere in the lower regions of hell (Geryon descends through the air, for example, swimming slowly as though through water; the monster backs off the cliff like a boat being launched, and its movements are compared to those of an eel). Beckett uses heaviness not for its association with sin but to suggest the weight of sorrow. Logic and convention notwithstanding, the coarse image of breaking wind (used variously in three different poems of *Echo's Bones*) fails to destroy the lyricism of the following two lines. It does, however, temper emotion and ward off the danger of sentimentality. "Mutes" in line 10 carries the connotation of "muffle," but its primary meaning is "voids." The term is used especially of birds and is another subtle allusion to the *Commedia*. The demons have wings, of course, and Barbariccia calls Farfarello an evil bird: "malvagio uccello" (XXII, 96). Then in two images Alichino is likened to a falcon, first diving after a duck and then defending itself against a second bird (XXII, 131, 139). Line 12 of "Malacoda" is especially worthy of note, because it exemplifies the tension (weighted on the side of acceptance) between revolt and resignation so typical of much of Beckett's work.

In sections two and three a second hoofed demon, Scarmilion, helps to put the body in the coffin and to secure the cover. As though trying to play his role in the unreal burial game in proper fashion, the son assists by holding Scarmilion's hat and his sulphur. All three sections of the poem are linked by a motif, not yet mentioned, that is part both of the son's attempt to spare his mother and of the calculated metamorphosis of reality:

> find the weeds engage them in the garden
>
> . . . .
>
> find the weeds engage their attention
>
> . . . .
>
> stay Scarmilion stay stay[55]
> lay this Huysum on the box
>
> (13, 17, 23-24)

The use of the metonymy (widow's weeds to suggest the widow)

[55] Almost a direct translation of Dante's "Posa, posa, Scarmiglione" (XXI, 105). In both lines the demon is halted in an act of cruelty: physical brutality toward Dante the pilgrim in one instance, premature departure with the coffin in the case of the narrator and his mother.

does not preclude a botanical overtone. The two plurals ("them" and "their") and the association with the garden support this secondary meaning. The natural plant that will meet the fate of all natural things, as the mother must follow the father to the grave, contrasts sharply with the Huysum that is laid by the son on the coffin. The floral painting by Jan van Huysum, the most famous painter of flowers in the Dutch School of the eighteenth century, enjoys a relative immortality. It, and the poem of which it is emblematic, are tributes of a son to his cherished father. The next line, "mind the imago it is he," suggests the only kind of permanence—in the mind and heart of a devoted son and in whatever art he can create—that a father may hope for. "Imago," the final, complete stage in an insect's life cycle (recalling Ovid's *Metamorphoses* and pointing beyond them to Beckett's poetry) is at the same time in psychological terminology the idealized image of the father retained from childhood by the son. It is in this double sense that the deceased is as "incorruptible" as the demon "in the vestibule." Henceforward, he is forever a figure in the world of poetry—hardly a glorious fate, to be sure, for the kingdom of art is a cemetery in which come to rest such paltry remains of a dead past as the bones of Echo.[56]

After one line of preparation a three-line conclusion ends the poem with the archetypal image of the voyage:

> divine dogday glass set fair
>
> . . . .
>
> all aboard all souls
> half-mast aye aye
>
> nay   (22, 27-29)

The coupling of "divine" and "dogday" is another of Beckett's ironical metaphysical thrusts, for the hot, breathless days of July and August have long been thought of as a time when malignant influences prevail. In using the voyage image, the poet departs from

---

[56] After this essay had been written, Beckett pointed out that his source for the "imago" was a butterfly poised on a flower in the Huysum painting. As the insect, in the beauty of its finished form, finds its eternity among the unfading flowers of art, so the father has his immortality in the idealizing memory of his son, in the son's poem, and among the incorruptible figures created by the most enduring of poets, Dante Alighieri.

his immediate model. The more or less demonic figure of the boat-
man Charon in Canto III may be partly responsible.[57] In any case,
the tradition of the posthumous voyage is ancient enough and suffi-
ciently widespread so that the combination causes no aesthetic problems. Lines 28 and 29 provide another example of the freedom the
poet assumes in the creative remodeling of his materials. Dante's
line refers to the grafters of Lucca and asserts that in that town
they can make yes out of no for money ("Del *no,* per li denar, vi si
fa *ita,*" XXI, 42). Beckett reverses the direction and changes yes
into no, but the sense of his lines is wholly different.[58] The final
"nay," set apart from the rest of the poem (like the last line of
"Sanies II"), negates not only the preceding line but the whole
poem. There is no reason to lower the flag to half-mast in sign of
mourning. Death is not a penalty but a welcome release from the
cruelty of life. Thus "Malacoda" is an ambivalent title, because for
the dead man at least the end is not an evil but a blessing. Logic,
of a kind, has come to the aid of art, and together they have tamed
the monster.

Although Dante, sometimes for good aesthetic and personal reasons, allows his alter ego, the wayfarer, to express sympathy for the
sufferers in hell, such feelings are really out of place in the theocentric world of the Italian poet. In Beckett's humanistic scheme,
however, compassion is central, compassion not for the dead, since
hell has become a literary fiction, but for the living, who suffer in
the earthly inferno of life. A similar contrast appears when we confront the first poem in *Echo's Bones* with its source. The starting
point for "The Vulture" is the opening stanza of "Winter Journey
to the Harz Mountains," the work of another great poet, Johann
Wolfgang von Goethe:

[57] In Etruscan paintings Charon appears as a winged demon, and in the
Christian framework many such figures of mythology were regarded as
demons.

[58] It is of course possible in a case like this that Beckett's starting point
was not in Dante at all, and that the "nay" simply follows, given the semantic
objective, from the nautical "aye aye." Similarly, it is conceivable, but not at
all certain, that Virgil's initial shielding of Dante from the *malabranche* may
have suggested to the poet the idea of the more reasonable son shielding his
distressed mother. Once again, however, major elements in the two situations
are neither analogous nor even related by meaningful opposition.

> As a vulture would,
> That on heavy clouds of morning
> With gentle wing reposing,
> Seeks for his prey—
> Hover, my song.[59]

The optimism, expansive joy, and religious mysticism of the original are missing in Beckett's poem. As Goethe defines himself by opposition to a morose recluse he knew, so the Irish poet reveals his personal and poetic orientation in the contrast between his poem and the German's. "The Vulture" might be called (by a critic) "The Artist on his Art." It is the most explicit account in *Echo's Bones* of the author's views on the nature of poetry. While the model and its offshoot have in common the theme of artistic creation, even here the views disclosed differ greatly. Goethe's "Geier" might well be a hawk in search of its prey, for there is nothing in the above lines that suggests the carrion-consuming Accipitridae of science. Even the "heavy clouds" are heavy only in order to furnish a stable resting-place, and the poet's heart is light. His poem is a song waiting to be born, and its author in his joyful moment of expectant creativity is in the state of poetic grace. There is little doubt that the poem will be born a healthy, happy offspring. Not so with the somber song of Samuel Beckett.

THE VULTURE

> dragging his hunger through the sky
> of my skull shell of sky and earth
>
> stooping to the prone who must
> soon take up their life and walk
>
> mocked by a tissue that may not serve
> till hunger earth and sky be offal

[59] *Poems of Goethe*, trans. Edwin H. Zeydel (Chapel Hill: University of North Carolina Press, 1957), p. 33. The first stanza of "Harzreise im Winter" reads:

> Dem Geier gleich,
> Der auf schweren Morgenwolken
> Mit sanftem Fittig ruhend
> Nach Beute schaut,
> Schwebe mein Lied.

Commenting on the poem, Zeydel writes (pp. 4-5): "Like the vulture, Goethe's creative urge is looking for prey."

Goethe's accidental image becomes the title and heart of this metaphor for a poet's hunger to create, frustrated by the recalcitrance of materials that are endowed with their own autonomous existence.[60] Here the bird is an authentic vulture, frightened off by the slightest sign of life in its intended prey. The focus is on need, even suffering, with the terms "dragging" and "mocked." While "stooping" (diving on a prey) is part of the technical vocabulary of falconry, it makes a clear link to the poet, as does the internalization of the outer world in the image of the skull. The whole of meaningful reality is encompassed in the earth and sky that exist inside the cranium, and "shell" cannot help but remind us of the related image of the egg in *Whoroscope*. Perhaps the most enigmatic aspect of the poem comes in the last line. We can understand, after acquaintance with some of the other poems and consideration of Ovid's tale of Echo and Narcissus, how poetry is a residue of life, how it feeds on death, and hence how the "earth and sky" of the mind, the substantial reality that comes alive only when it has been assimilated from the meaningless materials of the outer world, must in its turn perish and become offal before it can serve as material for poetry. Poetic creation, in other words, demands a double death. External reality must lose its autonomous, objective life by undergoing a subjective metamorphosis. But subjective reality must go the same way, must in a sense become detached from the subject in order to become object once again, the new object that emerges from the quiet chrysalis of the poet's mind. Thus larva gives way to pupa that becomes imago.[61] What is more difficult to

---

[60] Very early in "Dream of Fair to Middling Women" the narrator brings up the problem of the relationship between life and art in terms of irreducible complexity versus schematization. "John, most of the parents, the Smeraldina-Rima, the Syra-Cusa, the Alba, the Mandarin, the Polar Bear, Lucien, Chas, are a few of those that will, that stand, that is, for something or can be made to stand for something. It is to be hoped that we can make them stand for something. Whereas it is almost certain that Nemo cannot be made, at least not by us, stand for anything. . . . If all our characters were alike . . . [those mentioned above]—liŭ-liŭ-minded—we could write a little book that would be purely melodic, think how nice that would be, linear, a lovely Pythagorean chain-chant solo of cause and effect, a one-fingered teleophony that would be a pleasure to hear. (Which is more or less, if we may say so, what one gets from one's favourite novelist.) But what can you do with a person like Nemo who will not for any consideration be condensed into a liŭ, who is not a note at all but the most regrettable simultaneity of notes" (pp. 7-8).

[61] Cf. the views on pp. 59-60 of *Proust* (New York: Grove Press, 1957)

understand is the end of the hunger itself. Possibly the poet is saying that even the excitement that precedes poetic achievement, the urge to make a poem, the inspiration or unsettling emotion that comes before creation, must yield to the indispensable calm that is a kind of death of self and that accompanies the exercise of the poetic craft.[62]

Perhaps what distinguishes Beckett's poetic theory (as we can perceive it through the veil of his poetry) from similar theories and gives it real originality is this: the poetic death, which after all permits resurrection, since the poet as man can return to autonomously existing external reality and even resuscitate the prior life of the mind,[63] is for him very closely and it may be almost necessarily associated with real death, or at least with the process of dying that is made up of aging, absence, suffering, diminutions of all kinds. Real suffering and death seem both to precede their poetic counterparts and to take precedence over them. Poetic metamorphosis is not a magician's facile trick, somehow fortuitously analogous to the disastrous changes that are part of human destiny (although on occasion it may momentarily masquerade as such); it is their ritual reenactment. In the life-art relationship, art is the servant, and Beckett, ever aware of the servant's inclination to go her own independent way, suspiciously keeps her in menial and relatively unadorned subjection. The form of "The Vulture" is simple but functional. It ends as it started—and shortly thereafter—with no progress having been made. The circular structure that begins and ends with need in a closed universe reflects, or better, incarnates the theme: frustration of the poetic urge to make something out of words. As Mallarmé did before him, Beckett satisfies the need paradoxically, by turning it back narcissistically upon itself. The structure mirrors at once the sphere of earth, the dome of sky, and the closed microcosm of the skull. There is indeed a suggestion of linear movement of a sort, movement toward death that will take place sometime in the future when "hunger earth and sky" become offal, and this movement has its stylistic correlative in the succession

---

where Beckett introduces the following quotation: "Chi non ha la forza di uccidere la realtà non ha la forza di crearla."

[62] Cf. the analogous but quite distinct notion of "emotion recollected in tranquillity" in Wordsworth's 1800 Preface.

[63] For a discussion of the difference in point of view between Beckett and Proust on this possibility, see below, Chap. X.

made up of the initial word of each part of the poem: "dragging," "stooping," "mocked." The first two denote continuing, then downward, movement, brought to a halt with the past participle, which gives a sense of completion. Some twenty years later, in his masterpiece *En attendant Godot*, Beckett will still be using a combination of circular and linear patterns to express frustration heading toward extinction.

6. Religion and the Bible; Love and Dying

Of all the poems in *Echo's Bones*, only the two very short ones that conclude the collection are without at least an indirect reference to religion or the Bible. Of these two, "Da Tagte Es" stands in implicit opposition to the religious alba and the tradition that makes the dawn an image of hope, resurrection, Christ. The final poem, "Echo's Bones," contains a reference to maggots and rotting flesh reminiscent of a medieval poetic homily. Characteristically, however, concern for the fate of the soul is conspicuous by its absence. The dead, more than content with their lot, are taken by the maggots for exactly "what they are." We have already seen this rejection of transcendence worked out in "Alba," "Malacoda," and "Serena II." In this last poem, as darkness descends and blots out the vision of "Meath shining through a chink in the hills," the toads, figures of evil, "sidle up to their snares." The fairy-tales of Meath with their happy, nay impossibly utopian, conclusions are over. No one lives happily forever after. The ending of the day is also the ending of the illusions of childhood, among which the poet places religion. The ritual prayers are a last feeble attempt to hold onto the child's confident security, to ward off the phantoms of the night, but in ironic juxtaposition to the two phrases "knees of stone" and "bye-bye on the bones" the prayers go the way of the fairy-tales. The protective figure of the mother, with the coming of the nighttime of adulthood, has undergone a metamorphosis. As we noted above, she has become mother earth—but not as in the traditional figure, "the bosom of mother earth," which implies fertility, warmth, sustenance, safety. The bosom has been exchanged for the hard knees that suggest stones and bones, and we have left the nursery for the graveyard. Man's fate, when he emerges from the false light of childhood into the dark of maturity, is like that of a man alone at night in the wild desolation of the mountains with the signs of death about him.

116

When the narrator in "Serena I" curses the day he "was not born Defoe," when in "Enueg II" he confesses he is "tired of policemen," and when like the boy excluded from the enclosure where a game is going on, the hens shut out of their shed, and the goat out of his field in "Enueg I" he feels himself an exile in the midst of society, the reader may draw the conclusion that inability or unwillingness to accept social norms and organization lies at the heart of Beckett's poetry. There may be a good deal of truth in such a view, and we shall discuss the matter in greater detail shortly. In any case, however, Beckett's artistic response can hardly be called social satire. It is too drastic. He lacks the satirist's underlying belief in social institutions and his righteous indignation at their perversion. He has little faith that man's condition can be fundamentally improved by progressively better social organization. If he is capable of ironic thrusts at Victorian hypocrisy in Ireland ("Serena III"), he more often implies that the restrictions of society are a nuisance but are hardly the cause of the real trouble. In "Echo's Bones" the new liberty of the dead is the farcical freedom to break wind "without fear or favour."

More deep-seated, Beckett's rebellion has its source in man's suffering:

> Above the mansions the algum-trees[64]
> the mountains
> my skull sullenly
> clot of anger
> skewered aloft strangled in the cang of the wind
> bites like a dog against its chastisement
>
> ("Enueg I," 10-15)

As in "Dortmunder" with its reference to Habbakuk, the poet implies here that life is unmerited punishment. The reaction is sullen anger, a clenching of teeth. Earlier in "Enueg I" the reference to Dante's hell ("its secret things"), as we have seen, equates suffering and chastisement. In "The Vulture" the lines "stooping to the prone who must / soon take up their life and walk" (3-4) reverse the meaning of the Biblical injunction "Take up thy bed and walk."[65] Instead

[64] Used because of the similarity to the Greek *algos* ("pain") but possibly also for its association with the Old Testament (1 Kings 10:11; 2 Chron. 2:8 and 9:10, 11).

[65] Matt. 9:6; Mark 2:9, 11; John 5:8, Acts 9:34.

of a gift given by Christ, life is a burden. We find a parallel account in *Murphy*, written during roughly the same period: "Left in peace they [the inmates of the asylum] would have been as happy as Larry, short for Lazarus, whose raising seemed to Murphy perhaps the one occasion on which the Messiah had overstepped the mark."[66] To these illustrations we can add the examples of "Sanies II," where life is among other things a painful flagellation, and of "Serena II," where it is suffering, imprisonment, exile. If we take these two poems together, with their alternative religious responses—the cry for mercy of the kyrie as contrasted to the sardonic reproaches of the Zeus metaphor, the unfinished paternoster, and the "typhoid and mammon" allusion—we become aware of a certain ambivalence in the poet's attitude. To the apparently callous and indifferent deity that permits suffering (if indeed this incomprehensible being is not its very source) Beckett opposes an irony well aware of its own futility. For the Christ of mercy and compassion ("fingers of compassion / to endorse the dust" in "Alba"; "Jesus Christ Son of God Savior His Finger" in "Serena III"), he has only sympathy.[67] The problems of reconciling the two views have their solutions, but Beckett the poet is not interested in the answers of theologians nor in the intricacies of scholastic discussion on freedom, grace, and the existence of evil.

No doubt the most interesting use of religious materials that occurs in *Echo's Bones* comes in "Enueg II," the only one of the thirteen poems that relies on a religious event as a basis for its larger metaphoric structure. The middle section of the poem is clearly a *via dolorosa*:

> veronica mundi
> veronica munda
> give us a wipe for the love of Jesus
>
> sweating like Judas
> tired of dying
> tired of policemen
> feet in marmalade
> perspiring profusely
> heart in marmalade

[66] *Murphy* (New York: Grove Press, 1957), p. 180.

[67] In *Godot* Estragon says, "Toute ma vie je me suis comparé à lui [Jésus]" (p. 88).

smoke more fruit
the old heart the old heart
breaking outside congress
doch I assure thee
lying on O'Connell Bridge
goggling at the tulips of the evening
the green tulips
shining round the corner like an anthrax
shining on Guinness's barges   (9-26)

Veronica (popular etymology *vera icona*, "true image") according to legend wiped the face of Christ with a cloth as He carried the cross to Calvary. In a play on *mundi* and *munda* the figure of Veronica expands in time and space to become a universal figure of compassion who takes pity on every man as he trudges in spiritual and physical distress his painful way to the calvary of his death. It would perhaps have been surprising had not at least one among the several walks on which the narrators of Beckett's poem set out developed into this particular emblem of man's trip through life. Since the author views existence as a painful infliction, the trip easily enough turns into a via dolorosa. The "dying" narrator has his policemen, as Christ had the soldiers, to prod him on when, overcome with fatigue, he stops to rest.[68] Typically, the tone cannot remain anguished for very long without some form of relief. Here verbal derring-do brings together perspiration, boiling fruit, failing heart, and smoking, that sin of the long-distance walker. In his early taste for unlikely metaphor Beckett occasionally recalls the English metaphysical poets. The pendulum swings abruptly back, however, and the poet touches on the theme of old age, which will be so important in his later work ("I was born old," Beckett once said in an interview). The image of heartbreak suggests that the poet's calvary is more of the spirit than of the flesh. And once again, ever wary of sentimentality, the narrator (using the German *doch* for lack of an English equivalent of the strong contradictory positive) hastens in mock heroic manner to insist on the literal truth of what he has said. Prostrate finally on Dublin's main bridge over the Liffey, he stares at Hibernian tulips. Green in the light of the setting sun, they seem to shed a baleful light on the beer-bearing Guinness

---

[68] Policemen play a similar role in a number of Beckett's works, "A Wet Night" (in *More Pricks Than Kicks*) and "L'Expulsé," for example.

119

barges. In "Enueg I" beer is the opiate that brings forgetfulness. Here it is not exempt from the malefic influence. In "Enueg I" the color green, so often associated with spring, hope, rebirth, is linked with death and decay ("the stillborn evening turning a filthy green. . . . / the great mushy toadstool, green-black, oozing up after me"). The green tulips in "Enueg II" are also part of an atmosphere of physical and moral sickness and suffering.[69] Malignant pustules, they belong to the evening of death.

There is ample biographical reason for Beckett's choice of the simile likening the narrator to Judas. "Enueg II" was written late in 1931. At the end of that year the young professor left Ireland to spend the Christmas holidays in Germany. While there he "betrayed" his colleagues at Trinity by his resignation partway through the academic year and disappointed his family and friends by his "ingratitude" and "desertion." The poem paints a picture of the misery that preceded the break, and the simile suggests that the narrator already feels a sense of guilty estrangement. At the same time, in an enueg that is not only a list of the poet's grievances but also a funeral lament, the image of Judas brings in the motif of suicide that we noted in "Enueg I." But the general theme of dying can be better understood in the context of the poetic framework, the eight lines that precede the via dolorosa and the three lines that follow it and conclude the poem:

world world world world
and the face grave
cloud against the evening

de morituris nihil nisi

and the face crumbling shyly
too late to darken the sky
blushing away into the evening
shuddering away like a gaffe

. . . .

the overtone the face
too late to brighten the sky
doch doch I assure thee

(1-8, 27-29)

[69] For a more general discussion of Beckett's use of colors, see below, Chap. VIII.

Line 1 demonstrates that the poet's basic concern is metaphysical. The world is a place of woe and badly needs its "veronica." The time is evening (repeated in lines 3, 7, and 23), which reflects the theme of "too late" (lines 6 and 28) and provides a fit setting for disease, decline, and death. The latter are mirrored in the verbs of decomposition, "crumbling" and "shuddering away," which in turn suggest an analogy with the decomposing flesh, stewed in its sweaty juices like fruit boiled to the oblivion of marmalade. Even the bridge, so often a symbol of crossing over from life to death, finds a place in the general pattern of passing away that includes the clouds as well as the day. Finally, the Latin phrase "de morituris nihil nisi," a revealing transformation of Chilon's "de mortuis nihil nisi bonum,"[70] might be set off as epigraph not only to this poem but to all the author's works, for man facing his coming death is Beckett's great—and in a sense only—character.

While the various components of "Enueg II" invite interpretation from religious, philosophical, sociological, and biographical points of view, the "key" to this somewhat hermetic poem lies in a passage from the unpublished "Dream of Fair to Middling Women." Belacqua in his Irish purgatory has a platonic love affair with the Smeraldina-Rima, who reaches the western island by boat, as do the souls in Dante's *Commedia*. They meet again later in the less ethereal world of Hesse.

> To begin with, then, there was the Dublin edition [of the Smeraldina-Rima] that bewitched Belacqua, the unopened edition, all visage and climate: the intact little cameo of a bird-face, so moving, and the gay zephyrs of Purgatory, slithering in across the blue tremolo of the ocean with a pinnace of souls, as good as saved, to the landing-stage, the reedy beach, bright and blue, merging into grass, not without laughter and old K'in music, rising demitonically, we almost said: diademitonically, to the butt of the emerald sugarloaf. When she went away, as go she did, across the wide waters Hesse to seek, again Hesse, unashamed in mind, and left him alone and inconsolable, then her face in the clouds and in the fire and wherever he looked or looked away and on the lining of his lids . . . and the thought or dream, sleeping and waking, in the morning dozing and the evening ditto,

[70] In Stobaeus, *Florilegium* CXXV, 15 and Diogenes Laertius, *Lives*, "Chilon," p. 71. It was also one of Solon's laws; see Plutarch, *Lives*: "Solon," Sec. 21.

with the penny rapture, of the shining shore where underneath them the keel of their skiff would ground and grind and rasp and stay stuck for them, just the pair of them, to skip out on to the sand and gather reeds and bathe hands, faces and breasts and broach the foothills without any discussion, in the bright light with the keen music behind them—then that face and site preyed . . . on the poor fellow. . . .[71]

In this passage a reality seen through eyes in love with art ("edition," "cameo," "zephyrs," "Purgatory," "tremolo," "K'in music," "diadem") is the setting for idyllic young love. Once departed, the girl is even more securely a part of the poet's imaginary world. In the poem the tone is different. The "face in the clouds" is still there and the shy blush of innocent love, but in a real and cruel setting. Line 4, "de morituris nihil nisi," breaks in with its warning of coming destruction and echoes that other hint of tubercular disaster that opens "Enueg I" ("my darling's red sputum"). At the same time it brings up again the ethical and aesthetic problem posed in "The Vulture." What is the relationship of the poet to his materials? If, as Chilon affirmed, one should speak nothing but good of the dead, what can the poet say of the dying? Nothing except—that we are all dying? That each man suffers and dies a little when his love dies? Beckett says these things in his poem, and he also indicts the order of things. In our world, untimely death (Beckett's "Smeraldina" died at the age of twenty-four) seems to be a clumsy blunder—or perhaps the real gaffe is being born,[72] since, as in *Whoroscope*, we are never ripe for our own death. Lives are out of phase. Some system of synchronization that would match human trajectories is missing.

In the poem it is dusk. The cloud is "too late," literally, to have much effect on a sky that is already dark. There is a hint of red in the heavens, but not enough light remains to brighten the sky with the glorious colors of a full-fledged sunset. On the figurative level the poet seems to suggest that love at this late stage can mean only suffering with the suffering of the dying ("too late to brighten"). But the sky of his mind is long since somber with the certainty that the via dolorosa of man's existence takes place in the shadow of sorrow and loss ("too late to darken"). Turning again to line 24, we find the following elements of a likely interpretation. The name

[71] "Dream of Fair to Middling Women," p. 101.

[72] Beckett quotes Calderón in *Proust* (p. 49): "Pues el delito mayor / Del hombre es haber nacido."

"Smeraldina" ("little emerald") was chosen by Beckett because the girl in question was Irish, because of the greenish color of her eyes, and because she often wore green.[73] As the narrator in "Enueg II" sees her face in the cloud, so he sees her color in the tulips. As the cloud crumbles, the light of day gives way to the darkness of night and the girl's health to sickness; the color green, already infected by black in "Enueg I" ("a filthy green"; "green-black"), is here associated with anthrax.

Stylistically this poem is interesting and effective in good part because of its binary rhythm (reinforced by a pattern of repetition and broken periodically), which seems to suggest a dreary and difficult plodding, one foot dragged after the other with many halts on the way. Established at the beginning of the poem with the striking quadruple repetition, "world world world world," the rhythm begins again when line 2 is picked up in line 5 ("and the face grave"; "and the face crumbling"). The repetition of "away," "veronica," "tired," "marmalade," "the old heart," "tulips," "shining," and "doch" all add to the effect. Even when the words are different, as in "the overtone the face," the two-foot line continues the pattern. Especially during the central via dolorosa the short slow lines that begin with an accented syllable (for example, lines 12 through 15) create the feeling of a monotonous, mournful march. And when the rhythm is broken by the insertion of a line starting with an unaccented syllable (as in "perspiring profusely") and then returns to the former cadence, the reader has almost the physical sensation that the walker has staggered. Beckett is too sophisticated musically to overdo such imitative rhythms, and in any case perfect regularity would undo his design, but without the help of this poetic resource "Enueg II" would be a lesser poem than it is.

An allusion at the end of "Sanies I" and another that closes "Serena III" add a last note on the subject of religion. The first suggests a comparison between the narrator, who descends from his bicycle as he sees the girl he loves coming toward him, and Peter, who sees Christ walking on the sea and steps off the side of the fishing boat to go to Him in response to His summons:[74]

[73] See, for example, the short story "Draff" in *More Pricks Than Kicks* and the play *Krapp's Last Tape*, in which she appears as "A girl in a shabby green coat, on a railway-station platform."

[74] Matt. 14:25-31.

> her whom alone in the accusative
> I have dismounted to love
> gliding towards me dauntless nautch-girl on the
>   face of the waters
> (44-46)

But the narrator's doubts are more radical than Peter's. Better to risk the engulfment of solitude than allow himself to be "saved" by social conformity, to be caught in the web of religion, marriage, and other such entangling alliances:

> get along with you now take the six the seven the
>   eight or the little single-decker
> take a bus for all I care walk cadge a lift
> home to the cob of your web in Holles Street
> (48-50)

"Serena III" ends on a similar note. The tone of bitter revolt in the face of so much apparently senseless suffering has been muted. Religion appears as a refuge that the narrator cannot accept but would not deny to others. As his walk takes him through the town of Blackrock (known locally as the Rock) on the coast south of Dublin, he remembers a well-known Protestant hymn: "Rock of Ages, cleft for me, / Let me hide myself in Thee!"[75] His response in the poem is "hide yourself not in the Rock keep on the move / keep on the move." It would seem, finally, that Beckett has too much sense of the needs and sufferings of others, and too great a certainty that his way is neither the only nor the ideal way, to be either a true social reformer or a fire-eating metaphysical rebel. The range of his response extends from sardonic irony to irreverent puns to a sorrowfully resigned statement of disillusionment. For him neither institutional change nor religious faith provides an effective antidote to the malady of existence.

The Real Landscape and the Poet's Vision

As we observed at the beginning of this chapter, the literary heritage is at least as real for Beckett the young intellectual and erstwhile academic as the so-called real world outside his mind. We

[75] Words by Augustus Montague Toplady in *The Gospel Magazine*, Oct. 1775. "Rock of ages" is a rendering of the Hebrew text of Isa. 26:4, translated in the King James version as "everlasting strength," but in the *Jerusalem Bible* as "le Rocher éternel."

have dealt above with only those authors, genres, and specific works that play a major role in the poems discussed. In the course of the following remarks we shall be obliged on occasion to devote at least a brief note to some of the less important allusions with which the poems are liberally sprinkled. With the way of the poet, Beckett utilizes the tradition vitally, picking and choosing either those passages that reflect his own loves, admirations, convictions, anguish or else those to which he reacts ironically, and sometimes also nostalgically. Beckett has been accused of pedantry, but there is little that is truly pedantic in his use of the tradition. He is not a name-dropper, and we are not likely to find coolly objective views of literary figures in his writing. Fully aware both of his own strong subjectivity and literariness and of the importance to poetry of all that is objective and concrete,[76] he soon availed himself of the materials in his immediate surroundings. During the period from 1931 through 1934 when the poems of *Echo's Bones* were composed these surroundings included not only Dublin (city and county), Wicklow County, western Ireland, and London, but France and Germany as well. Of the thirteen poems, three ("Alba," "Dortmunder," and "Malacoda") make relatively slight use of a specific physical setting and three others ("The Vulture," "Da Tagte Es," and "Echo's Bones") almost none at all. In the seven other poems, however (the two enuegs, the two sanies, and the three serenas), the poet turns the literal landscape into an artistic asset. Several of the seven ("Enueg II" and "Sanies II," for example) also rely on the literary heritage, and these we have discussed in detail above. Of the remaining, "Enueg I" and "Sanies I" give a predominant role to the landscape and will therefore serve in the following discussions as prime illustrations of the ways in which Beckett bends external reality to his purposes.

At the beginning of "Enueg I," the first long poem in the collection, the narrator comes out of the somber stone building called the Portobello Private Nursing Home, not far from Merrion Square and Clare Street, where Beckett's father had his office. Still nearer is the Harcourt Street Station where as a boy, from about 1915 to 1919, the young Samuel would descend from the Dublin S. E. train (the Dublin Southeastern, but known to the boys as the Dublin Slow and Easy) to walk the short distance to the Earlsfort House School

---

[76] See the earlier remarks on his admiration for the writing of Defoe and the Aretino, pp. 88-89.

where he was a day student.[77] Just across the street from the nursing home is the Grand Canal and nearby a narrow footbridge (no longer in use) that crosses the canal above a modest waterfall caused by an abrupt drop of a few feet in the level of the canal. In 1931, when the poem was written, a high wooden structure protected a building site across the canal and probably bore advertisements of the sort seen still on billboards in the vicinity. Turning west, the narrator walks along the canal, which is crossed by a number of simple road-bridges that lead into the city of Dublin. One of these, Parnell Bridge, is mentioned in the poem. The area is flat and, these days, fairly drab, and the wind finds little to obstruct its path except the low buildings that thin out to the west and south to open a view across unkempt fields to the Dublin mountains in the distance. Only an occasional rather scraggly tree breaks the flatness of the landscape as the sidewalk along the canal gives way to a dirt footpath that soon peters out. Of such material Beckett makes the opening of "Enueg I":

> Exeo in a spasm
> tired of my darling's red sputum
> from the Portobello Private Nursing Home
> its secret things
> and toil to the crest of the surge of the steep perilous
>   bridge
> and lapse down blankly under the scream of the hoarding
> round the bright stiff banner of the hoarding
> into a black west
> throttled with clouds.
>
> Above the mansions the algum-trees
> the mountains
> my skull sullenly
> clot of anger
> skewered aloft strangled in the cang of the wind
> bites like a dog against its chastisement

---

[77] The information in the following pages comes from two sources: conversations with the author during 1961 and 1962 and personal investigations in the spring of 1962, when I was able to follow in Ireland, England, and France the itineraries sketched out in the poems.

I trundle along rapidly now on my ruined feet
flush with the livid canal;
at Parnell Bridge a dying barge
carrying a cargo of nails and timber
rocks itself softly in the foaming cloister of the lock;
on the far bank a gang of down and outs would seem
    to be mending a beam.

Then for miles only the wind
and the weals creeping alongside on the water
and the world opening up to the south
across a travesty of champaign to the mountains
and the stillborn evening turning a filthy green
manuring the night fungus
and the mind annulled
wrecked in wind.

(1-29)

The bridge today would certainly provide perilous crossing, and it probably did so even in 1931. As nearly always in these poems, the concrete starting point is real and not merely imagined, and it usually contains within itself the germ of its meaning in the poem. The part of invention lies first in the choice of details and then in the development of their poetic potential. The bridge is chosen for its peril, which is then magnified by focusing on the angle of inclination of its two sides.[78] Line 5 with its accumulation of anapests sets off the sharply accented series of monosyllabic words (except for one) indicating height and danger: "toil," "crest," "surge," "steep," "perilous," "bridge." The unusual repetition of three closely similar prepositional phrases and the use of "crest" and "surge," which suggest the foaming water below, increase the imitative effect of the line. The consonant clusters that link components of the line

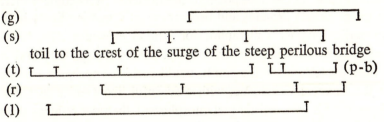

(g)
(s)
      toil to the crest of the surge of the steep perilous bridge
(t)   (p-b)
(r)
(l)

[78] It is broken in the middle to allow the passage of canal boats, and the two sides swing open to the vertical. Even when joined, however, they form at the bank angles of at least 30 degrees with the horizontal.

and the concentration of more or less frontal vowels in the accented syllables (*oi, e, u, ee, e, i*) combine with the rhythm, diction, and syntax to create an extraordinarily vivid picture of the risky climb. By contrast the almost equally effective line 6, with its three stressed monosyllabic words at the start, its heavy back vowels (except for "scream," which is there for other reasons) *a, o, a, u, oa,* and the rhythmic easing off at the end of the line, evokes the narrator's first braced steps as he descends and then his relaxation as he lets himself go toward the end of the descent and reaches the bank.

The poem is a funeral lament, so we should not be surprised to find all of nature molded to the mental state of the solitary walker. The wind around the boards of the hoarding is a "scream" and the hoarding itself a flag, stiffened as though rigor mortis had set in. The west, land of death, is dark before its time, "throttled with clouds." Real trees can be reminders of ruin, as the one in *Godot* is, and the walker feels in them the pain of the "algum-tree." His head is a "skull," his anger a "clot," the wind's punishment a "skewer" and a "cang." Whether or not the same barge of thirty years before, a barge was there near Parnell Bridge in 1961—and it was surely "dying." A little farther on there exists still on the far side of the canal a dilapidated building with lumber lying about, and on occasion workers, perhaps not unlike those the poet labels "a gang of down and outs," may be seen moving about. The water of the canal under the best of conditions hardly resembles the transparent blue of the southern seas and on a windy, cloudy day may not be far from the "livid" color the poet uses to describe it. But "livid" in line 17 forecasts "weals" in line 23, and both suggest a comparison between the surface of the water and flesh bruised, perhaps flagellated as in "Sanies II." The image of the "gauntlet of tulips" in that poem recurs for a third time as the "gantelope of sense and nonsense" in the final poem of the thirteen. In its context there, the image clearly expands and becomes what it was implicitly in the two earlier poems, a metaphor for human existence. One would hardly think that the green Irish fields, patchy though they may be as they stretch out to the south, could furnish appropriate matter for the funereal vision. Yet with a scornful jibe (and a metaphor suggesting his own artistic metamorphoses) the poet reduces them, by a comparison to more favored relatives, to "a travesty of champaign." Still not satisfied, he seizes upon the mangy coat of green and brown and blends its colors into an evening sky that comes out

128

of the cauldron "a filthy green." Another bold step and the evening, no sooner born than dead, becomes manure for the toadstool of night. The horrendous implications of this image, which must stand as a fitting culmination to a long Anglo-Saxon literary tradition that vilifies the hapless mushroom,[79] go beyond simple necrophagia of course. The night feeds on the defunct day and the nocturnal bard on the dead past. The flower blooms where Narcissus knelt near the pile of stones that once was Echo. Again, the poet is akin to the "vigilant gulls in the gray spew of the sewer" (72)—or to the scavenging vulture. Natural life, like poetic life, depends on death.[80] Besides the somber consistency of his powerful images, Beckett brings to his stripped-down poetry a canny sense of sound and rhythm. Although he eschews outright rhyme (except in "Da Tagte Es"), he never relinquishes the more subtle and wide-ranging effects of vowel and consonant combinations. Even a cursory examination of the important words in the eight short lines just discussed (22-29) reveals an unusual buildup of *m*'s and *n*'s, *l*'s and *w*'s: "miles," "wind," "weals," "water," "world," "champaign," "mountains," "stillborn," "evening," "green," "manuring," "night," "fungus," "mind," "annulled," "wrecked," "wind." And one could add subsidiary helpers like "then," "only," "creeping," "alongside," "opening," "turning," "and" (four times), and "in." In all, an extraordinary concentration of twenty-eight out of forty-eight words contribute directly to the phonetic-semantic fabric.

In the next section of the poem the narrator passes an old man, a group of players in a field, and a young child. In addition the poet reaches back into the past to retrieve a vision of gorse on fire in the mountains near Dublin, where he often walked with his father. An allusion to Sumatra, from a book he was reading at the time, completes the picture.

> I splashed past a little wearish old man,
> Democritus,
> scuttling along between a crutch and a stick,
> his stump caught up horribly, like a claw, under his breech,
> smoking.

[79] See V. P. and R. G. Wasson, *Mushrooms, Russia, and History* (New York: Pantheon, 1957).

[80] This view of things is not unrelated to Baudelaire's notion of flowers out of evil. Formally, on the other hand, Beckett and Baudelaire move in divergent directions.

Then because a field on the left went up in a sudden blaze
of shouting and urgent whistling and scarlet and blue ganzies
I stopped and climbed the bank to see the game.
A child fidgeting at the gate called up:
"Would we be let in Mister?"
"Certainly" I said "you would."
But, afraid, he set off down the road.
"Well" I called after him "why wouldn't you go on in?"
"Oh" he said, knowingly,
"I was in that field before and I got put out."
So on
derelict,
as from a bush of gorse on fire in the mountain after dark,
or, in Sumatra, the jungle hymen,
the still flagrant rafflesia.

(30-49)

Whatever appearance the old man of reality may have presented, the details selected by the author paint a uniformly distressing portrait. Being a man of Beckett's universe, he is little, sickly, old, crippled. With his claw and his scuttle, he is more crab than human. But, as so often, the ironic interpretation of reality gains a major assist from literature. Through the two key words in the passage, typically set off by themselves, the poet gives his own idea of the relative proportion of suffering and comfort in existence. According to a legend popular during the Renaissance, Democritus (in contrast to Heraclitus, the weeping philosopher) was pictured as reacting to human folly always with laughter. In fact, so the story goes, the end came when he burst his belly laughing. In ethics he was a precursor of the Epicureans. While Heraclitus lamented the passing of all things, Democritus sought to enjoy whatever he could in life. Hence the cigarette.

In the context of the whole poem, the game, watched from outside the enclosure by both the narrator and the child, takes on symbolic overtones. Inherently, of course, it suggests conflict, urgency, group activity, exclusion of the unqualified—characteristics easily associated with social existence or simply with life in general. Fearful, and already experienced, the child chooses to remain an outsider. The narrator too "set[s] off down the road" of a different existence. Lines 46 through 49 throw considerable light on the figure of the game and on the rest of the poem as well. "Derelict," abandoned, harks back to the "dying barge" that "rocks itself softly in the foaming cloister of the lock"; but also, in the larger setting of the poems as a whole, it points forward to the dying man in the narrow limits of his bed, the "sheet astream" in his hand ("Da Tagte Es"), as well as to another voyage in the still straiter confines of the coffin ("Malacoda"). And we might mention that other derelict of "Sanies II," "sailing . . . gliding / frescoward free up the fjord." In this poem the major theme of abandonment and the archetypal image of the voyage take on particular meaning and coloration. It is not so much the protagonist who abandons his beloved when he leaves the nursing home as the dying beloved who leaves *him* derelict and forlorn. Such is the message reiterated in lines 47 through 49. There is no night so black as the night into which one plunges after gazing on a fire in the wilderness. The yellow gorse seems more beautiful than ever in the dancing light that destroys it, red like the diseased sputum of his darling and the banner of meat bleeding, bright like the stiff banner of the hoarding, scarlet and blue like the blaze of jerseys—for the athletes too are consumed by the game. Yellow, perhaps by association with the sun, is traditionally emblematic of life, joy, happiness.[81] The islands in Clew Bay ("Serena II"), yellow with the last rays of the setting sun, gain a stay of execution, but their eventual fate is foretold in the image of the xanthic flowers. The yellow gorse goes the same way, and later the lights of the street lamps, sickly progeny of an illustrious solar parent, become upon their reflection in the river "Blotches of doomed yellow in the pit of the Liffey" (69). The Sumatra image adds to the color symbolism with the red of the jungle flower that will perish unpicked ("still," but not for long, alive), as though swallowed up by the dense darkness. Thus not only the virginal beloved but each man must die unfulfilled. "Flagrant," when we should expect fragrant, is a real poetic find. Not only does it balance *f*'s, *l*'s, and *r*'s in the harmony of "flagrant rafflesia" and carry on by its etymology the image of burning, but it suggests and yet disguises the word it replaces, as the beauty of the flower is a mask that belies the "fragrance" of putrefying meat that it gives off.

In the section of "Enueg I" just discussed, the outer world, neutral under the scrutiny of a scientific eye, provides the stricken poet with

[81] See, for example, the "Langage des fleurs" in the *Nouveau Larousse Universel.*

a mirror of his own misery. The theme of abandonment joins with images suggesting superficial optimism, vitality, or beauty dogged by the hounds of destruction. In the next section (50-60) the maggots of "Echo's Bones" are vermin attacking creatures still alive, chickens abandoned in a field that seems to share the depression of the narrator. The fungus of line 27 reappears, this time with gangrenous colors. As the dark waters of the Liffey drown the living yellow, so the green of hope and rebirth is infected by the black of despair and death. "The tattered sky" is sick, and the ichor that drips from its ulcers, like the verbal sanies discharged from the ailing heart and mind of the suffering poet, goes to sustain new life, the saprophytic horror of the "great mushy toadstool, / green-black" —not without analogy to the poem itself. As we look back on the opening lines of the book, we can see that the author is both vulture and victim, poet and man. The disease and death of others, omen of his own future disease and death, become now in the present his own dying, out of which that monstrous product, the poem, is born. The last lines of the section bring an internalization of the reality outside, through the same image of the skull that we saw in lines 12 to 15 and in "The Vulture":

> Next:
> a lamentable family of grey verminous hens,
> perishing out in the sunk field,
> trembling, half asleep, against the closed door of a shed,
> with no means of roosting.
> The great mushy toadstool,
> green-black,
> oozing up after me,
> soaking up the tattered sky like an ink of pestilence,
> in my skull the wind going fetid,
> the water . . .   (50-60)

This passage adds further to the pervasive color symbolism of "Enueg I" with "grey," which finds an echo in the "grey spew of the sewer" (72) and elsewhere. Part of the power of this poem comes from the interaction between the various colors and the four elements, perhaps suggested to the author by his readings in those ancient Greek philosophers concerned with the elemental building blocks of the universe. "Enueg II" begins "world world world

world," but "Enueg I" is perhaps in its way an even more "cosmic" poem. Here Democritus with his atomic theory suggests Heraclitus, who held that fire is the fundamental substance in the universe; but when all is said and done, "Enueg I" is no doubt chiefly under the sign of Thales, who argued the claims of water. We have already discussed the color red and its link to fire (as well as blood and carrion). Both yellow, the light that warms and nourishes the earth, and green, the mark of its vitality and fruitfulness, are associated with that second element. As we have seen, Beckett brings out the destructive effects of fire, while yellow and green are contaminated and endangered by gray and black. Similarly, we find no gentle zephyrs to represent the first element, air, but instead a punishing tyrant that skewers and strangles his victims, eliciting from them screams and clenching of teeth; that whips (the water, for the elements themselves are in conflict), annuls, and wrecks; and that dies, finally, in a fetid breath inside the tormented skull of the lonely walker.

Early in the poem, water shows its murderous colors as it lies in wait beneath the "steep perilous bridge" and in the form of clouds throttles the west until it turns black. In the canal it is the gray-blue-black color of livid flesh. In the lock it foams hungrily about the flanks of the dying barge. With the image of the walker splashing along past the crustaceous Democritus we get the first hint that the water has invaded the land. Far from bringing purification or fertility, it appears as an agent of putrefaction. In line 58 the rain is an "ink of pestilence" that spawns toadstools in the muddy ooze of decomposed earth. The unfinished line that ends the passage quoted above—"the water . . ."—seems at once a horrified indictment and a premonition. The four lines just before the allusion to Rimbaud that ends the poem make sense enough in human terms of all that has occurred heretofore on a cosmic scale. The call of the ladders is a summons to watery ruin in the pit below:

> Blotches of doomed yellow in the pit of the Liffey;
> the fingers of the ladders hooked over the parapet,
> soliciting;
> a slush of vigilant gulls in the grey spew of the sewer.
>
> (69-72)

Between line 60 ("the water . . .") and line 69 above comes a passage that provides perhaps the best illustration in "Enueg I" of

133

the poetic utilization and metamorphosis of an identifiable landscape. Skirting Kilmainham in a loop to the south, we walk through
a rural area and at a crossroads pass a sign indicating the tiny suburb
called the Fox and Geese. Not far beyond, the winding road cuts
down between banks lined with bushes and trees to the Liffey River.
Following the right bank of the stream upriver, away from Dublin,
we come to the town of Chapelizod, where a bridge crosses the
Liffey. We complete the journey with a right turn that puts us on a
main road leading past Phoenix Park on the left and the suburb of
Kilmainham up a hill on the right into the city of Dublin. There
are a number of suburbs in the general area and many landmarks
that might have been put to poetic use. Beckett chose and ordered
his choices as follows:

> Next:
> on the hill down from the Fox and Geese into Chapelizod
> a small malevolent goat, exiled on the road,
> remotely pucking the gate of his field;
> the Isolde Stores a great perturbation of sweaty heroes,
> in their Sunday best,
> come hastening down for a pint of nepenthe or moly
>   or half and half
> from watching the hurlers above in Kilmainham.
>
> (61-68)

The combination of fox and geese must have held the irresistible
suggestion of slaughter, echoed faintly in the ill will of the "malevolent goat." Chapelizod, literally the Chapel of Isolde, that doomed
lover from the Celtic past, provides a heroine to match the contemporary "darling" dying in the nursing home. The Isolde Stores have
gone the way of Isolde, but incredibly enough an Isolde Gas Station
joins life and literature near the bridge across the Liffey. The
"sweaty heroes" could hardly find forgetfulness there, but downstream, on the main road just before another bridge that leads down
from Kilmainham, the curious observer cannot miss the low building with its large block letters announcing "Athlete's Rest." The
need for liquid oblivion is still with us. Farther on, the ladders that
plunge the steel curves of their fingers into the concrete of the para-
pet are there yet; the sewers too, and the eternal gulls. For those
beyond all hope there is always the river.

Called a "puckaun" in Ireland, the male goat is still crowned at a yearly fair in the west that stems from ancient pagan festivals. Perhaps, nevertheless, he is "exiled" here, partly as a pagan presence in Christian Ireland. The author, himself in a minority group, suggests that the goat is only remotely interested in shifting his position from the outside to the inside. "Malevolent," touched on above, probably relates chiefly to "pucking." Besides a blow, a puck in its archaic sense of evil or malicious spirit[82] is not out of keeping in a poem so concerned with the problem of evil. These suggestions, however, are secondary to the central function of the image of the exiled goat. It chiefly serves to carry on the theme of abandonment that runs through the poem and that is repeated in the same passage by the name of the town and the stores, which recall the many exiles of Tristan and Isolde. The flowers that cannot exist in the arctic wasteland state the theme for the last time in the Rimbaud allusion that ends the poem—as it began, with the "exeo" of line 1.

> Ah the banner
> the banner of meat bleeding
> on the silk of the seas
> and the arctic flowers
> that do not exist. (73-76)

Exile can also be escape, of course. The goat may be just as well off outside his field as the "down and outs" are beyond the reach of the "ins." The modern "heroes" have escaped their weekly routine but need to flee even their Sunday freedom ("watching" the players as the narrator and the child did) in the magic of a "moly" or "a pint of nepenthe," not unrelated perhaps to the love potion that brought forgetfulness to Tristan and Isolde. Other "heroes,"[83] members of the Irish Republican movement, knew a different kind of exile in the Kilmainham jail, which long before their time had been —like the Portobello Private Nursing Home and bearing a similarly evocative name—a hospital.

As we look back over the poem and consider it as a whole, we can perceive in its structure the same combination of circular and linear movement that characterizes such plays of the mature years

[82] Cf. Shakespeare's character in *A Midsummer Night's Dream*.

[83] In quotes because Beckett, raised in the loyalist tradition of Dublin, the heart of the Pale, and educated partly in northern Ireland and then at Trinity, could hardly regard them as completely and unambiguously heroic. But then, Beckett does not seem to have been very much a political animal anyway.

as *Godot* and *Happy Days*. In the latter work, the existence of Winnie and Willie is played out within a circle of days and nights that come and go and simultaneously descend along a straight line on the inclined plane of time that leads to the grave. The playwright's fertile imagination finds a hundred and one ways of concretizing or specifying these abstract or mythic principles of overall structure. In "Enueg I" the narrator's walk begins in Dublin and after a circle to the south and west brings him back along the quays of the Liffey into the city. The circle is symbolic of frustration, as well, and reminds us on a formal level of the ironically "end-less" pilgrimage of the walkers in Dante's sixth *bolgia* of the eighth circle. Weighed down by their sins (figured by the leaden monk's habits), as the narrator by his sorrow, they find no escape from their punishment, nor he from his suffering. His exit from the Portobello Nursing Home is an attempt to flee the signs of decline and death, but hell exists on both sides of the gateway and the signs of decline are everywhere. He toils upward to the crest of the bridge only to "lapse down blankly." The reinforced sense of downward motion that comes from the first two words combines with the archaic but here primary meaning of "blank" ("lacking resource or answer"), which adds a note of psychological and spiritual depression. Like Winnie in her mound of earth, all things—not only the "down and outs"—are headed down and out. The field is sunk, the hens are down from their roosts and perishing, the "heroes" must at last come down from Kilmainham, and the end of the narrator's walk brings him down from the Fox and Geese to a final vision of the "pit of the Liffey."

In a still more organic way, however, each episode in the long string of encounters reduces the living landscape to its moribund essentials. Beneath the surfaces of life lie the sure signs of death. The structure of the poem is clearly indicated not only by typographical division into parts but also by introductory words or phrases, which, like milestones along a road, mark the progress of the poem: "Exeo," "I trundle along rapidly now," "Then," "I splashed past," "Then," "So on," "Next," "Next." Thus, little by little, each encounter with the outer world adds to the evidence that flight is futile. There is no escape from the universal plight of which the red sputum of his dying darling is only one among innumerable symptoms. And little by little, partly as a result of this evidence, we begin to realize that his trip through space is a metaphor that figures a segment of the declining trajectory of a human existence propelled through a brief stretch of time toward the tomb. Since each episode in space tells the same tale of disaster and since the journey in space gets nowhere but merely returns the traveler to his original starting point, real space tends to lose its ontological autonomy, to become time's vassal. The mountain resembles the plain and both repeat the sky and the river. Nature is of one voice. Space is perceived by a partisan viewer who sees only its temporal dimension and that in a partial way.

We would be saying something similar to this if we declared simply that for the poet inner reality can be more real than the world outside, that he is realms removed from the objective recorder. Still, for the poet more than for many another man, nature is of crucial importance, and not just as a source of materials. Traditionally, at least, art has involved some kind of collusion between two realities thought of as somehow both autonomous and interrelated: man and nature. If nature loses its substantive reality and is no longer scrutinized and probed for the independent mystery it seems to contain and conceal, if it becomes a storehouse of mere materials to be manipulated tyrannically to fit the needs of the artist's psyche, then does not art suffer and perhaps expire? This is a problem that Beckett recognized very early in his career as a writer and faced squarely in his critical essays, which we shall discuss in a subsequent chapter. The danger for art of epistemological idealism would seem to be a real one, and this appears to be the philosophical position toward which Beckett has evolved. The corner into which he has painted himself by progressively reducing the dependence of his art on external reality (and correlatively on the externals of poetic form) could mean silence and the end of his literary production. Already, however, Beckett's work stands as a monument to the creative potential inherent in such a philosophical position, even if it also testifies to certain limitations. At the other extreme, scientific positivism, which would seem equally sterile for the purposes of art, has produced the masterpieces of Zola. The reason in both cases, perhaps, lies in the authors' common failure to be wholly true to the theoretical views most congenial to them. The subjective intruders in Zola's laboratory find their opposite numbers in the faithfully observed if unwelcome guests in Beckett's mental microcosm. Even though the genial and dangerous power of a transforming subjectivity is clearly evident as early as "Enueg I" in the piti-

137

less consistency and univalence of the images drawn from the outer world, we can hardly grant in all fairness that nature has become "a storehouse of mere materials to be manipulated tyrannically." Things have not gone that far. At least at this early stage in his development as an artist, Beckett manages to render justice both to the oppressive foreign Caesar and to his own inner daemon.

"Sanies I," like its companion piece, provides some relief from the gloom of the enuegs and the anguish of the first two serenas. Once again the setting is Dublin and the immediate countryside around it. The overall structure is based on another excursion, this time along the shore to the north of the city as far as the beaches of the village of Portrane, then back through the towns of Donabete and Swords, passing by the domain of Turvey on the way, and so to Holles Street in Dublin. The poem begins:

> all the livelong way this day of sweet showers from
> Portrane on the seashore
> Donabete sad swans of Turvey Swords
> pounding along in three ratios like a sonata
> like a Ritter with pommelled scrotum atra cura on the step
> Botticelli from the fork down pestling the transmission
> tires bleeding voiding zeep the highway
> all heaven in the sphincter
> the sphincter (1-8)

In the first line, "sweet showers" alludes to the beginning of Chaucer's *Canterbury Tales*: "Whan that Aprille with his shoures sote / The droghte of Marche hath perced to the rote." It establishes an analogy between the pilgrims' journey to Canterbury and back and the ride of Beckett's narrator. The tale that the latter will tell along the way is the story of his own life. More specifically, Chaucer's description of nature's transition from death to life and in particular his mention of April, the month of Beckett's birth, sets the stage for the poet's reflections on his own nativity. The well-known lines in Eliot's *The Waste Land* include what is probably a recollection of Chaucer's opening verses. At any rate, the sentiments they express have a peculiar relevance to "Sanies I":

> April is the cruelest month, breeding
> Lilacs out of the dead land, mixing
> Memory and desire, stirring
> Dull roots with spring rain.

Elsewhere in the *Canterbury Tales* we can discover lines that further help to clarify the sense of pilgrimage as Beckett would doubtless understand it:

> This world nis but a thurghfare full of wo,
> And we ben pilgrimes, passing to an fro;
> Deeth is an ende of every worldly sore.
> ("The Knightes Tale," ll. 2847-2849)

With his fondness for puns and his interest in etymology, Beckett may very well have allowed the weather (which suggested Chaucer, or vice versa) to influence his choice of towns—very real ones that can be located on any map of the Dublin area. In any case the combination of Portrane ("poured rain") and Donabete ("don't abate") with the showers that continue during the entire excursion is more than a little suspicious. Such wanton wordplay often signals a mood of whimsy, even a kind of tragicomic abandon of the sort we observed in "Sanies II." It can be a symptom of the impulse to virtuosity, or of art liberated momentarily from its more serious duties, art indulging itself like an errant schoolboy. In support of such a view we can point to the opening transformation of the set expression, "all the livelong day," conceivably taken from the words of the popular "Levee Song."[84] The mutation calls attention to "way" by giving it priority over the expected word "day" and in so doing introduces the principal metaphor of the poem, the road— of both the excursion and the rider's life. In addition, the reference to art (however humble) by the artist suggests for the second time in a single line the virtuosity just mentioned. The similes in lines 3 and 4 comparing the gears of the bicycle to the movements of a sonata and the rider to a medieval knight on horseback have the same effect. So does the image in line 5, which likens the rider's

[84] Of unknown authorship, its first publication seems to have been in *Carmina Princetonia*, 1894. The immediate context is "I've been workin' on the railroad, all the livelong day. I've been workin' on the railroad just to pass the time away." The veiled allusion to another means of locomotion, if allusion it is, fits well in the general context of the poem. It brings with it the notion of "passing the time" while "waiting," a theme familiar to all who have seen or read *Godot*. Another word in "Sanies I," "slicker," will be familiar chiefly to Americans. Beckett learned it from a good friend, C. C. Clark, an American with whom he spent part of a summer bicycling through the Loire Valley in France in the days when he was a student at Trinity. The mode of travel in the poem may be the associative link with Clark, the raincoat, and the song.

overworked thighs to the outsize limbs of a Botticelli beauty. Finally, the reference in "atra cura" to the lines of Horace, "Behind the horseman sits black care,"[85] completes the collection of allusions that the author has managed to compress into the short space of a few lines. Poetry has joined hands with its sister arts, song, instrumental music, and painting, while invoking its own tradition in ancient and medieval times. For the moment at least to some degree disengaged from life (and death), it mirrors itself happily and with admiration. Even here, however, the detachment is not complete. Although "livelong" may have subtle connotations of lassitude, and showers even on the literal level can be sweet only just so long for a hatless cyclist, the first decidedly discordant note in the general exuberance comes with the "sad swans of Turvey." An extensive but run-down estate that speaks of former glory, Turvey boasts several noble gateways, one of them flanked with columns surmounted by stone swans. On a nearby wall the family coat of arms repeats the motif and displays the brave motto "Moriendo Cano," which neatly sums up the poet's view of the relationship between life and art. The tires are losing air, and the term he uses to describe the loss, "bleeding," looks back to "Swords" in line 2. From the term "pot-valiant" in line 18, from his concern about the reliability of the only sphincter that counts for him, his own, and from the "voiding" (6) that takes place later ("sucking in my bloated lantern," 40), we may surmise that the rider's verbal effervescence has been inspired by the foam of that drink so dear to the hearts of Irishmen, Guinness Beer (see also "Enueg II" [25] and the related "pint of nepenthe or moly or half and half" [67] in "Enueg I"). Masked by malt it may be, but a beating is endured by all and sundry on this road of life. From the rider and his steed to the walkers scattered by his passage, all are pounded, pommeled, and pestled.

The twin moods that intermingle in uneven balance at the beginning of the poem tend to sift themselves into a pattern of alternation as we proceed. Assisted by semantic clues like the series of "nows," we soon become aware of a dominant rhythm linked to the movement of the traveler:

3   pounding along in three ratios like a sonata

9   müüüüüüüüde now

[85] "Post equitem sedet atra cura" (*Odes*, Bk. III, Carm. 1, 1. 40). See also Montaigne, *Essays*, I, 38.

10   potwalloping now through the promenaders

14   ah to be back in the caul now with no trusts

16   belting along in the meantime clutching the bike

23   oh the larches the pain drawn like a cork

24   the glans he took the day off up hill and down dale

26   back the shadows lengthen the sycomores are sobbing

27   to roly-poly oh to me a spanking boy

33   tired now hair ebbing gums ebbing ebbing home

34   good as gold now in the prime after a brief prodigality

38   distraught half-crooked courting the sneers of these fauns
      these smart nymphs

42   flinging the proud Swift forward breasting the swell
      of Stürmers

45   I have dismounted to love

48   get along with you now take the six the seven the eight
      or the little single-decker

51   and let the tiger go on smiling

The most obvious contrast is between lines that introduce periods of vigorous pedaling (3, 10, 16, 42) and others that indicate moments of fatigue when the rider coasts along or has dismounted (9, 33, 38, 45). The regularity of the alternation is maintained, however, by other means as well. To lines that imply expansive spurts of energy we may add by analogy those that describe movement of another sort, walking cross-country (24) or riding the now-extinct trains between Dublin and Dun Laoghaire (48). In the first, "up hill and down dale" helps to reinforce the rhythmic alternation by its image of climbing and descent; in the second the list of possible choices is rhythmically not unlike the staccato repetition of downward thrusts on the pedals. Semantic analogy combines with the rapid run of monosyllables that seems to move into a higher gear and redouble its pace with the triad of bisyllabic words, "little single-decker." A similar combination of meaning and prosody, plus the sheer contrast with the context that immediately precedes, bring the sunny paratactic lines 27 and 34 into the same group. Associated with moments of fatigue and coasting, naturally enough, we have lines 14, 23, 26, and 51, which are more leisurely, lyrical (or simply contemplative), and legato. Perhaps the most striking contrast comes between the long, mellifluous phrases of line 26, where whispering sibilants supported by nasals and liquids succeed in softening even the accompanying *c*'s and *b*'s, and line 27 with its frank, jolly, activistic use of sound and sense, rhythm and syntax.

Most of the lines quoted above form boundaries for the subdivisions of the poem. If we consider the structure of these larger building blocks, again we note a symmetrical balance beneath the freewheeling contours of the imaginative surface.

> potwalloping now through the promenaders
> this trusty all-steel this super-real
> bound for home like a good boy
> where I was born with a pop with the green of the larches
> ah to be back in the caul now with no trusts
> no fingers no spoilt love
>
> (10-15)

In the first three lines above the Ritter describes his journey and his faithful steed and manages a playful parody of modern advertising. Then, switching from space to time, he evokes an impossible journey back through the years to the careless innocence of the womb. The pathos of the last two lines proves again the effectiveness of such tried and true contrasts between past happiness and present woe and recalls the poignant lines of Dante.[86] The larger space-time parallel continues and develops in the next section:

> belting along in the meantime clutching the bike
> the billows of the nubile the cere wrack
> pot-valiant waisted in rags hatless
> for mamma papa chicken and ham
> warm Grave too say the word
> happy days snap the stem shed a tear

---

[86] "Nessun maggior dolore / Che ricordarsi del tempo felice / Ne la miseria" (*Inf.* V, 121-123).

this day Spy Wedsday seven pentades past
oh the larches the pain drawn like a cork
the glans he took the day off up hill and down dale
with a ponderous fawn from the Liverpool London and
    Globe

                                            (16-25)

Lines 16 through 21 describe the real trip in space, heading home, while the last four lines take the rider back through time to the nuptials of his mother and father and to the period of his own birth. The pumping bicycle had already created vaguely erotic overtones in lines 4 and 5, above. In line 17 the ride is linked to the archetype of the voyage by the image of "billows"; at the same time, the curved handlebars suggest a woman's breasts (as did the harbor walls seen from the mountain in "Serena II"), while the image of the winding-sheet is discreetly indicated by "cere" (cf. cerement, cere cloth).[87] The skeletal frame of the vehicle is translated by "wrack," which brings with it the idea of pain and torture (cf. 23) as well as the meaning of "hulk" (used in the preceding poem, "Dortmunder"), which joins with "billows" to suggest the sea. Finally, the subliminal sense of "withered" comes through the homophone "sere." All this adds up to a macabre, almost medieval love-death interlude along the road traveled by everyman. The same double thread of pleasure and pain, joy and misery continues in lines 18 through 20 with alcoholic euphoria followed by the vulnerability of "caulless," "hatless," and "waisted in rags," which in turn gives way to the anticipation of a family reunion and celebration over good food and wine. The Irish toast "happy days" (followed shortly by "shed a tear") was used ironically by Beckett as the title of his 1961 play about Winnie and Willie (his own father's name) growing old together. Here it is part of the festivities recalling his parents' wedding (some "seven pentades" before the writing of "Sanies I" in the autumn of 1932) and his own birth in 1906.[88] Perhaps by coincidence, perhaps by design,

---

[87] "Cere" is also the term used to describe a waxlike membrane located near the base of the beak of certain birds, in which the nostrils are pierced. The context provokes an analogy with the hymen.

[88] In a pun that imitates a common Irish pronunciation, the poet links marriage to the betrayal of Judas (on "Spy Wedsday"), since wedlock prepares the way for the Good Friday crucifixion of being born.

he marks his entry into the world on April 13 in line 13 of the poem, where he describes the delivery "with a pop" that in line 23 we learn was more involved with pain (then and later) than the pop of the champagne cork or the snap of the goblet's stem (21). Again in lines 24 and 25 the holiday spirit is colored by the triple motif, "birth, copulation, and death": the "glans" is accompanied by a "fawn" from an insurance company. The larches beside the Beckett home in Foxrock were the first trees out in the spring, so it is natural that they are linked to his birth in that "cruelest month" of April.

The next section picks up again the contrast between the joy of his parents at the birth of their child and the pain of living that is his portion.

> back the shadows lengthen the sycomores are sobbing
> to roly-poly oh to me a spanking boy
> buckets of fizz childbed is thirsty work
> for the midwife he is gory
> for the proud parent he washes down a gob of gladness
> for footsore Achates also he pants his pleasure
> sparkling beestings for me
>
> (26-32)

We are once more in the world of the bicycle ride in line 26, with the rider reminding himself of his goal. He must be getting back. Evening is approaching. At the same time, however, the line has an unmistakable temporal dimension. The poem was written in the fall, and the shadows lengthen not only by reason of night's coming but also because the autumn is dying and winter draws on. Such an image almost automatically assumes eschatological significance, even without an added signpost like the sadness of the "sycomores." "Back," in this poetic climate, wears its ambiguity lightly, returning the rider through time as well as space to the home where he was born. The following lines continue the image of champagne ("fizz") and the theme of the voyage with a reference to the companion of Aeneas, faithful but "footsore" Achates. The double mood is maintained by the contrast between line 26 and those that follow, but even beneath the joyous clamor of festivities murmurs of coming misery can be heard in words like "gory" and "footsore." Not only does the term "beestings" suggest the homophonous "beast" (supported by "pants" in line 31, a word which itself is almost attracted by its proximity into the imagistic orbit of the tiring trip), but together with "sparkling" it evokes the notion of innumerable tiny darts and the idea of pain even within the pleasure of the champagne. The primary meaning of "beestings" is of course "the first milk from a mammal after parturition," but it also indicates "a disease from imbibing beestings." Here, naturally, the disease would be life itself. Perhaps this secondary sense is the hint that helps to mold the meaning of the following line, which begins the next section:

> tired now hair ebbing gums ebbing ebbing home
> good as gold now in the prime after a brief prodigality
> yea and suave
> suave urbane beyond good and evil
> biding my time without rancour you may take your oath
>
> (33-37)

We are back with the rider in the present, and on the surface only the reference to his "brief prodigality" links this present to the past. The undercurrent of disease we noted in "beestings," however, still flows in the term "ebbing," which denotes, besides its obvious meaning, "a disease of fruit-trees characterized by a morbid secretion of gum." Normally, one might be wary (even, or especially, after the work of Mr. Empson, depending on one's point of view) of utilizing alternative or subsidiary meanings. In the case of a poet like Beckett, however, one can scarcely afford to ignore them. An "adequate reader" of the Irish writer must share at least to some degree his fascination with words, their origins, organic development, and living potential. He was not for nothing, after all, a close friend of James Joyce. Both "beestings" and "ebbing" are diseases involving secretions of body fluid. The title of the poem is "Sanies," a fact that merits consideration even without other support such as the images of bleeding tires, the highway voided, urination, and indeed birth. And in the larger context we recall the evaporation of Echo's vital fluids and her consequent demise. "Ebbing" in its primary meaning adds one more sea image to those already noted in connection with the voyage of life. At the same time, the rhythm of ebb and flow reinforces the pattern arising out of the alternation of pedaling and coasting.

The "brief prodigality" can be understood on three structural planes. Closest to the literal level is the burst of energy between periods of coasting. Having been prodigal of his strength, the rider needs the rest suggested by line 33 in order to recuperate. Secondly, the "brief prodigality" suggests the excursion from Dublin to Portrane and back. Only the biographical level, however, can fully explain the three lines that follow. After resigning from Trinity and living and traveling in Germany, France, and England, the poet— suave and urbane now—has been forced back to his Dublin home by lack of money. "Good as gold" carries, besides its obvious sense, an allusion to this real-life situation. It is in this part of the poem that the important theme of "no return" begins to develop from the seed sown in lines 14 and 15. There we saw the vain longing to retreat to the comfort of the caul. The wanderer has indeed been brought back but, as "biding my time" indicates, not for long. Very often in Beckett's writing, the circle that he uses as a structural principle assumes negative value. It is motion getting nowhere. In "Enueg I" the points on the circle were all the same, and movement did not result in progress. Hence the words of the narrator in "Serena II":

> with whatever trust of panic we went out
> with so much shall we return
> there shall be no loss of panic between a man and his dog[89]

The prodigal has been set apart. Although he is back in Ireland, things will never be the same. He can no more become the Irishman he once was than he can recapture the world of his youth. The theme of love reappears in the next lines. The landscape is transformed by his erotic desires, but his own situation makes him a stranger among lovers:

> distraught half-crooked courting the sneers of these
>   fauns these smart nymphs
> clipped like a pederast as to one trouser-end
> sucking in my bloated lantern behind a Wild Woodbine
> cinched to death in a filthy slicker
>
> (38-41)

Like a deviate among the heterosexual, he is isolated. His is a "spoilt love" (15). Hiding behind his cigarette, he relieves himself by the roadside. The "Wild Woodbine" or *chèvrefeuille* reminds us at the

---

[89] Cf. the lines in *Godot*, p. 52: "Pour chacun qui se met à pleurer, quelque part un autre s'arrête. Il en va de même du rire."

same time of the eponymous *lai* of Marie de France, which recounts an episode from the story of Tristan and Isolde. Again we find the macrocosm stocked with signs that lead to literature. And literature in turn lends meaning to life. Like Tristan and Isolde, like Echo and Narcissus, the narrator and his love are destined to part, and to die. His fate is the embrace not of the amorous honeysuckle but of the solitary bicycle clip and the "filthy slicker." The double thread of union and separation dominates the final section of the poem. In the above lines the past participles "distraught," "clipped," and "cinched," coming after the long series of present participles, are stylistic correlatives of the brief halt. In the lines below, the syntax-conscious author playfully points to the final dismounting by underlining the fact that the main verb of this lengthy sentence has been postponed until now. (Beckett is not long back from Germany, as the series of German words in the poem testify, nor far removed from his work on Proust.)

> flinging the proud Swift forward breasting the swell
>   of Stürmers
> I see main verb at last
> her whom alone in the accusative
> I have dismounted to love
> gliding towards me dauntless nautch-girl on the face
>   of the waters
> dauntless daughter of desires in the old black and
>   flamingo
> get along with you now take the six the seven the
>   eight or the little single-decker
> take a bus for all I care walk cadge a lift
> home to the cob of your web in Holles Street
> and let the tiger go on smiling
> in our hearts that funds ways home   (42-52)

We have completed the geographical circuit and find ourselves back in Dublin. We have completed, too, the trip through time from the caul, to birth and childhood, to the recent expedition in foreign lands, to the return to Ireland, family, and girl. The sight of her red and black coat in the crowd on a Dublin street joins the two journeys through space and time and brings us into a single present moment. The voyage image recurs one last time in "breasting the swell" (the make of the bicycle provides both a bird image and the *s* and *f* that join the array of sibilants and fricatives to suggest the wind and wave). The related theme of the trip makes its final appearances in lines 48 through 50 and 52. Carrying through to the end, the rhythm of alternation based on pedaling and resting, like the systole and diastole of a pulsating heart, seems to reflect the ambivalence of desire and refusal. Others may love (the term *Stürmers*, "lady-killers" in the colloquial German, picks up the motif of the fauns and nymphs), and the narrator himself dismounts at the sight of the girl whose image has often been summoned by the call of his desire. He does not intend, however, to repeat the metaphysical betrayal of his own parents by entering into productive wedlock, nor allow himself to be caught like a fly in the web of social and religious conformity (50). Resisting attractions as compelling as those of the sensuous Indian dancers known as "nautch girls," the narrator suggests that she hustle on home to Holles Street. Why Holles Street, when in real life the girl's home was elsewhere? Rarely in these poems is the choice of a real landmark merely arbitrary. The presence of a number of German words in the poem ("Ritter," "müde," "Stürmers") and the overall semantic context make plausible an association with the German *Hölle*, or hell. Further, there was and is still a maternity hospital on Holles Street. If we add to these the image of the spider web, we may perhaps hazard a guess that the narrator is damning his love to the inferno of courtship, marriage, procreation, and death in Dublin, an inferno he prefers not to share. Refusing to perpetuate the pain that is life, he renounces his love and the ineluctable social cycle that continues man's misery. The last two lines seal their separation in the present and sever that present from a past when they were united in love. It might be nice to be back in the caul or back in love, but time moves in one direction only. Today and yesterday are irreparably two. The cord has been cut, and the circle in space is a fiction. Only the straight, descending line of a man's days is real. The memory of the single path they traveled briefly together may live on, but at the end of the poem each must go his separate way. No longer can the tiger of love fund ways home as he does in the limerick to which "Sanies I" alludes as it closes.[90]

[90] "Funds," from the Latin *fundere*, "to melt," is an archaic spelling of the verb "to found" (used chiefly in connection with metal and glass). The sense of "fusing" or "making into one" survives in "foundry" and compounds like "confound."

There was a young lady of Niger
Who smiled as she rode on a tiger;
They returned from the ride
With the lady inside
And the smile on the face of the tiger.

To sum up briefly before moving on to the last poem to be considered individually under this rubric, we recall that the real world around him with its occupants and furnishings speaks to the narrator consistently and powerfully on a limited number of topics: suffering before all others (the wind is a cang, a double row of tulips a gauntlet, and an ambulance an ambulance); then more specifically disease (the rain is an ink of pestilence and a flower an anthrax); death and dying very often (the world is an enormous nursing home filled with the perishing); exile (even the goat and chickens are outsiders); suicide (ladders down to the river beckon; asylum is available underground). Movement through this world is translated into man's trip through life (the narrow Rue Mouffetard, flanked by tall façades, becomes a fjord for the voyage of a human vessel). Immobile, man finds himself imprisoned (like the animals at the zoo) in a cage atop the Monument. Detached, viewing himself as occupant of this world, he is now the suffering and compassionate Christ, now the guilty Judas, now the loving, doubting, needing Peter. The city, London or Dublin, calls up the infernal prison of society; the woods, escape into solitude; the mountain peaks, monstrous claws from which no escape is possible; the western sea, a final refuge in death. Larches are a link to the narrator's childhood in "Sanies I" and "Serena II." A harbor is home and hospital. The name of a village, the frame of a bicycle, strolling couples, a fresco of Puvis de Chavannes call up love and sex. A cloud or thunder reveals religious attitudes. Hobbling along the road smoking, a cripple conjures up ancient and still meaningful philosophies. From caviar a lighter mood extracts henorrhoids, from Portrane and Donabete prolonged showers. Finally, the landscape leads to art: a nursing home to Dante, a mushroom to poetic "creativity," a town to a medieval tale of love, the color of the dusk to Homer, weeds to a Dutch painter. From these scattered examples, the reader can judge for himself the inventive agility of Beckett's imagination. He would exclude little in these early poems by reason of impropriety. There is pleasure to be had in the sheer spectacle

149

of such variety brought into meaningful coherence and unity, and indeed in each individual metamorphosis of neutral, obstinate reality. At the same time, the diversity of the materials admitted is likely to disturb many an amateur of classical purity. On the other hand, the major themes are few, and they have an archetypal universality and power: life, death, suffering, love, religion, exile, society, the self, escape, art. They are not only interwoven within individual poems but also bind one poem to another to form the harmonious tapestry of the whole collection. Consequently, the variety of materials is balanced by a thematic unity; the chaotic rhythms of multiform nature are measured to the composition of a man's mind and heart.

In "Enueg I" the narrator's walk took him to the west of Dublin, and then, inevitably, back into the heart of the city. The rider circles to the northeast and north in "Sanies I." The circle of impotence straightens into the line of a quest in "Serena III," and the direction is southeast along the coast, as though to forecast the poet's eventual migration to the Continent. To the west lay darkness and the ocean's void; to the southeast, perhaps, he will find the warmth and light of life. As the narrator says in "L'Expulsé," "Je pris la direction du levant, au jugé, pour être éclairé au plus tôt."[91] The walk begins at the first bridge east of O'Connell Street, Butt Bridge, which, besides its name, contributes to the ambivalent sexuality of lines 6 and 7 its salient feature, several concrete capitals that might easily have suggested stylized, flattened breasts ("or on Butt Bridge blush for shame / the mixed declension of those mammae"). Sometimes it is difficult not to believe that Beckett invents and names his geographical or urban landmarks to suit his aesthetic purposes. This is practically never the case, however. "The World's End" district of London, the setting for part of *Murphy*, to take one example, is a real section of Chelsea, where Beckett himself (perhaps with sardonic satisfaction) lived during his 1933-1935 stay in the city. From Butt Bridge one can look out over the dock area and, incredibly enough, over the authentic Misery Hill. From this last bridge over the Liffey before it empties into Dublin Bay one can also see the Bull and Pool Beg lighthouses. While the former easily enough represents the male element, the sense of the latter is buried for most non-Irish readers in the Gaelic. "Beg" means small

[91] In *Nouvelles et textes pour rien* (Paris: Les Editions de Minuit, 1958), p. 40.

and "poll," which becomes "poul" or "pool" in place names, indicates among other things a deep part of a river or an inlet of the sea. Its root meaning is pit, hollow, orifice. Even without such linguistic specificity, however, the symbol of eternal separation is clear and strong.

The last part of the poem continues the twin themes of desire and frustration:

> whereas dart away through the cavorting scapes
> bucket o'er Victoria Bridge that's the idea
> slow down slink down the Ringsend Road
> Irishtown Sandymount puzzle find the Hell Fire
> the Merrion Flats scored with a thrillion sigmas
> Jesus Christ Son of God Savior His Finger
> girls taken strippin that's the idea
> on the Bootersgrad breakwind and water
> the tide making the dun gulls in a panic
> the sands quicken in your hot heart
> hide yourself not in the Rock keep on the move
> keep on the move
>
> (16-27)

The alternative possibilities signaled by the conjunction "or" in lines 3 and 5 find an echo in the "whereas" that opens line 16. Why not avoid temptation or frustration by ignoring the message of puritan renunciation discovered in the Dublin landscape (11-15)? Why not be a bit reckless? Hogarth's curved line of beauty, the "pothook" of line 1, finds reflections in the "cavorting scapes." The local panorama *can* offer a gayer face to the determined seeker. Adding the archaic "o'er" to underline the Victorian atmosphere called up by this second bridge (across the Grand Canal), the poet rides roughshod over all that it symbolizes. The shame of "slink down" may be the natural reaction of a pro-English Irishman, himself an heir to the puritan tradition. On the level of biography and in conjunction with the verb "to bucket" (in the sense "to drive a car roughly and carelessly"), it recalls an accident on the narrow, bumpy, and antiquated bridge. Ringsend (a real road and small agglomeration near Victoria Bridge) suggests the end of more than one allegiance. In 1962 the bridge itself was down, but a rather perilous crossing for pedestrians and cyclists was possible on a very narrow temporary structure while the new bridge was being erected.

Beyond Ringsend, strung out along the coast to the south, lie a number of small towns and suburbs, among them Irishtown, Sandymount, Merrion, Booterstown, and Blackrock. Irishtown may have been chosen for juxtaposition with Ringsend in the poem (they are contiguous geographically) as an ironic commentary on widespread celibacy in Ireland. The theme of separation is stressed in other subtle ways as well. The "mount" of Sandymount recalls the "hill" of Misery Hill, crowned by the carnation-colored arch-gasometer, hyperbolic figure of solitary man's sexual frustration. From Sandymount one should be able to see the remains of the Hell Fire, a club for eighteenth-century libertines that once stood on a hill to the south of Dublin. The stone building is in ruins now, the blasphemous black masses over and the debauchery ended. The "puzzle" is whatever happened to such bohemian ways on the Emerald Isle. The next four lines (20-23) give a fairly clear answer. To the immaculate heart of Mary (13) the poet opposes the well-maculated Merrion Flats. Under the curved sign of love and beauty, they are "scored with a thousand sigmas," as though the sea were at once artist and lover. The poet proposes two responses to the profligacy of nature: compassion and forgiveness, the answer of Jesus Christ, who, as Hibernians profess to believe, is the Son of God and Savior of mankind; and condemnation and punishment, the effective answer of puritan Ireland. "His Finger" wrote love in the dust, love given even to the woman taken in adultery; the finger of the latter-day Pharisee is pointed in accusation at the "girls taken strippin." The phrase "that's the idea," used in both lines 17 and 22, clearly links Victorianism and the morals squad. Beckett builds his case by a quadruple repetition (21) that emphasizes the exemplary authority of the divinity. He adds two final thrusts in line 23: Booterstown becomes Bootersgrad, which suggests a Russian-style compulsory orthodoxy, and breakwater becomes "breakwind" in a final scornful salute to the Irish MKVD. Lines 24 and 25 recall both Sandymount and the Merrion Flats. Walking along the shore, the narrator imagines the amorous sea pursuing the gulls as the tide comes in over the beaches. And his poet's heart, longing for love and beauty, quickens and warms in sympathetic response, as sands under the sun's caress. But the landscape is ambiguous. Throughout the poem, asceticism vies with the erotic. Artist and lover, he would have rough sledding on the frigid terrain of puritanism, where the rock of religion provides cold comfort. His fears match the panic of the dun gulls. Better, he tells himself, to keep on the move.

The Personal Sources and the Unity of *Echo's Bones*

In *Echo's Bones*, as we observed at the beginning of this essay, the author makes use of his life in the world to a much greater extent than in *Whoroscope*. While both works are based on the literary and philosophical tradition, the poems in *Echo's Bones* are "personal" in a more immediate and tangible way. "Tangible" is no doubt an overly optimistic term to apply to the elusive relationships between art and life. Perhaps deterministic hypotheses have real validity only in the depths of an inner being where everything is (or was, in a past not always easy to retrieve, even for the poet) related to everything else. Beckett calls poetry a precipitate, i.e., a dead residue, a simplification and isolation, stabilized fragments left from an obscure and fluid complexity. To attempt a reconstruction seems more than rash, but to abandon all hope of relationship, however tenuous, is difficult. Some grounds for optimism can be found in the conviction that we are dealing not with pathologically repressed mysteries of an exceptional nature but with universal human experiences and problems, which, moreover, have reached the light of poetic day and at least to some extent appear to have surfaced as well in the early life of the author.

An investigation of Beckett's early life does not immediately unearth more than a fragile and paradoxical connection between his origins and *Echo's Bones*. His hardworking father while still quite young began practice as a "quantity surveyor."[92] He established his own firm and soon acquired an attractive home and property in the elegant suburb of Foxrock, south of Dublin. Sociable, athletic, almost always in good humor, he would take his younger son with him of a Sunday for long walks across the fields and over the hills. They swam together and played golf. William Beckett loved to tell amusing stories and had a large store of anecdotes. They laughed together and had long chats. The father had left school at the age of fourteen or fifteen but, intelligent and sensitive if not well educated, he encouraged his son's scholarly and intellectual tendencies and was very proud of his successes at school and

---

[92] A well-thought-of profession in Ireland. Its practitioners occupy an intermediary position between architect and builder, estimating the materials and labor required for a given project.

later at the university. A loving father, he carried his son's recent letters on his person until the day he died.

More austere and religious than her husband, Mary Beckett was no less tender and affectionate. Before their marriage she had worked as a nurse in a Dublin hospital. Calm and controlled, she was a pillar of strength and security during the inevitable small crises of family life—accidents, illness, the woes of childhood. Wholly devoted to her husband, her boys, her house and garden, she was respected and held in affectionate esteem in the circle of family friends.

Such an atmosphere, certainly conducive to happiness, extended beyond home and hearth. Samuel Beckett attended the best private schools, where he was as successful in athletics as in his studies. His talent at sports helped him make friends quickly, and he was certainly far from miserable. All in all, everything militated in favor of happiness. Suffering was to come, however, and nature had endowed him with a sensitivity that heightened it beyond measure, courage that kept him from turning aside, and an intellect that demanded and failed to find adequate reasons.

"You might say I had a happy childhood . . . although I had little talent for happiness. My parents did everything that could make a child happy. But I was often lonely." Little by little, through his studies and his voracious reading, the young man penetrated more and more deeply into a world that became less and less accessible to his parents. Progressively, the conventional side of their slightly bourgeois, a little-too-well organized life (which he never ceased to respect, however, and admires to this day) came to lend it an air of unreality. Already an abyss was opening between the inner and the outer worlds—an abyss that the study of Descartes was to widen and deepen. Prolonged stays in Italy, France, Germany, and England, preludes to the vagabond years to come, helped to undermine the stability of the Dublin macrocosm and reinforce the reality of the microcosm that was always available and more and more his true fatherland. And yet another element among those responsible for the January 1932 rupture with his past was probably decisive.

From a very early childhood, the future poet had been extremely sensitive to suffering of every kind.[93] This human and religious

[93] See, for example, the transposition of a real episode and feelings in the ending of "Dante and the Lobster," in *More Pricks Than Kicks.*

problem, perhaps the root problem, is worked out in explicit terms in "Ooftish," a poem published in 1938.[94] After an accumulation of miseries and misfortunes (not without a paradoxical relationship to certain hopefully pathogenic litanies of the medieval ascetic, Jacopone da Todi), the poem ends on the idea that all suffering can be reduced to "the blood of the lamb"—and we are reminded again of Estragon's line in *Godot*, "Toute ma vie je me suis comparé à [Jésus]," Jesus the prototype of the innocent victim. Obviously we are up against the ancient and eternally fresh enigma of the existence of evil. The event that exacerbated an already acute concern and prepared the terrain that was to produce the last six poems of *Echo's Bones* was the death of William Beckett from a heart attack in June 1933. Overwhelmed, the young man wrote to a friend, "What am I to do now but follow his trace over the fields and hedges." He left Ireland once again, after about a year at home, and went to London, where he spent two miserable years reading, walking, trying to write. Depressed, in what he was later to call "a confused state," searching, fleeing, tempted to end his stay in a cruel and incomprehensible world, he put together the collection called *Echo's Bones* and wrote the novel *Murphy*.

From these basic givens—a hypersensitivity to certain aspects of the external world as it impinged on his consciousness and led to his sense of the human condition; and the intensity of his emotional, voluntary, and intellectual responses to such experience—we can come to appreciate the closely woven unity of *Echo's Bones*, which on the surface may seem to be a chaos of conflicting or unrelated poems and themes. Once we have penetrated the veil of literary, geographical, and personal allusion and made our peace with the poet's use of language and form, we recognize that basically these poems are the record of a double initiation: the initiation of a young man into the stern realities of the world and man's condition and the initiation of a talent, an artistic potential, into the nature and uses of poetry. As "The Vulture," which opens the collection, introduces us to the latter, so the extended metaphor that is "Enueg I," the first long poem in the group, thrusts us harshly into the brutal setting of the former. All the world is a hospital. Those still able to move about ("who must / soon take up their life and walk" as Beckett puts it in "The Vulture") inhabit the outer chambers. Those in the inside rooms that face on the courtyard of death are prone,

[94] In *Transition*, No. 27 (April-May 1938), p. 33.

waiting. As in *Godot*, twenty years later, you stagger to the meeting or you wait for it to occur where you lie. Ovid used *abeo*, Beckett uses *exeo*; one way or another we are all on our way out. The young Samuel had more than his share of bedside vigils, and the Portobello passage is a kind of synthesis of these experiences and, as we have seen, a veiled commentary on the hellish nature of human existence here and now. We have evidence of the poet's vulnerability to suffering and dying in every poem of *Echo's Bones*. From the white rat in the adder's maw to Christ himself, innocence expires in pain. Such is the meaning of the simile in lines 12 to 15 of "Enueg I." The skull skewered and strangled "bites like a dog against its chastisement." Like the canine culprit, man is punished severely for crimes he fails to understand, offenses that can only be such for some unknown and mysterious master.

We can estimate the continuing importance for Beckett of the enigmatic experience of disease and death from the poem "Ooftish" ("auf dem Tisch," in the sense of "lay your money down, make your contribution"). The starting point for the poem was a sermon he had once heard in Ireland. The preacher, in describing his visits to the sick, confessed, "What gets me down is pain. The only thing I can tell them is that the crucifixion was only the beginning. You must contribute to the kitty." Here is what the skeptical poet makes of such counsel and of the view that suffering, accepted and offered up, has positive spiritual value:

OOFTISH

offer it up plank it down
Golgotha was only the potegg[95]
cancer angina it is all one to us
cough up your T.B. don't be stingy
no trifle is too trifling not even a thrombus
anything venereal is especially welcome
that old toga in the mothballs
don't be sentimental you won't be wanting it again
send it along we'll put it in the pot with the rest
with your love requited and unrequited
the things taken too late the things taken too soon
the spirit aching bullock's scrotum

[95] British: "a dummy nest egg for a fowl."

156

you won't cure it you—you won't endure it
it is you it equals you any fool has to pity you
so parcel up the whole issue and send it along
the whole misery diagnosed undiagnosed misdiagnosed
get your friends to do the same we'll make use of it
we'll make sense of it we'll put it in the pot with
   the rest
it all boils down to the blood of the lamb

We recognize the bitter irony that mimics cruelty partly in rage, partly in the certainty of understating the case, partly to jolt the reader into awareness; and we can guess the admixture of personal pain and pugnacious courage in a pun like "cough up your T.B." In *Echo's Bones* all things are "pressed down and bleeding." Several poems are filled with images of contortions and convulsions, of tremblings, shiverings, and shakings, of dissolution and crumbling, of stagnation, rotting, withering, and deterioration. Neither typhoid nor the ambulance is missing, and even the maggots are there.

If this is the dominant note in his poetry and the overwhelming fact to be coped with before any kind of *modus vivendi* can be won, the poet is far from insensitive to beauty, love, physical enjoyment, comradeship, affection. Indeed, it is no doubt his very awareness of the presence of such values and the high price he sets on them that exacerbates his misery at their fate. This tension between the "ideal" (the way things might be, ought to be, occasionally briefly are) and the "real" (more real finally because it always wins out) is everywhere in the poems: an unfairly balanced tension, a lopsided contest, but not total pessimism at any rate. One might object that others, perhaps equally sensitive, have accepted greater trials. Perhaps the poet tends to be a chronic idealist who cannot or will not avert his eyes from reality. The thin beauty of the silken seas and the arctic flowers must evaporate before the solid substance of bleeding flesh. Not for long, however. The scarlet beauty of the phlox catches his attention. But threatened by thunder it seems out of place in "our world dead fish adrift." The poems provide scores of examples of such nostalgia for an ideal world, always accompanied by a lucid realism. Hope is badly battered in the rough waters of Beckett's reality, but somehow it never quite goes under. Love, beauty, pardon exist in "Alba," but they are outweighed by the certainty of ultimate desolation. There is a "happy land" of

157

physical contentment, fun, and games. A make-believe realm, however, it soon dissolves in very real distress. And so, wrenched from his loves by his sorrows, yet loving still, tormented in his exile by vestiges of Eden, the poet somehow continues on his way.

His initiation into the savage realm of maturity discloses other aspects of reality. The world hides its horrors beneath the dress of euphemistic convention. The sounds of wailing and gnashing of teeth are muffled in the privacy of Portobello. Names mask the true nature of things. In *Murphy* the insane asylum is called The Magdalen Mental Mercyseat. Fiction imitates reality, for the official name of the London hospital popularly known as Bedlam is St. Mary's of Bethlehem. Like the anonymous popular poet responsible for this particular clarification, Beckett's X-ray vision pierces social pretense. The stylish young couples out for a walk are reduced to fauns and nymphs and the *paterfamilias* to the glans. In both cases sex is the essential. Athletic "heroes" are poor fellows in need of nepenthe (the real *raison d'être* of their drink). Their Sunday best disguises sweaty bodies. Religion is a refuge for the timorous. The city's surface dissolves beneath an acid gaze, revealing cruelty and baseness. On several occasions breaking wind is above all a way of cracking convention. Once in a while an unattractive envelope holds a hidden message of happiness ("slouching happy body / loose in my stinking old suit"), but this is the rare exception. Society is not the only hypocrite, however. Nature, too, masquerades under false colors: yellows, reds, blues, greens that blend into black, not white. And ultimately man as well, that inveterate optimist, deludes himself. He is not the creature of sunny surfaces he believes himself to be, but in essence an underground being (see the recent novel *Comment c'est*). When the flesh falls the maggots take him for what he is, a pile of bones like those of the once beautiful Echo, like those hidden beneath the stones of the cairn.

A good poet is by nature a seer in the literal sense of one who sees. In Beckett a keen vision cuts through the many veils men have used to make life easier and to hide the inescapable future. Perhaps this double-edged gift is responsible in part not only for what sometimes seems like an obsessive preoccupation with suffering and death but also for the sense of alienation that pervades many of these poems. Knowledge of evil, as in the original garden, is an exile. Pain can obscure beauty and happiness and lend them a dim unreality, until they seem part of the phantasmic surfaces. There are other, down-to-earth reasons as well that we have touched on earlier. The sickness and death of those one loves can produce a strong enough sense of loneliness. Then too, Beckett was a Protestant in Catholic Ireland, a southerner in a northern preparatory school, an introverted intellectual in the comfortably bourgeois family of an outgoing Dublin businessman, of loyalist parents in chauvinistic, anti-English Ireland, an artist miscast as a professor, and very much a foreigner as a down-and-out Irishman in London, Germany, and France. In the poems we become aware of exile and separation as important themes as early as the first word of "Enueg I"—"exeo"—and often again in that poem in images that range from social outcasts and a child excluded from a game, through chickens and a goat shut out of their enclosures, to the derelict narrator himself. The prey of policemen on the lookout for vagrants in "Enueg II," the narrator is like that other social misfit, Jesus Christ, and plods on until he lies exhausted on O'Connell Bridge. A diffuse impression of estrangement rises like a cold mist from the poems set in England, France, and Germany. The narrator is not "one of the gang" in the Paris brothel and pays for his intrusion with a whipping. The daytime world of "Dortmunder" is alien to him, and he seems a displaced person in the city of "Serena I," where exotic birds, captive in a foreign zoo, gaze westward in the direction of Ireland, his home. Even in Dublin, however, he remains the prodigal wanderer, held to the hearth by the bond of indigence. Out of his element at home and abroad, he has nothing to do but "keep on the move." And gradually we realize (it becomes clearest perhaps in "Sanies I") that he is the figure of the metaphysical misfit, man out of place on earth, out of joint in time.

Cut off from the context of *some* environment—national, social, religious, personal—the sense of self, of one's own existence and being, is weakened. Much of the later writing of Samuel Beckett will be a search for this missing self, missing in the unreality of the macrocosm but perhaps retrievable in the microcosm of the mind. The images of solitude and separation in *Echo's Bones* are ambiguous, however. The child, assured that he could indeed enter the field where the game is being played, chooses, after all, to remain outside, and the goat seems only half-decided to give up his liberty. Similarly, the darkness of the mountain or the jungle seems barely preferable to the fire that brightens as it destroys or the rotten beauty of the evil-smelling rafflesia. Only the beckoning river offers

159

momentarily a possible way out for one who knows neither how to accommodate himself to life nor how to accept total isolation. Nevertheless, the narrator does not respond to the call, and the poem remains without a true conclusion.

There are, in fact, other solutions, and a large part of *Echo's Bones* is devoted to an exploration of alternatives. Caught in such a bitter dilemma, what are the options open to a lucid and demanding mind and will? What are the possible courses of action for an initiate to whom the world seems intolerably cruel, far removed from the ideal, too thinly coated with the factitious gloss of health and happiness, and totally alien? First of all revolt, sometimes through violence and obscenity. In the wild mountains at twilight the Kerry Blue terrier, surrogate of the poet, is summoned to "snarl and howl," to "hound the harlots out of the ferns," to tear the heart from this "damfool twilight," "this crapulent hush." A masochistic flagellation can be a catharsis. Sarcasm and irony also serve, and sometimes classical understatement translates a response between resignation and revolt, a kind of refusal that is aware of its own futility in the face of what is unacceptable and at the same time inevitable. Overtones of such an attitude toward life are present in the simple "nay" that rejects mourning in "Malacoda."

At times religion holds out the hope of a reconciliation. The poet's sympathy for the suffering Christ is clear enough. But Christ in these poems is a figure of man, a victim, not a savior. Croagh Patrick is engulfed in the night that is the fate of all the condemned land. There is "no sun and no unveiling / and no host." Better not to hide in the rock of religion.

The quest that goes on after each failure does not exclude an effort to adapt to life in society. The adder is warm and well fed in her brightly lighted home. As far as the poet is concerned, however, it would seem (as the Pascal allusion suggests) that the whole earth has been usurped. He complains that he is not a Defoe or an Aretino able to live by the pen. Unwilling to prostrate himself abjectly before the altar of society, he is incapable of dominating the city by sheer brutality as Wren's giant bully seems to do.[96] Solitude seems desirable when difficult to come by and Ken Wood alluring when even "the canaille" will not leave him in peace to read his newspaper.

[96] Cf. Pope, *Moral Essays*, Epistle III, ll. 339-340: "Where London's column pointing at the skies, / Like a tall bully, lifts the head and lies."

... a guttersnipe blast his cernèd eyes
demanding 'ave I done with the Mirror
I stump off in a fearful rage under Married Men's Quarters

Society says join, share, adapt—in short, be sociable. The choice of a paper called the *Mirror* brings in narcissistic overtones and calls to mind an image of the poet as solitary introvert. A clash is inevitable. His response is rage at the invasion of his privacy. But it is not easy to escape the clutches of conformity, as the irony of "Married Men's Quarters" suggests. Not only does society arrange for singles to become couples, but it groups pairs into larger social cells as though solitude were a capital crime and segregation of the sexes a mortal sin against the canons of the group.

On the other hand, solitude can be as difficult as togetherness. In the wild Wicklow mountains at night where a misstep might mean a leg broken in a bog hole, where searching parties could easily arrive too late, in mountains populated by the phantoms of Celtic legend, the narrator is glad enough for a sign of civilization that "muzzles the cairn." The familiar cigarette package ("Churchman") calls up a Christianity that tamed the Celtic past. It succeeds now in quieting the voices from the grave and domesticating the awesome spectacle of the lonely mountains. Horace, attacking the urban vices that make for misery, proposed a rural-ethical solution and asserted he had found contentment in moderation and virtue on his Sabine farm. He knew the persistence of the "atra cura" he sought to elude, the black anxiety that can climb as high as successful ambition, that crosses the same seas traversed by the bronze-prowed trireme, that sits behind the flying horseman.[97] In "Sanies I," where Beckett quotes him, we recall that neither life in Dublin nor escape into the surrounding countryside could exorcize the demon. In "Serena II," the panic will not be effectively dissipated by a long hike in the mountains. Today Beckett divides his time between a Paris apartment and an isolated retreat in the Marne valley, but the nature of his writing has not changed. The problem for him is not ethical but metaphysical. Man is at home neither in

[97] . . . sed Timor et Minae
 scandunt eodem, quo dominus; neque
 decedit aerata trireme, et
 post equitem sedet atra Cura.
  (*Odes*, Bk. III, Carm. 1, ll. 37-40)

company nor alone. Anxiety is an ineradicable part of the human condition.

In a sense the collection of poems is divided between stasis and movement. Immobility can be prison or refuge: the cages at the zoo or the cage of the city on the one hand and Ken Wood, the caul, or the asylum of the tomb on the other. By the same token, movement can be quest or flight—or indeed, and ultimately, the movement through life that has ceased to be either quest or flight. One walks when sitting still can be endured no longer. One ceases to walk when exhaustion makes further motion impossible. And one moves through existence (walking or lying still) because one has no choice. Movement plays some part in twelve of the thirteen poems. It is of central importance in nine. A walk (or a ride in "Sanies I") is both symbol and structure in the two enuegs, the two sanies, and the first and third serenas. Even in the second serena, which unfolds in the mountains, going out and coming back (27, 35, 36) form a background framework that correlates with the earth's cycle of darkness and light and a man's emergence from and reabsorption into the night that frames his brief day. In "Malacoda" the voyage moves beyond life to a final destination. "Da Tagte Es" links that last journey to life's many surrogate trips in an explicit manner. Even in the three poems where art and stasis go hand in hand, there is some allusion to the archetypal journey. In "The Vulture" the prone "must / soon take up their life and walk." "Dortmunder" suggests the voyage by allusions to Homer and the "royal hulk"; besides, as the poem opens the narrator is walking down the street with a streetwalker. Even "Alba," with its pattern of imagery that includes allusions to Dante's symbolic journey, is not wholly static. If the poet insists that his trajectory is not an upward one, he only reiterates what we have observed several times. The spatial journey, usually circular, gets nowhere because it is above all a metaphor for man's trip in time.

> asylum under my tread all this day
> their muffled revels as the flesh falls
> breaking without fear or favour wind
> the gantelope of sense and nonsense run
> taken by the maggots for what they are
> ("Echo's Bones," 1-5)

The eponymous "Echo's Bones" concludes the collection appropriately by bringing together the major themes of the thirteen poems. The narrator has been walking all day; man is required by some mysterious power to "keep on the move" as long as he is alive. (We remember the policemen in "Enueg II," who are paradoxically like agents of this power.) His walk through life is painful, and the image of the gauntlet occurs again. "Sense and nonsense," curiously enough, recall the phrase "beyond good and evil" in "Sanies I." The distinctions between beautiful and ugly, good and evil, true and false fade before the fact of ultimate personal annihilation. In life, suffering puts all else in the shadow of insignificance, and death, far from being a final triumph or justification of values held during existence, is above all a release from suffering. The grave is an "asylum" that like the river in "Enueg I" arouses desire in the heart of the walker. The "revels" ruined by the misery of life are the part of the dead. No longer either cowed by conformity and convention nor crusaders against them, they share with an incorruptible Malacoda the symbolic freedom of organic decomposition, the privilege of the *peto*, the liberty of letting go below. They have descended beneath the surface and found their true meaning (the echo of wind broken) and their substantial selves (stripped bones). We have seen the poet as vulture. The magnetism of analogy pulls us toward an image of the poet-maggot, but the narrower context of the individual poem hardly supports the inference. However, while it is hard to see "Echo's Bones" as a poem on poetry, the author's artistic practice in this final piece is extremely instructive. Breaking conventions is not merely implied by breaking wind; it is imitated on the linguistic level. The closed syntax of the set phrase "break wind" is broken open by the inserted words "without fear or favour." Something similar happens in the next line, where "run" and "gantelope" are spread apart (like the two lines of the gauntlet itself) to admit the prepositional phrase "of sense and nonsense." The poet's imitative ingenuity does not stop there. "Gantelope" is obviously chosen over "gauntlet" for its running rhythm and the image it contains of the fleet-footed animal. Beyond sense and syntax, Beckett (obviously enjoying himself immensely) uses sound both to represent and to suggest. If he avoids the vulgar term itself, the accumulation of f's ("muffled," "flesh," "falls," "fear," "favour," not to mention the related *v* in "revels") certainly brings it to the reader's mind. More than that, the strategically situated cluster of fricatives (with the sibilants of "sense and nonsense" helping out)

163

imitates the very event, and playfully seduces the unwary reader into polite aesthetic participation. The characteristic combination of somber theme, irreverent farce (no pun intended), and imaginative verbal manipulation may on occasion get out of hand in *Murphy*. Here, miraculously, the tragicomic tone seems perfectly in keeping with the balance of moods in the rest of the collection and in a way sums them up.

The long walk in the wind that annuls and wrecks the ship of the mind ("Enueg I") makes it possible to continue the voyage of life to its welcome end. Fatigue brings release analogous to the ultimate release. Vulgarity is another form of letting go and so is the comic that disengages and lends distance. In this sense, they are all manifestations of art, an *art de vivre*. In "Sanies II" gay baroque surfaces conceal the skeletal scaffolding as laughter hides tears, at least for a while. Art can be the courage that helps an unhappy initiate to endure, to keep moving, even after he knows the quest will be fruitless and no cure short of the final healing more than temporary. *Echo's Bones* is the account of a double initiation. The first is prepared independent of the poet's will. He is the passive sufferer plunged into the world and society. During the second, which takes place on the basis of trial and error within the microcosm of his mind, he discovers ways of coping, the most important of which, for us as readers of his work, is the literary art. As we peruse the poems we become aware that the closed-in, protected place is not solely the maternal womb, nor the tomb that resembles it. It stands for something much more vital than these two symbols of a longed-for nirvana; it comes to represent the little world inside the skull.

While it recalls death, always present beneath the façades of life, the recurrent image of the skull also evokes the inner universe so well described in the contemporaneous novel *Murphy*: "who knows what the ostrich sees in the sand?" asks the narrator. Employed in an asylum for the insane, Murphy developed a decided loathing for "the complacent scientific conceptualism that made contact with outer reality the index of mental well-being. . . . [His] experience as a physical and rational being obliged him to call sanctuary what the psychiatrists called exile and to think of the patients not as banished from a system of benefits but as escaped from a colossal fiasco." For his part he thought of his mind not as an instrument to record the facts of the outside world but as a place from which he was exiled precisely because of those facts. For him a fundamental conflict existed between "the big world and the little world . . . [and] his vote was cast. 'I am not of the big world, I am of the little world.' "[98] The passage is an essential one, but the link between the inner asylum (*Murphy* opens with a description of the narrator's exotic method of shutting the outer world more thoroughly out) and artistic creation does not come in the novel but in the poetry of *Echo's Bones*. To isolate the microcosm completely is of course a vain hope, but a metamorphosis must occur, as we saw in "The Vulture," before materials from the macrocosm can become the stuff of art, and the metamorphic process is slow and difficult.

> ah across the way a adder
> broaches her rat
> white as snow
> in her dazzling oven strom of peristalsis
> limae labor[99]
>
> ("Serena I," 15-19)

The suffering and death of innocence, which is the way of the outer world, can be swallowed by the sensitive and compassionate initiate only after a prolonged and repeated effort that resembles peristalsis. It takes still longer for the mind to assimilate such raw material and change it into poetic substance. Nevertheless, in time the transformation can be accomplished. Life can be converted into art, and by art a poet lives. The passage is a kind of parable on aesthetic distance. Horace said that art is both *dulce* and *utile*. Beckett in his own way tells us something quite similar. Art is "sweet" because it removes us from a reality that is not. It disengages us temporarily from the *danse macabre* of life. It can turn a hospital or a brothel or a makeshift funeral parlor into a castle of words in the fabulous forest of a literary eternity where good works never die. It can make a poem out of pain. It is the flower that marks the spot where Narcissus knelt. Its words are the echo of a nymph's beauty. All this is not really very much, hardly the immortality claimed by the Renaissance poet. But as Beckett once said simply, "It is oxygen."

[98] Pp. 176-178. For a detailed description of Murphy's mind, see Chap. VI.

[99] Horace, in *Ars poetica*, ll. 291-292, wrote of the tedium of the poetic craft ("Non offenderet unum / quemque poetarum limae labor et mora"). Beckett is less concerned in this case with the toil required to perfect the formal aspects of art than with the transmutation of experience into poetry.

In *Happy Days* half-remembered lines help Winnie get through the day. If the microcosm is a place in which one can live, art is the record of the secret metamorphosis that occurs there and makes it fit for habitation.

Art is *dulce* in part because it substitutes other rules for the harsh and apparently arbitrary laws of life. The poet reigns as divinity over a cosmos of his own making, a cosmos ordered (and disordered) according to his whim. His is a world of play, and Beckett can be as playful as the next poet. We have observed his verbal antics in "Sanies II" and in "Echo's Bones." He signs his creation in a number of ways, notably, as we have seen, in "Sanies I." There he gives the month and day of his birth in the line number (13) and the reference to larches, "where I was born with a pop with the green of the larches," and recalls the event in line 23, where the gaiety of a champagne celebration has turned to the pain of childbirth: "oh the larches the pain drawn like a cork." The two tones correspond to the twin faces of art, both present in the collection viewed as a whole and signed again in the aggregate, for there are a total of thirteen poems. What the signature says is that it is "unlucky to be born on Friday the thirteenth; unlucky to be born at all." And yet at the same time chaos has been given a form and the absurd a meaning. Life has been forced into the human order of the game. Something similar occurs whenever the world of language is made to serve the special ends of the author. From a marionette moved by the strings of chance, the poet then becomes the master of a cosmos of verbal pawns. In the line "ah across the way a adder" the missing *n* is a clue that tips us off. Mouth open with the *a*'s at start and end of the line, the poet identifies himself with the adder in a common peristaltic *limae labor*—and simultaneously lessens the severity of his vision by the gentle irony of the almost comical duplication. Many of the echoing vowels and consonants in this poetry named after the nymph Echo have to some degree the same effect of playful mockery. "Oh things are not all that bad," the cavorting sounds seem to say.[100] While the narrator suffers

[100] We have analyzed several outstanding examples. Among hundreds of others one might cite, choosing at random: "bleeding zeep," "potwalloping," "promenaders" ("Sanies I"); "scuttling," "crutch," "stick," "breech" ("Enueg I"); "morning," "mysteries," "moon," "music," "morning" ("Alba"); "clew," "Croagh," "Xanthic," "Patrick" ("Serena II"); "perspiring profusely" ("Enueg II"); "stands," "stall," "sustaining splinters," "scarred signaculum"

166

anguish, his alter ego the poet withdraws far enough to view this being—partly a former self, partly an imagined creature—with a certain degree of detachment. Verbal artistry is the evidence of that withdrawal. Not only sounds but rhythms and the length and arrangement of lines play a part. "I break down quite in a titter of despite" ("Sanies II") groups plosives (*b, k, d, k, t, t, d, p, t*) into an accelerating rhythm that imitates stifled laughter finally breaking out of control. Lines 34 through 38 in the same poem conjure up chaos in the bordello by similar means. We have only to glance at the numerous examples of important single words or very short phrases set off by themselves and occupying a full line, in "Enueg I" for instance ("Exeo in a spasm," "its secret things," "smoking," "derelict," "green-black," "the water . . . ," "soliciting," among a number of others), to realize that the breakdown of regular versification in these poems is an artfully constructive way to more effective expression. In a collection that to a great extent does away with traditional punctuation and hypotactic grammatical organization in favor of staccato juxtapositions, it is extremely interesting to observe that "Alba," a poem dedicated to the hypnotic sorcery of art and music, makes abundant use of linking words to accompany the incantation of flowing sound and rhythm. The poem is composed of a single sentence, the segments of which are welded together by no fewer than nine "ands" plus "that," "who," "though," "whose," and "so that." The negative vision is blurred and anguish eased when desolation is a dulcet melody.

It would be a mistake to overemphasize the "art" side of Beckett's work, even though in general it has been badly neglected in criticism of his writing. He is a master of form, which at moments in a novel like *Murphy* can verge on the precious, the baroque, the rhetorical—whatever one is pleased to call those unsubstantial structures built by fancy when it tends to become gratuitous, an end in itself, when it forgets the serious purpose it is supposed to serve and takes delight in the frivolous interplay of sound and movement with whimsical image and flimsy sense. In his later writing Beckett becomes more and more suspicious of form, as though doing penance for an early exuberance. But even in *Echo's Bones* the *utile* dominates the *dulce*, as pain overshadows play. The seer's

---

("Dortmunder"). Sometimes the syllables are a lullaby, sometimes they sound reveille; always to some degree they draw attention to themselves and away from the realities of suffering and death.

talent that probes beneath pleasing appearances is more than a gift. It is also a stubborn will to know, a courage that refuses to accept easy anodynes, and perhaps a pride that balks at mystery and demands clarity and comprehension whatever the cost. Beckett's art is useful or instructive in that it restates in strong, imaginative, modern terms a part of the ancient wisdom that has always been the message of good art and remains the legacy of the literary tradition. We believe ourselves free; the poems tell of imprisonment. Life seems pretty good, all in all; "it is cruel," they say. We are too busy to sense the passage of time; it is passing, nonetheless. Our dreams will soon be realized; they are illusions. We are strong and young and beautiful; you are nervous, sweating, afraid, old, a cripple, in need of a drink. Around us are our friends and loved ones (dying), our country (in exile), society (alone). But, as we have seen, besides these and other ill tidings, the poems in *Echo's Bones* speak of love, compassion, perseverance, courage, and the consolations of humor and creative activity. On the formal side, the partial breakdown of traditional patterns has a double purpose. Not only does it provide scope for the play of art; it constitutes in itself, and this is its first function, a closer representation of the underlying nature of reality as the poet perceives it. If it is true that language itself is a human order, at least in part an artistic representation or version of the world, it is also true that everyday language drapes a veil of abstraction and generality over concrete experience and hides it from our view—which is both bane and blessing. Every poet makes contact with reality not only experientially but in one way or another by transmuting the language that both reveals and conceals it. The fragmentation of form into discrete particles in Beckett's poems is on the one hand a resolution of "no confidence" in the logical order of grammar and beyond this in the order of human rationality itself, and on the other an effort to transmit an experience of relative chaos perceived as more real. The paradox of art, often viewed as an ordering of chaos, used to destroy factitious harmonies and release more authentic anarchy is the familiar romantic reversal of a classical aesthetic. For Beckett, however, the paradox will become a haunting dilemma. Can language, which is form arising out of the formless, be used to express the formlessness of being?

We have hardly reached such an impasse in *Echo's Bones*, but the double tendency is clearly visible. Beckett is both maker and seer, but how can one compose decomposition? As we have seen, the stress falls on seeing rather than making, and poetry becomes the residue of the chemical reaction called either living or dying. It is the sanies produced by the wound of existence. Life prevails over art, realism over idealism. And yet the one has not destroyed the other. Indeed the very cruelty of the dark vision urgently demands relief. As with Henri Michaux, art is an exorcism. It bears witness to the need for a womb, a tomb, or a lost Eden. If tragedy has need of transcendence, the somber spectacle of life requires a comic interlude. The constant presence of suffering demands the distance of art. In *Happy Days* the refrain "Sing your song, Winnie," which recurs during the difficult moments when other resources fail, betrays a need and holds out a hope. Today, as some thirty years ago, the staff that helps the pilgrim "keep on the move" still seems to be the song that is art.

169

iii. Two Poems

Separated by a span of ten years, "Cascando" and "Saint-Lô"
illustrate both a continuity and a change.[1] The first comes out of a
period that was at once a prolongation of the earlier uncertain wanderings and the beginning of a new, if shaky, lease on life. *Echo's
Bones* was published in November 1935. Shortly afterward, "Cascando" completed, Beckett left Dublin, where he had spent a few
weeks with his mother and brother, for Germany. From Hamburg,
alone and often lonely, he zigzagged from town to town and from
museum to museum for some six months, visiting among other
places Lubeck, Luneberg, Brunswick, Leipzig, Halle, Naumburg,
Weimar, Wurzburg, Nuremberg, Regensburg and lingering especially at Hanover, Munich, Berlin, and Dresden. From previous
visits to relatives in Kassel he had picked up some German. Longer
stays in some towns, especially Dresden, where he made a number
of friends, enabled him to consolidate his knowledge of the language. Although at the time he had little contact with the ominous
political realities of Nazi Germany, he did hear Hitler howling over
the Dresden radio and reacted against pervasive National Socialist
propaganda. He filled three large notebooks with his observations,
mostly on the paintings he saw and the music he heard. Immersed
in a world of art, he became aware nonetheless of the threat from
another quarter of reality when he met "decadent" painters, often
Jewish intellectuals, whose works had been removed from museums
and who were forbidden to exhibit. He remembers the kindness of
the art critic Willi Grohmann, who had just been relieved of his
position as one of the directors of the Zwinger Gallery (bombed
out of existence during the war). In the summer of 1936 he flew
back to Ireland and after a visit returned to London. Around October of that year he made up his mind to try his luck in Paris and
took a room in the Hotel Libéria, Rue de la Grande Chaumière, in
the Montparnasse district.

The two commitments that we saw in *Echo's Bones*—to art with

---

[1] "Cascando" was first published in *Dublin Magazine*, XI, No. 4 (Oct.-
Dec. 1936), 3-4; "Saint-Lô" originally appeared in the *Irish Times*, 24 June
1946. They have been reprinted in *Poems in English* (New York: Grove
Press, 1961), pp. 49-51.

devotion and gratitude, to life with hesitancy and suspicion—are clearly present during this *Wanderjahr*. In Germany the worlds of beauty within the microcosms of the museums are balanced by the distasteful political macrocosm outside. Unlike the traditional *Wanderjahr* with its definite educational and professional purpose, Beckett's travels had no specific goal. Having sacrificed the long years of scholastic preparation by abandoning an academic career, uncertain of the future, he roamed partly to put off any decision, partly to escape into another linguistic cosmos (a way of softening reality with the veil of a less familiar language, of transforming the world through words much as the artist does in his own, more creative way), partly to follow his love of art wherever it might lead him.

"Cascando" presents a literary analogy to this coupling of commitment and indecision. *Echo's Bones* speaks of dying, spoilt love, endings. "Cascando" is about a new love. Life has reasserted itself in spite of all, but the poet is uncertain and hesitant.

> 1.
> why not merely the despaired of
> occasion of
> wordshed
>
> is it not better abort than be barren
>
> the hours after you are gone are so leaden
> they will always start dragging too soon
> the grapples clawing blindly the bed of want
> bringing up the bones the old loves
> sockets filled once with eyes like yours
> all always is it better too soon than never   10
> the black want splashing their faces
> saying again nine days never floated the loved
> nor nine months[2]
> nor nine lives
>
> 2.
> saying again
> if you do not teach me I shall not learn
> saying again there is a last
> even of last times

[2] Once again, as in "Sanies I," a reference to birth comes in line 13.

last times of begging
last times of loving   20
of knowing not knowing pretending
a last even of last times of saying
if you do not love me I shall not be loved
if I do not love you I shall not love

the churn of stale words in the heart again
love love love thud of the old plunger
pestling the unalterable
whey of words

terrified again
of not loving   30
of loving and not you
of being loved and not by you
of knowing not knowing pretending
pretending

I and all the others that will love you
if they love you

3.
unless they love you

"Cascando" is surely one of the finest poems Beckett has written. He has not forgotten the past with its pain and its lost loves, irretrievable now and forever. The bones are still with us (8). But the past confronts the present, the dead the living ("sockets filled once with eyes like yours"). It is the moment reached after the crisis is over, suffering has subsided, and the reality of young life can compete finally with receding memories and old loyalties. Formally, too, "Cascando" is several steps removed from the past—or rather it follows an aesthetic undercurrent present in *Echo's Bones*. There is a purity about "The Vulture," "Da Tagte Es," "Echo's Bones" and to some degree even "Dortmunder," "Alba," and "Malacoda" that is lacking in the more richly varied and "realistic" enuegs, sanies, and serenas. The beauty of "Cascando," as well, lies in its purity of tone, its more easily accessible unity, and its absence of referential diversity. There is nothing centrifugal about it. It has the kind of unity characteristic of a French classical writer like Racine. And it can hardly have been a coincidence that in the next year (1937) Beckett began writing in French. Fleeing not only his own early fondness for verbal and imaginative play but also the temptation to exuberance inherent in the richness and variety of the English language, he began a long trek toward the unadorned economy that has so often been a linguistic ideal of the French. This is not to say that "Cascando" lacks complexity. Its simplicity is deceptive. For literary and geographical abundance it substitutes psychological intricacy, and the problem of unity remains.

If there are no direct literary allusions in "Cascando," it nevertheless forms part of a long tradition, older and more important than that of the enueg. Although it may not be apparent at first glance, Beckett's poem is an authentic modern version of the *carpe diem* love poem that goes back to antiquity. In one of his most renowned poems Catullus stressed the joyous sensuality of love ("da mi basia mille, deinde centum, / dein mille altera, dein secunda centum, / deinde usque altera mille, deinde centum"), triumphant at least in the present and capable of exorcizing both the threat of time ("soles occidere et redire possunt; / nobis cum semel occidit brevis lux, / nox est perpetua una dormienda") and the envy of crabbed old age ("Vivamus, mea Lesbia, atque amemus, / rumoresque senum severiorum / omnes unius aestimemus assis").[3] The aging Ronsard in some of his better known sonnets shifted the focus to urgent and sometimes almost plaintive pleas ("Vivez, si m'en croyez, n'attendez à demain, / Cueillez dès aujourd'hui les roses de la vie"), pleas bolstered by prophetic portraits of his young *maîtresse* as an old woman ("Quand vous serez bien vieille, au soir à la chandelle, / Assise auprès du feu, dévidant et filant") and reinforced by the consolation and incentive of proud poetic immortality ("Direz, chantant mes vers, en vous émerveillant, / Ronsard me célébrait du temps que j'étais belle").[4] Andrew Marvell, among other English metaphysical poets, added a robust wit to his frank sensuality. Time is still central in "To His Coy Mistress," not only in the celebrated lines "But at my back I alwaies hear / Times winged Charriot hurrying near," but also in the closing that suggests the flexibility of psychological time: "Thus, though we cannot make our Sun / Stand still, yet we will make him run."[5] Beckett's

---

[3] *Carm.* V, 7-9, 4-6, 1-3.

[4] Sonnet XLIII, *Le Second livre des sonnets pour Hélène*, in *Oeuvres complètes de P. de Ronsard*, ed. Paul Laumonier (Paris: Lemerre, 1914-1919), I, 316. Ll. 13-14, 1-2, 3-4.

[5] *Miscellaneous Poems* (1681), ll. 21-22, 45-46. It would be possible, of

poem is strikingly original, but it includes the essential elements—and a few others besides. Love, time, and art are all present, but no one element of the triad can really be called the unifying concern, even though each is of major importance. As an entity, "Cascando" holds past and future, need and doubt in unstable equilibrium.

Traditionally, *tempus fugit* rationalizes *carpe diem*. Marvell imagines with smiling wit how love might be "Had we but World enough, and Time." Beckett is more desperately and painfully aware of the passing of days, as the title suggests. "Cascando," a musical direction indicating both diminishing volume and decreasing tempo, gives way to the even more explicit term "mancando" (defined as "dying away") in the poet's unpublished German translation. The past is dead beyond recall. The three images of retrieval or renewal in lines 12 through 14 are negated. The body of the time-drowned will not surface in nine days; nine months will not produce new life; nine lives are granted to cats, not humans. The future too is ominous. Tradition tells us that youth is the time of love. In "Cascando" the lover is fearful of never learning. Perhaps this is the last chance. The theme of "too late" runs like a leitmotif through this musical composition: "is it not better abort than be barren," "it is better too soon than never."[6] If the evidence of the present, past, and future urges love while there is still time, it does so with a voice considerably less steady and confident than in past ages—and this has to do with the nature of both love and art.

Beckett published his monograph on Proust in 1931. He was defining himself in terms of the French writer even before then (in *Whoroscope*, published in 1930), and *Echo's Bones* is an implicit rejection (or at best a radical revision) of Proustian ideas on recapturing the past. For Beckett, art is hardly a salvation that repairs the ravages of time. In "Cascando" we can perhaps detect echoes of Proust in the interference between memories of past love, fading but still painful, and the hesitant, uncertain new love (part 1); and

---

course, to cite hundreds of other well-known examples. Even in very recent times French poets have produced variations on the *carpe diem* theme that may well endure, among others "Le Pont Mirabeau" of Guillaume Apollinaire, "Si tu t'imagines" of Raymond Queneau, and "Les Feuilles mortes" of Jacques Prévert.

[6] Lines that recall those in "Ooftish": "with your love requited and unrequited / the things taken too late the things taken too soon."

also in the intolerable thought of future loves that will replace present love (31-32). In one of its dimensions, Beckett's poem describes the Proustian moment of painful but vital transition between an old self that is unwilling to die and a new self that has not yet found its new set of protective but dulling habits. During such a moment of partial detachment from past, present, and future, the lover in "Cascando" is lucid and capable of surveying the succession of loves, like beads on a string, extending out of the past and into the future. At the same time he is engaged to a considerable degree in past, present, and future. The result is neither the anguishing involvement of Swann nor the privileged serenity of the Proustian narrator who succeeds through involuntary memory in recapturing a past no longer subject to flux and fixing it forever in the timeless realm of art. Beckett's lover is caught somewhere in the middle, between commitment and detachment. His love has none of the joyous confidence in passionate sensuality we find in the poems by Catullus and Marvell. His term is not "lust" (Marvell) but "want," which puts the accent on suffering. Then there is, characteristically, the problem of what is real and what is mere illusion. The "knowing not knowing pretending" of line 21 ("Wissen Zweifel Trug," with its *zwei* mediating between knowing and deceit, catches the three moments more effectively) recurs in line 33, and line 34 throws the balance toward pretending. The lover is astonishingly honest in his proposition. In line 4 he makes his case in terms that hardly seem likely to win over a timid and wavering damsel. In the German, even he is frankly dubious about the answer, for the "not" is missing and the presence of the question mark seems to stress his doubt (*"Lieber* Missgeburt als keine?"). Once again in line 10 he undercuts his argument by admitting that it is "too soon." He does defend himself, weakly, when he says "all always" (10) and "I and all the others" (35). As the German makes clear ("So werden sie alle / immer beginnen / müssen," and "So begann ich, so werden sie alle / immer beginnen / müssen"), new love must always begin before old wounds are healed, can never develop except out of uncertainty or even pretense. Much of the strange beauty and pathos of "Cascando" depends on the very irresolution of the poet. He is reluctant to commit himself beyond the evidence of his mind and heart, however strong his desire. More than enjoyment is at stake, and his indecision is the guarantee of that something more.

175

The phenomenon of repetition in both time and love calls into question the uniqueness of the moment and the experience, and it gives them an air of unreality. Much of the poem works with and against love's age-old clichés: "I never knew what love was until I met you," "I love you and only you with all my heart," "I shall never love another." If built-in irony is a criterion of artistic maturity and excellence, then "Cascando" runs no risk of failing through naïve sentimentality. The feelings expressed include within themselves their correctives. In such an interplay of opposites we find the profound link between love and art that is perhaps the chief originality of the poem. This is a far cry from Ronsard's sturdy confidence in his poetic immortality. Art shares the equivocal status of time and love. The poem opens with the suggestion that love—true, false, or in-between—might perhaps be acceptable as a mere pretext for poetry, which the author has had trouble writing of late. Not only is love devalued, but so is poetry, in the slightly deprecating overtones of the term "wordshed." Marvell threatened that "Worms shall try / That long preserv'd Virginity." Beckett seems willing at first to leave it to their posthumous pleasure and avoid amorous bloodshed. When he unites Eros and the muse in the ambivalence of line 3, he suggests a degree of interpenetration that goes beyond simple analogy. "Cascando" is also about a young man's temptation to abandon his virginal neutrality and commit himself, before it is too late, to a career as a writer. Line 4 must be read not only in erotic but also in artistic terms: "Is an abortive literary production not better than poetic sterility?"

If each day is a repetition of the day before and new loves resemble old loves ("sockets filled once with eyes like yours"), language too sins against the unique and irreplaceable with its generalizing, abstracting clichés. With consummate skill Beckett works repetition into the fabric of his poem, where it suggests more effectively than semantic content the monotony of recurrence that robs reality of its substance. "Saying again" (12, 15, 17) in the German translation is "die alten Worte," "Die grauen Worte," "Die schalen Worte," which is more explicit but perhaps less artistically effective than the reiteration of identity. In a similar way, "last" is repeated six times and phrases on the model of "if you do not teach me I shall not learn" three times. "Love" itself appears fourteen times in the last twenty-three lines (parts 2 and 3), where the stylistic use of repetition is most extensive. There are a number of other examples,

176

including four lines (30-33) beginning, as lines 1 and 2 end, with "of" and four lines ending with verbal nouns (19-22). In the thirty-seven-line poem there are twenty-one such verbal nouns. They provide a sense of continuing action, always the same, that supports imitative recurrence. Finally the poem ends on a triple repetition ("love you . . . love you . . . love you") that echoes the "love love love" of line 26. Beckett, however, does not merely reproduce the phenomenon stylistically. He also works against it. Opposed to the seven verbal nouns in lines 17 through 22 are six "lasts" that threaten to terminate the continuing action. And the cliché that declares, "You are the last girl I shall ever love" is broken and recreated by reduplication: "a last / even of last times." Yet even this hard-won phrase undergoes the irony of repetition (17-18, 22). Every lover must discover the individual within the similarity of successive loves. Otherwise he will fail, and "knowing" will give way to "not knowing" and "not knowing" in turn to "pretending." The game will replace reality. And his task becomes more difficult with each succeeding love. Like the lover, the poet must find fresh forms among the stereotypes. He must make a new *carpe diem* poem, different from a thousand others. From the rigidly articulated fossil forms of syntax he must fashion other patterns. From faded images bright new figures must emerge. The lover-poet analogy goes still deeper. As lines 7 through 14 suggest, the lover who dredges up memories of lost loves is also the poet who salvages the few poems of *Echo's Bones*. The union of the two becomes clear in lines 25 through 28. Love is the force behind the poetic impulse. And here we can judge the distance traversed since *Echo's Bones*, for love is linked, however tenuously, to life as well as to dying.

> the churn of stale words in the heart again
> love love love thud of the old plunger
> pestling the unalterable
> whey of words

"Unalterable" looks back to "despaired of" in line 1 and together they form a poignant contrast to "cascando": continued poetic sterility while the clock ticks time away. Regarding love, too, the poet's terror (29) rises from the same source. The repetitions and the verbal nouns that dominate the poem and create an atmosphere of continuing, paralyzed stasis are set against the background of a title that figures the descending trajectory which leads to the grave.

While nothing is being accomplished, the hours are sweeping the lover-artist past the time of opportunity, beyond the occasions (2) for love and art. Within the text itself, time is present in both the principal images. "The old plunger" that thuds out "love love love," the heart using up its limited number of beats, inevitably brings to mind the clock that ticks its way toward silence.[7] In lines 5 through 14 time is a vessel that moves swiftly when the two lovers are together. In solitude it slows down, allowing the grappling hooks to sink to the bottom for a dredging operation that brings old bones to the surface.[8] "Dragging" (6) refers both to the hours that creep by and the hooks that scrape along the bottom. The passage is a metaphor for memory that depends on the ambiguity of words like "dragging," "grapples clawing" (ship's hooks and the lover's fingers), "blindly" (sightless hooks and closed eyes), "bed" (bottom and couch), "want" (water and desire). Simultaneously the passage calls up the archetypal voyage that occurs so often in *Echo's Bones* as a figure of man's trip through time.

The conclusion of the poem contributes another stylistic device, reservation or qualification, to the structure of oscillation that holds in tension doubt and desire, immobility and decline. The definite assertion "I and all the others that will love you" is called into question in the following line, "if they love you," which in its turn is modified by the alternative "unless they love you." The final line in Beckett's original typescript read "unless of course they love you." The omission is a happy one for several reasons but especially because the phrase "of course" introduces a note of certainty that is out of harmony with the minor mode of doubt. By itself and in juxtaposition with the preceding line, "unless" (except if) manages to keep the definite and the doubtful in balance. The narrator appears to be saying, "All love is uncertain of itself, if it is love." When he adds, "All love is uncertain of itself, unless it is love," he seems to contradict himself. In effect, however, he repeats one last time what he has been saying all along, that he is uncertain both of the nature of love and his own feelings ("if you do not teach me I shall not learn"). Contradiction, if it is simultaneous and not consecutive, is irresolution rather than decision. To some degree, how-

[7] Cf. the watch and heart routine in *Godot*, p. 77.

[8] For "float" (12) the German version has the verb *bargen* (*bergen*), which is used in a number of maritime situations, among them salvage operations.

ever, the lines are consecutive (they are separated by the break between parts 2 and 3 as well as joined semantically and formally), and to that degree the poet firmly refuses to commit himself even to the possibility that he might be in love. If love is sure of itself, then he cannot be in love.

"Saint-Lô" comes out of the period right after World War II, when Beckett was with the Irish Red Cross. The hospital in the French city had been demolished, and the French Red Cross had built a complex of thirty wooden huts as the basis for a field hospital to replace it. The Irish Red Cross provided food, supplies, and personnel to staff the new installation. At the suggestion of a close friend, the doctor heading the medical contingent, Beckett agreed to apply as interpreter and join the group. He was accepted on condition he would also run the hospital store. On the wharves in Dublin he helped assemble and list all the supplies ("a frightful job"). He left Ireland with an advance party in the charge of a Red Cross colonel. From Paris the expedition moved on to Saint-Lô, where they received trucks, ambulances, and supplies from Cherbourg and Dieppe. The hospital was in operation by the end of August 1945. The staff remained about two and a half years, but Beckett returned to his Paris apartment (from which he had fled just before the raid of the Gestapo in 1942) at the beginning of 1946.

While "Saint-Lô" commemorates the destruction of that city, it seems to sum up in its terse lines the human as well as physical destruction and chaos that the poet experienced during the entire period of the war years, from the June 1940 exodus from Paris, through the return to the misery of years in the famished capital under German occupation, to the work with a Resistance *réseau*, the flight from hiding place to hiding place when the group was exposed, and finally the years of bare subsistence in unoccupied France.

SAINT-LÔ

Vire will wind in other shadows
unborn through the bright ways tremble
and the old mind ghost-forsaken
sink into its havoc

The brief and unadorned perfection of this four-line poem characterizes the new poetic mode adopted by the author, but it recalls at the same time similar qualities in the last two pieces in *Echo's Bones*, "Da Tagte Es" and "Echo's Bones." Other Beckett hallmarks can be identified as well. First, the poem arises from a specific geographical source, in its title of course but also in "Vire," the name of the river that flows through the French town. Second, it divides neatly into two parts, the first two lines alluding to a form of the macrocosm, the city (which we saw in "Serena I"), and the second to the microcosm of the poet's mind. The Cartesian dualism that pervades *Whoroscope* and *Murphy* and makes itself felt also in *Echo's Bones* is still dominant in 1946. Third, we can observe the author's continuing fascination with etymology. The French *virer* (to turn) comes from the Latin *vibrare* influenced by the Greek *gyros* (modern Italian *girare*). *Vibrare* meant not only to vibrate or quiver but also to gleam or scintillate. Beckett exploits the three potential meanings in the words "wind," "bright," and "tremble." Fourth, the craftsmanlike precision that binds together the elements of an extended metaphor by semantic or phonetic associations between words is still quite apparent. "Wind" and "mind" form a rhyme that begins the parallel. The "shadows" of buildings that will rise from the ruins of Saint-Lô are analogous to the shade or "ghost." Once *it* has fled, however, there is no replacement. "Havoc," an unusual term to apply to the mind, is there to suggest the widespread destruction visited upon the city. In a similar way, "old" helps to further the poetic assimilation of this mind, conscious of its age from a very early date, to the venerable metropolis. Fifth, the central theme of life and death is the typical concern in Beckett's eschatological writing. Archetypal patterns that he often uses to give appropriate form to his theme can be perceived in "Saint-Lô"—although they remain largely implicit—in "sink" (ascension and fall), which helps to evoke its opposite, the rise of the new town, and in "shadows" and "bright," which contrast with the unbroken night (left unstated) to which consciousness must come. Sixth, the poem remains true to the aesthetic of *Whoroscope* and *Echo's Bones*: poetry is a product of dying. As in "Cascando," a phoenix-like rebirth is implied. There love, here the city rises again out of destruction. But in "Cascando" renewal is shrouded in doubt, and in "Saint-Lô" the human organism cannot find being in the ashes of annihilation. Only a city or a poem, products of art, can be built up by man—and what are the bones of art compared to living flesh and blood? Seventh, in this same theme of death and

180

resurrection we have the personal signature of a man born on Good Friday and unable to believe in the resurrection to follow on the morning of Easter Sunday. There will be a future Saint-Lô and other Vires, unborn as yet, from the constantly renewed waters of its source. Nature as well as art enjoys an immortality of sorts. Man is fated to sink, hurried on toward irredeemable havoc.

Finally, the poem demonstrates again Beckett's mastery at arranging combinations of sounds, sometimes as independent poetic values, more often as subtle servants of semantic patterns. "Vire will wind in" builds on four *i*'s, two *n*'s, the related liquids *r* and *l*, and of course the alliterative *w*'s and associated *v*. The attenuation of *t* into *th*, *s* into *sh*, the linking of *o*'s, and the presence of the relatively subdued *d* and *s* in "other shadows"—plus a linking to the first part of the line through the *r* and *d* common to both—help to create the harmony of easy phonetic flow appropriate to the gentle course of the meandering stream and the moderating influence of the shadows. In the next line a *w*, three nasals, two more variations of the *o* sound, an *i* to match the one in "wind," a variant *th* for the one in "other," three voiced *b*'s to support the voiced *d*'s above, five more liquids, and a corresponding voiced *s* continue the musical mood established at the start. The staccato *t* in "bright" introduces a different note, which helps to reinforce the onomatopoetic tendency of the term "tremble." "And the old mind," with its three nasals, three *d*'s, *th*, *o*, *l*, and *i*, utilizes the same group of sounds, and in addition it is associated with the preceding line by the connective "and." The prolonged use of a limited spectrum of related sounds that fuse with meaning to create an impression of low-key tranquillity broken by nothing more violent than the trembling of light on slowly moving water ends after the word "mind." Until that point even the syntax, winding unbroken from one line to the next, contributes its legato flow. ("Unborn," since it can apply as well to "shadows" as to "Vire," smoothes the transition from line 1 to line 2.) If there were punctuation, commas would set off "ghost-forsaken." Even without them, a break in the normal syntax, which would place an adjective before its noun, makes the separation required by the shift in sense and sound. Death and destruction are announced not only semantically but also by the introduction of new consonantal effects. A cluster of explosive unvoiced palatals joins with a group of voiceless, hissing sibilants in a harsh, disrupting intrusion that shatters the serenity of the earlier lines. This is an exaggeration, of course; Beckett's language does not really imitate the bombardment of Saint-Lô! It does perhaps suggest, however, its muffled repercussions in the microcosm of the skull. Better still, the contrast on the level of sound (in the consonants, not the vowels, which do not show any significant variation) between the first two and a half lines and the last line and a half is analogous within the realm of language, given the semantic and syntactic context, to the changes described in the two worlds of man. The sensitive reader is intuitively conscious of important harmonic shifts, so crucial in lyric poetry, but analytical verification is occasionally helpful in pinpointing the exact nature of the shift. To sum up the essential facts in this particular case, we may note that in the first part the ratio of voiced to unvoiced consonants is eight and a half to one (thirty-four to four), while in the second part a radical reversal results in a two to one ratio in favor of the unvoiced consonants (twelve to six). While the shift away from continuants and toward stops or plosives—almost two to one in part 1 (twenty-eight to ten) and hardly more than four to three in part 2 (eleven to seven)—is less striking, it is nevertheless decisive. Finally, among the thirty-eight consonants in part 1 there are no palatals at all, and the three sibilants ("shadows . . . ways") are lost in the overwhelming preponderance of liquids, nasals, and dentals. In part 2, on the other hand, the balance shifts to five palatals and four sibilants versus a total of nine others divided among four different classes. In reality the change is even more striking than it appears because of the near-absence of both palatals and sibilants in part 1.

A last brief observation on "Saint-Lô." The archetype of the voyage is conspicuous by its absence. True, the river is an ancient symbol of the flow of life toward the ocean of death, and the Vire unquestionably suggests the notion of constantly renewed life flowing even in the midst of desolation. The narrator, however, is set apart from the moving stream. The citadel of his mind will sink into ruin, but for the moment no other motion is ascribed to him. We shall have occasion to return to the theme of immobility apropos of the French poems and in connection with the years of lethargy and apathy that succeeded the years of wandering and searching in the life of the poet. In "Saint-Lô" one has the impression that life and the river are passing him by.

iv. Poems in French

1937-1939

In the spring of 1937 Beckett moved from his room in the Hotel Libéria to a seventh-floor studio at 6 Rue des Favorites in the fifteenth arrondissement.[1] Biographically there is little to note during this prewar period. Beckett describes it as a "period of lostness, drifting around, seeing a few friends—a period of apathy and lethargy." In 1936, at the turn of the year, he had narrowly missed death in a stabbing incident. It may be that the prolonged effect of this event contributed psychologically and physically to the depression suggested by such terms. During his convalescence he came to know the girl who visited him at the hospital and who is now his wife. Solitude, society, death, love—these are the dominant experiences of 1937-1939 and the chief themes of the twelve poems written during these three years.[2] Underlying all four is a general sense of lowered vitality.

Contacts With the Macrocosm

1. Love: The Experience of Sameness

Beckett has said that for him coming to Paris was like coming home. There, somehow, he no longer felt the need to seek, to flee,

[1] He lived there until 1961, when he took up residence in his present apartment.

[2] The twelve poems, which originally appeared in *Les Temps modernes*, No. 14 (Nov. 1946), pp. 288-293, have been collected in *Samuel Beckett, Gedichte*. Since most of the poems in this group are untitled, they will be identified in the text by numbers indicating the order in which they appear rather than by cumbersome references to first lines:

I	elles viennent
II	à elle l'acte calme
III	être là sans mâchoires sans dents
IV	"Ascension"
V	"La Mouche"
VI	musique de l'indifférence
VII	bois seul
VIII	ainsi a-t-on beau
IX	"Dieppe"
X	"Rue de Vaugirard"
XI	"Arènes de Lutèce"
XII	jusque dans la caverne ciel et sol

to hide. The agitation and movement, the interminable walks that recur in *Echo's Bones* are for the most part missing in these poems. Instead we find stasis. Most often the narrator is in a room, motionless at his worktable or in bed listening, watching, remembering, waiting. The first line of the first poem, given below in its entirety, is typical in that it represents the outside world coming in to him, in contrast to the *exeo* which begins *Echo's Bones*.

> elles viennent
> autres et pareilles
> avec chacune c'est autre et c'est pareil
> avec chacune l'absence d'amour est autre
> avec chacune l'absence d'amour est pareille

The turmoil and suffering and doubt that so often mix with a sense of the unique and irreplaceable in the experience of young love have already begun to wane in "Cascando." The narrator is conscious that time is dulling the heightened sensitivity, reducing both pain and passion. The process has reached an advanced stage in the above poem. Like Rodolphe in *Madame Bovary* and many another Don Juan, he discovers that with successive loves, the part of newness diminishes and the part of sameness increases. The promise of the initial encounter proves a deception, and little by little amorous experience is emptied of its substance and reality. Apparent diversity turns out to be quasi-identity, which repeated becomes paler and paler. Subsequent loves cannot fill the void left by the loss of first love, however unsure of itself that first love may have been. "L'absence d'amour" indicates a breakdown in spiritual communication with others and hence with the world outside the self. The phrase—and the poem—are a first approach to the central experience of the entire group of twelve, the withdrawal from the macrocosm into the microcosm of the mind. Murphy has found his rocking chair, the narrator of "Serena I" his Ken Wood in a seventh-floor studio in the Vaugirard district. The element of almost desperate hope that is present in "Cascando" has given way here to impassive resignation. No flashes of sardonic humor break the mood of listlessness in this portrait of physical presence accompanied by spiritual and emotional absence. The two halves of the old Cartesian dualism are further apart than ever.

Artistically, no such dichotomy exists. Form and content are one. Beckett has found the verbal structure of variation and repetition almost emptied of concrete particularity that perfectly stylizes the experience of amorous variety and identity without the participation of the inner self. "Elles," qualified only by "autres" and "pareilles," are general to the point of nonexistence; the act, also "autre" and "pareil," is infected with the same sense of unreality; and what is finally seen to be "autre" and "pareille" is absence itself! The pair (autre-pareil) is repeated three times and each time, thanks to the exigencies of French grammar, is varied slightly. The order of the terms is important. In love the perception of difference precedes the realization of similarity as "autre" precedes "pareil" in the poem. Similarity, benefiting from its decisive position at the end of lines and of the poem, has the last word. The effect of sameness is also heightened dramatically by a kind of structural crescendo. As though seen at first from some distance, "they" approach and are described in two very short lines. At closer range, in one longer line, the poet repeats the observation. Finally, through the mounting effect of repetition and variation along with an expansion into two lines, each slightly longer than the preceding, he produces a close-up view of considerable intensity. Not so paradoxically, the closer they come the less real it all seems—destruction of the illusion of novelty and difference, a build-up to nothingness. By their repetition the words almost cancel each other out. The only late new addition, in line 4, is eroded formally by recurrence in line 5, and semantically it already points to the void.[3]

While the experience of sameness that robs reality of its very essence is central in poem I, it plays an important role in other poems as well. In VI the poet writes of the "musique de l'indifférence" that is capable of drowning out the voices of society. Indifference, non-difference, reduces literally to sameness. In VI, IX, and XI the presence of sand or pebbles on a beach has such overtones.[4] The repetition of the tides in IX ("encore le dernier reflux") that reminds us of the "last . . . of last times" in "Cascando," and "la même lumière," "les mêmes lois" in XII produce a similar effect.

[3] No doubt this poem should also be considered in the light of Beckett's discussion in *Proust* of the deteriorating effects of habit. In *Godot* Vladimir says, "Mais l'habitude est une grande sourdine" (p. 157).

[4] In *Godot* Estragon says, "J'ai tiré ma roulure de vie au milieu des sables! Et tu veux que j'y voie des nuances!" (p. 103).

2. *Love: The Theme of "Too Late"*

"L'absence d'amour," can be laid to other causes. If poem I indicts satiety and monotony, II suggests that time is the villain. After all, the poet has passed a milestone. Beyond thirty a man's fancy turns, less than lightly, to more serious affairs. Not without a backward glance, however, for Eros still has its uses.

> à elle l'acte calme
> les pores savants le sexe bon enfant
> l'attente pas trop lente les regrets pas trop longs
>   l'absence
> au service de la présence
> les quelques haillons d'azur dans la tête les points
>   enfin morts du coeur
> toute la tardive grâce d'une pluie cessant
> au tomber d'une nuit
> d'août
>
> à elle vide
> lui pur
> d'amour

Although in a less striking way than in the first poem, the sense of two selves is quite strong here again. The body, aided by a temporary parting ("absence makes the heart grow fonder"), performs automatically, without passion. The calm act is his detached gift to her, but one apparently inspired more by something resembling friendship than by love. The uncertainty of the narrator in *Echo's Bones* and in "Cascando" about his capacity for love has been decided in the negative in this poem. She is "vide d'amour"—perhaps because she gave herself long before to another, perhaps because of the fact that she has just given herself to him—but he, "pur / d'amour," does not know love and possibly never has, though he gives himself as best he can (9-11).

Another kind of dualism, no doubt related more to the erotic rhythm than to a body-spirit division, informs the poem and can be followed in the phrasing that includes "les pores-le sexe," "l'attente-les regrets," "l'absence-la présence," "tête-coeur," and "elle-lui." Even the general structure of the poem before the postscript (9-11) suggests in its lengthening then shortening lines a brief prelude, a climax that brings rather negative benefits (5),

186

and a terminal subsiding. Semantically, beginning and ending are described by the "attente" and "regrets" of line 3. The sexual act has two effects. First, it does in this case penetrate the retreat of the inner being and establish at least fragmentary contact between the macrocosm and the microcosm. The cloudy sky of the mind is torn in places and a few "haillons d'azur" become visible.[5] Second, it stills the painful and persistent memories of love and death in the past, "les points . . . du coeur."

For Beckett a day of light rain with skies that clear just before sunset is a typically Irish phenomenon. From this climatic starting point he develops the theme of "too late," with all the reverberations it can take on in differing contexts. In "Enueg I" it is too late for the cloud that briefly suggests a human face either to darken the already dark sky or by its passing to brighten it, as might have happened had the sun been higher. The range of meaning possible in this situation is as great as the rich symbolism of darkness and light or the ways in which a man can receive or be denied enlightenment. "Sanies I" begins with day-long showers, and poignantly implicit in the poem is the narrator's realization of mistaken and irreparable decisions taken in the past. He remembers past happiness and longs to have it again, but he knows that a wrong fork in the road once taken and followed far enough precludes turning back. As we have noted before, part of Beckett's fascination with Dante stems from their common experience of exile. Dante's "Nessun maggior dolore" translates not only the despair of the damned, for whom it is "too late," but also his own hopeless yearning to return to his native Florence. In "Serena I," "the harpy is past caring" as it stares out toward Ireland and its lost home in the Andes mountains while the light fades. The time in eight poems of *Echo's Bones* is late in the day. In three it is night. The other two are poems on death, when the opportunity for love has gone forever. Since *Echo's Bones* is a young man's initiation, since it describes the cruel end of the "sweet showers" of youth—sweet by comparison with what follows—and a tardy awakening to the fact that life is a considerably darker sojourn than its overcast beginning might lead one to expect (first the sun is hidden, then it sets), we can understand the basic importance of the image under consideration. In a related form it is at the heart of *Whoroscope*. The chick is in the dark until

[5] Fragments of blue in the darkness is a recurrent image in Beckett's novel *Comment c'est*.

its shell opens. There is a brief moment of light, equivalent to the short span of a man's days, and then its life is extinguished.[6] The narrator of the poem undergoes a similar fate. He is allowed one "starless inscrutable hour" before he is murdered by "Christina the ripper" and her henchman Weulles. The second period of darkness may be either death or a darker period of life, but in Beckett's writing there is a strong tendency for the two to converge. Death-in-life shares many characteristics of the posthumous state.

While *Echo's Bones* and the writings of 1937-1939 both develop the theme of "too late," the earlier anguish is absent in the French poems. We no longer find the taut pull between longing and impossibility, desire and resignation, that was everywhere implicit, often explicit, and always deeply moving in *Echo's Bones*. There even poems like "Sanies II," with its undercurrent of horror, or "Dortmunder," which forecasts in its apparent quietude the almost emotionless acedia of the French group, must be seen as parts of a larger whole in which they are somber alternatives in tension with the lost loves of a dying and never to be recaptured past. The state described or sought after in most of the 1937-1939 poems is one from which desire has been drained away. It might well be epitomized by the lines of Leopardi, quoted by Beckett in *Proust*: "In noi di cari inganni / non che la speme, il desiderio è spento."[7] In lines 6 through 8 of poem II a similar state is linked to the theme of "too late." The rain that ceases at nightfall late in the summer season has a "tardive grâce," which suggests a benefaction that is more surcease of sorrow than positive pleasure. The fragmentary and darkening blue of such an August hardly brings ecstasy, but it does mute the voices of memory and soothe the pain of loss (5).

3. Love: The Related Theme of "Too Young"

By a slight shift of the kaleidoscope, related patterns that we may designate by the three words of line 8 in poem IV come into view. "Toujours trop jeune" is a theme that recurs often in *Whoroscope*. The chick, "this abortion of a fledgling," is thrust from its

---

[6] Cf. "Elles accouchent à cheval sur une tombe, le jour brille un instant, puis c'est la nuit à nouveau"; and "A cheval sur une tombe et une naissance difficile. Du fond du trou, rêveusement, le fossoyeur applique ses fers" (*Godot*, pp. 154, 156-157).

[7] From Leopardi's "A se stesso" (*Canti*, XXVIII), quoted in *Proust*, p. 7.

shell—and dies—too young. "The fourth Henry came to the crypt of the arrow" assassinated before his time by Ravaillac. Anna Maria Schurmann "bloomed and withered" prematurely, because she was too young to handle the large doses of theology administered by Voët. Descartes' daughter Francine dies at age six of scarlet fever, and of course Descartes himself perishes unnecessarily by reluctant subjection to a northern climate and unconscionably early hours. Almost as though trying to counter such unseemly haste, the narrator had made a practice of staying in bed until noon and refuses the proffered egg again and again until it is "ripe." We are ripe, alas, all too soon. Finally, in line 69 Beckett introduces the figure that for him, as we have seen in "Ooftish," is emblematic of mankind, Christ, the innocent victim who was taken from the world too soon. And we remember, again in "Ooftish," the lines that join both kinds of untimeliness, as in poem IV, to the theme of love: "with your love requited and unrequited / the things taken too late the things taken too soon." No doubt Beckett's sense in his twenties of his own aging and dying (in "Enueg II," for example) resulted in part at least from his experience of premature death among his close relatives and friends. By the same token, sentimental attachments broken off left him with a sense of man's fundamental unpreparedness to cope with the events of life, which always seem to occur out of season. In *Proust* he writes of this distressing *décalage*: "Moreover, when it is a case of human intercourse, we are faced by the problem of an object whose mobility is not merely a function of the subject's, but independent and personal: two separate and immanent dynamisms related by no system of synchronisation. So that whatever the object, our thirst for possession is, by definition, insatiable" (p. 7). Later, in the novel *Watt*, the same related themes occur, and we read of "the languor and the fever of the going of the coming too late, the languor and the fever of the coming of the going too soon" (p. 135). In poem IV the two experiences of love and death are closely linked to the theme of "trop jeune."[8]

[8] The author once remarked in a conversation, "Love and death, that's all there is. There's nothing else." He would no doubt more or less subscribe to Leopardi's view that love and death are brothers: "Nasce dall' uno il bene, / nasce il piacer maggiore / che per lo mar d'essere si trova; / l'altra ogni gran dolore, / ogni gran male annulla" ("Amore e morte," ll. 5-9, *Canti*, XXVII).

189

ASCENSION

à travers la mince cloison
ce jour où un enfant
prodigue à sa façon
rentra dans sa famille
j'entends la voix
elle est émue elle commente
la coupe du monde de football

toujours trop jeune

en même temps par la fenêtre ouverte
par les airs tout court
sourdement
la houle des fidèles

son sang gicla avec abondance
sur les draps sur les pois de senteur sur son mec
de ses doigts dégoutants il ferma les paupières
sur les grands yeux verts étonnés

elle rode légère
sur ma tombe d'air

Here the microcosm of the top-floor hotel studio, inhabited cor-
poreally by the narrator, and its correlative, the skull that houses
the mind, are linked to the death-in-life motif by the expression
"ma tombe d'air" (18). Motionless, passive, he is the instrument
that records impressions brought to him through space by the
medium of air (electromagnetic waves from the radio in the next
room [1, 5-7] or sound waves that reach him directly [9-12])[9] or
through time by means of memory (13-16). The time is Ascension
Thursday, which recalls Christ's return to the Father. The context
invites us to consider him in his youthfulness; as one prodigal of
his love, rejected by man, and finding death the response to his gift.
Those to whom he came had been expecting an older, more king-
like Messiah, and were themselves perhaps either unripe or overripe for a savior. Time's gears failed to mesh. The situation stirs
memories, and the narrator recalls his own prodigality (3) and
springtime return to his family, recounted in "Sanies I." In the
German translation, "ein Sohn" reinforces the motif of the prodigal

---

[9] "Tout court": "simply, merely" (without the intermediary of the radio).

son, but the French "enfant" supports better the main theme of "too young." Lines 13 through 16 bring in further associations: "doigts dégoûtants" (both dripping and disgusting) and "no fingers no spoilt love" ("Sanies I," 15); "son sang . . . les draps . . . son mec"[10] and death by phthisic hemorrhage in "my darling's red sputum" ("Enueg I," 2); "yeux verts" and the green-eyed Smeraldina, so prodigal of her love in "Dream of Fair to Middling Women."

Besides the parallel situations that carry the burden of the central poetic experience, "Ascension" sets forth three possible human attitudes. In ironic juxtaposition to the meaning of the day, it delineates first the complete indifference that finds its stimulation in spectator sports or, at one remove, in the radio report of one who watches the players imitating life's struggle without life's penalties; second, the religious faith of the "houle des fidèles"; and last, the response of the artist who provides a poetic ascension (17-18). The pathos of prodigality, as Beckett knew from experience, arises from temporal *décalage*. His own separation in space from his parents (an absence not unrelated to death) resulted in part from a separation in time, a difference in the education, taste, temperament, and needs of two generations. When love fails to bridge such gaps and communication breaks down, one may take refuge in the synthetic distractions of a surface existence, find solace in the hope of some hidden purpose and meaning behind it, or mitigate misery by reordering experience and giving it poetic form. In Beckett's final lines there is a switch that permits a "happy ending" corresponding to the ascension—or resurrection—of Christ. Poetically, the dead girl rises, comes back to life, while the live narrator is entombed.[11]

The sorrow at premature death would seem to contradict the view of death as a liberation, but in reality the sorrow is less for the fact of death than its inopportune arrival and the loss of what might have been. Beckett once said, in the heat of a discussion on censorship, "Give a person what he wants. If he wants pornography, give him pornography." Left unsaid was "before it's too late." William Beckett worked hard all his life and left himself little time for pleasure. After his heart attack he told his son that if he recovered he

---

[10] A slang word that has deteriorated in popular usage from the early meaning of *chef* to *homme quelconque*. Here the sense is "boy friend," but the term connotes at the same time someone inadequate to the situation.

[11] "Légère," while it suggests the unsubstantial spirit of the dead girl, also carries positive connotations of release from weight and care, from the burden of life.

planned just to lie on the hillside in the sun. He was dead a few days later. For many long years after his resignation from Trinity, Beckett—neither professor nor writer—must have asked himself often what kind of career he might have had, what kind of life and love had he married in Dublin. Similar feelings come through powerfully at the end of poem XI, "Arènes de Lutèce." As though he were watching a film in which he is the principal actor, the narrator observes the depressing and distasteful spectacle of his own perambulation as it occurred during the preceding five minutes or so. His telling comment is "le ciel . . . nous éclaire trop tard" (20-21).

In poem IV, "toujours" (8) has the sense both of "still" and "always." As it looks back to the radio broadcast the implication is that many are still unprepared. Were Christ to have waited two thousand years, the reception would not be different. It would still be too soon. But the situation of the young lovers broadens the meaning. We are always too young to cope. However, in one sense, for the "houle des fidèles," it is too late. Christ came, loved, was crucified, and departed two thousand years ago. It is too late to change that. Either we could but know too little, or we know enough and cannot. We are out of joint with time.

4. *Vanitas vanitatum et omnis vanitas*

Love is a tenuous link to the macrocosm. Repetition weakens it. Aging cools it. Time's *décalage* destroys it. Of the four poems on love in the French group, poem III first develops specifically the association between three motifs—the emptiness of life, love, and death—and links them to the Biblical tradition of the vanity of all things.

> être là sans mâchoires sans dents
> où s'en va le plaisir de perdre
> avec celui à peine inférieur
> de gagner
> et Roscelin et on attend
> adverbe oh petit cadeau
> vide vide sinon des loques de chanson
> *mon père m'a donné un mari*
> ou en faisant la fleur
> qu'elle mouille

> tant qu'elle voudra jusqu'à l'élégie
> des sabots ferrés encore loin des Halles
> ou l'eau de la canaille pestant dans les tuyaux
> ou plus rien
> qu'elle mouille puisque c'est ainsi
> parfasse tout le superflu
> et vienne
> à la bouche idiote à la main formicante
> au bloc cave à l'oeil qui écoute
> de lointains coups de ciseaux argentins

The man is lying in bed waiting for the woman, who is preparing herself for the sexual act ("qu'elle mouille"), to come to him. The bed, however, is not only the couch of love but at the same time the deathbed. The ambiguity is suggestive of many things, among others the death of love, the love of death, and the equal inanity of both. The objective of the poem is to fuse the experiences of life, love, and death into the single experience of emptiness. Baudelaire, in a similar vein, wrote of *L'Ennui* that would swallow the world. Prolonged inactivity and lack of commitment, whatever the cause, have a way of dissolving the reality of ordinary existence. In our busy, hurrying, crowded modern world the acedia of the desert monks is hardly a prevailing affliction. A part of Beckett's originality stems from his exploration of the values and woes of solitude against the background of a society in which it has become more and more infrequent. In the first line of poem III the emptiness of a mouth without jaws or teeth joins erotic overtones with an image of physical disintegration. The poem ends with a related vision of a mouth hanging open loosely, idiotically, and a cranium emptied of amorous thought (and, on a second level, of physical substance). Eros and Thanatos are represented simultaneously in a pun that Beckett develops almost twenty-five years later in *Happy Days*.[12] "Formicante" suggests not only "fornicante" but also, beyond the sensation it describes, the actual movement of ants over a corpse. Finally, the eye (which in the dark can only listen) focuses on the otherworldly sounds that tell of lives snipped off by the scissors of Atropos— whom we shall meet again in poem XII.

Between beginning and ending, life and love are reduced to *vanitas*. Winning and losing, whether in the game of love or of life and

[12] Pp. 29-31.

death, we play ourselves out and cease "là," on the bed of love-death. Losing is better than winning, in love probably because winning entails effort, while losing permits sleep or at least undisturbed solitude; in dying because the sooner over with, the better. Roscelin, the eleventh-century scholastic, founder of nominalism and teacher of Abelard, no doubt stands for philosophy, or more generally the intellectual life, a mode as vain as winning, losing, loving, living. There is something fitting in the choice of a nominalist, for whom the abstractions of thought are empty names corresponding to no reality. It is fascinating to discover in this early poem the little phrase of lines 5 and 6, "et on attend adverbe." A dozen years or so before *Godot*, the kernel of that play is clearly of central importance in Beckett's life and thought. "Adverbe" replaces any specific adverb and says, in effect, "It makes no difference how one waits or what one does while waiting; only the necessity of waiting has any significance." The steady passage of time, that is, cannot be objectively modified. Adverbs have negligible effect on verbs. While the juxtaposition of "adverbe" and "oh petit cadeau" suggests the same thing, the latter phrase has other meanings. It is the *expression consacrée* of the prostitute who collects the ticket before the performance begins. The image, prolonged by the slang expression "qu'elle mouille" (10, 15), serves to devalue love by pointing up its sterility and its separation from any spiritual or even emotive engagement. If lines 5 and 6 forecast *Godot*, lines 7 and 8 look beyond it to *Happy Days*. The narrator is empty save for snatches of half-remembered tunes, and Winnie relies again and again on fragments from forgotten plays and poems of the classical literary heritage. In the particular context of this poem the next line, which is the refrain of the song, provides a comic counterpart to the serious situation in the poem. The narrator's spiritual detachment is matched by the physical disproportion described by the dismayed girl in the song: "Quel homme! qu'il est petit!" In both cases, anything resembling what we usually think of as love seems out of the question. To help him while away the moments, the narrator has at his disposal, besides the "loques de chanson," the familiar pastime indicated by the French "faire la fleur" that consists of putting the ring finger over the little finger, the middle finger over both, and the index over all three, then in duplicating the process with the other hand.

194

Lines 10 to 14 establish periods of time. The girl may stay away preparing as long as she likes—until the sounds of the carts carrying produce from the surrounding countryside to the central market of Paris in the very small hours of the morning are heard, until the early risers, a few hours later, turn on the taps for morning ablutions, or until that distant moment when sound has ceased to penetrate. The net effect is the same as if one were to say, "I don't care if she never comes." While this disparagement of Eros is going on, the sounds filtering in from the macrocosm bring news of death (the horses' hoofs suggest a funeral procession, perhaps even tumbrils carrying prisoners to their execution), of complaint that a new day must begin (the sputtering of the water caused by air in the pipes seems a protest against invaded repose), and finally diminish into nothingness. In lines 15 through 17 the phrase "puisque c'est ainsi" and the word "superflu" administer the final touches to a portrait of the world's emptiness. The macrocosm, when all is said and done, tells of love and death. Compared to the *vanitas* of the former, the void of the latter seems almost inviting. In the "loin" of line 12 and the "lointains" of line 20 we can almost discern a regret that the wait for death is still so far from ended. If in spite of everything the narrator still says "qu'elle . . . vienne," we can be fairly certain that he agrees, because love, like art (if we can dignify the song [7-8] by calling it art), is a way of passing the time.

5. *Further Perspectives on the Macrocosm*

Life in Beckett's poetic macrocosm characteristically involves movement, usually walking, occasionally riding a bicycle. Even in the 1937-1939 poems, which are primarily concerned with the static life of the microcosm, we find a few examples of movement that to a certain degree recall *Echo's Bones*. "Arènes de Lutèce" is the most obvious case in point. Even here, however, the difference is decisive. It is true that a couple has been out walking, and the poem traces their course in detail as they enter the Roman arena and climb to seats above the ancient ruins. But their progress is seen not as it occurs but rather through the eyes of the seated narrator during a privileged moment of visionary self-detachment, as he watches himself and his companion approach, a few minutes earlier, his present vantage point. In a similar way the poem "Dieppe" involves the narrator in a walk along the seashore. But in four lines we can hardly expect the extended commentary of the enuegs, the sanies, and the first and third serenas. Length is revealing. The latter poems, six in all, average forty-seven lines in length, while the seven comparatively static, meditative, often art-centered pieces that comprise the rest of *Echo's Bones* average only eighteen lines. In the present collection of twelve the average drops to eleven lines. It is more than a mere quip to assert simply that the macrocosm is *bigger* than the microcosm! A like reduction in the length of the poems points to a progressive stripping down, the relinquishment and renunciation so well suggested by the French word *dépouillement*. It is no accident that these shorter poems are Beckett's first writings in French. When I asked him in 1962 (as everyone seems to, sooner or later) why he switched from English to French, he replied that for him, an Irishman, French represented a form of weakness by comparison with his mother tongue. Besides, English because of its very richness holds out the temptation to rhetoric and virtuosity, which are merely words mirroring themselves complacently, Narcissus-like. The relative asceticism of French seemed more appropriate to the expression of being, undeveloped, unsupported somewhere in the depths of the microcosm. While no doubt this is not the whole answer, it seems to fit the nature and evolution of Beckett's writing better than other explanations that have been proposed in recent years. To return to "Dieppe," we must add, finally, that the heart of the poem is not the stroll along the beach, but a moment of meditation between ocean and land before turning back toward the city.

In "La Mouche," which says in its more ascetic, economical way what "Enueg I" developed at length, we can admire again the astonishing ability, so characteristic of Beckett and surely a hallmark of greatness in a writer, to turn the most concrete and trivial incident of everyday existence into an emblem of man's condition and destiny.

> entre la scène et moi
> la vitre
> vide sauf elle
>
> ventre à terre
> sanglée dans ses boyaux noirs
> antennes affolées ailes liées

pattes crochues bouche suçant à vide
sabrant l'azur s'écrasant contre l'invisible
sous mon pouce impuissant elle fait chavirer
la mer et le ciel serein

As in the case of "my brother the fly / the common housefly" of
"Serena I," it is easy enough to discern a kinship between the fly
and man. Like the narrator alone in his room, for whom the world
outside has become more and more vaporous and unreal, the fly
exists in a kind of void (3, 7). "Ventre à terre" as though racing
about, it is as immobile as man waiting, even in the midst of his
most frenzied activity. Like man, the fly is imprisoned in the truss
of its own body (5) and, "ailes liées," escape is not possible. (Again
we are reminded of "Serena I" with its cages and prisons.) The fly's
antennae wave wildly in search of information, but it is up against
invisible, enigmatic forces beyond its comprehension. It would
obviously be better if it ceased the futile struggle and flew back into
the darkened room. It cannot know that, of course, and clinging
stubbornly to the glass with its "pattes crochues," desperately seeking nourishment from the sterile plane, it tries to reach the light
toward which it is irresistibly drawn. Near the end of this dense
modern parable of man's fate a dual perspective emerges. From a
seemingly objective description of the fly, the point of view expands
to include the narrator and the scene beyond the window pane. On
the one hand, the narrator plays the role of destiny in the universe
of the fly. While the serenity of sea and sky hold no threat of
danger, its end may come suddenly and unexpectedly out of the
darkness above its head. The parallel with Pozzo's speech in which
he recounts the passage of the daytime of a man's life is striking
(*Godot*, p. 61): "Il y a une heure . . . environ . . . après nous avoir
versé depuis . . . mettons dix heures du matin . . . sans faiblir des
torrents de lumière rouge et blanche, il s'est mis à perdre de son
éclat, à pâlir . . . à pâlir toujours un peu plus, jusqu'à ce que . . .
vlan! fini! il ne bouge plus! . . . —mais, derrière ce voile de douceur
et de calme . . . la nuit galope . . . et viendra se jeter sur nous . . .
pfft! comme ça . . . au moment où nous nous y attendrons le moins.
. . . C'est comme ça que ça se passe sur cette putain de terre." At
the same time, the fly plays a decisive role in the life of the narrator.
"Sabrant l'azur" and lines 8 and 9 must be understood from this
second point of view. The fly appears as a black slash against the

sea and sky in the background. But it causes them to totter and top-
ple (literally *chavirer*, from the Provençal *cap virar*, meaning to
turn upside down) only from the point of view of the narrator,
dizzy and close to fainting from the sudden emotion. He has been
unable to act the part of fate. At the critical moment his thumb
becomes paralyzed, incapable of visiting destruction on the helpless
fly. While the poet wisely leaves it at that, we can easily imagine the
experience preceding the poem, the sudden intuition of the unity of
all living creatures in a common earthly destiny. The metaphysical
criticism or at least suffering questioning implicit in the narrator's
inability to perform the function of almighty executioner is another
illustration of a religious position somewhere between revolt and
resignation. "La Mouche" reminds us again that if sameness diminishes the tenuous reality of the macrocosm and untimeliness thwarts
the hopes it holds, suffering and death destroy even the negative
value of the nirvana-like vacuum that remains.

The notion of inadequate knowledge that was an integral part of
the themes of "too late" and "too soon" in poems II and IV is
important also in "La Mouche." The sign of death in the macrocosm, overwhelming in the latter poem, appears in several others,
notably in III, IV, and XII, but more as leitmotif than as central
theme. A more all-pervasive experience recreated in the 1937-1939
poems is that of the unreal quality of the world outside. Such a feeling seems to stem in part from a natural dualism that separates
mind from body (no professor was ever more literally "absent-
minded" than many of Beckett's characters), in part from a psychological need to withdraw from the occasions of death, suffering,
violence (or simply overstimulation of a finely tuned sensibility),
and in part from a reasoned conviction that the macrocosm has
nothing worthwhile to offer. Beckett portrays this feeling in I, II,
III, and V but it is important also in VI, VII, and X. Perhaps it
emerges most frankly and definitely, though in a lighter vein, in the
last of these, "Rue de Vaugirard":

> à mi-hauteur
> je débraye et béant de candeur
> expose la plaque aux lumières et aux ombres
> puis repars fortifié
> d'un négatif irrécusable

From his apartment on the Rue des Favorites just off the Rue de

Vaugirard, which is the direct route to the Boulevard du Montparnasse with its literary and artistic cafés that he haunted through the years and still does ("La Closerie des Lilas," where Paul Fort had reigned over his "mardis," and "La Coupole" in particular), Beckett often walked or rode the now-famous bicycle toward the sixth arrondissement during the period before the war. In poem X we find an image taken from cycling. The walker "goes into neutral" (*débrayer*) and halts. "A mi-hauteur" (Rue de Vaugirard runs northeast from the Place de la Porte de Versailles on the outer boulevards as far as the Boulevard St. Michel) would place the poem between the Rue des Favorites and the Boulevard du Montparnasse. However, for this admirer of Dante it has literary echoes as well as a geographical setting. The Italian poet halved the traditional three score and ten years of a man's life when he wrote "Nel mezzo del cammin di nostra vita," and Beckett was close enough to thirty-five when he wrote "Rue de Vaugirard." By the use of such a literary echo he endows the Paris street with the archetypal value attached so often to the road and the voyage in *Echo's Bones*. Poem X is typical of the group as a whole in that, although the suggestion of movement through space occurs, it is built around a moment of stasis, the *point mort* of the gear system and a temporary halt in the narrator's progress. At a certain age along the way of life, the traveler stops and takes stock of the world around him. The momentary interruption of the trip, like times of stasis in certain poems in *Echo's Bones*, also figures the detachment from life required of the artist, and in this sense it mirrors one important meaning of the microcosm itself.

In "Rue de Vaugirard" the poetic technique brings out still more clearly the underlying theme of art. Like poem III, based on the love-death ambivalence, it makes use of an extended metaphor, in this case one that identifies walker and camera. Like an open shutter with virginal film behind it, the neutral narrator is the picture of wide-eyed innocence, ready to record objectively whatever the scene impresses on the "plaque" of his mind and heart. The archetypes of light and darkness (3) are common enough in the poems already discussed. Their human meanings are as crucial as their significance in photography. The walker starts off again fortified in the assurance he has unimpeachable negative evidence with which to convict the macrocosm. And we can be fairly sure that the process of development will never produce a positive portrait

199

from his negative judgment. Yet the claim to realism in this description of the poet as camera is undeniable.

Between Two Worlds

1. In an Alien Land

In poems II and IV the time is wrong, in poem VI the place. Out of his element, the narrator finds himself exasperated and silent in the confused babble of a social gathering.

> musique de l'indifférence
> coeur temps air feu sable
> du silence éboulement d'amours
> couvre leur voix et que
> je ne m'entende plus
> me taire

Behind the poem is the experience we might expect. Beckett, withdrawn and silent at a party,[13] carrying with him into the realm of noise the little world of silence, yearned "for the indifference of sand." The poem is an appeal from the animate to the inanimate, to the tiny voices that become audible when the louder ones are turned down by distance or, hopefully, indifference. In this theme of indifference, poem VI joins poem I. In the opening poem of the group, however, the phenomenon of sameness and its effect on reality is noted almost impassively. The only affective note discernible is the reserved understatement of an almost imperceptible nostalgia. Love would be desirable, were it possible. Noise is not. In poem VI indifference is no longer simply accepted as inevitable; it is actively courted.

Silence can be deafening, and for the narrator, very conscious of being out of place, his muteness competes in volume with the sound in the room. But if silence can be audible, so can the beating of the heart, time passing, the movement of air, a flame burning, sand settling, and even memories slipping further and further into the

---

[13] A close friend of Beckett's, A. J. Leventhal, speaks of evenings spent with the author in almost total silence, and in "Dream of Fair to Middling Women" we read, "The way people go on *saying* things . . ! Who shall silence them, at last?" (p. 167). Cf. also *More Pricks Than Kicks* (London: Chatto and Windus, 1934), p. 108, and the crucial distinction made between the observed couple (narrator and companion) and others in "Arènes de Lutèce": "aussi laids que les autres, / mais muets."

past. It is to these companions of solitude, to the microcosm of his mind and his lonely room, that he appeals from the insufferable tension and self-consciousness he feels. The list is a roll call of some of Beckett's favorite universals. We have seen the heart associated with time through the image of a ticking watch (*Godot*), with death in "Enueg II" ("the old heart the old heart / breaking outside congress"), and with love and art as "the old plunger / pestling the unalterable / whey of words" in "Cascando." It would be superfluous at this point to rehearse the uses of time in *Proust* and *Godot*, but we shall note its special place and its relation to both macrocosm and microcosm apropos of poem VIII. Already it has figured centrally in the themes of untimeliness in II and IV and of waiting in III. "Air feu sable" suggests three of the four elements in the cosmic landscape of "Enueg I." Only water is missing, and the music of indifference that is called upon to rise and cover the discordant babble of voices is not without analogy to a rising tide that submerges and mutes in the quiet of its depths. In poem IV the "tombe d'air" muffles as well as transmits sounds from the macrocosm, while the wind in VII blows through reeds that hear no other sound. The light and heat of fire recur in several poems, almost always in association with the passing of time but with nuances of meaning that range from enlightenment through destruction.

The crumbling away of loves (3), like the erosion of a pile of sand (or the cloud in "Enueg II") also suggests the passage of time. Perhaps these vast archetypal symbols share above all an eternal undifferentiated sameness. Silence is always silence, sand always sand. One heartbeat is like another. In their primordial and unchanging simplicity these elemental aspects of nature are indifferent to the ephemeral chatter of a cocktail party. The narrator would wish to partake of their ageless insensibility. "Sable du silence" suggests the great substratum of silence that survives the brevity of all sound. Longing for release, the narrator wills that his tiny silence, which looms so large, be subsumed into this cosmic quietude, that the din of voices be submerged in this ocean of stillness as a speck of time in the firmament of infinity.

Implicit in poem VI is a concern with art, which is linked to the microcosm. In choosing to associate music with indifference to the macrocosm of social existence, the poet intimates the possibility of creating art of his own silence, poems from the forces of indifference in himself and nature. And so he does in writing poem VI. Very often in the poems on poetry there is at least a bow in the direction of form. Here we can note a stylistic correlation between the two-to-one predominance of continuants over stops, the run-on lines (especially 2-3, 4-5, and 5-6), and the nature of the two principal metaphors. The idea of flux is present in the flow of music and time but especially in the phrase "éboulements d'amours," which, particularly in its juxtaposition with the image of sand, suggests an erosion that sends the stones and pebbles of past loves down the slope of time and into the abyss of forgetfulness. By calling upon such internalized sounds to mute intrusive voices from the outer world, the poet posts his discreet manifesto announcing a poetry of the microcosm.

2. *A Rueful Defense of Solitude*

Poem VII might be called a companion piece to VI. In it we find the same unresolved tension between the two worlds, the same appeal to the inanimate. However, back in the lonely microcosm, solitude seems only relatively more desirable than society.

> bois seul
> bouffe brûle fornique crève seul comme devant
> les absents sont morts les présents puent
> sors tes yeux détourne-les sur les roseaux
> se taquinent-ils ou les aïs
> pas la peine il y a le vent
> et l'état de veille

In lines 1 and 2 life is stripped down to its bare essentials: food and drink, desire, love, death. "Comme devant" is an allusion to La Fontaine and the expression, which has become proverbial, "être Gros-Jean comme devant" (*devant* in the old sense of *avant*). Like the disillusioned peasant of the fable, the narrator sorrowfully abandons his pretensions in favor of his true nature. After trying life in society he returns to his former solitary existence. There is no company to be had either from the absent (who are, or might as well be, dead) or from the present (who, as the ambiguous verb *puer* suggests, are moribund in one way or another). The alternative, as worked out in the somewhat involved grammatical structure of lines 4 through 7, is to make common cause with nature. The wind suffices for the reeds, which survive without the stimulation of other reeds, and the simple state of wakefulness provides quite enough excitement for the three-toed sloth. It should be possible, then, for the narrator to become a creature of the microcosm, divest himself of the trappings of society, and rid himself of the need for human companionship.

Beckett's choice of images is instructive. "Sors tes yeux" in line 4 is quite possibly a reminiscence of the Biblical passage, "And if thine eye offend thee, pluck it out."[14] We have seen in *Echo's Bones* that the world can be a source of "scandal" to the poet, but in this and the preceding poem we seem to be dealing more with a need-revulsion or desire-incapacity relationship than with the old problem of the existence of evil. The image of the reed suggests in a general way the theme of art and at the same time inevitably conjures up Pascal's "roseau pensant." Both art and the mind, as we have seen, are themes integral to the notion of the microcosm. Finally, the sloth recalls Dante's apathetic Belacqua and his spiritual descendant, Belacqua Shuah, the hero of *More Pricks Than Kicks* —as well as the poet himself, compared by Peggy Guggenheim to Goncharov's lethargic hero Oblomov, who shared with Descartes a propensity to remain in bed beyond the noon hour.[15]

3. The Divided Self

From something approaching an anguished revolt against life in society (VI) and from a rueful defense of solitude (VII), the tension between the two worlds reaches a relatively stable equilibrium in the dualism of poem XI.

ARÈNES DE LUTÈCE

De là où nous sommes assis plus haut que les gradins
je nous vois entrer du côté de la Rue des Arènes,
hésiter, regarder en l'air, puis pesamment
venir vers nous à travers le sable sombre,
de plus en plus laids, aussi laids que les autres,
mais muets. Un petit chien vert
entre en courant du côté de la Rue Monge,
elle s'arrête, elle le suit des yeux,
il traverse l'arène, il disparait
derrière le socle du savant Gabriel de Mortillet.   10
Elle se retourne, je suis parti, je gravis seul

---

[14] Matt. 5:29. See also Mark 9:47.
[15] *Out of This Century* (New York: Dial Press, 1946), p. 197.

les marches rustiques, je touche de ma main gauche
la rampe rustique, elle est en béton. Elle hésite,
fait un pas vers la sortie de la Rue Monge, puis me suit.
J'ai un frisson, c'est moi qui me rejoins,
c'est avec d'autres yeux que maintenant je regarde
le sable, les flaques d'eau sous la bruine,
une petite fille traînant derrière elle un cerceau,
un couple, qui sait des amoureux, la main dans la main
les gradins vides, les hautes maisons, le ciel   20
qui nous éclaire trop tard.
Je me retourne, je suis étonné
de trouver là son triste visage.

Hallucination or simply waking dream, an experience of *le double*
lies behind "Arènes de Lutèce." Seated on a bench above the old
Roman arena in Paris, the narrator watches himself and his companion as they enter a short time before, cross over, and separate.
He follows his own ascent to his present vantage point and experiences with a shudder the reunion of the two selves. He then surveys
the scene from another point of view. The poem ends on his aston-
ishment at finding his companion, who has rejoined him unper-
ceived, once again beside him. This final shock completes the return
to a more customary mode of vision. During conversations in 1961
and 1962 Beckett spoke more than once of "existence by proxy."
Quite often he is overtaken by a profound sense of the unreality
of the self called Samuel Beckett who goes through the motions of
day to day living, mechanically and without conviction. As he
walks down the street, this Beckett seems like another person, at
times almost as objectified as those who are indeed other. There is
no doubt that Beckett's early fascination with the dualism of
Descartes and Geulincx and his lasting espousal of a generally
dualistic point of view, both in his life and writing, are more than
mere intellectual conviction. They seem to correspond not only to
the decisive experiences of exile and alienation discussed earlier,
but also to deep tendencies in his own nature.

Beckett's dualism, however, is perhaps more important—at least
for readers of his poems, plays, and novels—from an artistic than
from a philosophical point of view. The analogy between the relationship of self to alter ego and that of author to character is very

close. Psychological and aesthetic distance or objectivity may indeed be interdependent to a considerable degree. The fact of this distance, while a commonplace of all art save perhaps the most outrageously romantic, in which the distinction between the I of the narrator and the I of the author tends to fade into insignificance, is unusually striking in Beckett's work. The frame of reference always involves macrocosm and microcosm. Beyond that, Beckett's extraordinary ability to suggest the universal through the particular, the "expansive" power of his writing, its strong tendency toward stylization, formal patterns, and finally ritual are very closely linked to a dualistic mode that in art maintains a tension between object and subject, real and ideal but moves always (and more strongly as his writing evolves through the years) in the direction of the latter. I was not surprised during a conversation in 1965 to hear him speak of a project for a new play in terms that irresistibly evoked the masks and the ballet-like movements of Greek tragedy.

In "Arènes de Lutèce" the split between the two selves acquires a dualistic resonance that owes much to, and may have been influenced by, the setting. We are in the presence of, in fact literally inside, two cities: modern Paris and ancient Lutèce (the former name of Paris). As poems VIII and XII (see below) make clear, time is in one sense abolished in the microcosm. The two cities that coexist only imperfectly in space may enjoy a much fuller simultaneity in the timeless eternity of the mind. However, they are also separate, and the sense of their separateness can be overwhelming when one leaves the busy, noisy modern city to enter this quiet oasis of sadness peopled by a few aimless phantoms drifting about beneath a drizzling sky. The two cities, joined yet separate, one within the other, are a figure of man, divided yet one. The names of the two streets from which one enters the Arènes de Lutèce reinforce the dualism. The Rue des Arènes (2) suggests the ancient, while the Rue Monge (7), named for Gaspard Monge (1746-1818), the founder of modern descriptive geometry, refers to the beginnings of present-day civilization. Gabriel de Mortillet (1821-1898), paleologist and paleoethnologist, a modern student of the ancient, combines the two in one. There is something whimsically appropriate about his eternalization in stone among the stones of the past—and something ironic in the reversal of roles between the living and the petrified that is suggested when the little dog disappears behind the pedestal of his statue.[16] The double reality is emphasized again in the phrases "la rampe rustique, elle est en béton" (13) and "les gradins vides, les hautes maisons" (20).

Much of the pathos and discreet nostalgia that "Arènes de Lutèce" elicits comes from the two visions made possible by the experience of *dédoublement*. Normally when we view the world as somber and unsatisfactory, we also view it as other. Our psychological defense mechanisms set us apart from the general fiasco, even as we project our own misery upon exterior reality. The illumination of lines 5 and 6 (which corresponds to the clearing of the sky in lines 20 and 21) enables the narrator to see himself as part and parcel of the world outside. He and his companion are "de plus en plus laids, aussi laids que les autres / mais muets." Part of the significance of "mais muets," set off and stressed by the *rejet*, becomes clear when we recall that close to ten years had passed since Beckett's resignation from Trinity, years during which a slim literary production caused scarcely a ripple of interest in the world of letters.[17] The muted anguish at the spectacle of an aging self, at the thought of time and opportunity lost, return us to the theme of "too late" (21) discussed above in connection with poem II. After a day of "bruine" (17) the sun comes out briefly, too close to setting to provide any real warmth or comfort. Probably the little green dog that appears and almost immediately disappears (6-10) is a related metaphor. We recall the green sunset in "Enueg II" and its association with the theme of "too late." Hope is a green tulip that shines "like an anthrax," a green dog that races out of sight (to join the bones studied by Mortillet, gone himself, like Echo, to bones and stone), a fleeting green twilight devoured by the black "night fungus" ("Enueg I"). The effects of the narrator's vision are prolonged beyond the duration of the vision, as the enlightenment of intuition extends into poetic creation. Lines 16 through 21 reduce the cluttered workaday world to its basic existential elements: the cycle of "birth, copulation, and death," here translated as a little girl with her hoop, a couple of lovers, and "les gradins vides."

---

[16] He fixed the generally accepted nomenclature for the prehistoric periods that play a part in poem VIII.

[17] Between 1931 and 1939 Beckett wrote one novel, a collection of short stories (based on the unpublished "Dream of Fair to Middling Women"), about ten pages of a play he never completed, a small volume of poetry, and a few scattered reviews, translations, pages of prose, and poems.

Beyond and out of the picture is the city, suggested by "les hautes maisons." Apart from love and death, there is only the sameness of somber sand (4, 17), the mirror of water ("les flaques d'eau"), the obscurity of the drizzle, and the poignant brevity of a futile penultimate clarification.

Life in the Microcosm

In the poems discussed so far, the poet has explored the shifting relationship between the two worlds to which, like it or not, he belongs—if only by virtue of possessing both a body and a mind. Within this dualistic framework certain themes predominate: alienation, solitude, suffering, death, memory, emptiness, love, nature, waiting, imprisonment, indifference, fatigue, knowing, time, and art. Two poems give us a somewhat different perspective on a number of these themes. In VIII and XII the equilibrium is upset, and we are allowed a glimpse of life lived almost wholly in the microcosm.

1. Tempus edax rerum

One important effect of studious and creative introversion is to abolish the sense of chronological interval and regular progression. As social contact is reduced, life in the world tends to become less real. As it recedes and is replaced more and more by fictional beings and events from the world of art and literature, new, various, and often highly flexible temporal systems come to interfere with the strict and exclusive clock-and-calendar time that organizes the macrocosm. Recent happenings easily become ancient history, and, conversely, ancient history may seem vividly present and actual. Time ceases to be irreversible, and only the quirks of memory prevent the absolute rule of simultaneity. Nevertheless, although the microcosm of the mind may be a privileged locus from which the effects of time and change have been banished, its eternity is a precarious and no more than relative one. Even if its tenant were capable of uninterrupted sojourn within such a citadel and even if memory were a docile servant, the penetrating voices of all-encompassing flux would still be difficult to muffle. As Pozzo points out in *Godot*, the light at a certain hour may seem unchanging, but "derrière ce voile de douceur et de calme la nuit galope" (p. 61). Such a tension between the ideal and the existential, between timelessness and flux, and ultimately between the inner and outer worlds mirrors in poem VIII the experience of anguish which we are no doubt justified in assuming preceded it.

> ainsi a-t-on beau
> par le beau temps et par le mauvais
> enfermé chez soi enfermé chez eux
> comme si c'était d'hier se rappeler le mammouth
> le dinothérium les premiers baisers
> les périodes glaciaires n'apportant rien de neuf
> la grande chaleur du treizième de leur ère
> sur Lisbonne fumante Kant froidement penché
> rêver en générations de chênes et oublier son père
> ses yeux s'il portait la moustache   10
> s'il était bon de quoi il est mort
> on n'en est pas moins mangé sans appétit
> par le mauvais temps et par le pire
> enfermé chez soi enfermé chez eux

Lines 4 through 11 describe an inner universe that has little in common with any of the three levels of Murphy's mind. Its owner and occupant does not appear able to rearrange its image to his liking. There are no forms without correspondents in either the bookish or the social worlds and no joy in contemplation or in volitionless immersion in a flux of generation and dissolution. Instead, memory mixes learning and experience, preserving intact the recollection of a long-ago (pre-Miocene!) first kiss along with vivid images of extinct mammals, while capriciously consigning to quasi-oblivion the likeness of a cherished father, only a few years gone. The narrator's pain at this reversal of values calls into question the desirability of the solitary life. After the movement backward in time in lines 4 and 5, from the mammoth (Pleistocene) to the dinotherium (Miocene and Pliocene) to "les premiers baisers," we return to the Quaternary period with its glaciers that bring nothing new—except man! The narrator's scorn is clear as he skips to the thirteenth century A.D. The Christian era is "theirs," not his.[18] From the thirteenth we move to the eighteenth century and finally to 1933, the date of William Beckett's death, about five years before the writing of this poem. Above all, these lines suggest "a fly . . . in the ointment of Microcosmos." Although the depths of the past may be available in

---

[18] Cf. "au septième de leur ère" in Lucky's speech (*Godot*, p. 74).

an eternal present, memory is quite capable of producing the frivolous, erasing the essential, and resurrecting past suffering. It spans the enormous stretches of time represented by "générations de chênes," while yesterday slips into the abyss of forgetfulness.

At the same time this central section of the poem develops the theme of the weather. "Le temps," the key word in both the opening and closing lines of the poem, has the sense of both time and weather, which indeed amount to no more than the temporal and spatial aspects of a single phenomenon. From line 4 to line 8 the poet sketches in rough outline a cyclical pattern in the weather. The alternating rhythm of hot and cold begins with the preglacial age, and continues with the glacial ages that destroy one species and favor the development of another. In historic times two colder periods are broken by the great heat wave of the thirteenth century. In prehistoric times the devastating effects of these changes is suggested by the extinction of dinotherium and mammoth. In historic times the catastrophe involves man, who is at once the victim and the analyst of the elemental forces of nature. Line 8 evokes the disastrous Lisbon earthquake and subsequent fire of November 1, 1755 (which moved Voltaire to his relatively pessimistic attack on Leibnitzian complacency in *Candide*). In that same year, 1755, interested in natural philosophy and still under the influence of the monadism of Leibnitz, Kant published his treatise on fire (*De igne*). The juxtaposition of the Lisbon fire and Kant's essay functions in several ways in the poem. Primarily it serves to carry on the heat-cold alternation and at the same time to give it more than mere meteorological significance. The poet is obviously no cold philosophical analyst. For him fire is an aspect of time-weather, a destroyer of human beings, a creator of suffering, part of the mystery of life and death. The unfeeling and futile manipulations of icy reason seem, within the framework of the poem, as destructively impersonal as the action of glaciers, the servants of all-devouring time. The monad of Leibnitz was an isolated, self-contained microcosm reflecting the world with more or less clarity from a particular point of view. The poet's negative reaction to reason and implicitly to the Leibnitz-Kant monadism is a measure of his own dissatisfaction with life in the "little world." A gulf separates the narrator of this poem from Murphy.[19] Lines 4 through 8 are summed up in

[19] Kant's mature position as the founder of German idealism and in particular the limits he set upon pure reason are much closer to views expressed

209

line 9, which establishes at the same time a poignant contrast between the vast but secondhand vision of the geological epochs and the only relatively shorter span of the A.D. centuries on the one hand and the brief years of a man's life on the other. The emotional impact of lines 4 through 11 derives chiefly from this three-stage narrowing of focus. Considered in the perspective of eons, a human trajectory from womb to grave is a brief moment indeed, and the more precious for its brevity. We might even assert that in terms of the values implied in the poem there is an inverse relationship between duration and worth.[20] Finally, we should note in passing the similarity between the cyclic pattern of this poem and the clonic rhythm suggested in the cosmic imagery of "Serena II."

Perhaps the most interesting facet of this unusually interesting poem is to be found in another aspect of its structure. In effect it is a kind of poem within a poem, or better, a world within a world. The first three lines and the last three compose a framework that encloses the little world of remembrance as the macrocosm encloses the microcosm. The prison image ("enfermé") that is repeated at start and at end gives semantic backing to the formal arrangement, but "le temps" is still more crucial in this respect. While some limited degree of simultaneity is possible in the microcosmic center of the poem, time moves inexorably and irreversibly forward on the outside (and of course this movement is in part reflected even within the microcosm). Since the macrocosm encloses and imprisons the little world of the mind and carries it along on its one-way journey, even imperfect freedom from flux is seen to be illusory. Such is the basic meaning of the expression "a-t-on beau," which opens the poem by ironically undercutting the *beau* of "par le beau temps." It is vain to recall bygone ages, summoning them into an eternal present, and likewise unimportant, for the immediate past slips irretrievably away. While we dream of immobility, we are being carried along in the stream of time to our certain end. The sense of time as flux underlies lines 4 through 11, and it is implicit also in the

---

by Beckett in his discussion of the theory of art in articles on the Van Velde brothers in 1945, 1948, and 1949. Both subscribe to the fundamental notion that the subject is incapable of knowing the essence (*noumena*) of the object. The senses report only on surfaces (*phenomena*). As always, Beckett is true to his generally dualistic mode of thinking and feeling.

[20] Thornton Wilder makes effective use of a similar poetic structure at the beginning of *Our Town*, but the stress is more spatial than temporal.

transition from "par le beau temps et par le mauvais" in line 2 to "par le mauvais temps et par le pire" in line 13, a transition that suggests the decline of the later years. And the simple fact of changing weather conditions works in the same direction. However, the spatial aspect of "le temps" dominates in the striking image of Time the eater in line 12 (which recalls the image of Descartes and the chick in its microcosmic egg in *Whoroscope*). *Tempus edax* as the weather (heat, cold, glaciers, earthquakes) gnaws away insatiably and indiscriminately at the macrocosm of the world and the body, the double prison of society and the self evoked by the phrase "enfermé chez soi enfermé chez eux" (3, 14). It is appropriate in this series of static poems, and especially fitting in VIII, which is a formal and semantic representation of the two worlds as analogous to concentric circles, that the spatial aspect of *le temps* should prevail over the temporal. The double fortress is eroded as by sun and frost, wind and rain. Few poems are wholly original and Beckett is no doubt indebted for the image of *tempus edax* to the memorable lines of Swift's "On Time":

> Ever eating, never cloying,
> All-devouring, all-destroying,
> Never finding full repast,
> Till I eat the world at last.[21]

2. Death in Life

The last poem in this group of twelve, like the ending of *Whoroscope* and like "Echo's Bones," which gives its name to the collection that it concludes, brings the narrator face to face with death. However, while Beckett's Descartes asks vainly for a "second / starless inscrutable hour," the narrator of "Echo's Bones" contemplates with a certain envy the imagined freedom and revels of those who have reached the asylum of death. In poem XII the narrator

[21] Swift in turn may have borrowed the image from Ovid's "Tempus edax rerum" (*Metamorphoses* XV, 234) or from the Latin lines by an unknown author translated by John Addington Symonds in *Wine, Women, and Song* (London: Chatto and Windus, 1884), p. 140:

Lauriger Horatius	Laurel-crowned Horatius,
quam dicisti verum:	True, how true thy saying:
fugit Euro citius	Swift as wind flies over us
tempus edax rerum.	Time, devouring, slaying.

See also *Nouvelles et textes pour rien*, p. 204.

has moved closer to the somber object of his desire. Existence in the little world has become a kind of death in life. Only an occasional recollection from distant days in the world outside intrudes.

> jusque dans la caverne ciel et sol
> et une à une les vieilles voix
> d'outre-tombe
> et lentement la même lumière
> qui sur les plaines d'Enna en longs viols
> macérait naguère les capillaires
> et les mêmes lois
> que naguère
> et lentement au loin qui éteint
> Proserpine et Atropos 10
> adorable de vide douteux
> encore la bouche d'ombre

As in poem VIII, the structure is circular, illustrating once again the formal repercussions of the shift from dynamism in *Echo's Bones* with its quests and flights and restlessness to immobility in the 1937-1939 collection.[22] While the structure in both poems is circular and in both reflects the enclosure of the two worlds, poem XII differs decisively from poem VIII. In the earlier piece the macrocosm envelops and ultimately controls the inner world. The concluding poem reverses this situation. The framework—"la caverne" (1) and "la bouche d'ombre" (12), both figures of the microcosmic nirvana—is still controlling, but now it represents the engulfing potential of the little world. At the center of the poem (2-10) old voices from the world outside penetrate, then die away, extinguished like rays of light by the deathlike darkness inside the skull. Things have been turned inside out. The image of the eater survives in "la bouche," but time no longer consumes all, even the inner self. Instead, vestiges of outer reality are swallowed and obliterated in the microcosmic maw. Ultimately, of course, the two ways to nothingness converge. Time leads to death, and only death can destroy time. Psychologically, withdrawal is a lessening of life but by the same token a lessening of tribulation. The figures of death follow logically, as does the "death wish," which in these poems is clearly a longing for the cessation of persistent suffering.

---

[22] Cf. the presence and interrelationship of both the "travel" and the "waiting" archetypes and their structures in *Godot*.

As often in *Echo's Bones*, the narrator is willing to give up a great deal, if not all, of life as the price of respite from pain and sorrow. Although he relinquishes memories of a loved father only reluctantly in VIII, in XII he welcomes the *néant* that blots out recollection of the deaths of loved persons (10).

The universalizing tendency that we have often observed in Beckett's poetry is evident and very effective here. The personal situation of the narrator is expanded and becomes a generalized human predicament primarily through the use of time, metaphoric analogy, and mythology. "Les vieilles voix" (2) are the voices of memory that reach him in his cavern-tomb from the world above, which he once inhabited. We can imagine similar voices reaching Proserpina in her infernal abode after her ravishment by Pluto, which according to the tradition took place as she was picking flowers with her companions on the plains of Enna in Sicily. The individual is generalized still further, however, in lines 4 through 6. The symbolism of darkness and light is of central importance, and since darkness is associated with the cavern, the "bouche d'ombre," the tomb, and death, light would naturally suggest life even if it were not so clearly associated with the living world above the cavern. But the light in line 4 is the strong Sicilian light of the Enna plains, and it slowly (in long "viols" that recall the fate of Proserpina) wastes away the delicate maidenhair ferns that can survive only in shaded areas. The name of the plant in English makes the link with Proserpina, as do the geographical location and the image of ravishment. The name in French, "capillaires," calls to mind not only the fragile fern but secondarily the tiny capillaries that carry the blood of life in the human body. The light, then, which is life itself, destroys man. He is too fragile a being to survive the glare of the day for very long[23]—and he will probably yearn for the shadows after he has been exposed for a while to such a sun. The adjective "longs" (5) suggests an association between time and the light, and in effect the light assumes in XII the role played by time in VIII. Through this pattern of interrelated images the destiny of the narrator becomes that of Proserpina and ultimately of man.

Other images involve time. "Les vieilles voix" in the context are as much the old voices of mankind as those of the narrator. Similarly, the laws of life and death are the same now as in centuries past (7-8). In poem VIII, as in XII, Beckett universalizes the indi-

[23] Cf. the use of light in *Happy Days*.

vidual by alluding to a human condition unchanged over long periods of time. Something of the same result is achieved by reducing the clutter of life to a few essentials. In line 1, "ciel et sol" provide the stripped-down setting for the play of life (again, cf. especially *Happy Days*). "Ciel" supports the imagery of light, and "sol," the surface of man's earthly arena, makes the transition easy to the cavern—or "sous-sol" as Estragon calls it in *Godot* (p. 103). Another pairing (10) eliminates all but the basic events in human existence. "Proserpina and Atropos" very probably stand for love and death, even though Proserpina in herself might well combine the two. We remember the association of sky and love in *Comment c'est* and again in the "haillons d'azur" of poem II. The link of "sol" and death needs no further comment, but we might recall the specific combination of love and Atropos in poem III, where the narrator as he lies waiting in the darkness of his microcosm is quite definite about the fact that he is much less interested in the macrocosmic love that is on the way than in the "ciseaux argentins" of the third sister.

The last lines of the poem are fairly clear once the somewhat tangled syntax is unraveled. It is the "bouche d'ombre" with its compelling attraction and with its uncertain void (11) (uncertain since voices do invade its emptiness) that, like dark waters slowly flowing back in after the ebb tide, gradually extinguishes the memories of old loves and old deaths (10). Finally, we should attempt a defense of the syntax. Beckett practically never in his serious writing chooses complication or obscurity for its own sake. The inversion of grammatical order in this case allows him to end the poem with the subject, "la bouche d'ombre," and thereby makes possible the crucial circular structure. We need only note the presence in line 12 of "encore," which links the "bouche d'ombre" to the "caverne" in line 1, to perceive that the inversion is both poetically functional and, on whatever level of consciousness, poetically willed.

3. *Und dann der Steg*

Even though the microcosm may have the last word in the 1937-1939 poems, the world of men is never wholly blotted out by the darkness and silence and solitude. The cavern resembles death, but as long as a man is alive, the uneasy companions of an ancient dualism stubbornly resist definitive separation. The little

214

poem "Dieppe," the ninth in the series, strikes a balance. At first it seems to be out of place, with its walk along the seashore, among these poems of immobility and contemplation. In truth, however, the heart of the poem lies at the still point between the second and third lines, unexpressed yet compellingly present. On either side loom archetypal figures of the two worlds, the one again associated with darkness and death, the other with light and communion with other beings. The still point is a long moment of meditation and a weighing of alternatives. Finally, desire gives way to some unnamed instinct or necessity and the narrator wearily turns in the direction of the light.

DIEPPE

> encore le dernier reflux
> le galet mort
> le demi-tour puis les pas
> vers les vieilles lumières[24]

Between the ocean and the city runs the sterile beach on which the narrator stands. It belongs to the water and will soon be covered by the incoming tide. To stay longer there in the domain of death would be a symbolic suicide, just as remaining too exclusively in the microcosm would mean a possibly irreversible renunciation of life in the world outside (or as poem XII and *Comment c'est* put it, in the world above). The force that impels or decides the narrator to turn toward the light seems to be the same force that brings the fly in "Serena I" out of the darkness into the sun and that drives his brother in "La Mouche" against the pane of glass. Perhaps it is natural law that sends the tide eternally out and brings it everlastingly back again in a dualistic parody of the human condition. Again in "Serena I" the light "sucks" the narrator after it as though he had no more choice than the fly, and in "Serena II" man seems to be caught up in the clonic rhythm of light and darkness that rules his mother the earth. Still more explicitly, the narrator in the short story "L'Expulsé" expresses his knowledge of a power that

[24] Beckett's English translation appears in *Poems in English* (New York: Grove Press, 1961), p. 55:

> again the last ebb
> the dead shingle
> the turning then the steps
> towards the lighted town

he does not understand but which he obeys, a power that keeps him going until the light fails.[25] "I leave when the pub closes," said Churchill with considerably more enthusiasm. But not even water is available to the hero of "Act without Words I," so we can perhaps comprehend his ultimate retreat into immobility and self-contemplation. In Beckett's experience, first comes the death of Echo and only then the withdrawal of Narcissus.

The narrator in "Dieppe" accepts life among men but without joy. It is a poem of fatigue, and all the efforts of the poet are bent to recreating stylistically this feeling of lassitude. "Again the last ebb" recalls the "last even of last times" in "Cascando." There, however, the poet feared that last time would come without his having loved. Here we sense in the word "encore" (more than in the English "again") the weariness that would welcome a last of last times. "Le galet mort" speaks again of finality, and "les vieilles lumières" (lost in the English translation) evoke the great age of the European town and the burden of continued existence. More than anything else, however, the cadence of the lines contributes to the stylistic effect. The lines, like the poem itself, are short, as though greater length would require more effort than is available. But the first and fourth lines are further subdivided. A slight pause is required after "encore" to allow its full meaning to emerge. Similar pauses should come before and after "puis." One has only to imagine the substitution of "et" for "puis" to appreciate the labored, halting effect created by the latter. "Le demi-tour" seems to suggest that a turn of more than 180 degrees would exceed the strength of the walker, and line 3 as a whole almost imitates his tired, hesitant movements. When we attempt to assess the part played by sound groupings in "Dieppe," we are immediately struck by the overwhelming preponderance of continuants over stops (twenty-four to seven). Three of the seven stops are absorbed easily, one per phrase in the first two lines, but the four others (including three of the four unvoiced stops in the poem) are concentrated in line 3. This series of plosives (d, t, p, p) coming at the moment of decision and action, serves to accentuate the impression of great effort involved in the accomplishment of even these minimal movements. The ratio

[25] "Je pris la direction du levant, au jugé, pour être éclairé au plus tôt. J'aurais voulu un horizon marin, ou désertique. Quand je suis dehors, le matin, je vais à la rencontre du soleil, et le soir, quand je suis dehors, je le suis, et jusque chez les morts" (*Nouvelles et textes pour rien*, p. 40).

216

of stops to continuants in line 3 is four to four, but the stops occupy the critical initial positions in each of the four nouns in the line. By contrast, the ratio is two to seven in line 1, one to four in line 2, and zero to seven in line 4. The predominance of continuants in the first two and the fourth lines, paradoxically perhaps, also expresses the narrator's fatigue. Given the semantic context, these consonants suggest with their easier, smoother flow within each syntactic group a lower energy level than the relatively vigorous plosives. The unbroken course of line 4 is like the sigh of a slow diminuendo, legato after the staccato of line 3.[26] Finally, the syntactical organization of the poem plays its role, which is closely associated with the pattern of sounds. Of the thirty-one consonants in "Dieppe," about half (fifteen) are liquids. The *l*'s and *r*'s alone, then, account for five-eighths of the continuants (fifteen out of twenty-four). While it would no doubt be a mistake to take the metaphoric term "liquid consonant" too literally, a certain tradition of literary association does exist.[27] We could perhaps make a case for a link between the psychological pull of the sea—the temptation of the narrator to allow himself to slip into the slumber of will-lessness—and the effortless flow of continuants, especially the liquids, in the poem.

At the same time, this configuration of consonants leads us to an observation on syntax. Five of the *l*'s are there because of the presence of an unusually high proportion of definite articles (*le* occurs three times and *les* twice). Except for "puis" and "vers," these articles and their substantives are juxtaposed to form the static structure of the poem. The absence of verbs reduces the sense of vitality, slows down the poem, and in general contributes considerably to the overall sense of fatigue. Each syntactical block is like a difficult obstacle. Each pause is a needed respite before the next exhausting expenditure of verbal and psychic energy. For the narrator of "La Fin" the alternatives are the same, but in his vision the

[26] The English version works on the basis of a different sound structure. Plosives are crucial in line 3 (*t, t, p*) but also, and even more so, in line 4 (*t, d, t, d, t*). The result is an impression of increasing energy and resolution (abetted by the absence of an adjective suggesting great age), and something of the sense of enormous weariness is sacrificed. Translation of poetry, even by the author himself, inevitably results in certain losses.

[27] One random example from modern French literature: François Mauriac's "La vitre ruisselait comme un visage plein de larmes . . ." (*Enfant chargé de chaînes* [Paris: Ferenczi, 1929], p. 115).

balance is tipped in the other direction. His last words as the sea slowly enters his boat are these: "Je songeai faiblement et sans regret au récit que j'avais failli faire, récit à l'image de ma vie, je veux dire sans le courage de finir ni la force de continuer."[28] Unlike his narrator, Beckett did write such a story, which he called "La Fin." In the lyric poem, where the distance between poet and narrator is less, both manage to go on (though barely), the narrator in his symbolic act of turning from the sea toward the town and the poet in writing the four lines of "Dieppe."

As with most of the poems in *Echo's Bones*, this ninth poem in the 1937-1939 group has both a biographical-geographical and a literary source. Beckett had been in Dieppe in the latter thirties, and later, after the war and after the poem had been written, the Irish Red Cross set up headquarters at the Hotel des Arcades. He met arrivals from Ireland there and drove them back through Rouen to the Irish Hospital that had been organized in Saint-Lô. In retrospect, the narrator's coming back toward the town from the sea and the poet's emergence from the microcosm into the larger world outside seem strangely prophetic. The literary starting point is a poem by Friedrich Hölderlin called "Der Spaziergang," or rather a single passage in it. The German poem draws a parallel between the artist and God, the primordial painter. It speaks of rest after the labor and pain of writing, the thorn in the heart and darkness in the mind. It suggests a parallel, that may also have inspired Beckett, between the blue skies of nature and a man's youth on the one hand and darkness and advancing age on the other. The particular passage that moved Beckett deeply sums up this larger contrast:

> Ihr lieblichen Bilder im Tale,
> Zum Beispiel Gärten und Baum,
> Und dann der Steg, der schmale,
> Der Bach zu sehen kaum. . . .[29]

[28] In *Nouvelles et textes pour rien*, pp. 122-133.
[29] The complete poem follows:

> Ihr Wälder schön an der Seite,
> Am grünen Abhang gemalt,
> Wo ich umher mich leite,
> Durch süsse Ruhe bezahlt
> Für jeden Stachel im Herzen,
> Wenn dunkel mir ist der Sinn,
> Denn Kunst und Sinnen hat Schmerzen
> Gekostet von Anbeginn.

After a vision of the beauty of nature arranged by the divine artist, the poet turns to the small, scarcely visible path by the brook that suggests his own narrowing, darkening future.[30] The transitional phrase "und dann" that so affected Beckett no doubt suggested many things to him but above all a hesitation and a great weariness. From it comes the "puis" in "Dieppe."[31]

Although the 1937-1939 poems mark a moment of withdrawal and *recueillement* by comparison with *Echo's Bones*, the double source of "Dieppe" reminds us again of the continuing tension between macrocosm and microcosm. Even today the two worlds of Samuel Beckett—on the one hand his Paris apartment, social and intellectual life in the nocturnal cafés of Montparnasse, and correspondence and meetings with editors, producers, and critics; and on the other his periodic escapes to the solitude of his lonely retreat

---

> Ihr lieblichen Bilder im Tale,
> Zum Beispiel Gärten und Baum,
> Und dann der Steg, der schmale,
> Der Bach zu sehen kaum,
> Wie schön aus heiterer Ferne
> Glänzt einem das herrliche Bild
> Der Landschaft, die ich gerne
> Besuch in Witterung mild.
> Die Gottheit freundlich geleitet
> Uns erstlich mit Blau,
> Hernach mit Wolken bereitet,
> Gebildet wölbig und grau,
> Mit sengenden Blitzen und Rollen
> Des Donners, mit Reiz des Gefilds,
> Mit Schönheit, die gequollen
> Vom Quell ursprünglichen Bilds.
> (*Friedrich Hölderlins Sämtliche Werke* [Leipzig: Insel-Verlag, n.d.], p. 1005.)

[30] This late poem was written during the poet's insanity, which lasted from 1802 until his death in 1843.

[31] In a review of poetry by Denis Devlin (*Transition*, No. 27 [April-May 1938], p. 293) Beckett wrote, "First emerges. With what directness and concreteness the same totality may be achieved appears from the exquisite last stanza of *The Statue and the Perturbed Burghers*, which with its repetition of 'crimson and blind' and the extraordinary evocation of the unsaid by the said has the distinction of a late poem by Hölderlin (e.g. 'Ihr lieblichen Bilder im Tale . .')." Some five years later, in writing *Watt*, he had not forgotten the Dieppe experience: "on the dark shingle the turning for the last time again to the lights of the little town . . ." (p. 40).

219

in the Marne Valley, where he does his writing within the walls of a small house set on a piece of land enclosed by another wall almost as high as the sides of the house—these two worlds, the city and the country, society and the self, are the fields of attraction and repulsion for the armature of an existence and for the inner movements of a continuing literary and dramatic effort.

v. Poems in French

1946-1948

After his resignation from Trinity College in January of 1932, Beckett wrote a short poem called "Gnome," which was published some time later in *Dublin Magazine*.[1] The title, from the Greek verb *gignoskein*, "to know," refers to an aphorism or other writing characterized by sententious wisdom. Beckett's poem not only illustrates the genre; it takes knowing as its theme.

> Spend the years of learning squandering
> Courage for the years of wandering
> Through the world politely turning
> From the loutishness of learning.

Characteristically, the poet's thought frames itself in a dual mode that opposes inner and outer reality, "learning" and "world," the years of apprenticeship (*die Lehrjahre*) and the years of travel (*die Wanderjahre*). The phrase "squandering / Courage" suggests that the years of learning have diminished his capacity for living. While "politely turning" evokes the worldly goals of polish, sophistication, and flexibility, there is about the phrase a certain undertone of ineffectuality, as though the "wandering" and the "turning" were aimless and superficial. At the same time, learning is boorish. All in all, the poet seems to paint a bleak picture of wasted years behind him and hollow times without purpose ahead. "Gnome" foreshadows some of the poems in the 1937-1939 series, perhaps especially VI and VII, which offer as an alternative to social ineptitude the "loutishness" of a solitary Gros-Jean. It is prophetic, too, that structurally the poem incorporates a conflict between microcosm and macrocosm in which the balance shifts first from the inner life of "learning" to "wandering" in the big world and then swings back from "turning" to end where it began. All the while, the poet avoids end-stops and takes full advantage of present participles in prominent rhyme position to express formally, but not without a touch of irony, a sense of continuing movement and smoothly adroit reversals.

[1] IX, No. 3 (July-Sept. 1934), 8.

221

As Beckett once said, he "lost the best" when he resigned from Trinity, after which he spent the following years "not knowing what to do." How does one come to know? In one of its dimensions *Whoroscope* denies that intellect is the way. The searchings of *Echo's Bones* are fruitless, and the return to the inner world described in the 1937-1939 poems seems more an imperfect escape than an answer. From the beginning, but more and more as we follow the evolution of Beckett's poetry, the other question, "How do I manage to live," rivals the first in importance. It moves into the foreground as the first recedes. Beckett had suspected for a long time that the answer to the second question was to be found, ideally, in making things with words. From one point of view, working in the evenings on *Watt* in Roussillon during the war was only "a game"; from another it was a means of "staying sane" and a way "to keep [his] hand in." Unfortunately, the years had brought forth little to verify his growing certainty that his way was writing. Leaving Trinity—partly because he felt unsuited to a life of learning, teaching, and scholarship—left him with the feeling that these years had been "wasted." The anguish and the effort of the next five years (1932-1936) in Germany, France, England, and Ireland produced principally *More Pricks Than Kicks*, *Echo's Bones*, and *Murphy*. The physical and emotional demands of these years took their toll, and the period of lethargy between late 1936, when he settled down in Paris, and the exodus before the invading German armies in June of 1940 added little to his meager output. Except for *Watt*, the period of the war—spent chiefly in occupied Paris, the Vaucluse, and Saint-Lô and taken up with efforts to obtain enough food for survival, work in the resistance movement, and labors with the Irish Red Cross in France—was more or less a time of enforced artistic sterility. Such was the situation when Beckett returned to his Paris apartment (which had been searched and looted by the Gestapo) at the beginning of 1946. In April he was able to look back from the vantage point of forty years over his life as a writer. The perspective can hardly have been reassuring. In any case, his sense of time lost and talent frittered away unproductively, the moment in history that closed an epoch and began another, and the trauma of turning forty must have combined to help produce what he has called "the frenzied activity" of the next four years. Between 1946 and 1950 he wrote the unpublished novel

"Mercier et Camier" as well as the trilogy *Molloy* (begun earlier), *Malone Meurt*, and *L'Innommable*; the unpublished short story "Premier Amour" and three other short stories that appeared in their definitive versions as the *nouvelles* in *Nouvelles et textes pour rien* (1955) under the individual titles "L'Expulsé," "Le Calmant," and "La Fin"; an unpublished three-act play called "Eleuthéria" and *En attendant Godot*; six poems in French; and, finally, two important essays and three dialogues on art and criticism.[2]

The cliché "life begins at forty" seems almost literally true for Beckett. During the years that gave birth to the postwar world, he also took or was given a new lease on life. He appears to have discovered within himself a source of energy in the concrete application of his more or less theoretical answer to the question "How do I manage to live?" After four decades of apprenticeship—learning and seeking, wandering and waiting and working, loving and suffering and dying—he seems to have freed himself to a considerable degree of intruders (out of the past at least), and in effect to have mastered his microcosm. For the new life he finds is in a world of the imagination, a world partly given and partly brought into being through words. While the six short poems written during this period give subtle evidence of this change, they can hardly be called optimistic pieces overflowing with joie de vivre. Their author has learned how to manage, how to survive, no more. On the whole, the 1946-1948 group represents a developing continuity more than a break. The same themes are present; the same sadness, deeper yet more resigned, permeates most of the poems. There is a greater unity of tone, fewer prosaic lines, less narration and description. The flow of sound is less often broken. In short, the 1946-1948 poems are the culmination of a poetic evolution toward the pure lyric. Almost every word carries an affective charge and a power to expand poetically beyond itself. Meaning and feeling emerge together almost miraculously from verbal counters that are normally no more than references to neutral things in the world of uncommunicative objects. Beckett has achieved over the years in his poetry some of the distinctive qualities that will characterize the poetic prose of his stories, novels, and plays from this period on.

[2] For an analysis of these critical and theoretical writings, see Chap. X.

223

Continuity: The Two Worlds, Love and Death, Suffering, and Time

All six poems in this group,[3] the first five quite explicitly, the sixth less directly, are concerned with the enduring dualism of macrocosm and microcosm. Using images taken from the outer world, poem III describes the inner realm. The mind has only one season, but it holds in timeless suspension the antinomies of natural succession.

> vive morte ma seule saison
> lis blancs chrysanthèmes
> nids vifs abandonnés
> boue des feuilles d'avril
> beaux jours gris de givre

Life and death, beginning and ending are suggested by the first two words, "vive morte," which also establish the vocalic structure of the poem with their contrast between front and back vowels. The opening and closing seasons, spring and fall, follow in abrupt juxtapositions in each of the following lines, as though living itself were squeezed into nothing more than a brief pause between contraries. The spring flower gives way to the fall flower, the nest containing life to the empty nest; the living leaves of spring decompose in the fall rains, and sunny days are turned gray with frost announcing winter. On the level of sound a series of similar juxtapositions occurs. One or more *i*'s are followed in the first three lines and preceded in the last two by the darker back vowels. This reversal in order is matched by another shift, for the *i*'s that are associated with the beginnings of life in the first four lines are linked to death in the

---

[3] These poems, like those of 1937-1939, have been collected in *Samuel Beckett, Gedichte*, where they may be found on pp. 79-91. References will be by number, as follows:

> I   bon bon il est un pays
> II   "Mort de A. D."
> III vive morte ma seule saison
> IV   je suis ce cours de sable qui glisse
> V   que ferais-je sans ce monde sans visage sans questions
> VI   je voudrais que mon amour meure

The first three originally appeared in *Cahiers des saisons*, No. 2 (Oct. 1955), pp. 115-116; the three remaining poems were first published in *Transition Forty-Eight*, No. 2 (June 1948), pp. 96-97.

last. No doubt these changes help to suggest a world in which there is but a single season, where no fixed order or stable relationships or temporal priorities exist, where an eternal present constitutes the space for a "flux of forms,"[4] and the mutually exclusive modes of nature coexist. Like the mind, the poem is a world in which beginnings and endings can switch places and time can be abolished. And within the larger entity of the whole poem each line unites opposites. Moving one step further, we can note that on the level of sound in line 2 each of the internally rhyming combinations "lis blancs" and "chrysan-" contains in itself the vocalic antitheses. There are worlds within worlds within worlds.[5]

In one of the finest lyrics he has written, Beckett uses a walk along the sea to express the isolation of his inner existence. The walk is no longer a quest as it sometimes was in earlier years. In "Echo's Bones" and in the fourth poem of the 1946-1948 group, "je suis ce cours de sable qui glisse," the theme of the walk through life is coupled with a desire for death. But between 1934 and 1948 the tone has changed. At first the attitude toward life falls somewhere between revolt and revulsion. The narrator envies the dead, and the poet does not hesitate to join a hint of suicide and just a touch of rhetoric. By 1948 the compass of existence has narrowed. It no longer seems so acutely distressing, and the thought of death is accompanied not so much by compelling desire as by what can only be described as a kind of anticipatory relish.

> je suis ce cours de sable qui glisse
> entre le galet et la dune
> la pluie d'été pleut sur ma vie
> sur moi ma vie qui me fuit me poursuit
> et finira le jour de son commencement

[4] *Murphy*, p. 112.

[5] Cf. the related view of the artist as excavator, probing toward the depths of the microcosm, a view set forth repeatedly in *Proust*. For example: "The only fertile research is excavatory, immersive, a contraction of the spirit, a descent. The artist is active, but negatively, shrinking from the nullity of extracircumferential phenomena, drawn in to the core of the eddy" (p. 48). And again: "—the heart of the cauliflower or the ideal core of the onion would represent a more appropriate tribute to the labours of poetical excavation than the crown of bay" (pp. 16-17).

cher instant je te vois
dans ce rideau de brume qui recule
où je n'aurai plus à fouler ces longs seuils mouvants
et vivrai le temps d'une porte
qui s'ouvre et se referme[6]

From the end of the war until she died in 1950 Beckett spent a good part of each summer with his mother in Ireland. His brother had a house at Killiney, on the coast south of Dublin. Walking on Killiney beach on a misty day under a gentle Irish rain with the visibility extending perhaps no more than ten yards in any direction gives the walker an impression of moving within the circumscribed limits of a world that moves along with him. Out of such a walk along Killiney beach under such characteristically Irish conditions came the present poem. We have seen a similar situation, sun breaking through a mist as the rain ends in the late afternoon, give rise to the theme of "too late" in several earlier poems. Here the sense of enclosure provided by the mist and rain becomes a natural figure for the microcosm. Poem IV adds to this feeling. Not only do the mist and rain limit vision above and around the walker; his course is confined by the shingle on one side and the sand dune on the other. From the poet's development of this objective correlative of his existence, we can draw a number of inferences. The poem begins with the ambiguous "je suis," in the German translation "ich bin" and in the Italian "seguo." The French verb for "be" and "follow" is the same in the first person singular, and Beckett manages to keep both meanings in English too with "my way is in." The possessive and the preposition establish an adequate degree of assimilation between the walker and his way, neither the total identification of "I am" nor the total separation of "I follow." What is common

---

[6] Beckett's English translation, which first appeared in the issue of *Transition Forty-Eight* just cited, follows:

my way is in the sand flowing
between the shingle and the dune
the summer rain rains on my life
on me my life harrying fleeing
to its beginning to its end
my peace is there in the receding mist
when I may cease from treading these long shifting thresholds
and live the space of a door
that opens and shuts

to the walker's life and the sand is sameness and flux. "My way" in addition makes possible the very effective parallel with "my peace," the first beginning the part of the poem on life, the second the part on death. "Flowing," too, with the participial form reflecting the meaning, is in one way an improvement over the French. At the same time, line 1 in the English loses the slipping of the four *s*'s that embodies the sense of "glisse."

The enclosure and the river of sand, static sameness and flux, bring together the immobility that characterizes the microcosm and the movement through time that carries the inner world along toward oblivion. It is the same combination we saw most recently in "ainsi a-t-on beau." The melancholy and the sweetness of the summer rain shrouds this life, which has been reduced to no more than the present moment. This narrowing in time that corresponds to the narrowing in space caused by mist and rain and pathway (with ocean beyond on one side and town on the other, as in "Dieppe," but blotted out here) is perhaps the great advantage of the microcosm. We noted life squeezed between contraries in the last poem. Such a diminishing has its sadness, but its compensations too. If the macrocosmic arrangement is a "colossal fiasco" (*Murphy*, p. 178), obliteration by withdrawal is the part of wisdom. Here (5, 6) the mist performs this service. It closes in behind the walker and recedes in front of him. It spares him a vision of his future and painful memories from the past. If life can be anywhere restricted to the present moment with its blessed freedom in this double absence, it is in a microcosm walled around more securely than appeared possible in poems VIII and XII of the 1937-1939 group. The repetition "sur ma vie / sur moi sur ma vie" is a stylistic device that suggests an identity between a whole lifetime and the present, momentary "moi." The same effect is achieved in line 6 by a temporal telescoping that joins beginning and ending. Each day dawns on the dead dust of yesterday and sinks into extinction, leaving no trace for tomorrow. Time has become discontinuous. Yet paradoxically, the narrator is caught up in flux. The image of the river of sand suggests this, but the idea is developed more fully in the metaphor of the moving mist. As he walks toward the curtain of mist ahead, it recedes before him; as he walks from the curtain of mist behind, it follows him. He remains within his little world as though stationary, but all the while he and the world are moving on together. In an analogous way, life pursues him, harries him onward, all the while fleeing ahead of him. Life in effect escapes him. Past and future are hidden, and the present is reduced to the sameness of sand and mist, so that one day is no different from another and time collapses into an undifferentiated bleakness. All lines of supply from the macrocosm cut, the microcosm and "le néant" become almost indistinguishable.

The choice between suffering existence and unfeeling nirvana having been made in favor of the latter, the next step is a small one. The longing for death asserts itself in the beautiful images that conclude the poem. As though the ten-yard threshold of death's door were a treadmill, the narrator yearns for the moment when the moving path will come to a stop, allowing him to reach the door at last and pass through it into the mist. It is interesting to note that "instant" (6) has been eliminated in the English version and "le temps" (9) replaced by "the space," which can of course carry a temporal meaning. Similarly, the time verb "finira" (5) has given way to a spatial use of the nouns "beginning" and "end." No doubt much of the art of making a poem that at heart is about human existence in time consists in finding (consciously or unconsciously) concrete spatial correlatives for temporal phenomena. If this is true —and requirements of idiom in the two languages aside—we perhaps have the right to prefer the English version in these instances. Beckett takes full advantage of present participles available in English to suggest indirectly the passing of time ("flowing," "harrying," "fleeing," "receding," "treading," "shifting"), and for once the English surpasses the French in the proportion of continuants to stops, although it is high in both cases (two and a half to one in French and almost three and a half to one in English).

In the sixth and last poem of the 1946-1948 group, several of these same themes occur. The poet joins love and death in an apparently paradoxical combination.

> je voudrais que mon amour meure
> qu'il pleuve sur le cimetière
> et les ruelles où je vais
> pleurant celle qui crut m'aimer[7]

---

[7] Beckett's translation, below, originally appeared in the same issue of *Transition*, pp. 96-97:

> I would like my love to die
> and the rain to be falling on the graveyard

As a love poem, "je voudrais . . ." strikes an original and strangely moving note. It recalls "Cascando" in the ambiguity of "crut," which, in spite of the past definite tense that strengthens the affirmative aspect of *croire*, remains slightly equivocal. She had no doubt, but the narrator does—perhaps about the very possibility of love. The exclusive force of "celle" ("the one") implies, as the English also suggests, that she is the only one to have loved him, if she loved him. Along with the impersonal character of the pronoun "celle," the tense, which places the event in the distant past (even while she is still alive!), expresses the pain of a loss that is forever irreparable, a loss of what is finally understood as uniquely precious. The effect is greatly heightened by the juxtaposition of presence and felt absence to come. Beckett associates the tense of "crut" with a celebrated passage in Racine's *Phèdre*: "Ariane, ma soeur! de quel amour blessée, / Vous mourûtes aux bords où vous fûtes laissée" (I, iii, 253-254). The allusion to Racine suggests a parallel between the narrator and Thésée and brings in the motif of ingratitude. The poet's mother died shortly after this poem was written (in 1950), after a long illness, and she had been left "aux bords" of another island by a son who in spite of annual visits to see her in Ireland cannot now wholly ward off the pangs of self-reproach. In "Krapp's Last Tape" we read, "When I look . . . —back on the year that is gone . . . there is of course the house on the canal where mother lay a-dying, in the late autumn, after her long viduity and the . . . —bench by the weir from where I could see her window. There I sat, in the biting wind, wishing she were gone."[8] In Phèdre's horror at the "love" visited upon her sister and herself by Venus ("de quel amour blessée") we can also read the Irish poet's metaphysical protest.

"First and last" (used in the English translation), as an idiom meaning all-inclusive, tends to rule out "last" in the sense of "most

---

and on me walking the streets
mourning the first and last to love me

[8] In *Krapp's Last Tape and Other Dramatic Pieces* (New York: Grove Press, 1958), pp. 17-19. On these same pages there is a reference to "Malacoda" and to "Serena I." Krapp reads from his dictionary under the word "viduity": "State—or condition of being—or remaining—a widow—or widower . . . Deep weeds of viduity . . . Also of an animal, especially a bird . . . the vidua or weaver-bird . . . Black plumage of male . . . (He looks up. With relish.) The vidua-bird!"

recent." This conviction that the time of love is over adds to the pathos of its rarity in the past, its uncertainty, and its transience.[9] If there is any doubt about the woman's feelings, what can we say of a lover who desires death for his beloved? In the light of other Beckett poems, we immediately understand that he could wish her no greater good. If life is unbearable suffering, then the release from life that is death must be prized above all things. What is so affecting in the lover's words is that her death, the disappearance of the origin of his only experience of another's love, will be an enduring source of suffering for him. The gift he would give her, then, is the only gift love knows, the sacrifice of self to the good of the other. He offers to assume the burden of suffering she lays down. At the same time, the lover suffers from the beloved's suffering, and her release is at least a partial release for him.

While poem VI recalls the "darling" sick in the Portobello Nursing Home, it also reminds us more generally of themes and images from earlier works. Here, as in so many poems of *Echo's Bones*, the narrator walks the streets trying to ease his pain. Again we find the rain, accompanying his tears as his solace accompanies his grief. He wanders in the macrocosm, but the setting suggests the microcosm, filled again with renewed memories of love and death, to be exorcized finally by the magic formula of mind-annulling fatigue. The peace of exhaustion will have to do until that desired day when he too is granted the gift of death.

Between Past and Future: A Transitional Poem

"Mort de A. D.," poem II in this group, is similar to VI. It recounts another invasion of the little world the poet has chosen for his earthly asylum. However, even though the elements of continuity are still predominant, we begin to perceive more clearly the new nervous energy that makes creative effort possible and at the same time increases the poet's capacity for suffering. Even more than in poem VI, the narrator's helpless anguish before the suffering

[9] In the expression "first and last" there may be an echo of the same phrase in *Proust*: "Albertine is the first and the last, the Bacchante of the shore, as seen by the narrator in that pure act of understanding—intuition, and the captive that has recovered liberty and life, possessed of herself among the young laundresses, bathing in the Loire" (pp. 44-45). In both cases love and death, past and present come together in the insight that precedes artistic creation.

and death of A. D. (a friend who was with Beckett at the Irish Hospital at Saint-Lô) evokes certain passages in *Echo's Bones*.

> et là être là
> pressé contre ma vieille planche vérolée du noir
> des jours et nuits broyés aveuglément
> à être là à ne pas fuir et fuir et être là
> courbé vers l'aveu du temps mourant
> d'avoir été ce qu'il fut fait ce qu'il fit
> de moi de mon ami mort hier l'oeil luisant
> les dents longues haletant dans sa barbe dévorant
> la vie des saints une vie par jour de vie
> revivant dans la nuit ses noirs péchés
> mort hier pendant que je vivais
> et être là buvant plus haut que l'orage
> la coulpe du temps irrémissible
> agrippé au vieux bois témoin des départs
> témoin des retours

"Mort de A. D." has much in common with poems VIII and XII of the 1937-1939 group. It employs their framework structure that so well suggests the limiting circle of the cosmos. As in XII ("jusque dans la caverne . . ."), beginning and ending place the reader in the little world of the narrator, while the center of the poem is given over to bad news and painful memories from outside. For the first time we have a picture of activity within the microcosm, the "là" of lines 1, 4, and 12. During a 1962 conversation at his Marne Valley retreat (which I was generously allowed to invade on a number of occasions), Beckett confessed that as a younger man he had rarely been able to remain in isolation for more than a week at a time.[10] In lines 1 through 4 and 12 through 15 we witness his struggle with himself. Line 4, especially, translates vividly his effort to remain at his worktable and his need for relief from the prolonged concentration of writing.[11]

At the same time a certain passivity, reflected in the series of past participles ("pressé," "vérolée," "broyés," "courbé," and even

[10] While longer periods are easier for him today, the problem now is to find more than a week, or indeed even a week, free from professional, administrative, and social obligations.

[11] According to his old friend A. J. Leventhal, Beckett drives himself very hard during periods of work.

231

to some extent in "agrippé") makes itself felt. This tension between activity and passivity is an interesting development of the tension between flux and stasis in "ainsi a-t-on beau" (VIII). There the narrator's escape into a timeless realm could not completely muffle the telltale sounds of voracious *tempus edax*. His illusion of immobility failed to mask the evidence of the passage of time. Here, dreaming of the past has given way to active effort, which might well be a more effective mute. It is activity within a larger passivity, however. While he is working on time in his writing, time is working on him. We suspect that it, as much as his own will, presses him down, bends him over, brings him to an admission that for him it is running out, forces him to clutch at the worktable as a drowning man at a spar. His close association with the table allows it, poetically, to serve as his surrogate. Old as it is old, marked as it is marked by the disease that comes through long intercourse with time, the whore that infects all men impartially, he is somehow still afloat. The "mangé sans appétit" of poem VIII, which translates time's lack of discrimination, finds an echo here. Chained to his table, deep in his shadowy inner world, he is blind to the distinction between days, between nights, between day and night. In a striking image, the poet pictures them ground up automatically, without preference or prejudice, into a pepper of virulent pocks that eat into and scar the table, and by implication the worker before it.

The imagery carries with it a built-in ambiguity. Since time and man are both inseparable and, ultimately, separable, time is both victim along with man and destroyer. Time is dying (5), the days and nights are demolished (3). But time is also the pathogenic and unpardonable (13) power that has sickened and finally brought low the narrator's friend and that stands accused at the end of the poem. In an extended metaphor the writer becomes the prosecutor who has before him a confession, his own, to be sure, but also the confession of expiring time (5). The criminal assassin cannot be pardoned and must die (13). But the writer is writer as well as prosecutor and the "aveu" is his poem, which is above all the recognition that if time and his friend must die, so too must he. This seems to be the sense of the expression "buvant . . . / la coulpe du temps irrémissible," which is on the pattern of the French idiom "boire un affront," to swallow or accept an insult. There is nothing for it but to resign oneself to the damage done and being done.

The identification of the narrator and his friend is suggested still more strongly in lines 6 and 7. The confession, or poem, is about himself as well as his friend. Their lives were parallel. He has been and done what his friend was and did. While "d'avoir été" depends grammatically on "aveu," its position following "mourant" suggests (somewhere on the periphery of the reader's consciousness) that he too is dying—from having been living. The parallel comes to a sharp halt in line 11, with an anguished question implied: "Why should he die and not I too?" We feel both the writer's sorrow and his sense of guilt at living in the protected calm of his little world while his friend succumbed in the gale of life outside. Nonetheless, the evidence of flux penetrates even into his refuge in the ticking of a clock, suggesting here a clenched fist striking the breast in the *mea culpa* of guilty Time. Line 14 implies that he is holding on for not-so-dear life to his worktable, which reminds us again of Beckett's belief that for him writing is a way of surviving. The nautical overtones in the image are strengthened in the idea of "départs" and "retours" (recalling "Da Tagte Es"). The terms relate to line 4 and his own departures from and returns to his worktable, but they move us especially because they evoke his friend, who has departed and will not return again. "Témoin" carries on the legal metaphor and concludes the poem on the theme of art, art that is a witness to living and dying, to love and suffering, a witness that testifies against time.

At the heart of the poem, in lines 7 through 10, we are in the macrocosm with the narrator's moribund friend. The poet gives a brief description of visible symptoms during the later stages of tuberculosis—eyes bright with fever, emaciation, the panting for breath as the lungs fail—a description that serves symbolically at the same time. All of the symptoms taken together may be interpreted as a portrait of avidity: shining eyes, hunger (the French idiom "les dents longues"), the hard breathing of desire—and the beard which the sick man allows to grow, on the one hand because he is too sick or weak to shave, on the other in order not to take time from the object of his desire. Now what the patient is eager for is not nourishment for his ailing body but food for his spirit. As time consumes him, he devours the lives of the saints. There is just a hint of protest hidden beneath this subtle use of ambiguity. The sicker his friend is, the more religious he becomes, to state the case baldly. Something of Beckett's gentle and suffering irony is apparent in the phrase "une vie par jour de vie." The narrator is concerned about his friend's life, not the lives of the saints. It pains him that the dying man's sufferings should be increased at night, when instead of the peace of sleep he experiences the agony of "reliving" the sins of his past. His friend is not to blame. If anyone has a "noir péché" (10), a "coulpe" (13) to account for, it is the culprit time.[12] Beginning with "luisant" (7) and ending with "noir" (10), these lines utilize the imagery of darkness and light, night and day. The dying man makes the traditional association between good and the light, evil and the dark. The lines also contribute to the cohesion of the poem by picking up the same motif from lines 2 and 3, where dark days and nights form the neutral, monochrome background of the narrator's twilight existence.

"Mort de A. D." is among other things a catalogue of Beckett's dual perspectives: macrocosm and microcosm, activity and passivity, flux and stasis, departure and return, day and night, light and darkness, good and evil, self and others, guilt and innocence, life and death. At the same time it gives proof of a new adaptation to the microcosm through work. While the solution is not achieved without struggle, the expenditure of energy seems to open up new sources of energy. A quiet, almost despairing resignation pervaded the poem "ainsi a-t-on beau" and others in the 1937-1939 group. Given *tempus edax*, the order of existence was *vanitas vanitatum*. Here, however, a certain anguish that is something more than despair if less than revolt replaces hopeless lassitude. Time is cruelly brief but no longer wholly unmanageable. The themes of "too late" and "too soon" are superseded by a theme that only by the wildest stretch of the imagination could be identified as *carpe diem*. Nevertheless, the poet is now making something—a lifeboat at least—out of time. He is no longer prone and waiting, but seated and working.

The Part of Innovation: Life in the Microcosm, A Defense of Solitude

To date we have learned that the little world is an asylum with certain disadvantages attached to it. It can be penetrated all too

---

[12] Even in the title one suspects the presence, in a pun, of antireligious irony. "Mort de A. D." is not only a curious reduplication—"mort-dead"—but may be read "Mort de A[nno]. D[omini].," i.e., "What death is like in the Christian era."

easily by painful memories or painful news from the big world out-side. It resembles death, but it can be a way of living. From it comes poetry. One can work there but not without interruption and not without a considerable effort of the will. So far, however, we have been given only occasional hints of what life inside the microcosm is like. Beckett's prose and especially the later novels will paint the inner landscape and populate (if that is the word) its emptiness. They will give us some idea of "what the ostrich sees in the sand" (*Murphy*, p. 176). The poems cannot do that, but two of them in the 1946-1948 group do suggest more compellingly and clearly than others the "feeling" of the poet's preferred habitat. The initial poem in the group was written under even more inauspicious circumstances than *Whoroscope*. The painter Geer van Velde, younger brother of Bram, asked Beckett to write a text to be used in association with one of his paintings. Reluctantly, Beckett agreed. As it turned out, however, the text was never used, and some time later the young painter Avigdor Arikha, who illustrated *Nouvelles et textes pour rien*, obtained Beckett's permission to include it in a London showing of his own work. Far from being a transposition of an individual painting or even an attempt to capture the essence of a body of paintings, the poem is first an expression of irritation at the prospect of a disagreeable chore and second an attempt to explain why the task is so onerous. The situation presents itself to Beckett in the familiar terms of an intrusion from the public macro-cosm into the private realm where he has come to spend more and more of his time.

> bon bon il est un pays
> où l'oubli où pèse l'oubli
> doucement sur les mondes innommés
> là la tête on la tait la tête est muette
> et on sait non on ne sait rien
> le chant des bouches mortes meurt
> sur la grève il a fait le voyage
> il n'y a rien à pleurer
>
> ma solitude je la connais allez je la connais mal
> j'ai le temps c'est ce que je me dis j'ai le temps   10
> mais quel temps os affamé le temps du chien
> du ciel pâlissant sans cesse mon grain de ciel
> du rayon qui grimpe ocellé tremblant
> des microns des années ténèbres

vous voulez que j'aille d'A à B je ne peux pas
je ne peux pas sortir je suis dans un pays sans traces
oui oui c'est une belle chose que vous avez là une
    bien belle chose
qu'est-ce que c'est ne me posez plus de questions
spirale poussière d'instants qu'est-ce que c'est le même
le calme l'amour la haine le calme le calme   20

In its number of lines, curiously, the poem resembles a sonnet with two sestets.[13] The structure that is poetically effective, however, is built on dramatic dialogue. Each of the three divisions of the poems begins with a reply that is at the same time a defense. The first section, lines 1 through 8, begins with an expression ("bon bon") of exasperated resignation: "All right, all right, I'll give you a text." The remainder of this section is devoted to a slightly petulant evocation of the narrator's private world. As we learn, the very nature of this private environment tends to disqualify him for the task he is being asked to perform. First of all we should note that for him it is an authentic world, a true alternative to the one outside. He thinks of it in spatial terms, as a "pays." Similarly, Murphy's mind is described as functioning "not as an instrument but as a place" (p. 178). The narrator's "place" is characterized by its isolation. The muffling effect of watery distances protects it. Voices from the dead die as they reach its shores (6-7), while merciful forgetfulness lies like an Irish mist about other worlds that once were or still are (2-3). And as we learn later (16), egress is very difficult. Like Dante's dark and trackless wood, it is a "pays sans traces."

Besides the double absence of isolation, in time from the past and in space from the macrocosm, other negative qualities distinguish this *pays*. "Innommées" (3) (which immediately calls up the title of the third novel of Beckett's trilogy, *L'Innommable*) may refer to prior selves and the reality attached to each. Beckett, after all, is the author of *Proust*. At the same time, these "mondes innommés" suggest worlds of painting, perhaps not only those of Van Velde and Arikha but also the many worlds in the National Gallery

---

[13] Another curious fact, which seems however to be equally without significance (Beckett's interest in Dante notwithstanding), is that in five of the poems presently under consideration the total number of lines is divisible by five. This is true of only one poem, the last, in *Echo's Bones*, of neither of the next two poems, and of only four in the 1937-1939 group: all in all, five out of twenty-seven compared to five out of six in the 1946-1948 poems.

that Beckett came to know so well as a young man in Dublin. Beyond its objective reference, however, the term tells us something about existence in the microcosm. Although etymologically there may be no relationship between "name" and "knowledge," epistemologically "unnamed" and "unknown" are close indeed. Since *Whoroscope*, the need for and unavailability of knowledge of ultimate things has been a recurrent theme. In this solitary land the dilemma dissolves. Need ends and the ceaseless activity of the conceptual intellect comes to a halt. "La tête est muette" (4). At first the end of frustration seems to resemble the satisfaction of the need to know: "et on sait" (5). But no, although the gnawing has stopped, still "on ne sait rien." Finally, the feeling of this inner existence is translated by images of silence (4, 6) and insensibility (8). Once inside the frontiers of solitude, it becomes clear that the dead are not to be mourned. They have completed the rough voyage of life and, like the narrator, have found peace. The list of negatives is impressive: absence of the past, absence of outer reality, absence of thought, absence of knowledge, absence of need, absence of sound, absence of feeling, and, one is tempted to say, absence of life. We can understand his attitude toward the deceased. The lonely country in which he lives seems to resemble the state of nonbeing more than the land of the living.

The second section makes it clear, however, that the resemblance is not complete. The alter ego of the narrator—whose conscience, torn between personal desire and the wish to help a friend, is giving him trouble—takes the part of the persistent petitioner and suggests that he can always come back to his familiar world. Writing the text will take only a short time. The narrator rejects both arguments. First, the world is not all that familiar. In line 9, the interjection has the force of a negation on the order of "nonsense": "allez je la connais mal." From this simple but decisive assertion we can infer that the narrator's solitude is not merely a state of total quietude. It differs from the absence characterizing the void and indeed is less a condition than a site, a site to be explored. The result of these explorations will provide the substance of the author's art. He refutes also the argument that he has plenty of time to carry out these explorations. Lines 11 through 14 attempt to explode this myth with a series of images that reduce a man's brief moment to its true dimensions. He is at once the eater and the eaten. Skeletal, starved, he consumes time insatiably. But the metaphor of the "os affamé" calls up the canine. Time is in turn a dog that devours the bone that is man. The next line employs a similar double reduction. The sky of life is fading fast and that part the narrator can call his own is a tiny "grain," an image which brings to mind the "quelques haillons d'azur" in poem II of the 1937-1939 series. But a more striking parallel can be found in *Godot*. In Pozzo's speech (p. 61), quoted above apropos of "La Mouche," the passage of time is rendered through this same image of a continually dimming sky, and we recall that *Godot* was also written during this period.[14] Finally, the precarious ("tremblant") ray of light, many-eyed like the allegorical peacock which represents the *Commedia* in Boccaccio's *Vita di Dante*,[15] seems to suggest the little the poet manages to dredge from the darkness of the depths he probes for materials to be used in his future opus. In the metaphorical equation that brings together poet and universe (14), a few thousandths of a millimeter of creative progress corresponds to light-years. This systematic contraction of time translates the narrator's anxiety. *Ars longa, vita brevis*, and if the need to know has been exorcized from the microcosm, the need to make—his hold on life—has not. More clearly than in "Mort de A. D.," time is seen in a *carpe diem* perspective. It may not after all be too late, but only by defending his solitude can the writer hope to snatch the day for his work.

The dialogue continues in section three with the antagonist becoming more precise in his demands. He insists that the narrator act the part in which he has been cast, that of art critic. There must be categories and orderly transitions. Analytical reason must follow its rules of logic. Not unjustifiably, the poet pleads inability. He is imprisoned in a world cut off from other worlds. The discursive language that simplifies and makes communication between men possible is foreign to him. His is a speech without critical pigeonholes. In lines 17 and 18 this same conflict between logic and art continues. Before the stubborn questions of his pursuer he hopefully

---

[14] Cf. also the image of the "os affamé" and the heartrending comedy of the chicken bones in *Godot* (pp. 40-43). Man is given so little, and even this little will be taken from him, perhaps through the unconscious cruelty of a fellow sufferer who is nearly as needy as he. Estragon, who asks politely for Lucky's chicken bones, is like the imagined antagonist of our present poem, and the poem is the kick he receives in return. There is neither right nor wrong, only two conflicting needs.

[15] Used by Beckett in the poem "Text," discussed below in Chap. VII.

grants the propitiatory offering of enthusiastic appreciation: "une bien belle chose." But this extracted admission fails to halt the cross-examination. His interrogator will settle for nothing but critical analysis, and finally the poet, like a hunted quarry, begs for an end to questions. Faced with such an unrelenting onslaught, in the end his resistance crumbles and he makes the supreme effort. While the last two lines of the poem do bear some relationship to a description of the painting of Geer van Velde contained in Beckett's 1945 essay, which we shall discuss in Chapter X, they are more obviously an imagistic transposition of his own views on human existence. "Spirale" is an immediate perception of form and sensation and not an analysis. The image is especially interesting for another reason, however. Containing within itself the linear and the circular, the spiral conveys progress and limitation and brings to mind the union of flux and immobility that we have seen in "ainsi a-t-on beau," "je suis ce cours de sable . . . ," "Mort de A. D.," and other poems. "Poussière d'instants" translates a preoccupation with the passage of time, suggesting a debris of yesterdays. The beleaguered poet's response to a final question, "c'est le même," implies that there *is* nothing else besides waiting and the voyage, circular stasis and linear descent. Line 20 with its own "circular" arrangement that puts first things first *and* last sums up the essence of the two worlds. Outside is the realm of relationship, where man exists in the society of his fellows. Two reactions are possible: attraction and revulsion, love and hate. Only in the land of the self can one find the absence of relationship, the calm that makes creation possible. The last words of the poem, "le calme le calme" are almost a prayer to be allowed his brief time in that land.

The conversational style of the poem is appropriate, of course, to the dialogue form. It is vivid and effective and forecasts the mastery to come in *Godot*. There are other, less obvious but important stylistic characteristics present in the poem, however. In line 2 the poet seems to catch himself, as one does in conversation, and rephrase. At the same time, the line betrays an impatience with grammatical order and structure. These belong to the language of communication used in society. We note a similar inclination, which is typical of a more poetic popular language, to place the noun object first and repeat it with a pronoun immediately preceding the verb: "là la tête on la tait." Another example of this trend occurs in line 9: "ma solitude je la connais." The tendency to give an unusually important role to the substantive and to loosen grammatical order reaches its climax in the last lines of the poem, where a poetic style of imagistic notations completely does away with the logic of syntax. More prosaically, these false starts and repetitions express the poet's hurry to finish with his ordeal. Often, too, they imply the inadequacy of language. The poet catches himself in a poor rendering of his inner reality and changes the course of the sentence: "et on sait non on ne sait rien." Just as intellect is not an instrument adequate to the knowledge of the microcosm, so the tool of intellect, structured language, fails in its attempt to capture that trackless, unstructured inner world. The theme of the woeful shortcomings of language is one that Beckett will develop in later works, *L'Innommable* and *Comment c'est* in particular. In this poem we see already the beginnings of the style that is used there, the same false starts followed by new attempts, the same preference for substantives, the same qualification of inadequately expressed vision, the same disappearance of connectives, the same breakdown in syntactical order. Nevertheless, Beckett does not entirely shun the expressive use of sound that we have seen so often in his poems. In line 4, six *t*'s help to create a monosyllabic patter of plosives that succeeds in suggesting the meaningless jabber of reason that the poet would quiet. Again in lines 6 and 7, the idea of a song sets off a series of imitative harmonies, vocalic modulations, and consonantal correspondences that overflow the end-stopped line. Even as he destroys form, the true poet recreates it.

"Que ferais-je sans ce monde . . . ," the fifth poem and the last to be considered in the 1946-1948 group, is in one respect at least the most significant poem that Beckett has written. It contains in embryonic form the essentials of the artistic enterprise to come. Like poem I of the same group, it bears a certain relationship to the sonnet. Its "octave" has one line too many, but its single sestet conforms with regulations as to length. Like a good number of sonnets, its internal structure is based on the device of question and answer. More basically, however, it simply shares with the sonnet the crucial two-part structure. Abandoning the framework arrangement that enclosed microcosm within macrocosm (or vice versa), in forthright fashion Beckett devotes the first part of the poem to the former and the second to the latter. The new organization reflects a shift in emphasis. No longer does each world tend to encroach upon the domain of the other and preempt the author's energies and exist-

240

ence. Here the very architecture of the poem presents them as clear-cut alternatives. In the first section the poet not only evokes his inner sanctum; he also imagines the possibility of its elimination. Without it he would be driven back into the "life" he describes in section two.

> que ferais-je sans ce monde sans visage sans questions
> où être ne dure qu'un instant où chaque instant
> verse dans le vide dans l'oubli d'avoir été
> sans cette onde où à la fin
> corps et ombre ensemble s'engloutissent
> que ferais-je sans ce silence gouffre des murmures
> haletant furieux vers le secours vers l'amour
> sans ce ciel qui s'élève
> sur la poussière de ses lests   9
>
> que ferais-je je ferais comme hier comme aujourd'hui
> regardant par mon hublot si je ne suis pas seul
> à errer et à virer loin de toute vie
> dans un espace pantin
> sans voix parmi les voix
> enfermées avec moi[16]

Typical again of many sonnets and of Beckett's highly developed sense of organization is the subdivision of lines 1 through 9 into four clearly distinct parts. In each we find a metaphoric equivalent

---

[16] The author's English translation appeared on pages 96-97 of the issue of *Transition* cited above:

> what would I do without this world faceless incurious
> where to be lasts but an instant where every instant
> spills in the void the ignorance of having been
> without this wave where in the end
> body and shadow together are engulfed
> what would I do without this silence where the murmurs die
> the pantings the frenzies towards succour towards love
> without this sky that soars
> above its ballast dust
>
> what would I do what I did yesterday and the day before
> peering out of my deadlight looking for another
> wandering like me eddying far from all the living
> in a convulsive space
> among the voices voiceless
> that throng my hiddenness

of the poet's asylum: "monde," "être," "instant," "onde," "gouffre," "ciel," and "poussière." "Monde" repeats the image of poem I. It indicates a place one can live in, an alternative to the everyday world. Significantly enough, the term is not used in section two; the derogatory phrase "espace pantin" replaces it. In this context, then, "monde" denotes "the true world" as opposed to the puppeteer's artificial and limited stage space. Authentic existence is possible inside the mind and not outside, where bodies go about mechanically performing their preestablished functions. Once, in a discussion on this general subject, Beckett quoted the following limerick from memory.

> There was a young man who said, "Damn!
> I suddenly see what I am,
> A creature that moves
> In predestined grooves,
> In fact not a bus but a tram."[17]

"Etre" confirms the idea that this is the realm of "being," not "acting." "Instant" echoes line 6 of poem IV ("cher instant je te vois") and makes explicit what was only implied there: the "cher instant" is the present moment. Being is inconceivable in either past or future. While "onde" suggests secondarily a muffling effect on sound and the feeling of depth, in the present circumstances it is most closely associated with the notion of death. The stock poetic phrase "sur la terre et sur l'onde" brings to mind the duality of land and sea we discussed in connection with "Dieppe." There the sea was linked to death and the land with the lights of the city and life in society. In the third subdivision of part one, "gouffre" repeats the image of depth, descent, and engulfment. In lines 8 and 9 this world is equipped with its sky. "Poussière de ses lests" recalls the "poussière d'instants" in poem I. Each day rises, like a balloon lightened

---

[17] This limerick on predestination may have held special appeal for Beckett because of his interest in the occasionalist philosophy of Geulincx, which tends to undermine the efficacy of free will because it relies on God to produce in the physical realm actions corresponding to those willed by the mind of man. (See Victor Vander Haeghen, *Geulincx, étude sur sa vie, sa philosophie et ses ouvrages* [Ghent: Ad. Hoste, 1886], Part II, Chaps. 2, 5, and 6.) The bus-tram limerick is popularly attributed to Ronald Knox, but the original was written at Oxford between 1906 and 1909 by Maurice E. Hare. (See Langford Reed, *The Complete Limerick Book* [New York and London: The Knickerbocker Press, 1925], pp. 37-38, for the original version.)

of its ballast, above the jettisoned dust of the annihilated past. The first section ends as it began, with the assertion that in the microcosm only the present exists.

The portrait in part one is completed, as in the first poem, through a series of negations. While the first nine lines are structured by a succession of "sans" that carries out the central poetic stratagem, which is the hypothetical destruction of the inner world, the last two "sans" in the first line are not part of this stratagem. They serve, rather, along with the negative phrases that follow, in the portrait itself. The double use of "sans" in line 1—besides establishing a phonetic echo pattern at the level of individual sounds, syllables, and words, a pattern that continues throughout the poem— faces the reader immediately with a compelling if veiled statement of the paradoxical point of the whole poem. Each world excludes the other. The microcosm is by definition a negation of the macrocosm, and the answer to the hypothetical question suggests that the negation of the microcosm would return the poet to the macrocosm. The central tension of the poem might be stated as a competition between illusion and reality. Because it is defined as a negation, is the microcosm less real? Would the negation of this negation return the narrator from illusion to reality? Such is the question raised by the three "sans" in line 1 and answered implicitly, through a description of a return to the macrocosm, in part two.

There is little doubt about the negative nature of the portrait. This faceless world is "sans questions." Communication with others has been eliminated. "Ne . . . que" in line 2 rules out past and future, and in line 3 the past in particular is consigned to the void, to the oblivion of forgetfulness. Lines 4 and 5 look forward to the elimination of life itself and establish once again the relationship we have seen earlier between the inner world and death. "Corps et ombre" (the last, significantly enough, replacing "âme") repeat the familiar dualism. When asked during a conversation in 1961 to describe his manner of setting about writing, Beckett said that he would sit at his table sometimes for two or three hours without putting down a word, trying to "descend into the darkness." The idea of a descent and an engulfment seem to apply equally well to life in the microcosm, to artistic creation, and to death—perhaps Beckett's three main concerns, at least in his later prose. "Ce silence" in line 6 reiterates "sans questions." The sound of voices is swallowed up by the "gouffre." Line 7 gives us an insight into the often unavowed function of speech in the big world. "Haletant" implies desire. "Furieux" would appear to have its original sense of "mad," or quite literally (and very appropriately in this context) "out of one's mind." The term suggests that life in the macrocosm is an alienation from the true self and perhaps also that attempts to communicate with others are insanity. Such attempts are more than idle conversation. They are abortive cries for help, another term for love. Pessimistically, or perhaps realistically, Beckett recognizes that love is more often a selfish need than a selfless impulse directed toward the good of others. Pressed about the nature of an early affection, he once confessed, "I suppose I was in love. To the extent that I was capable of love." Finally, in lines 8 and 9, each new day eliminates its predecessor and consigns it to a dusty destiny.

The second part of the poem recalls the question in line 1 and gives it an answer. Were this land of the mind unavailable to him, and line 10 indicates that this is sometimes the case, the narrator's eye would turn outward toward the macrocosm. As we understood from the goings and comings in "Mort de A. D." and from other poems, the unbroken solitude of the inner world can weigh heavily at times. Line 11 conjures up an extraordinary vision. Sealed in as though in a one-man submarine or a diving suit,[18] the narrator peers out in search of other similarly isolated individuals. "Enfermées" in line 15 does double service. Individuals are shut off from each other, but all are imprisoned together in the somewhat larger space of the macrocosm. "Errer" and "virer" in line 12 combine in a figure that performs the function of the spiral in poem I. Aimless, more or less linear movement is further vitiated by the curve that changes direction. Closed in, one must eventually and repeatedly circle back into known space and re-trace old paths.[19] Line 13 is perhaps the most important line in the poem. The image of an "espace pantin" is the clearest statement thus far in the poetry of a conviction of the unreality of life on the little stage where marionettes go through their motions.[20] In this Kafkaesque realm there are many voices but

[18] Beckett's English translation for "hublot" is "deadlight," which has both the meaning of "porthole" and "skylight," the latter term suggesting the microcosm of his studio apartment. "Deadlight" also has the advantage of reinforcing the phrase "far from all the living."

[19] The English translation for "virer" comes even closer by evoking the double movement of the spiral in the incipient whirlpool of an eddy. It also strengthens the notion of someone out of the mainstream of life.

[20] "Convulsive space" in the English translation catches the basic idea of

little communication, and the narrator, as in "musique de l'indif-férence . . ." and "Arènes de Lutèce," is silent. More than most people, the poet seems aware that social conversation consists of stereotyped gambits. We all adopt roles and pronounce the expected words that fit the conventional situations. Most of us, however, are less sensitive to the loss of self that such role-playing involves. For Beckett, the unreality of a worldly surface life leads to a search for a lost self in the depths of the mysterious inner world. Now, as at the beginning, we find the ancient archetype of the quest. To over-simplify, pain and sorrow plunge the poet toward asylum; boredom and loneliness send him up into the world; anguish at the passage of time, a sense of the unreality of social existence bring him back into the microcosm again. These and other forces we have discussed eventually determine a continuing *va-et-vient*. His life is lived within the bounds of two incompatible yet paradoxically allied worlds. His true home, however, is down inside. While he needs air, he must sound to survive. If he comes to the surface periodically, it is in order to dive more deeply and remain submerged longer.

It would be improper to end this discussion of the French poetry without stressing one last time that it is indeed poetry and not merely a catalogue of ideas related to a general philosophical dualism. Musically talented himself and coming from a family background including several professional musicians, Beckett understandably writes poetry in which sound and rhythm are of the greatest impor-tance. In "que ferais-je sans ce monde . . . ," words that are of key semantic importance determine the dominant sound patterns. In their vicinity we find words chosen in large part as "phonetic helpers." By reinforcing the sounds present in a key word they strengthen its total impact. This is one reason for the reader's sense that such poetic statement is more vivid, moving, and meaningful than prose. A kind of phonetic revitalization, it can at times liberate meaning and emotion through music and restore lost evocative power to worn-out clichés. "Monde" by itself, for example, is trite

---

movement unwilled and uncontrolled by the individual. The choice of these words is a good example of the great importance the author attaches to rhythm and sound. The extra syllable in "convulsive" makes up for the loss of one syllable in "space," so that the total number remains the same in both the French and English versions. At the same time, "convulsive" brings to three the number of *s* sounds in the line, matching roughly the one voiced and two unvoiced *s*'s of the French.

and vague. The phrase "sans ce monde," however, brings echoing *s* sounds and variant nasal vowels together to form a semantic and phonetic unit. The negative quality of this "monde" is emphasized partly by semantic repetition but even more strongly by the reverberations of *s*'s and nasals in the succeeding phrases "sans visages" and "sans questions." Not only the negative quality is stressed, however. After all, the harmony of fluid and resonant sounds is itself a figure of this world from which the "stenches, asperities, ear-splitters and eye-closers" have been banished (*Murphy*, p. 246). It is easy enough to follow analytically the musical incantation that lulls the reader into the calm of the poet's inner world, for it is indeed the incantation, poetically inseparable from the intuition, that immerses the reader and transmits to him on a nonconceptual level something of the poet's experience of that world.

Besides the density of vowel and consonant correspondence, the poet utilizes repetition of whole words within single lines: "sans," "instant," "dans," "vers," "ferais," "comme," "voix." The web of sound has a warp as well as a woof, and vertical echoes are as profuse as horizontal: "ferais-je" (1, 6, 10;) "monde," "onde," "ombre" (1, 4, 5; here the less poetic "monde" gets two assists); "s'engloutissent," "gouffre des murmures," "amour" (5, 6, 7); "ferais . . . gouffre," "furieux" (6, 7); "qui s'élève," "de ses lests" (8, 9); "hui," "vie" (10, 12); and "voix," "moi" (14, 15). Probably, however, the dominant tone in the tapestry of sound is the dark nasal, which is present and often repeated in thirteen of the fifteen lines of the poem. The interruption (9-10) in the pattern of nasals reflects the passage from part one to part two, from one world to the other. In the second section the nasals cluster about the key word "pantin," preparing its way and prolonging its effect. In the first they are the mainstay of a remarkably homogenous phonetic and semantic group including nearly all the key words ("sans," "monde," "instant," "onde," "fin," "silence") with the notable exceptions of "ciel" and "poussière." These two (as well as "silence") benefit from the support of the numerous *s*'s they attract to themselves. The *s* sound functions very effectively in line 1, drops off in the next three lines, and comes back strongly in the last five lines of part one. Of the thirty-two unvoiced *s*'s in the poem, five occur in line 1, five reinforce the *s* sounds of "silence" (5, 6), and six crowd around "ciel" and "poussière" in lines 8 and 9: a total of twenty. In part two there are only six *s*'s, three associated with solitude in the last part of

246

line 11 and three with the notions of negation and lifeless space in the words "espace pantin / sans." Rarely in Beckett's best poems does a word that is semantically crucial find itself phonetically isolated.

Beckett on Life and Art

Analysis of the poems has brought us to a point where the poet should perhaps be allowed to speak directly in his own behalf. During conversations in 1961 and 1962 Beckett frequently expressed himself on his activity as a writer and its relation to his existence as a human being. In the following pages I transcribe some of his remarks as they were recorded in notes taken during these conversations. They fill out and make explicit views that in the poems are often no more than underlying assumptions or fugitive allusions. The poems help us to understand the origin and development of these views and show us something of their aesthetic potential, but they come to full flower only in the later novels and the plays.

An image Beckett used repeatedly to express his sense of the unreality of life on the surface was "existence by proxy." Very often one is unable to take a single step without feeling that someone else is taking the step. Going through the motions, "being absent," are common experiences. This notion led him to describe a schizophrenic in a London mental institution where, like Murphy, he worked for a time. The patient seemed like a lump of meat. There was no one there. He was absent. On another occasion he made an association between this feeling and the idealist philosophy of Berkeley. Perhaps it was an Irish thing, basically a skepticism before nature as given, complicated by a skepticism about the perceiving subject as well. Along with this sense of existence by proxy goes "an unconquerable intuition that being is so unlike what one is standing up," an intuition of "a presence, embryonic, undeveloped, of a self that might have been but never got born, an *être manqué*."

Beckett spoke also of the attempt to find this lost self in images of getting down, getting below the surface, concentrating, listening, getting your ear down so you can hear the infinitesimal murmur. There is a gray struggle, a groping in the dark for a shadow. On another occasion he said the encounter was like meeting oneself, like approaching home. And then one comes face to face with one's stupidities, one's obscenities, and one becomes convinced of the

247

authentic weakness of being. In a sense Beckett's 1957 radio play *All That Fall* is a parable about this abortive being. It is Minnie, the little girl that Mrs. Rooney lost. It is the dying child of whom the "mind doctor" says, "The trouble with her was she had never been really born!"[21] And finally, it is the little child that fell out of the train in which Mr. Rooney was riding and disappeared under its wheels.

Even when Beckett succeeds in getting beneath the surface, a prerequisite to writing, the problem is far from solved. With both object and subject, nature and agent, called into question, materials are lacking. "What complicates it all is the need to make. Like a child in mud but no mud. And no child. Only need." At this point I take the liberty of inserting an important related passage from *Murphy*:

> Then this [an after-image of Mr. Endon's finery] also faded and Murphy began to see nothing, that colourlessness which is such a rare postnatal treat, being the absence (to abuse a nice distinction) not of *percipere* but of *percipi*. His other senses also found themselves at peace, an unexpected pleasure. Not the numb peace of their own suspension, but the positive peace that comes when the somethings give way, or perhaps simply add up, to the Nothing, than which in the guffaw of the Abderite naught is more real. Time did not cease, that would be asking too much, but the wheel of rounds and pauses did, as Murphy with his head among the armies [on the chessboard] continued to suck in, through all the posterns of his withered soul, the accidentless One-and-Only, conveniently called Nothing. Then this also vanished, or perhaps simply came asunder, in the familiar variety of stenches, asperities, ear-splitters and eye-closers, and Murphy saw that Mr. Endon was missing. (p. 246)

In Murphy's microcosm and in the interior world evoked in the last two poems discussed, perception does not cease, but the usual objects perceived by the senses dissolve into a positive nothingness. Repeated experiences of passage from one world into another, from an "espace pantin" into a "monde sans visage," increase one's sense of the unreality of these dissolving objects (of which the subject himself, as inhabitant of the physical world, is one). But the bric-a-

[21] *All That Fall*, pp. 50-52.

brac of the macrocosm normally furnishes the materials of poetry. If the conditions of creation exist only in the microcosm, can the nothing serve as material? "Insofar as one *is*, there is no material," said Beckett. If one remains at this deep level of the need to make, one can't perceive objects, one is shut away from the world. In this realm "the writer is like a foetus trying to do gymnastics." This collision between a need to make and a lack of materials accounts for a characteristic quality in the writing of Beckett's maturity.

The problem of the absence of materials extends to language and form, both of which are associated with the macrocosm. "Joyce believed in words. All you had to do was rearrange them and they would express what you wanted." Beckett, however, has less confidence in language. "If you really get down to the disaster, the slightest eloquence becomes unbearable. Whatever is said is so far from experience." Beckett's dilemma is almost the dilemma of expressing the inexpressible. The need to express is as real as the obstacles to expression. On one occasion Beckett said, "I write because I have to," and added, "What do you do when 'I can't' meets 'I must'?" He admitted to using words where words are illegitimate. "At that level you break up words to diminish shame. Painting and music have so much better a chance."

On the other hand, he vigorously denied that his enterprise had anything at all to do with surrealist formlessness. At this deeper level "there is a form, but it doesn't move, stand upright, have hands. Yet it must have its form. Being *has* a form. Someone will find it someday. Perhaps I won't, but someone will. It is a form that has been abandoned, left behind, a proxy in its place." While the situation of a writer caught in such a dilemma is a distressing one, it also has about it the excitement of exploration and discovery. "Being," according to Beckett, has been excluded from writing in the past. The attempt to expand the sphere of literature to include it, which means eliminating the artificial forms and techniques that hide and violate it, is the adventure of modern art. Someday someone will find an adequate form, a "syntax of weakness." Beckett has too anguished a sense of the tremendous gulf between words and reality, art and being, too keen an awareness of the temptations and risks of language to underestimate the difficulty of the undertaking or overestimate what has so far been achieved. ("I can't let my left hand know what my right hand is doing. There is a danger of rising

249

up into rhetoric. Speak it even and pride comes. Words are a form of complacency.") Yet for his readers the task has surely been accomplished by Samuel Beckett. No one has succeeded as he has in winning for literature lands as strange and unknown as those conquered only in recent years by music and painting.

Part 2 • The Early Fiction and Criticism:
Apprenticeship and Vision

INTRODUCTION

In the preceding pages we have dealt with the poems in French and in English that Beckett permitted to be republished. They cover the period that extends from 1929 to 1948, from *Whoroscope* to the last poems in French. While we have been concerned above all with individual poems, which we have attempted to illuminate chiefly by formal analysis and only in a very limited way through recourse to biographical information, we have sought at the same time to discover within the poems the main lines of an evolution, both in form and in meaning. In the following chapters the focus will be rather less on the poem as an artistic entity and more on central preoccupations, both thematic and aesthetic, that appear both in the poems and the prose and that are of decisive importance in the masterpieces of Beckett's maturity. We will not, as in Part 1, trace a gradual evolution covering a span of some twenty years, but rather will place in sharp juxtaposition (1) the literary beginnings that include unpublished and "not-to-be-republished" poems and fiction, some of which antedate *Whoroscope*, and (2) the last of the works written before Beckett's adoption of the French language, in which the major novels and plays that brought him worldwide renown during the fifties first appeared.[1] Such a juxtaposition should bring into clear relief the distance traversed from the first start (in English) to the second (in French) and allow us to measure the part of influence and the part of originality in Beckett's philosophical position and literary production.

[1] Since life is never as neatly organized as art, we shall include, for the sake of generic completeness, all the known reviews and essays, which stretch from the late twenties into the fifties, and which in the latter years are written in French.

vi. *Fictional Elaboration of Some Early Poems*

THE BELACQUA PROSE
AND *ECHO'S BONES*

As we read Beckett's unpublished first novel "Dream of Fair to Middling Women" (written in the summer of 1932) and the stories assembled and elaborated from it and published in 1934 as *More Pricks Than Kicks*,[1] we quickly realize that words, phrases, lines, even whole paragraphs were lifted from these sources and utilized in the collection of poems called *Echo's Bones* (1935). An examination of these correspondences illuminates not only the poetry but Beckett's life and psychology at the time. At the basic level of vocabulary, the kinship between "Dream" and "Enueg I," for example, is striking. "Fetid head" ("Dream," p. 15) recalls the line "in my skull the wind going fetid." "Belacqua sprained the rim of his belly" (p. 33) is an allusion to Democritus, who in the poem is found "scuttling along between a crutch and a stick." "Algor" (p. 75) calls up "algum-trees." "Bleeding like a banner" (p. 88) repeats "the banner of meat bleeding." "The gulls . . . are grey slush in the spewing meatus of the sewer" (p. 139) suggests "a slush of vigilant gulls in the grey spew of the sewer." "Throttled west" (p. 155) is very close to "a black west / throttled with clouds." The unusual term "cang" (p. 167) occurs in both novel and poem. In "Dream" the rain falls upon "the champaign-land and the mountains" (p. 213), recalling the "travesty of champaign to the mountains" in the poem. Some of the above phrases occur also in *More Pricks Than Kicks*, and this work furnishes additional examples of coincidence of vocabulary. In the story "A Wet Night" we read "a

[1] The collection has not been republished since this original London edition by Chatto and Windus (hereafter cited as *MP*), which contains the following stories: "Dante and the Lobster," "Fingal," "Ding-Dong," "A Wet Night," "Love and Lethe," "Walking Out," "What a Misfortune," "The Smeraldina's Billet Doux," "Yellow," and "Draff." Page numbers given for these stories refer to the Chatto and Windus edition.

fungus of hopeless green" (p. 61), which parallels the lines "and the stillborn evening turning a filthy green / manuring the night fungus" and with the term "hopeless" comments at the same time on the symbolism of Beckett's off-colors. In the next story, "Walking Out," we find the "Enueg I" substantive "down and out" (p. 145), and the "pale wales" (p. 239) of dawn in the story "Yellow" suggest the wind's "weals" in the poem.

While the similarity of the vocabulary is revealing, it is considerably less important than cases of more extensive overlapping. The story "A Wet Night" contains a conversation between a character called the Polar Bear and a Jesuit. The latter concludes the conversation with the remark, "In just such a Gehenna of links I forged my vocation" (*MP*, p. 77), which recalls "its secret things" at the beginning of "Enueg I" and suggests again that for Beckett, hell exists in the here and now. It is in "Dream," however, that we find whole fragments of the poem:

"ENUEG I"	"DREAM"
and toil to the crest of the surge of the steep perilous bridge/ and lapse down blankly under the scream of the hoarding/ round the bright banner of the hoarding/ into a black west/ throttled with clouds./ Above the mansions the algum-trees/ the mountains/ my skull sullenly/ clot of anger/ skewered aloft strangled in the cang of the wind/ bites like a dog against its chastisement. (ll. 5-15)	There the wind was big and he was wise who stirred not at all, came not abroad. The man, Nemo, to be precise, was on his bridge, curved over the western parapet. High over the black water he leaned out, he let fall a foaming spit, it fell plumb to the top of the arch, then was scattered, by the Wild West Wind. He moved off left to the end of the bridge, he lapsed down blankly on to the quay, where the bus rank is, he set off sullenly, his head sullenly, a clot of anger, skewered aloft, strangled in the cang of the wind, biting like a dog against its chastisement. (p. 48)

255

and the stillborn evening
turning a filthy green/
manuring the night
fungus . . . the great
mushy toadstool,/ green-
black,/ oozing up after
me,/ soaking up the
tattered sky like an ink
of pestilence. . . .

(ll. 26-27, 55-58)

. . . when Nemo is in position, when Night has its
nasty difficult birth all
over the sheets of dusk. . . .

(p. 155)

Behind him, spouting
and spouting from the grey
sea, the battalions of night,
devouring the sky, soaking
up the tattered sky, like an
ink of pestilence. The city
would be hooded, dusk would
be harried from the city.

(p. 25)

The following paragraph is punctuated by phrases indicating that
the walk through Dublin is similar if not identical to the one
described in the poem:

the Isolde Stores a great
perturbation of sweaty
heroes,/ in their Sunday
best,/ come hastening down
for a pint of nepenthe or
moly or half and half/
from watching the hurlers
above in Kilmainham.

(ll. 65-68)

From the bridge . . . as far
as the Park Gates. . . . At
Island Bridge . . . at
Chapelizod. . . . The snug
chez Isolde was a great
perturbation of sweaty heroes
come hastening down from
watching the hurlers above in
Kilmainham in time for a pint
of nepenthe or moly or half-
and-half.

(p. 25)

The question of suicide, which is hinted at in lines 69-71 of the
poem, is taken up in considerable detail on pages 162-164 of
"Dream." There we find also a reference to the Fox and Geese
(mentioned in line 62 of the poem) and the pub below Kilmainham,
which is described in these words: "Belacqua took cognisance of
this corpulent reportage on his way home from the Fox and Geese
over cheese and porter in the tabernacle of a wayfarers' public near
the Island Bridge that has since been destroyed and consumed
utterly by brimstone the bishops all say." "Enueg I" ends with a

vision of the Liffey and a quote from Rimbaud. The corresponding fictional fragment comes to a more prosaic close: "There [in the pub] he would have one or two and then he would tram back and go to the pictures, he would slip into the womb of the Grand Central burning on the waterside, and then he would crawl back home across the cobbles and his heart is a stone" (p. 25). The elements of "Enueg I" are scattered through the novel and the stories, where their effect is considerably diluted, if not wholly destroyed, by the self-conscious verbal horseplay that mars both works but especially the earlier "Dream." In the poem these elements are fused into a relatively sober unity. The poet increases the effectiveness of the somber funeral lament by his use of the first person. In the poem it is no longer the half-pitiful, half-comic Belacqua speaking but someone closer to the author himself.

Most of the early poems have fragments in common with the early prose, and parallel passages often help to elucidate details in the verse, but only for "Dortmunder" and "Alba" does the prose significantly extend the meaning of the poetry. Stripped to its essence, "Dream of Fair to Middling Women" is a discourse on love. It takes a fictional form in which there are three main characters: Belacqua, in part a figure of the young Beckett and in part his imaginative extension into the realm of might-have-been, and two girls, modeled in a similar way on women that Beckett knew and loved in real life but stylized in his writing until they come to represent diametrically opposed possibilities. Roughly speaking, one is a type of the physical and the other of the intellectual. Biographically, "Dream" covers the two-year period in Paris when Beckett was a *lecteur* at the Ecole Normale, the two academic years 1928-1930. He had received his degree from Trinity College at the end of the spring term in 1928. Later that summer he spent about a month in Germany (late August to late September). In the story, he meets the Smeraldina-Rima in Germany. Ten days in Germany during Christmas vacation 1928 correspond to a similar visit by Belacqua. Beckett spent the summer of 1929, following the first year at the Ecole Normale, in Ireland and in Germany. In the novel he meets the other girl, the Alba, during that summer in Ireland. During the summer of 1930 Beckett remained in Paris and wrote *Proust*. As we recall, he spent 1930-1931 teaching at Trinity and resigned after the fall term of 1931-1932, spending the next six months of 1932 in Germany. It was in Paris at the Trianon Hotel, on the Rue de Vaugirard near its junction with the Boulevard St. Michel, that he wrote "Dream of Fair to Middling Women" during the summer of 1932.

"Dortmunder" is related to the German experience and indirectly to the Smeraldina-Rima and the Alba. The vocabulary and allusions of the poem recur in "Dream": "the Homer dusk" (pp. 25, 155), "the magic, the Homer dust of the dawn-dusk" (p. 28), "plagal" (p. 43), "Schopenhauer" (p. 55), "K'in music" (p. 101), "the magic hour, the magic tragic prépuscule" (p. 155). In *More Pricks Than Kicks*, too, we find the evening hour poetically evoked in such expressions as the "Homer hour" (pp. 64, 268). Moving beyond the simple correspondence of vocabulary and considering the crucial lines of "Dortmunder"—"the eyes the eyes black till the plagal east/ shall resolve the long night phrase"— we are led to the story "Walking Out." In this sixth episode in the adventures of Belacqua as recounted in *More Pricks* the reader learns that the hero is on occasion given to voyeurism. Lucy, his betrothed, suspects as much, but before her suspicions can be confirmed she is crippled when the horse she is riding is struck by an automobile. For Belacqua at least, all ends well. The lover he had suggested Lucy should take after their marriage will no longer be necessary, thanks to her accident. Belacqua can settle down to enjoy undisturbed the quasi-mystical experience for which her presence is a prerequisite. "What a Misfortune" is taken from the Italian lines of Voltaire's *Candide* (Chapter XI): "Che sciagura d'essere senza coglioni."[2] In this story we learn that Lucy lived on only two more years, no doubt as a result of the accident, and that "Belacqua [began] to feel more and more the lack of those windows on to better worlds that Lucy's big black eyes had been" (p. 163). During the story this is remedied when he meets another girl, Thelma bboggs, and eventually marries her. The story ends as they leave for a honeymoon in Connemara. Their concluding conversation as they drive toward the West sums up in symbolic form the tension between physical and "ideal" love that makes Belacqua what he is. He asks Thelma whether she has ever heard of a "babylan" (a pagan priest, priestess, or medium in the central and south Philippines). Unfortunately she has not. This particular attempt to

[2] Beckett published a fictional dialogue on contraception in the Trinity College newspaper (14 November 1929) entitled "Che Sciagura" and signed D.E.S.C.

explain his view of woman as the key that opens the gate to his visionary paradise fails. She asks if a babylan is something to eat. He replies, ". . . you're thinking of a baba." In its Polish origins "baba" had the meaning of "old woman," and elsewhere in the stories Beckett calls Belacqua a combination of old woman and ephebe. Our hero gives up for the moment his attempt to explain his double nature, closes his eyes, and sees "clearer than ever before, the mule, up to its knees in mire, and astride its back a beaver, flogging it with a wooden sword" (p. 214). Belacqua's vision refers to the legend of the beaver hunted for its testicles, which were used in the making of perfume. According to tradition the beaver would cut them off in order to save its life. As we shall see in a moment, Belacqua has reason to fear the physicality of woman, and in his vision he obviously identifies himself with the pursued creature whose escape is impeded by the mire in which his sterile mount is bogged down (Thelma's last name, we recall, is bboggs). A final bit of erotic symbolism ends the story. Thelma had asked for the little flower Belacqua wore in his buttonhole. She had hoped to keep it forever. " 'Your veronica,' she said, 'that I wanted so much, where is it gone?' . . . Alas! the tassel had drooped, wormed its stem out of the slit, fallen to the ground and been trodden underfoot."

Belacqua's peculiar combination of virility and microcosmic sublimation is most frankly explained and developed not in *More Pricks Than Kicks* but in the earlier work "Dream of Fair to Middling Women." In the first part of that work Belacqua falls in love with the Smeraldina-Rima because of her beautiful eyes and face. To his later sorrow, he fails to note beneath the tiny head (which, characteristically, he assimilates to a Pisanello portrait) a body that is all ardent, ripe physicality. "Because her body was all wrong . . . Poppata, big breech, Botticelli thighs . . . mammose, slobbery-blubbery . . . a real button-bursting Weib, ripe. Then, perched aloft on top of this porpoise prism, the loveliest little pale firm cameo of a birdface he ever clapped his blazing blue eyes on" (p. 12). Belacqua is happy in his world of art and platonic ecstasies—that is, "until she rape[s] him" (p. 15). From then on the affair becomes a "gehenna of sweats and fiascos and tears" (p. 16).

To appreciate fully the significance of what happens in "Dream" we must realize that Belacqua is among other things a figure of the poet. At the entrance to Dante's purgatory the indolent Belacqua sits dreaming his life over again. It is this detached contemplation, so crucial for the poet, that Beckett's Belacqua seeks and from which he is kept on a number of occasions by the passionate advances of less than ethereal and definitely predatory females. When gazing into the eyes of the Smeraldina (p. 84) has given way to more prurient pastimes, Belacqua's curious solution is the brothel (p. 94). Yet this is understandable, for if it necessitates a physical starting point, it also allows for contemplation without engagement. This is the situation in "Dortmunder." With the satisfaction of physical desire ("the scarred signacuum of purity quiet" [7]), and music aiding, other worlds may be glimpsed in black eyes. The expression "to look babies at him" recurs a number of times in the prose works. Belacqua's contemplation, then, has narcissistic overtones, for he sees himself in miniature in the eyes of his partner. At the same time the brothel has its disadvantages, as a very important passage in "Dream" (pp. 33-38) makes clear. After his stay in Germany, Belacqua, like Beckett, returns to Paris, where he spends the money that comes from home (Ireland) on "concerts, cinemas, cocktails, theatres, apéritifs" but not on opera nor "after a bit on brothels" (p. 32).

Following on the heels of the brothel solution in Germany, this aboutface requires some explanation, as the author realizes. He begins his six-page apologia for his hero's actions with two phrases: "love condones . . . narcissism" (p. 33), and "love demands narcissism" (p. 34). He then proceeds to assert that the "mystical experience" is available as well from the whore as from the Smeraldina.[8] The physical act nullifies both desire and the girl and makes possible the spiritual vision: "The usual over, its purveyor null as before, there began the other outpour, streaming into the parched sanctuary, a gracious strength and virtue, a flow of bounty" (pp. 35-36). Unfortunately, Belacqua at this stage insists on maintaining both the idealization of the girl and his inner experience. Since the same inner experience can be evoked by the girl or the prostitute, the former tends to be assimilated to the latter, to be de-idealized and degraded in his mind. So he abandons the brothel. But since the ecstasy of spirit can be released only through the flesh, he adopts

[8] The terms used in the pages following these (pp. 35-36)—"sanctuary," "banquet of music," "gift of magic from her," "red-lamp," "Beatrice lurked in every brothel," "null," "bounty"—coincide with those in "Sanies I," "Alba," and "Dortmunder," the poems in *Echo's Bones* that are most directly concerned with the relationship between physical and ideal love.

in its place "a fraudulent system of Platonic manualization, chiro-platonism" (p. 37) while postulating the physical encounter with the Smeraldina.[4] In this way she alone remains associated with the inner vision. The sex act (in imagination together with her, in fact alone) is used only as a springboard. This is what the author terms Belacqua's "certain system of narcissistic manoeuvres" (p. 34). In a similar way, the object for the poet must be obliterated in one way or another in order to be possessed spiritually.[5]

The experience of physical love, the microcosm of the mind, and art, especially music, are of central importance not only in "Dort-munder" but also in "Alba." In "Dream" the girl called the Alba is directly associated with Belacqua's experience of his "womb-tomb." When the physicality of the Smeraldina, "like collops of pork gone greasy" (p. 99), begins to nauseate Belacqua, he turns to the Alba, to whom Beckett refers in the words of "Dortmunder": "the eyes the eyes black till the plagal east shall resolve the long night-phrase" (p. 99). Later he writes, "Many a time had Belacqua, responding to the obscure need to verbalize a wombtombing . . . , murmured a syllable or two of incantation: . . . 'Before morning you shall be here . . .'" (p. 131). This is the opening line of the poem entitled "Alba," which, as other passages from "Dream" demonstrate conclusively, is meant to be exactly that: a verbal representation of the experience of the microcosm, growing out of the need to make with words, the need specific to the artist. Apropos of a picnic shared by Belacqua and the Alba, another term from the poem is used. Belacqua interprets the actions of two gulls moving around a sandwich on the sand as a love-game. "They were not hungry, they were man and wife." "Alas," writes Beckett, "cang of emblem" (p. 167). In the poem, too, the girl is a sign set against the emblem, or intellectual symbol. Her beauty is "a statement of itself drawn across the tempest of emblems" that are the stock in trade of the macrocosmic mind. For Belacqua the Alba will "remain quite useless and beautiful, like the very best music that could be had." He does not propose "to Blake her" or "plaster [her] with . . . tempests" (p. 172). Beckett associates the girl with music in the

---

[4] Cf. "no fingers no spoilt love" in "Sanies I."

[5] See above the discussion of destruction and creation (pp. 114-115) and in the final chapter the consideration of the influence of Proust, in whose analysis the object, apparently consigned to oblivion by the screening action of practical reason, is resurrected by involuntary memory and fixed forever as the "ideal real" in the work of art.

poem, as well, and refuses to trade the experience of her mysterious beauty, which is akin to the experience of the microcosm that art makes possible, for an abstract counter in a mystical or theological system. She will not be his Beatrice. If he will not Blake her in the prose, he will not Dante her in the poem.[6] Earlier in "Dream" her mere name, tossed off during a conversation, provokes a Proustian response in Belacqua: "It was the miracle . . . taking him down from his pangs, sheathing him in the cerements of clarity. It was the descent and the enwombing, assumption upside down . . . the hush and indolence of Limbo in his mind . . . , lounging against the will-pricks. It was the mercy of salve on the prurigo of living . . ." (p. 162). Immediately upon this passage follows another that amounts to a first version of the poem to the Alba in *Echo's Bones*, a poem that attempts to put into words the experience of release into a kind of absence that is at the same time a mysterious presence, the experience of an extratemporal reality.

> Plane of white music, warpless music expunging the tempest of emblems, calm womb of dawn whelping no sun, no lichen of sun-rising on its candid parapets, still flat white music, alb of timeless light. It is a blade before me, it is a sail of bleached silk on a shore, impassive statement of itself drawn across the strata and symbols, lamina of peace for my eyes and my brain slave of my eyes, pressing and pouring itself whiteness and music through blindness into the limp mind. It is the dawn-foil and the gift of blindness and the mysteries of bulk banished and the mind swathed in the music and candour of the dawn-foil, facts of surface. The layers of Damask fused and drawn to the uttermost layer, silken blade. Blind and my mind blade of silk, blind and music and whiteness facts in the fact of my mind. Douceurs. . . .
>
> (p. 162)

Sooner or later someone is bound to apply Freud in an attempt to get at the psychological origins of Beckett's art. The evidence is not lacking. Belacqua's sexual reluctance, his voyeurism, his auto-

---

[6] In "Dream" the Alba has her say. She is far from wholly sympathetic to what she calls Belacqua's "pallor and umbilicism à deux." If she can become convinced she is right in thinking he is "too permanently selfish, faithful to himself . . . , inextricably Limbese, then that [is] where she step[s] off" (p. 173). Beckett is capable of self-criticism, or to put it in another way, Belacqua is only one fictional facet of a many-faceted Beckett.

eroticism are not without correlation to the use he makes of the brothel in "Dortmunder" and the Alba in the poem by that name. In both cases woman is no more than a pretext. "Dream" begins with a vision of Belacqua as an "overfed child" fascinated with buttocks, surprised "climbing trees in the country and in the town sliding down the rope in the gymnasium." The Alba calls him *niño* and the Smeraldina dreams he turns into a baby. He appreciates women only when he can associate them with art. Masturbation plus imagination appear preferable, in his view, to the brothel.

The year Beckett published *More Pricks Than Kicks* he also gave to the public a short story entitled "A Case in a Thousand,"[7] in which one Dr. Nye, "a sad man," delves into his own past in an attempt to discover the origins of his melancholy, which he considers not "as natural and proper" but "as a disorder." Chance brings him into contact with his old nanny, Mrs. Bray, whose sick child Dr. Nye is unable to save. Eventually she relates to him "a matter connected with his earliest years, so trivial and intimate that it need not be enlarged on here, but from the elucidation of which Dr. Nye, that sad man, expected great things." Another line in the story helps to elucidate matters for the reader: " 'Yes,' said Mrs. Bray, 'you were always in a great hurry to grow up so's you could marry me,' but did not disclose the trauma at the root of this attachment." Here and elsewhere in Beckett's early writing, we find hints of the child's erotic attachment to a mother figure, an attachment which later partially interferes with normal heterosexual relationships. This story ends on the suggestion of a contrast between Dr. Nye and "an old schoolfellow" who has other problems. Dr. Nye leaves to "carry out Wassermann's test" on him. At the same time, Mrs. Bray leaves "to go and pack up her things and the dead boy's things," which she had been unable to do before her confession to Dr. Nye. Now, finally, her vigil outside the hospital ends. Her own boy is buried, and the child who continued to live on in Dr. Nye, arresting his emotional and sexual development, has been laid to rest. The imagery of the story supports such an interpretation and, further, suggests links between Belacqua's limbo and Murphy's microcosm on the one hand and on the other a journey back through time in the direction of the womb to try to recover a lost child, who himself longed perhaps to recover the lost Eden of the prenatal state. Dr. Nye needs the help of Mrs. Bray, and like a good Freudian

[7] In *The Bookman*, 86 (August 1934), 241-242.

ponders the proposition, "Myself I cannot save." He hears "the distant furious crying of a child," no doubt unhappy at having been born! Watching from the hospital a group of people observing a barge pass through the canal lock, he notes that they have crossed over to the near side, "with the result, most pleasing to [him], that where formerly he had seen their faces, now he enjoyed a clear view of their buttocks, male and female." Most important, however, is the following passage that clearly associates Dr. Nye and Mrs. Bray's son and suggests an inner experience that is almost a communion with a lost self, symbolized by the sick boy.

> He took hold of the boy's wrist, stretched himself all along the edge of the bed and entered the kind of therapeutic trance that he reserved for such happily rare dilemmas.
>
> Mrs. Bray, noting the expression, at once aghast and rapt, that overcame his face, was moved in a number of ways: to trouble, at such dissolution of feature; to gratification that at last she saw him as she could remember him; to shame, as the memory grew defined; to embarrassment, as though intruding on a privacy or a face asleep.

Equivocal erotic attitudes, infantilism, nostalgia for the womb are of course motifs that run through the later works too. In "L'Expulsé," one of the 1945 *nouvelles*, to take a single example, the protagonist says, "j'abhorre les enfants," and of a particular child he asserts, "Je l'aurais écrasé avec joie . . . ç'aurait été d'ailleurs lui rendre service . . ." (*Nouvelles et textes pour rien*, p. 22). He notes that the coachman's wife is "extraordinairement fessue" (p. 37), and speculates that a woman who sent him money might have been the object of his infantile eroticism: "Peut-être qu'elle m'avait pris sur ses genoux quand j'étais encore dans les langes et que je lui avais fait des mamours. Cela suffit quelquefois. Je dis bien, dans les langes, car plus tard ç'aurait été trop tard, pour les mamours" (pp. 29-30). While the term "mamour" derives from "mon amour" through "m'amour," the present context clearly makes another association: between *mam(an)* and *(am)our*. Finally, the "expulsé" of the title is a man ejected from the room he rented, but this room is clearly a figure for the womb that sent him forth into life—the French verb used is "émettre" (p. 16): "Je regardai au troisième et dernier étage ma fenêtre, outrageusement ouverte. Le nettoyage à fond battait son plein. Dans quelques heures on refermerait la fenêtre, on tirerait les rideaux et on procéderait à une pulverisation au formol. Je les connaissais. Je serais volontiers mort dans cette maison. Je vis, dans une sorte de vision, la porte s'ouvrir et mes pieds sortir" (p. 17). Earlier, in fact, the narrator had made a similar association between this room (and all the others he had known) and "le berceau [et] le tombeau" (p. 16). Later he confesses, "je n'admettais en fait de meubles, dans ma chambre, que le lit, et qu'il fallait en retirer tous les autres, et jusqu'à la table de nuit, avant que je consente à y mettre les pieds" (p. 33). The search for a "womb-tomb," an unfurnished, quiet, sheltered, isolated place reproducing as nearly as possible the privileged prenatal conditions goes on through both "L'Expulsé" and the third *nouvelle*, "La Fin."

An ambiguous attitude toward love is apparent in a number of the poems: in "Cascando" in a line like "if you do not teach me I shall not learn" or in the very pattern of alternation, "knowing not knowing," or in the suggestion of love's unreality in "pretending"; in the poems "elles viennent" and "être là . . . ," where the phenomena of sameness, repetition, and boredom rob amorous reality of its substance; in "Sanies I" in the tension between the image of sneering fauns and nymphs and the image of the bicycle rider as pederast or in the opposition between platonic love and sensual love in the erotic pun "her whom alone . . . / I have dismounted to love" (which recalls the androgynous "concierge" of the *Whoroscope* joke). The examples of equivocation, with desire and indifference in the scales, could be multiplied, but—and this is important—not only in the realm of Eros but also when it comes to a choice between society and solitude ("Gnome," "bois seul," "musique de l'indifférence," "bon bon il est un pays," "que ferais-je . . . ," and elsewhere).

Similar concerns are present in later works. In the 1957 radio play *All That Fall*, for example, Mr. Rooney asks, "Did you ever wish to kill a child? Nip some young doom in the bud" (p. 74). He refers to "Dante's damned, with their faces arsy-versy" and adds, "Our tears will water our bottoms" (pp. 74-75). Mr. Rooney has his womb-tomb too, his "silent, backstreet, basement office, with its obliterated plate, rest-couch and velvet hangings." "Nothing . . . ," he asserts, "not even fully certified death, can ever take the place of that" (p. 79).[8] Mrs. Rooney tells of attending "a lecture by one

[8] Later Mrs. Rooney refers to a "hot-cupboard" (p. 87) in which they hang wet clothes, and we are reminded of the microcosm image of *Whoroscope*, the *poêle* of Descartes.

265

of these new mind doctors" in the hope "he might shed a little light on [her] lifelong preoccupation with horses' buttocks" (p. 83). As mentioned above, the doctor tells her a story of a little girl who is dying for no apparent reason except, as he suddenly exclaims "as if he had had a revelation," that "she had never been really born!" (p. 84).[9] Once again the motif of sterility—linked here to religion —appears in the discussion: "Can hinnies procreate, I wonder? . . . You know, hinnies, or jinnies, aren't they barren, or sterile, or whatever it is? . . . Yes, it was a hinny, he rode into Jerusalem or wherever it was on a hinny. That must mean something" (pp. 85-86). At the end of *All That Fall* a messenger boy returns to Mr. Rooney a lost object, which he refuses to identify. Mrs. Rooney notes that "it looks like a kind of ball. And yet it is not a ball," and we may speculate that it is another of Beckett's eggs (cf., for example, those in *Whoroscope* and *Happy Days*). In *All That Fall*, in any case, it seems to be an analogue of the image on which the play ends. The messenger reveals what Mr. Rooney had not: that his train was late because "a little child fell out of the carriage . . . On to the line . . . Under the wheels . . ." (pp. 89-91).

It would be unusual, even allowing for prerogatives of imagination and the necessities of fictional elaboration, if these persistent themes had no correlatives in the life of the author. Like Dr. Nye, Beckett had a nanny, one who refused to use the term "bottom" but substituted for it (as does the narrator in "Serena I") the euphemistic "btm." The Portobello Nursing Home on the Grand Canal in Dublin played an important part in the author's life as well as in "Enueg I," "A Case in a Thousand," and *Krapp's Last Tape*. Beckett knew of Freudian psychoanalysis at least by the early thirties, when he visited Bedlam (St. Mary of Bethlehem) in London, where a close friend from Trinity was working in preparation for a career as a psychiatrist (cf. *Murphy*). In Beckett's mind Italy (like Germany in "Dream") tends to be associated with physicality, while France (and Ireland in "Dream") suggests various forms of anti-physicality. His views on procreation and the lost self have already been noted. In her memoirs Peggy Guggenheim writes of Oblomov-

---

[9] Beckett used the identical expression during a 1962 conversation when he described his own sense of existing "by proxy," as an unreal being replacing a lost self, an "abortive" or "stunted" self, an "embryonic" being that was somehow kept from developing. See above, pp. 54-55, 247-248.

Beckett's amorous indecision, of his mistress who sounded "more like a mother than a mistress," and so on.[10]

However suggestive the case for psychological sources may be, we should be careful to avoid the temptation to reduce and oversimplify. Philosophy and art marked Beckett profoundly. Experience of the intellectual, literary, and artistic tradition may have been as important an influence on his writing as experience of "nature" (in the broadest sense). If we grant that the narrator in "L'Expulsé" is to some degree the voice of the author, then the warning against interpretation in terms of reductive psychological systems is clear enough. After laying his "rigidité de base" to a diaper-changing complex and explaining his "balancement désespéré du buste" as a compensation designed to create a false impression of nonchalance, gaiety, and high spirits and to render plausible a public posture ascribing this basal rigidity to "rhumatismes héréditaires," he continues as follows: "Mon ardeur juvénile, dans la mesure où j'en avais, s'y usa, je devins aigre, méfiant, un peu avant l'heure, fervent de la cachette et de la station horizontale. Pauvres solutions de jeunesse, qui n'expliquent rien. On n'a donc pas à se gêner. Ratiocinons sans crainte, le brouillard tiendra bon" (*Nouvelles et textes*, pp. 21-22). Whether or not such an approach, amusingly satirized in this passage, disperses any mists or not, Beckett's writings provide ample evidence that the subconscious of the author is in any case not the only possible source for the sexual dualism that we find in the poems and early prose works, where it is associated with the macrocosm and the microcosm, concepts developed in part at least under the philosophical influence not only of Schopenhauer but of Descartes, Geulincx, Berkeley, and others. In 1962 Beckett remarked that if he were a critic setting out to write on the works of Beckett (and he thanked heaven he was not), he would start with two quotations, one by Geulincx: "Ubi nihil valis ibi nihil velis," and one by Democritus: "Nothing is more real than nothing." The first suggests that to Murphy (and perhaps to a lesser extent to Beckett), the body, that part of him which exists in the macrocosm, is of negligible value. Indeed, it is primarily a source of suffering. And where no value is attached, no desire is possible. The quotation from Democritus refers to the reality of a "void

[10] *Out of This Century*, pp. 205-207; and *Confessions of an Art Addict* (New York: Macmillan, 1960).

that is filled with atoms. Beckett applies the words of the Greek philosopher to the microcosm of the mind. The first phrase, then, condemns external existence while the second proposes a truer inner reality. Similarly, Berkeley's "being is being perceived" ("*essere est percipi*"), discussed briefly above in connection with *Murphy*, is a key phrase in a radical idealism that stresses the mind of the subject and like Cartesian dualism relies on God to guarantee the objective reality of the macrocosm. The important final scene in *Murphy* shows the protagonist holding Mr. Endon's face close to his own and looking deep into his unseeing eyes. There Murphy perceives, "horribly reduced, obscured and distorted, his own image." He sees himself "stigmatized in those eyes that did not see him." Murphy's attempt to escape *being* in the macrocosm is a figure of the attempt to escape self-consciousness. Even should our self-image not be determined by the image others have of us, we are at the mercy of our own self-judgment. The crucifixion image implicit in "stigmatized" is one more among many examples of a recurrent figure that associates a suffering Christ with the protagonist. Being is being perceived, and being perceived is painful. We are crucified by others or by ourselves. Only when he can enter his unselfconscious inner world can Murphy find peace—an intermittent achievement at best. In his recent *Film* (1965) Beckett takes up again from the starting point in Berkeley. In a few lines at the beginning of his notes for the film, he sums things up: "*esse est percipi*. All extraneous perception suppressed, animal, human, divine, self-perception maintains in being. Search of non-being in flight from extraneous perception breaking down in inescapability of self-perception."

Credible psychological and equally credible philosophical sources for Beckett's writing are not lacking. Nonetheless, the more strictly artistic motivations are perhaps the most telling. Although Belacqua unquestionably has a good deal of Beckett in him, he is by no means simply a psychological self-portrait. The author makes the point in the story "Ding-Dong" when he says, "I know all this because he [Belacqua] told me. We were Pylades and Orestes for a period, flattened down to something very genteel; but the relation abode and was highly confidential while it lasted. I have witnessed every stage of the exercise. . . . He was an impossible person in the end. I gave him up in the end because he was not *serious*" (*MP*, pp. 44-46). Any attempt to determine exactly to what degree Belacqua is a creation of the imagination would be futile. If we remain within the character himself and abandon the referential point of view, it immediately becomes apparent that his erotic eccentricities are more a function of his poetic nature than the reverse. In the course of the stories we learn that Belacqua is indeed a poet, but we hardly need this information to realize that his is a highly developed artistic nature. In the story "Fingal," Winnie Coates is totally incapable of understanding that the landscape is meaningful to Belacqua not in itself but as poeticized by association with MacPherson's poems. The magic of the area around Portrane is dependent on the fact that Swift took his "motte," Stella, to a tower there.[11] The unremitting assimilation of natural reality to painting, literature, and music is a dominant and often exasperating characteristic of Belacqua's personality. Even buttocks are less a psychological than an artistic phenomenon:

> "The human bottom," he proceeded, "is extremely deserving of esteem, conferring as it does the faculty of assiduity. The great Lawgiver urged his pupils to cultivate an iron head and a leaden posterior. The Greeks, I need hardly tell you, entertained a high notion of its beauty; and the celebrated poet Rousseau worships in the temple of Venus Callipyge. The Romans bestowed upon the part the epithet of 'fair,' and many have thought it susceptible, not only of being beautiful, but even of being endowed with dignity and splendour. Thus M. Pavillon, academician, bel esprit and nephew of a bishop, in his noble *Métamorphose du Cul d'Iris en Astre*." ("Dream," p. 87)

Beckett describes Belacqua as follows: "At his simplest he was trine. . . . Centripetal, centrifugal and . . . not. Phoebus chasing Daphne, Narcissus flying from Echo and . . . neither" ("Dream," p. 107). Belacqua pursues the Smeraldina to Vienna, then escapes from her by retreating to Paris, where he immures himself in his "dark gulf . . . limbo . . . wombtomb." Reality is cast in terms of art, but the myths themselves suggest desire, beauty, *and* non-consummation. It is their elaboration in the microcosm, where imagination can be enjoyed and art fashioned, that interests Belacqua. In the myths we can find the universals of man's sexuality and his antisexuality, of action and contemplation, of the macrocosm

---

[11] We are reminded of the telling phrase in Beckett's *Proust*: "the infinite futility—for the artist—of all that is not art" (p. 51).

and the microcosm—which are also linked explicitly to Schopen-hauer's philosophy, Eros to will and struggle, Anteros to the con-templative ataraxy that is a condition of art. In "Serena III" the poet suggests that consummation with ensuing commitment can be a disaster for the artist: "or leave her she is paradise and then / plush hymens on your eyeballs." Sex can be a set of blinders, happi-ness a handicap for the thinker in search of understanding and the artist in need of experience and creative freedom. If he is to honor his commitment to art, he cannot allow life in the macrocosm to become an end in itself. It must be merely experience, materials for a poetic metamorphosis.

On page 22 of "Dream" we read: "it was not when he .. er .. held her in his arms, nor yet when he remained remote and shared, so to speak, her air and sensed her essence, but only when he sat down to himself in an approximate silence and had a vision on the strength of her or let fly a poem at her, anyhow felt some reality that somehow was she fidgeting in the catacombs of his spirit, that he had her truly and totally, according to his God." Exile, whether voluntary or involuntary, the death of those he loves, separation—all these are painful and at the same time necessary and desirable for the artist. They correspond to the aesthetic distance that is a prerequisite of art, and the suffering they bring is the price the artist must pay. Belacqua's onanism is only one of many forms of detachment that are figures of the detachment of the artist. While such a point of view is quite explicit in "Dream" and *More Pricks Than Kicks*, it is also present in *Echo's Bones*. We have only to remember the troubadour titles, the enuegs, the serenas, the alba, to realize that there is a profound link between Beckett and the Cathar poets of southern France, for whom the idealized lady is above all a catalytic agent crucial in the chemistry of the imagina-tion, which can produce the precipitates that are poetry. It is not Echo but Echo's bones, not the physical Smeraldina but her trans-muted image the poet seeks. Art, no less than love, demands narcis-sism. Belacqua puts the same dualism in terms of medieval romance when he suggests on several occasions that life is all "temptation and knighthood," and the same theme turns up unexpectedly many years later in "L'Expulsé" in the song of the *cocher de fiacre*: "Elle est loin du pays où son jeune héros dort" (*Nouvelles et textes*, p. 34). In the final analysis, a deterministic psychological explanation tends to enclose the poet in the prison of a too narrowly conceived nature and experience, allowing little room for imaginative freedom. Whatever its psychological origins, it is clear that the poet does not consider his "split personality" as an aberration to be remedied but as a condition to be exploited. Far from desiring to change it, he finds justifications in psychology for the dualism of macrocosm and microcosm, primarily because it provides the conditions under which his art may flourish. Surely for the artist the most meaningful correlative of the two worlds is material and form, experience metamorphosed by imagination into art.

vii. The Jettisoned Poems

The meaning and implications of "Alba" and "Dortmunder" become more readily accessible when these poems are juxtaposed with certain pasages of the early prose. This is true to a lesser degree of "Enueg II," the two sanies, the three serenas, "Malacoda," and *Whoroscope*—and to a still lesser degree of other poems in *Echo's Bones*. As might be expected, later poems in English and the poems in French are much less directly related to the early prose on the level of vocabulary. Themes from *all* the poems, however, are present in the early prose, and in Chapter VIII we shall give some attention to the more important thematic developments.

Besides the poems examined thus far there exist twelve others, which Beckett includes in what he calls his "jettisoned works," and which he declines to republish. Of the twelve, two—"Gnome" (1934) and "Ooftish" (1938)—have already been discussed. Seven others belong to the period of *Whoroscope* and were published in 1930 and 1931. One is an acrostic, "Home Olga," written to James Joyce and first published in 1934. Two others, "Calvary by Night" and a sonnet to the Smeraldina, appear in the unpublished "Dream of Fair to Middling Women," written in 1932. Both in spirit and chronologically the ten jettisoned poems we have yet to consider belong to the period of apprenticeship. Some of these were written before *Whoroscope* and are the best examples we have of Beckett's earliest style and preoccupations. Two final poems, printed in the Addenda to the novel *Watt*, belong to the end of the twenty-year period we are considering and illustrate even more effectively than the last French poems the concerns and art that will prevail in the writing of Beckett's maturity. They will be discussed in Chapter IX.

Many of the jettisoned poems are directly related to the prose. In those that take us back to *Whoroscope* and earlier, we find the familiar predominance of virtuosity, verbal play, and literary and artistic allusion. Most of these poems are divorced from substantial and significant human experience, and more specifically they are not marked by the suffering felt so often in the poems of *Echo's Bones*. They are important because the incipient artist is everywhere evident in them. At that time Beckett was a young man fascinated with ideas and in love with literature, a being for whom the reality of words and the possibilities of language were at least as absorbing as the world outside. Like Joyce, Beckett was a gifted "wordman." His meeting and acquaintance with the master in Paris during the years when he was a *lecteur* at the *Ecole Normale* heightened this natural predisposition.

The Beckett of today is severe in his judgment of the young poet in his twenties. He either dismisses the poems as worthless or with a great effort at impartiality describes them as "the work of a very young man with nothing to say and the itch to make." He deplores their self-consciousness and display of literary and artistic erudition, which he terms "showing off." Still, we have only to read *Transition* during those years to realize that verbal play plus semigratuitous allusiveness was in fashion. And, of course, the work of Eliot, Pound, and Joyce was hardly free of such "flaws." The personal element in Beckett's "Hell Crane to Starling" (more a lecherous leer than the recalled emotion of authentic experience) is all but submerged by the Biblical and Dantesque materials used by the poet. "Calvary by Night" conceals elements of poetic authenticity by masquerading (more effectively in the second than in the first version) as part of a larger satire directed against the "homespun" Irish poet. Although the satirical element is somewhat less evident in Belacqua's sonnet to the Smeraldina, the context is less than conducive to aesthetic contemplation. "Home Olga," written to Joyce, is the young poet's farewell to Joycean virtuosity, but it is written in the virtuoso mode. "Text" leans heavily on Proust, the mythology of *Tiresias*, the Bible, and Dante; "Return to the Vestry" on Ronsard; "From the Only Poet to a Shining Whore" on Dante and the Bible; and "Casket of Pralinen" on Beaumarchais, the Bible, Dahlberg, Proust, Wordsworth, and others. In this last poem, after allowing himself a fleeting exposure of heart and mind, the poet writes: "Melancholy Christ that was a soft one! / Oh yes I think that was perhaps just a very little inclined to be rather too self-conscious." He is all too keenly aware of his reliance on materials of the literary tradition and his lack of a personal stake in his own writing, and he both adores and abhors the verbal play that is art in a vacuum. Confessing as much at one point in "Casket of Pralinen," he writes: "Oh I am ashamed / of all clumsy artistry / I am ashamed of presuming / to arrange words / of everything but the ingenuous fibres / that suffer honestly." But if the young poet

273

sins against art by relying far too heavily on the verbal machinations of conceptual intellect, he also sins on occasion in the opposite direction. The last stanza of "Casket of Pralinen" and the entire poem "For Future Reference" are the poet's own recurrent dreams, or nightmares, raw materials for poetry passed off as poetry itself. The reader sees the top and bottom of the poet's mind, but the twilight zone between, from which poetry emerges and to which Beckett is so faithful in his later writing, is only rarely glimpsed in these pre-poems.

Notwithstanding very considerable defects, Beckett's early efforts fail to smother completely the poetic impulse. The poems unquestionably provide at least isolated moments of real poetic pleasure for a reader who is not put off by the linguistic and literary exhibitionism. Beyond such moments, the little group of a dozen poems, remarkably homogeneous in subject matter, reveals that the poet's mature concerns were with him already in these early years. Three themes dominate: religion, love, and art. Only suffering is for the most part absent—except in the later poem, "Ooftish" (1938). Life has not yet penetrated the natural defenses of youth.

Love and the Rational Mind

Even though "Calvary by Night" is in part an intellectual exercise, illustrating the "aquatic manner" ("A Wet Night," *MP*, p. 80) of the homespun poet, it is interesting for several reasons. It shows Beckett's early concern with form, and here with the circular form that begins and ends on the same note and that we have seen in a number of poems in *Echo's Bones*. Another aspect that will endure in Beckett's writing is the portrait of life as a brief flowering between birth and death. Even his characteristically desolate landscape finds its aqueous counterpart here in the "waste of water." As elsewhere, he juxtaposes and almost identifies womb and tomb ("from the spouting forth / to the re-enwombing"). His love of alliteration shows itself in "water . . . waste . . . womb." Traits of satire occur in the archaic "an pansy" and both more and less subtly in other lines. We can see a development from the lyric toward satire by comparing the original version with the version published in "A Wet Night."[1] "Bow of petal and fragrance" in the original becomes

---

[1] The original version is quoted from "Dream," p. 190; for the revised version of 1934 see "A Wet Night," *MP*, pp. 79-80.

"bow of petaline sweet-smellingness"; "Lamb of my insustenance" becomes "lamb of insustenance mine"; "blue flower" becomes the comical "blue bloom." The title, "Calvary by Night," which remains unchanged in the later version, may well suggest everyman's hard journey through the darkness of life to his destiny as victim, but it can also slip toward the satirical, for it is vaguely reminiscent of travel posters advertising tourist delights: "See Paris by Night."

CALVARY BY NIGHT

the water
the waste of water

in the womb of water
an pansy leaps

rocket of bloom flare flower of night wilt for me
on the breasts of the water it has closed it has made
an act of floral presence on the water
the tranquil act of its cycle on the waste
from the spouting forth
to the re-enwombing   10
an untroubled bow of petal and fragrance
kingfished abated
drowned for me
Lamb of my insustenance

till the clamour of a blue flower
beat on the walls of the womb of
the waste of
the water   18

Built both semantically and structurally (and even typographically) around the image of an ephemeral blooming and fading like the still briefer burst of beauty in some nocturnal fireworks display, when the brilliant shower of an exploding rocket paints a momentary floral pattern against the black sky, this early poem reminds us of the long tradition of literary comparison between the lives and destinies of flowers and men. Differences are immediately apparent, however. Except for the occasional rise and fall of a blue "flare flower," the human landscape is a black waste. (The blue of happiness, beauty, love against the overwhelmingly predominant darkness recurs, as we have noted, from the early poems to *Comment*

275

c'est.) The religious imagery chosen by the Good Friday poet suggests a resurrection to come, and indeed lines 15 through 18 look forward to at least a floral rebirth. The evidence from "Dream," however, indicates that the metaphor does not point to the sacred or transcendent but rather to the erotico-mystic mechanism that Belacqua tries unsuccessfully to explain to the Smeraldina (p. 22) and that the narrator develops at length in passages on love and narcissism (pp. 33-38) and Beatrice and the brothel (pp. 89-92). The chief difficulty in associating "Calvary by Night" with these early episodes in "Dream" involving the Smeraldina is the poem's position. It appears near the end of "Dream" (p. 190), in a section dominated by the Alba and in a context of satire. Its presence there suggests that Beckett had already decided to abandon the poem as a serious lyrical effort, an impression reinforced by the more satirical version published later in "A Wet Night." Vocabulary, however, is decisive in associating the original poem with the Smeraldina and in establishing it, along with "Alba" and "Dortmunder," as a poetic transposition of "mystic" experience made possible through erotic or semierotic encounter ("The true Shekinah is Woman," says Belacqua ["Dream," p. 94]). In passages referring unequivocally to the Smeraldina we find references to such experiences couched in the key words of "Calvary by Night." "Bloom," "fragrance," and "floral" occur early in "Dream" (pp. 35-36), and in another section Belacqua refers colorfully to the Smeraldina as "his darling blue flower" (p. 63). The erotic origins of "Calvary by Night" are perceptible in the motif of fertility ("womb . . . breasts") and in the general love-death theme, supported by the religious imagery, a theme that is central again in Belacqua's sonnet to the Smeraldina. But water, suggestive here of sterility as well as fertility, is significant too in the aesthetic domain. "Flower . . . petal . . . fragrance" are most at home in the realm of beauty and pleasure, and the reappearance of the blue flower is forecast (15-16) in a way that evokes not only the idea of poetic inspiration but also (as do related passages in "Dream") the Proustian experience of involuntary memory with its concomitant implications for artistic creativity. Beckett had very recently published his monograph on Proust, and both the terminology and experiential content of Belacqua's escapes from the workaday world into his private *sanctum sanctorum* recall the Irish author's analyses of related episodes in *A la recherche du temps perdu.*

While the use of religious materials for the purposes of art no doubt of itself implies neither belief nor disbelief, it does seem to indicate concern with a religious dimension. This preoccupation becomes overriding in "Ooftish," but it is important in other early poems too. The religious theme provides whatever unity exists in the loosely constructed poem "Casket of Pralinen for a Daughter of a Dissipated Mandarin."[2] The poet comes to the crux of the matter after a somewhat rambling introduction in lines 41 and 42: "Fool! do you hope to untangle/ the knot of God's pain?" As we have seen before, this is the metaphysical problem that plagued the young Beckett: How can an all-loving and all-merciful God permit the existence of pain and suffering in the world? We have hints of this central theme earlier in the poem. It begins with a conversation between mother and daughter on the suitor who has gone back to Paris after a holiday. The daughter (the Smeraldina, to whom this "box of chocolates" is addressed) is writing him a letter and recalls the New Year's Eve they spent together. The religious imagery in lines 13 and 14, used to describe the experience of young love, is followed in lines 15 through 24 by a verbal transposition of a painting by Dahlberg, *Das Abendmahl* (*Last Supper*). From line 25 on, the poet-suitor in Paris muses and embroiders on his own, more or less abandoning the fictional mother-daughter point of view. He ponders over the days in Germany and the relationship between beauty, love, pain, and memory. Lines 13 and 14 suggest already that innocent young love is somehow related to religious experience, and the transposition of Dahlberg's painting calls up various possible relationships between man and God in the relationships of some of the apostles to Christ. In lines 27 through 34 the poem moves into high gear. The experience of beauty is painful, but there is a metaphysical anguish that is worse. "A stitch in the hem of the garment of God" is insufficient contact. The gaze of the beloved is at times no more fulfilling than the sunlight that filters through bars to a caged lark that has lost its heaven. In these images the poet manages to suggest both the need for and the impossibility of spiritual fulfillment. Neither beauty nor God can be possessed wholly, yet nothing less than full possession is enough.

Already in such lines we can see what is perhaps the central experience evoked in the corpus of Beckett's writing: the deep and

[2] In *The European Caravan* (New York: Brewer, Warren, and Putnam, 1931), pp. 476-478.

painful consciousness of loss, absence, separation, exile. As though ashamed of this avowal of his suffering, as well as of his "clumsy artistry," the poet puts on an exhibition of virtuosity which includes an extraordinary metaphor that calls into question the whole idea of beauty as a value and at the same time impugns the authenticity of the Proustian experience of a substitute paradise. The poem ends in a series of allusions and images that cast some doubt on both the possibility of human love and the power and mercy of God.

CASKET OF PRALINEN FOR A DAUGHTER OF A DISSIPATED MANDARIN

Is he long enough in the leg?
Già[3] but his faice[4] . . . .
Oh me little timid Rosinette
isn't it Bartholo, synthetic grey cat, regal candle?
Keep Thyrsis for your morning ones.[5]
Hold your head well over the letter darling
or they'll fall on the blotting.[6]
Will you ever forget that soupe arrosée
on the first of the first,
spoonfeeding the weeping gladiator[7]   10
renewing our baptismal vows
and dawn cracking all along the line
Slobbery assumption of the innocents
two Irish in one God.[8]

[3] Italian for "yes."

[4] Spelling mimics English accent.

[5] Mother replies to daughter that if her Irish suitor is not too handsome, he will do for dates in the evening; she can save her handsome friends for the full light of morning. Rosine is the heroine and Bartholo her severe tutor in Beaumarchais' *The Marriage of Figaro*. Thyrsis is the name of many a young protagonist of pastoral and tragicomedy. Note, in connection with line 4, the proverbial French expression "La nuit, tous les chats sont gris."

[6] Motherly advice to daughter as she writes a letter to the departed suitor, more fully developed in "The Smeraldina's Billet Doux," which appears in both "Dream" and *More Pricks Than Kicks*.

[7] Self-caricature through allusion to the statue of the dying gladiator at the Roman Capitolium.

[8] Not only the suitor but the Smeraldina (as the "emerald" in her name indicates) is Irish. The narrator in "Dream" uses the term "assumption" to

Radiant lemon-whiskered Christ
and you obliging porte-phallic-portfolio[9]
and blood-faced Tom
disbelieving[10]
in the Closerie cocktail that is my[11]
and of course John the bright boy of the class[12]   20
swallowing an apostolic spit
THE BULLIEST FEED IN 'ISTORY[13]
if the boy scouts hadn't booked a trough
for the eleventh's eleventh eleven years after.[14]

---

describe Belacqua's experience of release: "It was the miracle . . . taking him down from his pangs, sheathing him in the cerements of clarity. It was the descent and the enwombing, assumption upside down. . . . It was at last the hush and indolence of Limbo in his mind . . . lounging against the will-pricks. It was the mercy of salve on the prurigo of living . . ." (pp. 161-162).

[9] Judas with his scrotum-shaped purse.

[10] Doubting Thomas.

[11] Omitted is "blood." The Closerie is the Closerie des Lilas, a bar and restaurant that stands at the corner of the Boulevard St. Michel, the Avenue de l'Observatoire, and the Boulevard du Montparnasse, still frequented by Beckett.

[12] John, the Beloved Disciple, seen as the teacher's pet.

[13] The Last Supper.

[14] An Armistice Day celebration on November 11, 1929, eleven years after the end of World War I. In "Dream of Fair to Middling Women" Belacqua describes the world as divided into "temptation and knighthood," by which he means love and idealism, body and spirit. One of the several pairs of polar opposites he uses to describe this dualism is "bloomers" and "boy-scouts" (pp. 39-40). In lines 15 through 24 of the poem the Apostles are crusaders for an ideal, and in line 23 the boy scouts who made the world safe for democracy no doubt provide another example of the spirit of idealistic crusade.

This third section of the poem (15-24) is expanded to some three pages in "Dream," pages that are of considerable importance for the understanding of Beckett's later religious and artistic position. Belacqua is in front of the painting in question: "He goggled like a fool at the shrieking paullo-post-Expression of the Last Supper hanging on the wall fornenst him, livid in the restless yellow light, its thirteen flattened flagrant egg-heads gathered round the tempter and his sop and the traitor and his burse. The tempter and the traitor and the Jugendbund of eleven. John the Divine was the green egg at the head of the board. What a charming undershot purity of expression to be sure! He would ask for a toad to eat in a minute . . ." (p. 69). Further on we have the portrait of Judas and doubting Thomas: "Pink of course for the insidious chairman, the perfidious very much more than

> Now me boy
> take a hitch in your lyrical loinstring.
> What is this that is more
> than the anguish of Beauty,

---

papal key, with the little phallic pouch trapped in his plump pink palpers, his lips parted for the garden, or was it vinegar and gall maybe, a boil on his neck that I cannot see, his Gilles de Rais orbs, quite too Rio-Santo, *focused* on the patibulary melancholy of the lemon of lemons, was it vinegar then or hyssop or the sponge or the reed of hyssop, and of course before gliding on to more pleasant topics allusion must be made to blood-faced Tom with his bow-tie moustache disbelieving in the Sherry Cobbler that is my. A masterly study, boys, there's no getting away from it, of what I once saw described as the bulliest feed in 'istory if the boyscouts 'adn't booked a trough for th'eleventh's eleventh eleven years after . . ." (p. 71). To be noted in this passage is the "boil on his neck," corresponding to the anthrax on Belacqua's neck and a nonmalignant tumor which Beckett had removed from his own neck. This is one of many hints of the relationship between Belacqua, Judas, and Beckett. The description of the painting is no more important in this respect than other sections of this three-page interlude that show quite clearly: (1) the conflict in the young poet's mind between love for his Irish *Fräulein* and his loyalty to Christ: "and let me tell all you boys what it feels like to be in Old Nick's bath. I am in the extreme centre of Old Nick's bath, I have gone light in the centre, I am at the frontiers of the boundless, I am the scourged cream of human adversity, yes, the quintessence and the upshot. A whore, boys, in a deep ditch of diabolic water, there am I, shall I then be hot in a cold cause, is it fair to expect that, would it not be much nicer to know a few good digs of compunction and clip Jesus straight away and stand fast for ever? Oh sometimes as now I almost think: nothing is less like me than me. It must be either that I am not adequately alkaline or that there is a cavity needing filling under my navel spiral where the big weight ought to be. Fire and stone and torment by skewering" (p. 69); (2) the conflict between opposed loyalties to art and to Christ: "I go as it is written of me. A fico and a fouter for your stags of amber and your pines of bronze and your marble love-potions and your frozen fugues, as it is written so help me but woe to that man, and your mard of gold sculpppt and foil of silver painted and the swivelling snivelling miracle of your belly-cum-bum totalities and realities . . . Who are your patrons? Greeks? Kings? Lovers? . . . You can keep your George Bernard Pygmalion . . . The man of my peace . . . Hath lifted up his heel against me. Wet doom of lime. That thou doest do quickly. A ewe can grow cold. And it was night. Oh the moon shines bright on Aceldama . . ." (p. 70); and (3) the dilemma of the existence of evil, which recurs in Beckett's early writing in the image of Christ writing in the dust when the woman caught in adultery is brought to him ("A dream of lines palped the dust of the ground" [p. 69]), the old problem of the mysterious coexistence of God's justice and His mercy.

this gale of pain that was not prepared
in the caves of her eyes?[15]   30

Is it enough
a stitch in the hem of the garment of God?

To-night her gaze would be less
than a lark's barred sunlight.

Oh I am ashamed
of all clumsy artistry
I am ashamed of presuming
to arrange words
of everything but the ingenuous fibres
that suffer honestly.   40

Fool! do you hope to untangle
the knot of God's pain?

Melancholy Christ that was a soft one!
Oh yes I think that was perhaps just a very little
    inclined to be rather too self-conscious.

Schluss![16]
Now ladies and gents
a chocolate-coated hiccough[17] to our old friend.[18]
Put on your hats and sit easy.
Oh beauty!
oh thou predatory evacuation,   50
from the bowels of my regret—
readily affected
by the assimilation of a purging gobbet
from my memory's involuntary vomit—
violently projected,
oh beauty!
oh innocent and spluttering beautiful!

[15] "The dark pangs of the sons of Adam" ("Dream," p. 38).
[16] "Conclusion!"
[17] From eating the candy in the "Casket of Pralinen."
[18] I.e., beauty.

What price the Balbec express?[19]
Albion Albion mourn for him mourn
thy cockerup Willy the idiot boy   60
the portly scullion's codpiece.[20]
Now who'll discover in Mantegna's
butchery stout foreshortened Saviour[21]
recognitions of transcendent
horse-power?[22]
Sheep he wrote the very much doubting
genial illegible landscape gardener.[23]
Gloucester's no bimbo
and he's in Limbo
so all's well with the gorgonzola cheese of human   70
    kindness.[24]

Though the swine were slaughtered
beneath the waves
not far from the firm sand

[19] I.e., "How do you like that rendition of Proust? What's it worth to you?" Behind this bit of virtuosity we can note the difference in point of view that marks the two authors. For Proust involuntary memory could resuscitate the past, concrete and entire, freed from time, ready to be set down forever in the immutable realm of art. For Beckett involuntary memory stimulates sorrow to produce waste materials that exercise a sinister attraction ("predatory"). The process eventuates not in a glorious resurrection but in the anguish of certain loss. Bones or feces (another "precipitate") serve only to remind us that Echo is gone and irretrievable.

[20] An allusion to William Wordsworth, the pampered ("cockerup") child of England ("Albion").

[21] In the painting by Mantegna entitled *Cristo morto e le Marie* (in the Pinacoteca, Milan).

[22] Allusion to Wordsworth's "intimations of immortality."

[23] Reference to the story that Wordsworth's famous phrase "fields of sleep" was due to the error of a printer who misread "fields of sheep."

[24] An obscure allusion, possibly to Edmund, son of the Earl of Gloucester, the villain in Shakespeare's *King Lear*. The events of the play occur before Christ's birth, so perhaps the bastard Edmund, on the basis of his charitable act just before he dies, might conceivably qualify for limbo. If such an out-and-out villain can make it, then no matter the turned milk of human kindness. We too have a chance at that neutral realm. If such a reading is accurate, these lines would represent another appearance of the theme of God's mercy and His justice.

282

they're gone they're gone[25]
my Brussels Braut![26]

The Smeraldina's love letter to Belacqua appears in both "Dream" and *More Pricks Than Kicks*. In the former she writes, "I am longing to see the 'thing' you wrot about my 'beauty' (as *you* call it) I must say (without wanting any complements) I cant see anything very much to writ about except the usual rot men writ about women" (p. 53). Beckett did in fact write three sonnets to the girl he knew in Germany, one of which found its way into "Dream" (p. 63). As so often in that work, the poet protects himself by undercutting the expression of sincere feeling. He introduces this sonnet with the following paragraph: "By Jove when we look back and think how chaste was the passion of mutual attraction that juxtaposed those two young people in the first instance! It is out of the question, it is beyond our poor powers, to give you any idea of the reverence with which they—how shall we say?—clave the one to the other in an ecstasy and an agony of mystical adhesion. Yessir! An ecstasy and an agony! A sentimentical coagulum, sir, that biggers descruption. . . . [Later] Belacqua inscribed to his darling blue flower some of the finest Night of May hiccupsobs that ever left a fox's paw sneering and rotting in a snaptrap" (pp. 62-

[25] Lines 71 through 74 appear to refer to Matt. 9:28-32: "And when he was come to the other side into the country of the Gergesenes, there met him two possessed with devils, coming out of the tombs, exceeding fierce, so that no man might pass that way. And, behold, they cried out, saying, What have we to do with thee, Jesus, thou Son of God? Art thou come hither to torment us before the time? And there was a good way off from them an herd of many swine feeding. So the devils besought him, saying, If thou cast us out, suffer us to go away into the herd of swine. And he said unto them, Go. And when they were come out, they went into the herd of swine: and, behold, the whole herd of swine ran violently down a steep place into the sea, and perished in the waters."
The narrator's regret at the perplexing slaughter (cf. the deaths of canary and lobster mentioned above) is outweighed by his relief. In the context of the poem, he may have murdered the muse, but at least the demons of his metaphysical anguish have been exorcized. Writing has been therapeutic, and he can now give his attention, in a playful pun, to the lesser complexities of amorous relationships.
[26] A pun on the German word for "betrothed" that through the English suggests the French term of endearment *choux*. It is used by Belacqua in "Dream" as one of several affectionately ironic names for the Smeraldina.

63). For all that and in spite of the something less than mystical images that follow the poem, the poem itself, like "Calvary by Night," is parody only in part.

> At last I find in my confusèd soul,
> Dark with the dark flame of the cypresses,
> The certitude that I cannot be whole,
> Consummate, finally achieved, unless
>
> I be consumed and fused in the white heat
> Of her sad finite essence, so that none
> Shall sever us who are at last complete
> Eternally, irrevocably one,
>
> One with the birdless, cloudless, colourless skies,
> One with the bright purity of the fire
> of which we are and for which we must die
> A rapturous strange death and be entire,
>
> Like syzygetic stars, supernly bright,
> Conjoined in One and in the Infinite![27]

The link between platonic ecstasy and young love in the mystic experience is established on numerous occasions in Beckett's early writing. In "Dream" we find the following passage: "Unfortunate Belacqua, you miss our point, *the* point: that beauty, in the final analysis, is not subject to categories, is beyond categories. There is only one category, yours, that furnished by your stases. As all mystics, independent of creed and colour and sex, are transelemented into the creedless, colourless, sexless Christ, so all categories of beauty must be transelemented into yours. Take it, deary, from us: beauty is one and beauties uni generis, immanent and transcendent, totum intra omnia, deary, et totum extra, with a centre everywhere and a circumference nowhere. Put that into your pipe, dear fellow, and smoke it slowly" (p. 31). The theme of love and death is suggested in line 5 and lines 11 and 12 of the poem in the implied

---

[27] The sonnet to the Smeraldina was published as part of "Sedendo et Quiesciendo" [sic] (taken in its entirety from "Dream of Fair to Middling Women") in *Transition*, No. 21 (The Hague: The Servire Press, March 1932), p. 17. Except for minor changes in punctuation, only lines 12 and 13 were altered in this later appearance—in the direction of simplicity: "A strange exalted death and be entire, / Like two merged stars, intolerably bright. . . ."

image of the phoenix. The same love-death theme, in a slightly less mystical key, is suggested in the very title of one of the short stories in *More Pricks Than Kicks*, "Love and Lethe," at the end of which the author quotes from Ronsard: "l'Amour et la Mort—caesura—n'est qu'une mesme chose" (p. 138).[28] As we saw in lines 13 and 14 of "Casket of Pralinen" ("Slobbery assumption of the innocents/ two Irish in one God"), the access to an otherworldly realm has parallels both with profane love and religion. In Beckett's own writings and particularly in his *Proust* he points out the relationship of art to a similar experience:

And now, on the outskirts of this futility, favoured by the very depression and fatigue that had appeared to his disgust as the aftermath of a minute and sterile lucidity (favoured, because the pretensions of a discouraged memory are for the moment reduced to the most immediate and utilitarian presentification), he is to receive the oracle that had invariably been denied to the most exalted tension of his spirit, which his intelligence had failed to extract from the sismic enigma of tree and flower and gesture and art, and suffer a religious experience in the only intelligible sense of that epithet, at once an assumption and an annunciation, so

[28] On page 65 of "Dream" (and page 19 of "Sedendo et Quiesciendo") allusions to Zurbaran, Statius, and Valéry continue the love-death motif: "J'aime et je veux pââââlir. Livid rapture of the Zurbaran Saint-Onan. Schwindsucht and pollution in the umbra in the tunnel in the Thebaid. Rapturous strange death! Plus précieuse que la vie, the dirty dog."
  The line from Ronsard is taken from the final poem (LXXVII) of *Le Second livre des sonnets pour Hélène* (*Oeuvres complètes*, ed. Laumonier, I, 340-341):

> Je chantois ces Sonnets amoureux d'une Helene,
>   En ce funeste mois que mon Prince mourut:
>   Son sceptre, tant fust grand, Charles ne secourut,
>   Qu'il ne payast la debte à la Nature humaine.
> La Mort fut d'un costé, et l'Amour qui me meine,
>   Estoit de l'autre part, dont le traict me ferut,
>   Et si bien la poison par les veines courut,
>   Que j'oubliay mon maistre, attaint d'une autre peine.
> Je senty dans le coeur deux diverses douleurs,
>   La rigueur de ma Dame, et la tristesse enclose
>   Du Roy, que j'adorois pour ses rares valeurs.
> La vivante et le mort tout malheur me propose:
>   L'une aime les regrets, et l'autre aime les pleurs:
>   Car l'Amour et la Mort n'est qu'une mesme chose.

that at last he will understand the promise of Bergotte and the achievement of Elstir and the message of Vinteuil from his paradise and the dolorous and necessary course of his own life and the infinite futility—for the artist—of all that is not art.   (p. 51)

Here again, as in "Casket of Pralinen" and "Dream," we find the term "assumption" and a religious figure used to describe a very earthly paradise. The first short story that Beckett published carries the title "Assumption."[29] Similar lines appear there: "Before no supreme manifestation of Beauty do we proceed comfortably up a staircase of sensation, and sit down mildly on the topmost stair to digest our gratification: such is the pleasure of Prettiness. We are taken up bodily and pitched breathless on the peak of a sheer crag: which is the pain of Beauty" (p. 269). There are other clues in the story that lead us to believe that the girl involved is once again the Smeraldina: descriptions of the lower lip, low, broad brow, the green-flecked eyes, and the hat of faded green felt tally with the portrait in "Dream," and again we find the term "blue flower." The protagonist of "Assumption" is a figure of the poet: "In the silence of his room he was afraid, afraid of that wild rebellious surge that aspired violently towards realization in sound. He felt its implacable caged resentment, its longing to be released in one splendid drunken scream and fused with the cosmic discord. . . . he dreaded lest his prisoner should escape, he longed that it might escape; it tore at his throat and he choked it back in dread and sorrow" (p. 269). Then the girl arrives and her eyes are "pools of obscurity." "SO each evening in contemplation and absorption of this woman, he lost a part of his essential animality: so that the water rose terrifying him" (p. 270). Beckett goes on to describe the mystic experience, the increasing need of the poet for self-expression, and finally his emblematic death. The ending of the story is obviously a transposition of Belacqua's sonnet to the Smeraldina (of note especially is the phrase common to story and poem, "one with the birdless cloudless colourless skies"):

Until at last, for the first time, he was unconditioned by the Satanic dimensional Trinity, he was released, achieved, the blue flower, Vega, GOD . . . After a timeless parenthesis he found himself alone in his room, spent with ecstasy, torn by the bitter loathing of that which he had condemned to the humanity of silence.

[29] In *Transition*, Nos. 16-17 (June 1929), pp. 268-271.

Thus each night he died and was God, each night revived and was torn, torn and battered with increasing grievousness, so that he hungered to be irretrievably engulfed in the light of eternity, one with the birdless cloudless colourless skies, in infinite fulfillment.

Then it happened. While the woman was contemplating the face that she had overlaid with death, she was swept aside by a great storm of sound, shaking the very house with its prolonged, triumphant vehemence, climbing in a dizzy, bubbling scale, until, dispersed, it fused into the breath of the forest and the throbbing cry of the sea.

They found her caressing his wild dead hair.   (p. 271)

The story is a parable of the poet, who is possessed by an overwhelming need to speak. Woman is the catalyst that increases this need. He fights to remain silent not only from a realization of the inadequacy of language or simply out of discretion but also, and more basically, because when the poet, like the lover, does speak, he loses something of himself, is emptied, dies. Like the act of love, the act of verbal creation is a giving of the self in the most literal sense, that is to say a dying. In "Assumption" the relationship between love, mysticism, and artistic creation becomes clear. Neither love of woman nor the mystic experience is the end, although the anguish and doubt of the poet are evident on numerous occasions in Beckett's early prose and poetry. It seems fairly certain that the tale told is of the making of an artist. The end, the ultimate loyalty, is art; the rest is means. We are in the presence of courage and terror and the danger of self-destruction. *Homo faber* in one perspective is no man (Nemo in "Dream"). He separates himself from himself again and again as each successive being becomes material for art. He is a crucible repeatedly emptied of its contents.

The poem "Text"[30] belongs, along with "Ooftish," to that early writing concerned with the religious problem of suffering. Pity given and pity withheld are the twin themes that unify the poem; Proust, Dante, the Bible, and mythology provide the texts for "Text." The first section (1-10) describes the quality of human compassion. Like Belacqua, Françoise, the family cook in Proust's novel, is overcome with pity on hearing of suffering in China but is

---

[30] In *The European Caravan*, pp. 478-480. Reprinted in *The New Review, An International Notebook for the Arts*, I, No. 4 (Paris, Winter 1931-1932), 338-339.

incapable of sympathy for the misery of her pregnant helper.[31] The ambiguous term "miserere," at once a painful affection due to intestinal obstruction, especially in the ileum, and an appeal to God for mercy, brings up the enigma of the existence of evil in the world.

> Miserere oh colon
> oh passionate ilium[32]
> and Frances the cook in the study mourning
> an abstract belly
> instead of the writhing asparagus-plumer
> smashed on delivery
> by the most indifferential calculus[33]
> that never came out[34]
> or ever disdressed[35]
> a redknuckled slut of a Paduan Virtue.[36]
>
> (1-10)

Section two (11-19) suggests filial compassion in the devotion of Tiresias during seven years as a female giving suck to a starving father in prison.[37]

> Show that plate here to your bedfruit[38]
> spent baby
> and take a good swig
> at our buxom calabash.
> There's more than bandit Glaxo[39]
> underneath me maternity toga.
> So she sags and here's the other.

[31] Beckett writes in *Proust* (p. 30): "So, unlike Miranda, he [the narrator] suffers with her whom he had not seen suffer, as though, for him as for Françoise, whom Giotto's charitable scullion in childbirth and the violent translation of what is fit to live into what is fit to eat leave indifferent, but who cannot restrain her tears when informed that there has been an earthquake in China, pain could only be focussed at a distance."

[32] The "iliac passion" is another name for "ileus" or "miserere."

[33] A play on the term "differential calculus" and on "calculus" in the sense of stone, referring to the dead foetus.

[34] The mother died in childbirth.

[35] Joycean combination of distressed and undressed.

[36] Françoise reminded Proust of a Virtue in Giotto's Paduan frescos.

[37] Suggested by Apollinaire's play, *Les Mamelles de Tirésias*.

[38] Fruit of the bed or offspring.

[39] A brand of baby food smuggled into the prison.

That's the real export or I'm a Jungfrau.
Now wipe your moustache and hand us the vaseline.

(11-19)

Section three brings in Job and the nagging riddle of a God who allows the innocent to suffer. Again we see the theme of pity withheld. In the Biblical narration Job repents and acknowledges his ignorance and his presumption. In Beckett's version Job remains unreconciled to his sufferings and laments the fact that he, as man, supposedly the masterpiece of the creator, has not been accorded the same physical equipment as the other creatures, equipment that might enable him to bear up under the afflictions that rain down on him.

> Open Thou my lips[40]
> and
> (if one dare make a suggestion)
> Thine eye of skyflesh.[41]
> Am I a token of Godcraft?[42]
> The masterpiece of a scourged apprentice?[43]
> Where is my hippopot's cedar tail?
> and belly muscles?[44]
> Shall I cease to lament
> being not as the flashsneezing[45]
> non-suppliant airtight alligator?[46]

(20-30)

[40] Job 42:4: "Hear, I beseech thee. . . ."

[41] Job 10:3-4: "Is it good unto thee that thou shouldest oppress, that thou shouldest despise the work of thine hands, and shine upon the counsel of the wicked? Hast thou eyes of flesh? or seest thou as man seeth?"

[42] Job 10:8: "Thine hands have made me and fashioned me together round about; yet thou dost destroy me." Even though their conclusions are different, Beckett begins from a point of view close to that of the suffering Job. In Job 10:18-19 we read, "Wherefore then hast thou brought me forth out of the womb? Oh that I had given up the ghost, and no eye had seen me! I should have been carried from the womb to the grave."

[43] I.e., the prime example in man's history of the suffering servant.

[44] Job 40:15-17: "Behold now behemoth, which I made with thee; he eateth grass as an ox. Lo now, his strength is in his loins, and his force is in the navel of his belly. He moveth his tail like a cedar: the sinews of his stones are wrapped together."

[45] Job 41:18: "By his neesings a light doth shine. . . ." More clearly in the Knox translation, Job 41:9: "Let him but sneeze, the fire flashes out."

[46] Job 41:15-16: "His scales are his pride, shut up together as with a

The reply to Job comes in lines 31 through 36 by way of Boccaccio's account of Dante's dream, in which he compares the four qualities of the peacock to the characteristics of the *Commedia*. The sense of these lines seems to be the following: although there is cold comfort for suffering man in a knowledge of God's power as revealed in the awesome aspects of natural creation, there may be some consolation in the products of man's art.

> Not so but perhaps
> at the sight and the sound of
> a screechy[47] flatfooted Tuscany[48] peacock's
> Strauss fandango and recitative[49]
> not forgetting
> he stinks eternal.[50]
>
> (31-36)

Section five (37-53) is a transposition of parts of Canto XX of Dante's *Inferno* and of the mythological account of the life of Tiresias. The first five lines refer to the soothsayers, who were punished for fraud in the fourth ditch of the eighth circle. They claimed to see ahead into the future during their lives, so now in death their heads are twisted in pain toward the rear as they walk weeping around their *bolgia*.[51] Their torment arouses Dante's compassion

---

close seal. One is so near to another, that no air can come between them." Leviathan is usually identified with the crocodile.

[47] The harsh cry of the peacock corresponds to Dante's voice chastising sinners.

[48] The unattractive feet of the peacock suggest Dante's use of the vernacular language.

[49] Allusion to a semipopular dance rhythm and a language closer to everyday speech than the more classically elegant rhythm and music of Latin. "Strauss" is also used for the German meaning, "ostrich"—a creature with a walk perhaps recalling that of the peacock. The "eyes" on the feathers of the strutting peacock are interpreted as corresponding to the one hundred cantos of the *Commedia*.

[50] The bad-smelling flesh of the peacock was reputed to be incorruptible, suggesting the immortality of Dante's poem.

[51] Cf. in *Watt* (p. 58) Arsene's description of himself and Erskine as "little fat shabby seedy juicy or oily bandylegged men, with a little fat bottom sticking out in front and a little fat belly sticking out behind" and later (p. 162) Sam's description of Watt: "he came, awkwardly buttoning his trousers, which he was wearing back to front, out from behind a tree, and then backwards, guided by my cries, painfully. . . ."

and he weeps with the sufferers, so that Virgil reprimands him severely: "'Ancor sei tu de li altri sciocchi?/ Qui vive la pietà quand' è ben morta./ Chi è piu scellerato che colui/ Che al giudico divin passion comporta?" (XX, 27-30). The same conflict between justice (or simply the withholding of pity) and pity is of central importance in "Dante and the Lobster," one of the best of the stories of *More Pricks Than Kicks.* Not only does it determine the metaphoric structure that includes Cain and the problem of the moon spots, the episode of the sandwich, the imagery of crucifixion in the grocery store, the news of McCabe's execution, the assignment given Belacqua by his Italian teacher ("Dante's rare movements of compassion in hell"), and the concluding crisis, when the lobster is boiled alive; it also provides a key to Belacqua's sensibility and many of his actions in other stories as well. And it shows the decisive importance Beckett attached to these lines that Dante puts into the mouth of Virgil and that Belacqua quotes in the story. The religious implications of the conflict are apparent in Belacqua's thoughts as he walks toward his aunt's house with the doomed lobster: "Why not piety and pity both, even down below? Why not mercy and Godliness together? A little mercy in the stress of sacrifice, a little mercy to rejoice against judgment. He thought of Jonah and the gourd and the pity of a jealous God on Nineveh" (p. 18).

The last twelve lines of section four describe the unusual adventures of Tiresias (who also appears among the soothsayers in Canto XX). While walking one day on Mount Cyllene (Cithaeron in some versions of the story), he came upon two snakes joined together. He separated them, whereupon he was changed from male to female. A repetition of the episode seven years later (50, below) gave him back his original sex. Dante wrote:

> Vedi Tiresia, che mutò sembiante,
>   Quando di maschio femmina divenne,
>   Cangiandosi le membra tutte quante;
> E prima poi ribatter li convenne
>   Li duo serpenti avvolti, con la verga,
>   Che rïavesse le mascili penne.
>   (*Inf.* XX, 40-45)

Later Zeus and Hera sought Tiresias' answer, as one who should know, on the question of whether men or women derive more pleasure from the act of love. His reply, that if love were divided into

291

ten parts (in most versions) man would have one and woman nine (48, below), so enraged Hera that she blinded him (51). Zeus took pity on him and gave him compensating gifts, among others the gift of prophecy.

> Alas my scorned packthread![52]
> No blade has smoothed the furrowed cheeks
> that my tears corrode.[53]
> My varicose veins take my kneeling thoughts
> from the piteous pelican.[54]

[52] Among the soothsayers is the poor cobbler of Parma, Astente, who now wishes he had stuck to his trade. Cf. the proverb: "Cobbler, stick to your last" (Pliny the Elder, *Historia naturalis*, Bk. 35, Chap. 10, § 36: "Ne sutor supra crepidam." Also in Lucian and Martial). Dante writes:

> Vedi Bruno Bonatti, vedi Asdente,
>   C'avere inteso al cuoio ed a lo spago
>   Ora vorebbe, ma tardi si pente.
> Vedi le triste che lasciaron l'ago,
>   La spuola e 'l fuso, e fecersi 'ndivine;
>   Fecer malìe con erba e con imago.
>   (*Inf.* XX, 118-123)

[53] Dante writes:

> Ma io nol vidi, nè credo che sia.
>   Se Dio ti lasci, lettor, prender frutto
>   Di tua lezione, or pensa per te stesso,
> Com' io potea tener lo viso asciutto,
>   Quando la nostra imagine di presso
>   Vidi sì torta che 'l pianto de li occhi
>   Le natiche bagnava per lo fesso.
> Certo io piangea, poggiato a un de' rocchi
>   Del duro scoglio. . . .
>   (*Inf.* XX, 19-26)

In *All That Fall* Mr. Rooney, who like the soothsayers is blind, suggests to his wife that they walk "arsy-versy" like Dante's damned. Here the implication that earth is hell recalls the beginning of "Enueg I" ("its secret things").

[54] Beckett imagines a soothsayer kneeling and thus viewing the veins in his legs. This line introduces a new variation on the theme of pity. The pelican brings up food for its young from its pouch by pressing its beak against its breast. Hence the legend that it sacrifices itself for its starving offspring. In "La Nuit de Mai" Musset wrote:

> Lorsque le pélican, lassé d'un long voyage,
> Dans les brouillards du soir retourne à ses roseaux,

Quick tip losers narcissistic inverts.[55]
Twice I parted two crawlers
dribbling their not connubial strangles
in Arcadia of all places.
Believe me Miss Ops
swan flame or shower of gold.[56]
its one to ten at the time
(no offence to your noble deathjerks)[57]
I know I was at it seven . . .[58]
the bitch she's blinded me!
Manto me dear
an iced sherbet and me blood's a solid.[59]

(37-53)

In the final section of the poem (54-69) the poet abandons
burlesque in a serious and moving passage that reveals his own
compassion and his difficulty in accepting the notion of eternal
punishment. In lines 54 through 63 he identifies himself to a considerable degree with the souls of the lukewarm, the slothful, those
who in life took neither side but remained neutral, those who, as
Virgil says to Dante, were neither rebels nor disciples but were
faithful to themselves only. Beckett, not Dante, attributes their

---

Ses petits affamés courent sur le rivage
En le voyant au loin s'abattre sur les eaux.

. . . .

Pour toute nourriture il apporte son coeur.
Sombre et silencieux, étendu sur la pierre,
Partageant à ses fils ses entrailles de père. . . .

(Alfred de Musset, *Poésies complètes* [Paris: Gallimard, 1957], pp. 308-309.)

[55] This line refers to a joke on circumcision once current in Ireland,
which Beckett uses in "Home Olga" (see below). There may have been
some superstition according to which premature circumcision leads to sexual
withdrawal and introversion, both suggested by the myth of Narcissus. Or
perhaps the line may refer to the fate of Narcissus, forecast by Tiresias.

[56] Various forms assumed by Zeus to facilitate seduction.

[57] Once again the ambiguity between love and death (see the analysis of
"Assumption," above).

[58] During seven years as a female, Tiresias became a famous harlot.

[59] Manto was the daughter of Tiresias. They fled together from Thebes
after its conquest. Thirsty from the journey, Tiresias one morning drank
the icy water of the spring Telphoussa and died.

sloth (55) to their clear-sightedness. These are the souls who will be accepted neither by hell nor by heaven but must remain in the vestibule of the inferno. Such souls are obviously close spiritual kin to Belacqua. He too is negligent, lazy, intelligent in his ironic mode, and concerned with the life of the self. He occupies a position analogous to theirs in the *Antipurgatorio*, where he must remain for a second life span. We may also recall again Beckett's interest in Descartes, who stayed in bed until noon, as the author points out in *Whoroscope*. Murphy loved his rocking chair and, as Peggy Guggenheim notes, Oblomov-Beckett was himself a later riser. In lines 64 to 69 Virgil speaks to Dante, chiding him. His opening invocation, "Lo-Ruhama Lo-Ruhama," is taken from the Old Testament prophecy of Hosea 1:6: "And God said unto him, Call her name Lo-Ruhamah: for I will no more have mercy upon the house of Israel. . . ." The central theme of "Text" is emphasized once again, for the prophecy of Hosea deals from beginning to end with the Lord's justice and His mercy. In Hosea 11:9 we read, for example: "All at once my heart misgives me, and from its embers pity revives. How should I wreak my vengeance, of Ephraim take full toll?"[60]

The poem ends with Virgil's restatement of line 28 from Canto XX of the *Inferno*: "Qui vive la pietà quand è ben morta." He urges Dante, foolishly compassionate in Beckett's version, to suppress his sentimentalism and come along through the inferno and purgatory to paradise. "Stand cold/ on the cold moon," the last lines of "Text," recall once again "Dante and the Lobster," which opens with Belacqua reading the *Commedia*. He is "stuck in the first of the canti in the moon," where Beatrice gives Dante the true explanation of the moon spots. According to popular belief they were Cain and his bundle of thorns, a figure of the unacceptable offering to God. In "Dante and the Lobster" we read: "The spots were Cain with his truss of thorns, dispossessed, cursed from the earth, fugitive and vagabond. The moon was that countenance fallen and branded, seared with the first stigma of God's pity, that an outcast might not die quickly" (p. 5).

> We are proud in our pain
> our life was not blind.[61]

---

[60] Knox translation.

[61] For Beckett the lukewarm are those who avoid fanaticism. It need hardly be stated that such was not Dante's position.

Worms breed in their red tears[62]
as they slouch by unnamed[63]
scorned by the black ferry[64]
despairing of death
who shall not scour in swift joy
the bright hill's girdle
nor tremble with the dark pride of torture
and the bitter dignity of an ingenious damnation.[65]
Lo-Ruhama Lo-Ruhama
pity is quick with death.
Presumptuous passionate fool come now[66]

[62] Dante writes: "Elle rigavan lor di sangue il volto,/ Che, mischiato di lagrime, ai lor piedi,/ Da fastidiosi vermi era ricolto" (*Inf.* III, 67-69).

[63] Although Dante names none of the lukewarm, he suggests in lines 59 and 60 ("Vidi e conobbi l'ombra di colui/ Che fece per viltà il gran rifiuto") that one of them is Celestine V, a pope who abdicated the papacy after five months in office.

[64] Charon refuses to allow them across the Acheron into hell proper.

[65] They are denied death (59), entrance to purgatory, which leads to heaven (60-61), and admission to hell (62-63). Dante writes of them:

> . . . 'Questo misero modo
> Tengon l' anime triste di coloro
> Che visser sanza infamia e sanza lodo.
> Mischiate sono a quel cattivo coro
> De li angeli che non furon ribelli
> Nè fur fedeli a Dio, ma per sè fuoro.
> Caccianli i ciel per non esser men belli;
> Nè lo profondo inferno li riceve,
> Ch'alcuna gloria i rei avrebber d'elli.'
> (*Inf.* III, 34-42)

He also mentions that they have no "speranza di morte" (III, 46), and Beckett seconds him. He calls their lives blind ("lor cieca vita" [III, 47]), but here Beckett contradicts him in line 55. The lukewarm run hither and thither following an inconstant banner, a fittingly ironic punishment for those who refused to follow a single ideal in life. Because of their former immobility now they are "stimolati molto/ Da mosconi e da vespe" (III, 65-66). Virgil claims that they were never really alive: "mai non fur vivi" (III, 64). If as much cannot be said of Belacqua and Murphy, at least their earnest desires tend in that direction.

[66] Dante has no pity for the lukewarm. These lines are a transposition of his compassion for the soothsayers. As we have seen, it is there that the phrase "Qui vive la pietà quand' è ben morta" (*Inf.* XX, 28) occurs. Dante's pity in "Text" is presumptuous because it is incompatible with divine justice. "Passionate" stems from "passion comporta" (XX, 30), "fool" from "sciocchi" (XX, 27).

> to the sad maimed shades
> and stand cold
> on the cold moon.[67]   (54-69)

Above Poetry and Beneath It

The next two pieces to come up for brief consideration can scarcely be called poems at all. They are interesting as documents, however, for they illustrate Beckett's intellectualism in one case and his recognition of the importance of the subconscious in the other. The acrostic "Home Olga" is in essence an admirer's farewell to the master.[68] Beckett is "getting off the Joyce bandwagon."

HOME OLGA[69]

> J might be made sit up for[70] a jade of hope (and exile,
>   don't you know)[71]

[67] The moon, so often associated with love, becomes in the popular belief that its markings represent Cain and his bundle of thorns an emblem of God's justice. Thus the moon is cold because pity for Cain is withheld. Virgil urges Dante to imitate the impassivity of the moon.

[68] First published in *Contempo*, III (Chapel Hill, N.C., 15 Feb. 1934), 3. The poem is also mentioned by Joyce in a letter dated July 22, 1932 and is reprinted in Richard Ellmann, *James Joyce* (New York: Oxford University Press, 1959), p. 714.

[69] According to Beckett, the phrase "Home Olga" was a private joke shared by a circle of friends in Paris in the early 1930's. It originated at an earlier party in Ireland when a bored husband, unable to contain himself any longer, got his coat and his wife's, said to her, "Home Olga!" and swept her out the door without so much as a word of farewell to the hostess. At subsequent parties the phrase signaled ennui and became a covert call for relief and regroupment at a pre-selected cafe. The application to the present poem is clear, but Joyce never indicated to Beckett that he was aware of the meaning of the title.

[70] "To stand for."

[71] The colors traditionally associated with the theological virtues: green for hope, red for charity (4), and white for faith (7). They are linked in the poem to corresponding qualities, "silence, exile, and cunning," which figure in the strategy of Stephen Dedalus in *A Portrait of the Artist as a Young Man*: "—Look here, Cranley, he said. You have asked me what I would do and what I would not do. I will tell you what I will do and what I will not do. I will not serve that in which I no longer believe, whether it call itself my home, my fatherland, or my church: and I will try to express myself in some mode of life or art as freely as I can and as wholly

And Jesus and Jesuits juggernauted in the haemorrhoidal
    isle,[72]

Modo et forma anal maiden,[73] giggling to death in
    stomacho.[74]

E for the erythrite of love and silence and the sweet
    noo style,[75]

Swoops and loops of love and silence in the eye of the
    sun and view of the mew,[76]

Juvante Jah and a Jain or two and the tip of a friendly
    yiddophile.[77]

O for an opal of faith and cunning winking adieu,
    adieu, adieu;[78]

Yesterday shall be tomorrow,[79] riddle me that my
    rapparee;[80]

Che sarà sarà che fu, there's more than Homer knows
    how to spew,[81]

Exempli gratia: ecce himself and the pickthank agnus—
                              e.o.o.e.[82]

---

as I can, using for my defence the only arms I allow myself to use—silence, exile, and cunning" (New York. The Viking Press, 1964), pp. 246-247.

[72] The Catholic Church in Ireland.

[73] The unnatural sterility of the country.

[74] *In petto.* Allusion to a certain atmosphere then prevalent in Dublin pubs, described by Beckett as "miserable, provincial sneering and quipping at everything."

[75] The *dolce stil novo* of Dante and Joyce's hope of creating an original mode of expression.

[76] The bird imagery suggests Daedalus, the high-flying experimenter, a figure of Joyce the artist in *A Portrait of the Artist as a Young Man.*

[77] With the help of Yahweh, a couple of adherents of the Indian religion Jainism, and a God seen (in *Ulysses*) as a collector of prepuces. This last refers also to a joke current in Ireland at the time: "Take a tip from me— as the Jew said to the Rabbi."

[78] The jewel glinting suggests the wink, related to Stephen's cunning. The triple adieu is from one of Joyce's favorite songs (in his *Chamber Music*).

[79] Time telescoped in *Finnegans Wake*, reiterated in Italian at the beginning of line 9.

[80] Here no doubt in the sense of vagabond, recalling exile in line 1. The phrase is an echo of a line in the Anna Livia fragment of *Finnegans Wake*: "Latin me that me Trinity scholard."

[81] Satirical thrust at the Irish poet who compared himself to the blind bard of Greece.

[82] At the end of his half-ironic poem *à la maniere de* Joyce, Beckett pre-

"For Future Reference"[83] is a dream recorded by the poet and left, as the title indicates, for possible use in the years to come. In many of its details the poem is obscure, but the general sense is clear enough. If we are to judge by the poem, Beckett must have suffered as a youth from contact with certain of his professors. Fear of the teacher is associated in the poem with fear of high places. Beckett was plagued by a recurring nightmare in which he was required to dive into a small and distant pool closely ringed by jagged rocks. In *Watt* (p. 222) he writes of "an uneasy sleep, lacerated by dreams, by dives from dreadful heights into rocky waters, before a numerous public." He attributes such dreams to diving lessons he received at the age of six from his father at the "Forty-foot Hole," a rocky swimming spot on the coast south of Dublin. He learned to dog-paddle, but paid the price in dreams that shrank the pool, sharpened the rocks, and elevated the diving board. While Beckett holds no grudge, he is not today an advocate of the sink-or-swim method of instruction. These events are no doubt related to an unusual sport which strangely enough delighted him as a boy. He would climb a tall fir tree on the grounds of Cooldri-nagh, the family home, and project himself from its upper reaches to crash through branches to the earth. In spite of what would seem to be traumatic experiences of heights, Beckett came to love high diving, in which he continued to indulge until very recent years. In "Dream of Fair to Middling Women" we read: "To take her arm, to flow together, out of step, down the asphalt bed, was a foundering in music, the slow ineffable flight of a dream-dive, a launching and terrible foundering in a rich rape of water. Her grace was supplejack, it was cutty-stool and cavaletto,[84] he trembled as on a springboard, jutting out, doomed, high over dream-water. Would she sink or swim in Diana's well? That depends what we mean by a maiden" (pp. 29-30). Again, on page 39, Belacqua's microcosm ("going back into one's heart") is described as "not sleep, not yet,

---

sents the poem ("Exempli gratia"). *Ecce homo* becomes *ecce* Joyce in an analogy between Christ the Word and Joyce the wordman. But Beckett the young disciple is also responsible for the poem, and he pictures himself as the lamb following the shepherd, an ungrateful lamb who has decided to leave the flock. The poem ends with the initials e.o.o.e., errors or omissions excepted.

[83] In *Transition*, Nos. 19-20 (June 1930), pp. 342-343.

[84] Note the correspondence to the vocabulary of "Sanies II."

nor dream, with its sweats and terrors." And at the beginning of
"Yellow" the author writes: "He waked with it [a line from Hardy's
Tess] now in his mind, as though it had been there all the time he
slept, holding that fragile place against dreams" (*MP*, p. 229). The
terror of dreaming is a leitmotif that runs through Beckett's writing
as a kind of subterranean analogue to the misery of living. The
reality of the subconscious life of the mind probably has a bearing
on the notion that all life does not immediately cease upon death,
which we find in the early unpublished short story entitled "Echo's
Bones" and in the recent dramatic work *Play*.

FOR FUTURE REFERENCE

My cherished chemist friend
lured me aloofly
down from the cornice
into the basement[85]
and there:
drew bottles of acid and alkali out of his breast
to a colourscale accompaniment
    (mad dumbells spare me!)
fiddling deft and expert
with the doubled jointed nutcrackers of the hen's ovaries   10
But I stilled my cringing[86]
and smote him
yes oh my strength!
smashed
mashed
    (peace my incisors!)
flayed and crushed him
with a ready are you steady
cuff-discharge.
But did I?   20

And then the bright waters
beneath the broad board
the trembling blade of the streamlined divers
and down to our waiting
to my enforced buoyancy

[85] A clear analogy to diving from a height and penetrating beneath a
surface.

[86] The chemist has plainly become a threatening figure.

came floating the words of
the Mutilator
and the work of his fingerjoints:
observe gentlemen one of
the consequences of the displacement of   30
(click)!
the muncher.[87]
The hair shall be grey
above the left temple
the hair shall be grey there
    abracadabra!
     sweet wedge of birds faithless!
God blast you yes it is we see
God bless you professor
we can't clap or we'd sink   40
three cheers for the perhaps pitiful professor[88]
next per shaving? next per sh. . . . . ?
Well of all the . . . . !
that little bullet-headed bristle-cropped
red-faced rat of a pure mathematician
that I thought was experimenting with barbed wire in
    the Punjab[89]
up he comes surging to the landing steps
and tells me I'm putting no guts in my kick.
Like this he says like this.
Well I just swam out nimbly   50
blushing and hopeless
with the little swift strokes that I like and . . . . . .
Whoops!
over the stream and the tall green bank
in a strong shallow arch[90]
and his face all twisted calm and patient

[87] Lines 21 through 32 evoke the swimming and diving situation. Here the threatening figure takes the form of the "Mutilator" and seems to be a professor giving a lecture on anatomy ("displacement of" the jaw).

[88] In these lines (39-41) we have the professor and students attempting to placate him.

[89] The swimming and diving experience continues with a new teacher, a Trinity friend of Beckett's who went into the Indian Civil Service.

[90] Again the danger of landing not in the water but on solid land. See also line 59, below.

and the board ledge doing its best to illustrate
Bruno's identification of contraries[91]
into the water or on to the stones?
No matter at all he can't come back   60
from far bay or stony ground
yes here he is
(he must have come under)
for the second edition
      coming
house innings set half or anything. . .[92]

if he can't come twice
or forgets his lesson
or breaks his leg
he might forget me   70
they all might . . . . ![93]

so the snowy floor of the parrot's cell
burning at dawn
the palaiate of my strange mouth.[94]

Eros and the Need for Liberating Experience

The first four poems discussed (and "Ooftish") are concerned with the metaphysical problem of God's mercy and justice and in general with the relationship between a kind of "mysticism" and feminine beauty and love. The concern with art that we noted there becomes dominant in the last four jettisoned poems. In "Home Olga" the poet expresses his need to free himself from literary masters and strike out on his own. In "Gnome," as we saw, this need becomes quite explicit. There Beckett turns his back on the years

[91] This poem, written when Beckett was at the Ecole Normale, is of the same period as his essay on Joyce, "Dante. . . Bruno. Vico. . Joyce," in *Our Exagmination* . . . (pp. 3-22). In that essay he analyzes Bruno's theory of the identification of contraries, here suggested by the diving board that vibrates so rapidly that its highest and lowest points seem to coincide.

[92] The second half in theater, cricket, tennis, and rugby.

[93] Hopefully the professor will not return, and the pupil will be spared further torture.

[94] An image used by Beckett ("Dream," p. 27) to describe the reveler's morning mouth and at the same time a somewhat gratuitous allusion to a line of Verlaine.

of study and accuses the intellectual life of jeopardizing direct experience of existence. The following poems either propose the erotic as such experience or else indict it as simply another shackle that the poet in search of varied materials for his art must break. One of the four poems in this group is wholeheartedly under the sign of Eros. The title, "Hell Crane to Starling," is taken from Canto V of Dante's *Inferno*, where we find the moving episode of Paolo and Francesca and another example of Dante's pity for the damned. Those who have sinned out of carnal desire are blown through the air by powerful winds that are emblematic of passion. The birds—cranes, starlings, and doves—are associated with incontinence:

> E come li stornei ne portan l'ali
> Nel freddo tempo, a schiera larga e piena,
> Così quel fiato li spiriti mali.
> Di qua, di là, di giù, di su li mena;
> Nulla speranza li conforta mai,
> Non che di posa, ma di minor pena.
> E come i gru van cantando lor lai,
> Faccendo in aere di sè lunga riga,
> Così vidi venir, traendo guai,
> Ombre portate da la detta briga.
>
> . . . .
>
> Quali colombe dal disio chiamate,
> Con l'ali alzate e ferme, al dolce nido
> Vegnon per l'aere dal voler portate. . . .
>
> (*Inf.* V, 40-49; 82-84)

Beckett quotes the same Canto (V, 24) in "Dream of Fair to Middling Women" to castigate the eroticism of women in general: "Grit in the mistral, tattered starlings in the devil's blizzard . . . sniffing at you and snatching at you and committing decorous nuisance with the nozzle. 'Vuolsi così colà, dove si puote/ ciò che si vuole, e più non dimandare' " (p. 32). Having provided the background to the poem, Dante gives way to Beckett's other important source of material for his early writing, the Bible. In essence the poem is an invitation to erotic fun and games proffered to a lusty female, along with a denunciation of a possible rival as much too effeminate for her tastes.

HELL CRANE TO STARLING[95]

Oholiba charm of my eyes[96]
there is a cave above Tsoar[97]
and a Spanish donkey there.[98]

You needn't bring wine to that non-relation.

And he won't know
who changed his name
when Jehovah sprained the seam of his haunch
in Peniel in Peniel
after he's sent on the thirty camels
suckling for dear death   10
and so many fillies
that I don't want log tablets.[99]

---

[95] In *The European Caravan*, p. 475.

[96] Ezek. 23:1-4: "The word of the Lord came again unto me, saying, Son of man, there were two women, the daughters of one mother: And they committed whoredoms in Egypt; they committed whoredoms in their youth: there were their breasts pressed, and there they bruised the teats of their virginity. And the names of them were Aholah the elder, and Aholibah her sister: and they were mine, and they bore sons and daughters. Thus were their names; Samaria is Aholah, and Jerusalem Aholibah."

[97] Gen. 19:22-24, 30-32: "Haste thee, escape thither; for I cannot do any thing till thou be come thither. Therefore the name of the city was called Zoar. The sun was risen upon the earth when Lot entered into Zoar. Then the Lord rained upon Sodom and upon Gomorrah brimstone and fire from the Lord out of heaven. . . . And Lot went up out of Zoar, and dwelt in the mountain, and his two daughters with him; for he feared to dwell in Zoar: and he dwelt in a cave, he and his two daughters. And the firstborn said unto the younger, Our father is old, and there is not a man in the earth to come in unto us after the manner of all the earth: Come, let us make our father drink wine, and we will lie with him, that we may preserve seed of our father."

Cf. three related pieces on sex in Ireland: "Che Sciagura," in *T.C.D., A College Miscellany*, XXXVI, No. 622 (Dublin, 14 Nov. 1929), p. 42; "Censorship in the Saorstat," an unpublished essay written about 1936; and the passage on Bando in *Watt*, p. 170.

[98] Ezek. 23:20: "For she doted upon their paramours, whose flesh is as the flesh of asses, and whose issue is like the issue of horses." See also line 23, below.

[99] Allusion in lines 5 through 12 is to Gen. 32, where Jacob comes bearing gifts (camels, cattle, and other livestock) for his brother Esau and wrestles

Mister Jacobson mister Hippolitus-in-hell Jacobson
we all know
how you tried to rejoin your da.
Bilha always blabs.[100]

Because Benoni skirted aftercrop
of my aching loins[101]
you'll never see him
reddening the wall in two dimensions[102]   20
and if you did
you might spare the postage to Chaldea.[103]

---

with the angel, who puts his thigh out of joint. There Jacob's name is changed
to Israel, and he calls the place Peniel. See also Gen. 35:10.

[100] Gen. 35:22: "And it came to pass, when Israel dwelt in that land, that
Reuben [son of Israel] went and lay with Bilhah his father's concubine: and
Israel heard of it."

[101] Benoni (literally, "son of pain") was Jacob's last child by Rachel. Gen.
35:18: "And it came to pass, as her soul was in departing (for she died)
that she called his name Benoni: but his father called him Benjamin." In this
last section of the poem Benjamin is seen as an effeminate type, perhaps
because the name has become synonymous with the youngest child in a
family, who may be coddled and spoiled by parents and older brothers and
sisters. It seems that the only Biblical justification for the poet's interpretation
is the fact that Benjamin did occupy a special place in the affections of Jacob
and was protected by him as well as by his older brother Joseph, and, it
would seem from Moses' blessing as described in Deut. 33:12, by God also:
"And of Benjamin he said, The beloved of the Lord shall dwell in safety by
him; and the Lord shall cover him all the day long, and he shall dwell
between his shoulders."

[102] As an alternative to the poet's portrait of a somewhat less than virile
Benoni we find wall-paintings in vermilion of Chaldeans, pictures that held a
powerful fascination for Aholibah according to Ezek. 23:14-15: "And that
she increased her whoredoms: for when she saw men pourtrayed upon the
wall, the images of the Chaldeans pourtrayed with vermilion, girded with
girdles upon their loins, exceeding in dyed attire upon their heads, all of them
princes to look to, after the manner of the Babylonians of Chaldea, the land
of their nativity."

[103] Ezek. 23:16-17: "And as soon as she saw them with her eyes, she doted
upon them, and sent messengers unto them into Chaldea. And the Babylonians came to her into the bed of love, and they defiled her with their
whoredom, and she was polluted with them, and her mind was alienated from
them."

But there's a bloody fine ass
lepping[104] with stout and impurée de pommes[105]
in the hill above Tsoar.

It was in reference particularly to the 1931 "Hell Crane to Starling" that Beckett spoke of himself as "a young man with nothing
to say and the itch to make." Nevertheless, there is one line in the
poem that has a certain significance. As in other instances, the
April 13 poet chooses to make a personal statement in line 13 of
his poem. Mr. Jacobson (the son of Jacob, i.e., Reuben, who
seduced his father's concubine, Bilhah) is analogous to the composite figure of Hippolitus-in-hell, or chaste innocence in search of
amorous experience. Recalling the poet's sympathy for Paolo and
Francesca in "Text" and the amorous adventures of Belacqua, that
innocent abroad,[106] not to mention line 13 of "Casket of Pralinen"
("assumption of the innocents"), the poem "Gnome," and others,
we realize that Beckett, the young Irishman recently arrived in
Paris, where wild oats are traditionally sown, must have been well
aware of the choices facing him. Perhaps the use of the erotic *and*
the Biblical in "Hell Crane to Starling" reflects the uncertainty of a
puritan conscience anxious for amorous experience yet not unfamiliar with religious scruples.

In any case, one of the better jettisoned poems seems to mirror
such a conflict. In "From the Only Poet to a Shining Whore,"[107]
the only (i.e., greatest) poet, Dante, addresses Rahab, the harlot
of Jericho, in the first ten lines and Beatrice in the last seven. In
the Bible, Rahab is a figure of the saving power of faith. In Hebrews
11:31 we read: "By faith the harlot Rahab perished not with them
that believed not, when she had received the spies with peace."
Dante puts her in the heaven of Venus among those whose love was
too much of the flesh. In Beckett's poem her love and confident
faith are contrasted with the attitude of Beatrice. As a figure of

[104] Irish for "leaping." In "Dante and the Lobster" Belacqua muses over
the meaning of the word as applied to a crustacean. Unlike a fish, a "lepping
fresh" lobster is still alive.

[105] Without the *im*, the French equivalent of mashed potatoes.

[106] See p. 33 of "Dream," for example.

[107] Written in the Dôme Café in Montparnasse and published in *Henry-
Music* (Paris: The Hours Press, 1930), which contains music by Henry
Crowder and poems by Samuel Beckett and others.

respectable woman ("mother, sister, daughter, beloved"), Beatrice lacks the unquestioning acceptance shown by Rahab, the social outcast. Beatrice is a figure of angry doubt, resembling the Beatrice who rejected the pre-*vita nuova* Dante. The beautiful concluding lines of the poem are a reproach to Beatrice. God seems disappointed in her lack of faith in the young Dante sowing wild oats with the dissolute Forese Donati. After all, was He not capable of bringing Rahab to salvation? Surely He can do the same for Dante —or for the companion of a "dissipated mandarin." In the last line, "and my sorrow," we can imagine a fusion between the narrator Dante and the poet Beckett. The poem, then, seems to be a gentle reproach on the part of the Irish poet to loved ones in Ireland who fear for him in his descent through the various circles of the Parisian "inferno."

FROM THE ONLY POET TO A SHINING WHORE

For Henry Crowder to sing.

Rahab of the holy battlements,[108]
bright dripping shaft[109]
in the bright bright patient
pearl-brow dawn-dusk lover of the sun.[110]

[108] See Dante, *Par.* IX, 112-125 and Josh. 2 and 3.

[109] Cf. *Par.* IX, 114: "Come raggio di sole in acqua mera."

[110] A description of the planet Venus (Cantos VIII and IX of the *Paradiso*), the bright "star" that patiently follows the sun and can be seen at dawn and at dusk near the horizon. The image "pearl-brow" is taken from *Par.* III, 14: "Debili sì che perla in bianca fronte. . . ." Like a pearl against a white brow, souls in the moon, Piccarda Donati among others, appear as faint, translucent images of human beings, like reflections in water or glass. Beckett applies the image to the planet Venus as it appears against the background of the sun's light at dawn or dusk, light against light and visible only as a faint image of its real splendor.

In "Dream of Fair to Middling Women" (pp. 155-156) we read, "Her great eyes went as black as sloes. . . . Pupil and white swamped in the dark iris gone black as night. . . . Now under the threat of night the evening is albescent, its hues have blanched, it is dim white and palpable, it pillows and mutes her head. So that as from transparent polished glass or, if you prefer, from tranquil shining waters, the details of his face return so feeble that a pearl on a white brow comes not less promptly to his pupils, so now he sees her vigilant face and in him is reversed the error that lit love between the man . . . and the pool. For she had closed the eyes. 'Spirit of the moon' he said." In *Watt* the same image is used, not to describe an attenuated (and

306

Puttanina mia!
You hid them happy in the high flax,[111]
pale before the fords
of Jordan, and the dry red waters,[112]
and you lowered a pledge
of scarlet hemp.[113]   10

Oh radiant, oh angry, oh Beatrice,
she foul with the victory
of the bloodless fingers
and proud, and you, Beatrice, mother, sister,
    daughter, belovèd,
fierce pale flame
of doubt, and God's sorrow,
and my sorrow.

Anteros and the Trap of Love

Eroticism may offer a corrective to Irish puritanism, but it has
its own dangers. It can lead to carnal enslavement, boredom (see
the poem "elles viennent"), or to psychological and even marital
commitment (see "Sanies II": "get along with you now"). From
this point of view the last two poems, "Return to the Vestry" and

---

hence more desirable) vision of the self or the other, but to express the negative mystery of Mr. Knott: "Add to this that the few glimpses caught of Mr.
Knott, by Watt, were not clearly caught, but as it were in a glass, not a look-
ing-glass, a plain glass, an eastern window at morning, a western window at
evening" (p. 147).

[111] Cf. Josh. 2:6: "But she had brought them up to the roof of the house,
and hid them with the stalks of flax, which she had laid in order upon the
roof."

[112] Cf. Josh. 2:9-11 (the fear of the inhabitants of Jericho), 3, and 5:1:
"And it came to pass, when all the kings of the Amorites, which were on the
side of Jordan westward, and all the kings of the Canaanites, which were by
the sea, heard that the Lord had dried up the waters of Jordan from before
the children of Israel, until we were passed over, that their heart melted,
neither was their spirit in them any more, because of the children of Israel."

[113] Josh. 2:18-21: "Behold, when we come into the land, thou shalt bind
this line of scarlet thread in the window which thou didst let us down by. . . .
And she sent them away and they departed: and she bound the scarlet line
in the window."

"Yoke of Liberty," are in tension with the two preceding, "Hell Crane to Starling" and "From the Only Poet." During 1926, the year before he graduated from Trinity, Beckett spent the summer in Tours. He stayed at a *pension* called Le Petit Belmont on a hill outside town, and it was there that he met Charles C. Clark. Together they bicycled through the Loire Valley visiting the châteaux. Later Clark visited Beckett's family in Ireland (1927) and they drove together through the Wicklow mountains. During his summer in the Loire Valley, Beckett made an artistic pilgrimage to the burial place of Ronsard at the Prieuré de Saint-Cosme near Tours. Excavations were being carried on at the time to find the remains of Ronsard. The poet's chapel had been made into a kind of stable with hay on the floor and agricultural implements here and there. Beckett was saddened by the signs of neglect and indifference in the ruined chapel of the great French poet. In the first stanza of "Return to the Vestry" the young Irish poet hides his emotion beneath a mask of burlesque. He stems his sadness by reducing Ronsard's noble, flowing language to rough, abrupt phrases. His colloquial realism muffles the soaring, sorrowful song of the French poet much as the "factorized" indifference of the modern world has abolished the ancient aristocracy of beauty. Lines 1 through 4 and 21 through 33 are a transliteration of Ronsard's description of his trip up a mountain and the ancient purification rites he performed there, contained in the ode entitled "Magie, ou delivrance d'amour." In the last stanza of the poem we can easily detect the characteristic Beckett note of sorrow and withdrawal. Ronsard's clarion call to a warlike Anteros, the god of antilove, becomes a plea to a gentle, dark, and dispassionate divinity for help and a hiding place from Eros.

RETURN TO THE VESTRY[114]

Lover
off with your braces
Slouch in unbuttoned ease

[114] In *The New Review, An International Notebook for the Arts*, I, No. 3 (Paris, Aug.-Oct. 1931), 98-99.

fill a sack take a porter climb a mountain[115]
as he did[116]
the deaf conceited lecherous laypriest[117]
the vindictive old sausage-sprinkler
   dirt in a dirt floor
   in a chapel barn
   by a stifled stream.[118]   10
Zoroaster
politely factorized[119]
and a hay-rake
guarantee his siesta
except during the harvest season when the
   latter is removed.
I may be mistaken
but—

[115] Ronsard, "Magie, ou delivrance d'amour," *Oeuvres complètes*, ed. Laumonier, II, 457-460:

> Sans avoir lein qui m'estraigne,
>   Sans cordon, ceinture ny nouds,
>   Et sans jartiere à mes genous
>   Je vien dessus ceste montagne:
> A fin qu'autant soit relasché
>   Mon coeur d'amoureuses tortures,
>   Comme de noeuds et de ceintures
>   J'ay le corps icy detaché.
>
> . . . .
>
>   Sus, Page, verse à mon costé
>   Le sac que tu as apporté,
>   Pour me guarir de ma folie.
>   (1-8, 26-28)

Beckett refers three times to this particular ode in "Dream of Fair to Middling Women" (pp. 25, 61, 156). Note also the pun on "sack" and "porter."

[116] The poet-lover addresses himself: "Off with the suspenders and into hiking clothes. A porter needed to carry the equipment. Then up the mountain to repeat the ritual climb Ronsard made."

[117] Ronsard became deaf after a grave illness; was convinced his work would enjoy immortal fame; gave a great role to love in his life and poetry; was tonsured and received minor orders and ecclesiastical allowances.

[118] Good lines that express Beckett's sorrow at the fate of the French poet, whose chapel has become a barn and whose voice, like the stream, has been stifled.

[119] A sundial, possibly.

tears covering all risks—[120]
I took a time exposure   20
and wept into my hat
So
swell the cairn[121] and spill the doings.[122]
Burn sulphur![123]
Juniper flame to a swirl of ashes![124]
Drown the Singer[125]
I'm done with stitch anguish.[126]
Now a compress of wormwood and verbena
on my fiery buttocks[127]

[120] Perhaps the remains of Ronsard are not in the chapel, but the poet's emotion is its own justification.

[121] The Irish tradition of adding a stone to any cairn one happens on.

[122] Empty the knapsack.

[123] In "Magie . . ." we read:

> Brule du soufre et de l'encens:
>> Comme en l'air je voy consommée
>> Leur vapeur, se puisse en fumée
>> Consommer le mal que je sens.
>> (29-32)

[124] Another herb used in purification rites. In "Magie . . .":

> Laisse dans ce Genievre prendre
> Un feu s'enfumant peu à peu;
> Amour, je ne veux plus de feu,
> Je ne veux plus que de la cendre.
> (41-44)

[125] No more love poems. Possibly from "Magie . . .":

> Verse moy l'eau de ceste esguiere:
> Et comme à bas tu la respans,
> Qu'à bas s'espande le Megere
> De l'amour dont je me repans.
> (33-36)

[126] A pun combining the anguish expressed in love songs and a reference to the Singer sewing machine.

[127] Medicinal herbs mentioned in "Magie . . .":

> Vien viste, enlasse moy le flanc
> Non de Thym ny de Marjolaine,
> Mais bien d'Armoise et de Vervaine,
> Pour mieux me refraischir le sang.
> (45-48)

The reduction of the noble "flanc" of the tradition to a crudely realistic "buttocks" is a typical example of Beckett's purposeful stylistic and semantic strategy.

Smother the place in Cerebos it stinks of breeding.[128]
Here's the mange of beauty in a corporation bucket!   30
Shovel it into the winds![129]
Loose the sparrows.
Pluck that pigeon she dribbles fertility.[130]
Mumps and a orchid to Fräulein Miranda.[131]
Gentle Anteros[132]

[128] Cerebos is a brand of salt, used here as a purifying agent. In "Magie . . .":

> Verse du sel en ceste place:
> Comme il est infertile, ainsi
> L'engeance du cruel soucy
> Ne couve plus en moy de race.
> (49-52)

[129] The souvenirs of love which Ronsard brought with him in "a corporation bucket" (Irish term for ash can) and which he throws to the winds. In "Magie . . .":

> Apporte moy tous ses presens,
> Ses cheveux, ses gans, sa peinture,
> Romps ses lettres, son escriture,
> Et jette les morceaux aux vents.
> (53-56)

[130] Symbols of love and lasciviousness. In "Magie . . .":

> Vien donq, ouvre moy ceste cage,
> Et laisse vivre en libertez
> Ces pauvres oiseaux arrestez
> Ainsi que j'estois en servage.
> Paisseteaux, volez à plaisir,
> De ma cage je vous delivre,
> Comme desormais je veux vivre
> Au gré de mon premier desir.
> Vole ma douce Tourterelle,
> Le vray symbole de l'amour,
> Je ne veux plus ny nuict ny jour
> Entendre ta plainte fidelle.
> Pigeon, je te veux desplumer,
> Et respandant au vent ta plume,
> Puissé-je en forceant ma coustume
> Me plumer les ailes d'aimer.
> (57-72)

[131] The amorous heroine of Shakespeare's play, *The Tempest*. Here the poet wishes for her betrothed, Ferdinand, the sterility engendered by mumps. "Orchid" suggests the same idea through its etymological link with "orchitis."

[132] Antilove, the Greek divinity, son of Ares and Aphrodite, daughter of

dark and dispassionate
come a grave snake with peace to my quarry
and choke my regret[133]
noble Anteros
and coil at the door of my quarry tomb   40
and span its rim with a luminous awning
shallow and dim
as a grey tilt of silk
filtering sadly
the weary triumph of morning.[134]

Or mock a duller impurity.[135]

Perhaps the little poem "Yoke of Liberty"[136] sums up better than

---

Zeus and Dione. He was sometimes represented arguing with his brother
Eros. In "Magie . . .":

> Anterot, preste moy la main,
> Enfonce tes fleches diverses:
> Il faut que pour moy tu renverses
> Cet ennemy du genre humain.
>
> .   .   .   .
> Je veux à la façon antique
> Bastir un temple de cyprés,
> Où d'Amour je rompray les traicts
> Dessus l'autel Anterotique.
> (21-24, 73-76)

[133] Anteros is a dark and dispassionate god, against life and love. The poet
both regrets giving up his love and longs to escape from it to the peace of
solitary seclusion. Like Belacqua he is both Phoebus and Narcissus, the
pursuer and the pursued, who would stem the outward-turning of the self,
who would keep apart and avoid involvement. These lines of Beckett are
wholly original. At age twenty-five he could hardly follow Ronsard in lines
77-80 of "Magie . . .":

> Vivant il ne faut plus mourir,
> Il faut du coeur s'oster la playe:
> Dix lustres veulent que j'essaye
> Le remede de me guarir.

[134] A sentiment typical of Beckett: morning begins the whole miserable
business all over again. We recognize in this line the antidawn note in both
"Alba" and "Dortmunder."

[135] That is, either protect me or go mock some more naïve servant of Eros.
The narrator admits to impurity but is aware of its price.

[136] In *The European Caravan*, p. 480. The title is taken from a passage in
Dante's *De Monarchia* (Bk. II, Chap. 1): "ad ostendendum genus humanum

any other this whole group of twelve. At least implicit in each of these poems is the tension between body and spirit, between Eros and Anteros, between the bonds of love and religion and a lonely freedom that is only half wanted. "From the Only Poet to a Shining Whore" reminds us of "plush hymens on your eyeballs" in "Serena III." The young poet needs and demands an untrammeled time. The quest for experience means abandoning for a time at least—whatever the cost—the ways of home, religion, countryland, and love. It is to Beckett's artistic credit that the tension is never wholly resolved, that the complex relationship between man's freedom and his servitude is never grossly oversimplified in favor of one side or the other. As we saw in prior poems, the need for solitary independence is only relatively stronger than the need for social intercourse. One does not eliminate the other. Even in a poem like "Hell Crane to Starling" the joyful burlesque and delighted game with words and allusions give the lie to what might otherwise seem to be a complete dedication to the lascivious little god. We are much more in the realm of play than of serious intent. The same ambiguity is present in the final alternative of "Return to the Vestry": "or mock a duller impurity." "Yoke of Liberty" owes its excellence in good part to the fact that the poet maintains as part of the very fabric of the poem this paradoxical union of contrary needs.[137] Except for the title, which he owes to Dante, the poem is wholly Beckett's. As later, when he abandons literary allusion in favor of simplicity and personal statement, there is a great gain in quiet beauty. The title makes the initial statement of ambivalence. In the poem itself the trapping and hunting images suggest the captivity, suffering, or death that awaits the prey of beauty. Their readiness to succumb accounts for the weariness of the huntress.

---

liberum a iugo ipsorum, cum Propheta sanctissimo meme subsequentem hortabor, subsequentia subadsumens: 'Dirumpamus,' videlicet, 'vincula eorum, et proiciamus a nobis iugum ipsorum.' " This passage in turn is drawn from Psalms 2:1-3.

[137] Beckett is well aware of the importance of an aesthetic of tension, as we can judge from a passage in "Dream" where he lightheartedly admits, apropos of "Return to the Vestry": "we have a little note somewhere on Anteros we do believe, in fact we seem to remember we once wrote a poem . . . on him or to him cogged from the liquorish laypriest's Magic Ode and if we don't forget we'll have the good taste to shove in the little ducky-diver as a kind of contrapuntal compensation do you comprehend us and in deference to your Pisan penchants for literary stress and strain" (p. 61).

313

Her triumphs come too surely over too-willing victims. A number of words in the poem suggest that the poet himself is not insensitive to her compelling attractions. But he is "watchful" and has mastered his longing for amorous defeat. His sorrow has been "tamed" (11). At the same time, her failure—linked by the image of a crescent to the waning moon of love—arouses his pity and is his own certain loss as well as his gain. The liberty he guards so jealously is not only a need but also an unwelcome burden. Once again we find the dilemma of a young man at a crossroads, torn between Phoebus and Narcissus, temptation and knighthood, Eros and Anteros.

YOKE OF LIBERTY

The lips of her desire are grey
and parted like a silk loop
threatening
a slight wanton wound.
She preys wearily
on sensitive wild things
proud to be torn
by the grave crouch of her beauty.
But she will die and her snare[138]
tendered so patiently
to my tamed watchful sorrow
will break and hang
in a pitiful crescent.

[138] The erotic aggression of the Syra-Cusa is translated in "Dream" (p. 44) by the images of "a coiled spring, and a springe, too, to catch woodcocks."

314

viii. Early Prose & Poetry: General Themes

Certain passages in "Dream of Fair to Middling Women" and a smaller number in *More Pricks Than Kicks* are of considerable importance to an understanding of Beckett's early poetry as well as his later drama and fiction. Since he has decided, for the present at any rate, not to permit publication of "Dream" nor republication of *More Pricks*, we shall set down in this chapter a few pertinent excerpts in order to provide some access to these materials. "Dream" is a storehouse of Beckett viewpoints, on five topics in particular. Love, death, and religion we have already discussed at some length. Here we shall limit ourselves to two other themes with a future in his writing, the microcosm and art, and comment briefly on motifs related to each. At a certain moment in his career, toward the end of World War II, Beckett decided he wanted to become the artist of the inner world—and he has surely done so in the years since that decision. The following selections will show how surprisingly prominent these two themes are even in his earliest writing.

Four Motifs Related to the Microcosm:
Absence, Silence, Time, Space

—The real presence was a pest because it did not give the imagination a break. Without going as far as Stendhal, who said . . . that the best music . . . was the music that became inaudible after a few bars, we do declare and maintain stiffly . . . that the object that becomes invisible before your eyes is, so to speak, the brightest and best. ("Dream," pp. 9-10)

So she had been, sad and still, without limbs or paps in a great stillness of body, that summer evening in the green isle when first she heaved his soul from its hinges; as quiet as a tree, column of quiet. Pinus puella quondam fuit. Alas fuit! So he would always have her be, rapt, like the spirit of a troubadour, casting no shade, herself shade. Instead of which of course it was only a

315

question of seconds before she would surge up at him, blithe and buxom and young and lusty, a lascivious petulant virgin, a generous mare neighing after a great horse, caterwauling after a great stallion. . . . Only the spirit of the troubadour, rapt in a niche of rock, huddled and withdrawn forever if no prayers go up for him, raccolta a se, like a lion. And without anger. It is a poor anger that rises when the stillness is broken, our anger, the poor anger of the world that life cannot be still, that live things cannot be active quietly, that the neighbor is not a moon, slow wax and wane of phases, changeless in a tranquility of changes. But without measure, all anyhow. I, he thought, and she and the neighbor are cities bereft of light, where the citizen carries his torch. I shall separate myself and the neighbor from the moon, and the lurid place that he is from the lurid place that I am. . . .

("Dream," pp. 20-21)[1]

"Not a clock" he implored, "don't say a grandfather clock."
"The grandfather and mother" she did say "of a period clock."
He turned his face to the wall. He who of late years and with the approval of Lucy would not tolerate a chronometer of any kind in the house, for whom the local publication of the hours was six of the best on the brain every hour, and even the sun's shadow a torment, now to have this time-fuse deafen the rest of his days. It was enough to make him break off the engagement.

(MP, p. 183)

. . . she . . . does not really care about moving . . . she puts not her trust in changes of scenery, she is too inward by a long chalk, she inclines towards an absolute moral geography, her soul is her only poste restante.   ("Dream," p. 157)

"Where were we?" said Belacqua.
But Neapolitan patience has its limits.
"Where are we ever?" cried the Ottolenghi, "where we were, as we were."   (MP, pp. 17-18)

The quotations given above suggest themes that are basically forms of negation: the abolition of presence and of sound, the abolition of time and of space. "Ding-Dong," the third story in More Pricks Than Kicks, illuminates the nature of these negations

---

[1] Cf. "musique de l'indifférence" and "Arènes de Lutèce."

perhaps better than any other of Beckett's early works. It is an elaboration of the theme of motion and stasis, and the motion described is a kind of moving immobility,[2] a state that annihilates time and space and releases one from normal activity in the macrocosm. The poems in *Echo's Bones* provide hints, but little more, of a relationship between movement and the microcosm in such phrases as "mind annulled/ . . . in wind" ("Enueg I"). In the later poems, where immobility is central, the relationship becomes obvious. During the long walks of the enuegs, the sanies, and the serenas in *Echo's Bones* the macrocosmic mind of the learner, lover, and sufferer works away in pain. Its activity blocks access to the site of a "flux of forms" where Murphy will find sporadic peace (p. 112).

"Ding-Dong" opens by relating motion to the inner self. "My sometime friend Belacqua enlivened the last phase of his solipsism, before he toed the line and began to relish the world, with the belief that the best thing he had to do was to move constantly from place to place" (*MP*, p. 43). Very early in the story we encounter, too, the motif of sameness (familiar from the poem "elles viennent"), which appears here as the abolition of geographical differences:

> He did not know how this conclusion had been gained, but that it was not thanks to his preferring one place to another he felt sure. . . . one was as good as another, because they all disappeared as soon as he came to rest in them. . . . Thus it is clear that his contrivance did not proceed from any discrimination between different points in space, since he returned directly, if we except an occasional pause for refreshment, to his point of departure, and truly no less recruited in spirit than if the interval had been whiled away abroad in the most highly reputed cities.
>
> (pp. 43-44)

This dismissal of geographical distinction is echoed later in the absence of distinguishing traits in the face of the woman peddler hawking "seats in heaven": "The features were null, only luminous, impassive and secure, petrified in radiance . . ." (p. 56). The movement described by Belacqua is set apart from ordinary movement in a number of ways. "The mere act of rising and going, irrespective of whence and whither, did him good. . . . Hither and thither on land and sea! . . . It was a most pleasant street, despite its name, to

---

[2] Cf. lines 10 and 90 of *Whoroscope*: "That's not moving, that's *moving*"; and "Then I will rise and move moving. . . ."

be abroad in, full as it always was with shabby substance and honest-to-God coming and going" (pp. 43, 49).[3] This to-and-fro movement, already related to the form of the circle in that it returns to the same point, becomes curvilinear in an early image of an "exercise of the boomerang, out and back" (p. 44), and explicitly circular in the image of the "spheres" that go nowhere, "only round and round" (p. 47). "Heaven goes round," says the peddler, whirling her arm, "and round and round and round and round and round" (p. 56). Essentially, the images of oscillating and circular motion are simply metaphors for directionless movement, "pure blank movement, . . . 'gress' or 'gression' " (p. 46). Thus on occasion Belacqua, at a standstill, is incapable of deciding which direction to choose and must wait for "a sign": "Now the summons to move on was a subpoena. Yet he found he could not, any more than Buridan's ass, move to right or left, backward or forward" (p. 47). When he receives a sign he inevitably goes in the opposite direction, no doubt in a kind of perverse but consistent rejection of signs, of directed movement.

The story is sprinkled with horrible examples of the unseeing but ordered motion that is characteristic of life in the macrocosm. With disenchanted irony Beckett paints a portrait of human beings with blinders on; mechanically or avidly zeroed in on paltry targets, they are oblivious to the suffering they may cause themselves or others. Human willfulness is suggested in an incident involving a blind paralytic and again when a little girl in a hurry to reach her destination is run down by a bus:

> Turning aside from this and other no less futile emblems, his attention was arrested by a wheel-chair being pushed rapidly under the arcade of the Bank, in the direction of Dame Street. It moved in and out of sight behind the bars of the columns. This was the blind paralytic who sat all day near to the corner of Fleet Street, and in bad weather under the shelter of the arcade, the same being wheeled home to his home in the Coombe. It was past his time and there was a bitter look on his face. He would give his chairman a piece of his mind when he got him to

[3] The continuing importance of this motif for Beckett is attested by the title of the very recent playlet, *Come and Go, Dramaticule*, in which this movement out and back clearly takes on symbolic resonance, suggesting the coming into life and the going forth into death.

himself. This chairman, hireling or poor relation, came every evening a little before the dark, unfastened from the beggar's neck and breast the placard announcing his distress, tucked him up snugly in his coverings and wheeled him home to his supper. He was well advised to be assiduous, for this beggar was a power in the Coombe. In the morning it was his duty to shave his man and wheel him, according to the weather, to one or other of his pitches. So it went, day after day. (p. 48)

All day the roadway was a tumult of buses, red and blue and silver. By one of these a little girl was run down, just as Belacqua drew near to the railway viaduct. She had been to the Hibernian Dairies for milk and bread and then she had plunged out into the roadway, she was in such a childish fever to get back in record time with her treasure to the tenement in Mark Street where she lived. (p. 49)

People waiting in line for the show at the Palace Cinema remain immobile, held in place like marionettes supported by pulls from opposite directions. Except in the case of a "debauched girl," the vectors of desire cancel each other out:

The .queue standing for the Palace Cinema was torn between conflicting desires: to keep their places and to see the excitement. They craned their necks and called out to know the worst, but they stood firm. Only one girl, debauched in appearance and swathed in a black blanket, fell out near the sting of the queue and secured the loaf. With the loaf under her blanket she sidled unchallenged down Mark Street and turned into Mark Lane. When she got back to the queue her place had been taken of course. But her sally had not cost her more than a couple of yards. (p. 50)

Even more interesting than the nature of the movement is the motive behind it. Although Beckett has explained his own long walks as a need for physical exercise that fatigues, calms vibrating nerves, and puts an end to the torment of thought, Belacqua, anxious to distinguish himself from the mob of common humanity, rejects such explanations: "He was at pains to make it clear to me, and to all those to whom he exposed his manoeuvre, that it was in no way cognate with the popular act of brute labour, digging and such like, exploited to disperse the dumps, an antidote depending for its efficaciousness on mere physical exhaustion, and for which he expressed the greatest contempt" (p. 45). As is very apparent in the poems of *Echo's Bones*, however, walking can be linked to surcease of suffering, and so it is for Belacqua: "these little acts of motion he was in a fair way of making, and they certainly did do him some good as a rule. It was the old story of the salad days, torment in the terms and in the intervals a measure of ease" (p. 44). The suffering in question is mental. It arises, no doubt, from prolonged hyperactivity of the conscious intellect and will that must determine directions, judge the weight of conflicting desires, decide. "Was it not from sitting still among his ideas, other people's ideas, that he had come away? What would he not give now to get on the move again! Away from ideas! . . . all he could say was that the objects in which he was used to find such recreation and repose lost gradually their hold upon him, he became insensible to them little by little, the old itch and algos crept back into his mind" (pp. 48, 53). We can note here and in "Gnome" the suffering of the poet who longs for self-expression and who has been cast as an intellectual, a learner and analyst of the ideas of others.[4] The notion of escape from intellectualism is also implicit in the narrator's accusation of Belacqua as someone who excels in wriggling out of a logical impasse: "But notice the double response, like two holes to a burrow." A secondary reason for these long walks is that they promote an increase in sensitivity favorable to poetic contemplation and eventual creativity:

> Not the least charm of this pure blank movement, this "gress" or "gression," was its aptness to receive, with or without the approval of the subject, in all their integrity the faint inscriptions of the outer world. Exempt from destination, it had not to shun the unforeseen nor turn aside from the agreeable odds and ends of vaudeville that are liable to crop up. This sensitiveness was not the least charm of this roaming that began by being blank, not the least charm of this pure act the alacrity with which it welcomed defilement. But very nearly the least. (p. 46)

The primary goal of such random wanderings is release into the microcosm, a world out of this world where time and space are suspended. Belacqua uses an image, to appear later in Beckett's

---

[4] Cf. also such parallel phrases as "keep on the move/ keep on the move" in "Serena III" and the image of "algum-trees" in "Enueg I."

letter to Axel Kaun, of a "Beethoven pause" (p. 45) in the flow of music. A "moving pause," says the protagonist, and the narrator mimics and mocks him (but at the same time suggests his own partial identification with him) by noting wryly that his friend "had a strong weakness for oxymoron" (p. 46). In the other world of the microcosm Belacqua can avoid the art that is mere disputation and the love that is exhaustion. A public house in Lombard Street, frequented by him, is another such world within a world: "Here also art and love, scrabbling in dispute or staggering home, were barred, or, perhaps better, unknown. The aesthetes and the impotent were far away. These circumstances combined to make of this place a very grateful refuge for Belacqua, who never omitted, when he found himself in its neighbourhood with the price of a drink about him, to pay it a visit" (pp. 50-51). There he enters a heaven and finds a beatitude that may not be wholly unrelated to mystical bliss but is much more the profound pleasure to be found in aesthetic experience.

Curiously enough, in the final analysis immobility provides the open sesame to the microcosm. Near the beginning of "Ding-Dong" Belacqua expresses his preference clearly:

> Being by nature however sinfully indolent, bogged in indolence, asking nothing better than to stay put at the good pleasure of what he called the Furies, he was at times tempted to wonder whether the remedy [aimless walking] were not rather more disagreeable than the complaint. But he could only suppose that it was not, seeing that he continued to have recourse to it, in a small way it is true, but nevertheless for years he continued to have recourse to it, and to return thanks for the little good it did him.
> (p. 44)

Later, inert in the pub, Belacqua hears the incantation of the ticket-selling shawlie, which, like a Proustian stimulus, releases him into a world of serenity and happiness:

> . . . he would say that the only place where he could come to anchor and be happy was a low public-house, and that all the wearisome tactics of gress and dud Beethoven would be done away with if only he could spend his life in such a place. But as they closed at ten, and as residence and good faith were viewed as incompatible, and as in any case he had not the means to

consecrate his life to stasis, even in the meanest bar, he supposed he must be content to indulge this whim from time to time, and return thanks for such sporadic mercy.   (pp. 52-53)

The association between life and literature becomes apparent when the shawlie makes her appearance. She offers seats in heaven, and her radiance evokes the blessed of the *Paradiso*, and especially Beatrice. To make sure we do not miss the allusion the narrator uses the term "petrified," recalling Dante's *Rime petrose*, and requests that the reader "take notice that this sweet style [*dolce stil novo*] is Belacqua's" (p. 56). The shawlie's revolving heavens, "tiresome Ptolemy" to Belacqua, and the melody of her voice, which he "tarried a little to listen to" (pp. 57, 58) after her departure, together bring to mind the music of the spheres and the Italian poet, while the impassivity of her face suggests in general a stylization that moves her out of the macrocosm into the microcosm of art. The title "Ding-Dong" sums up these related motifs: music of bells, a to-and-fro motion along the arc of an inchoate circle, moving immobility, and a pause before return that mirrors the pause in the pub, the microcosmic moment Beckett will make a lifetime project of exploring. The story itself goes a long way toward explaining the psychological origins of the project.

Representations of the Microcosm in the Early Prose

The starting point is a dualism that splits a young lover's universe into macrocosm and microcosm: "I admit Beatrice . . . and the brothel, Beatrice after the brothel or the brothel after Beatrice, but not Beatrice in the brothel . . ." ("Dream," pp. 91-92). Belacqua opposes Apollo, or love for a beauty beyond, to a modern, introverted Narcissus, or love for the psychic self. The third possibility entails the abolition of both other and ego in favor of unselfconscious existence in inner space among the phantom forms of a timeless flux: "the emancipation, in a slough of indifference and negligence and disinterest, from identity, his own and his neighbor's, suits his accursed complexion much better than the dreary fiasco of oscillation that presents itself as the only alternative" ("Dream," p. 108). For Belacqua the physical self is almost as alien as his neighbor, so that a sharp separation between mind and body goes along with the division between self and other. In "Fingal" we read

322

that "he scoffed at the idea of a sequitur from his body to his mind" (*MP*, p. 32).

While it is quite clear that Belacqua has a decided preference for his microcosm, in reality he spends very little time there. For the most part he does indeed oscillate between Apollo and Narcissus in a macrocosm where identity is a social relationship. "He is sorry it [his descent into the microcosm] does not happen more often, that he does not go under more often. . . . But when, as rarely happened, he was drawn down to the blessedly sunless depths . . . then he knew . . . that if he were free he would take up his dwelling in that place" ("Dream," pp. 108-109). By such passages we are made aware that Belacqua is at least a potential denizen of these depths. He exhibits again and again a decided preference for the inward-turning Narcissus over the extroverted Apollo, but beyond Narcissus he yearns for release from the macrocosm into various forms of contemplative selflessness. He wishes he could move among "all the articles of bric-a-brac" of the big world as though they were "so many tunics of so many onions" ("Dream," p. 142). Similarly, the dead Belacqua in the unpublished short story entitled "Echo's Bones" looks back on surface existence in these terms: "Sometimes he feels as though this old wound of his life had no intention of healing. . . . He has tried everything from fresh air and early hours to irony and great art" (p. 23). And in "Fingal" he says to Winnie, "And then . . . I want very much to be back in the caul, on my back in the dark forever. . . . No shaving or haggling or cold or hugger-mugger, no . . . night-sweats" (*MP*, p. 32). Paradoxically, the various girls with whom Belacqua is associated in the early prose are above all a means of escape from living in the external world. The dark eyes of a girl are doorways to a better realm. Just in case the reader should confuse metaphor and reality and take Belacqua for a religious mystic and the microcosm for a place of encounter with the Divinity, Beckett writes in "Dream":

> . . . he felt himself heavenly enflamed as the Cherubim and Seraphim for all the world as though his mouth had been tapping the bung of the heavenly pipe of the fountain of sweetness instead of just coming from clipping the rim of a pint pot of half-and-half. For about two minutes he floated about the snug as Gottesfreund and disembodied as you please. This sudden strange

sensation was of a piece with the ancient volatilisation of his first
communion, long forgot and never brought to mind in all the
long years that had run out with him since and rolled over that
delicious event. Alas! it was a short knock and went as it had
come, like that, it vacated him like that, leaving him bereft and
in his breast a void place and a spacious nothing.   (p. 165)

Among the many images used to evoke escape from the macrocosm into quietude, two of the most impressive occur early in
"Dream." In the first, Belacqua stands in a courtyard in Vienna,
the walls around him like a funnel. Atypically, release in this case
comes in an upward thrust:

> Wien, biding her time, and the terrible Wienerwald, the fields
> receding like a brow in sleep to the dark fringe of trees, crowded
> in upon him now and dehumanised the last days. He was no
> longer detached, nor ever almost at one with the girl,[5] but an
> item in the Hof's invisible garrison, going siege-crazy. There was
> the jungle of stone and the other jungle, crowding in to invest
> them, soaking up the frivolous wild life of the park. He fidgeted
> by night in the dark room and the rats were with him, now he
> was one of them. He was anxious with their anxiety, shuffling
> and darting about in the room. Outside the battalions were mass-
> ing, a heavy disorder of thicket and stone. He would not go out,
> though the girl still came, unscathed, from without. He stood in
> the courtyard, doomed. The fragile dykes were caving in on him,
> he would be drowned, stones and thickets would flood over him
> and over the land, a nightmare strom of timber and leaves and
> tendrils and bergs of stone. He stood amidst the weeds and the
> shell of the Hof, braced against the dense masses, strained out
> away from him. Over the rim of the funnel, when he looked up,
> the night sky was stretched like a skin. He would scale the inner
> wall, his head would tear a great rip in the taut sky, he would
> climb out above the deluge, into a quiet zone above the
> nightmare.   (p. 23)

The labour of resting in a strange place is properly extenuat-
ing. The first week and more went to throwing up a ring of earth-
works; this to break not so much the flow of people and things
to him as the ebb of him to people and things. It was his instinct

[5] Cf. "Sonnet to the Smeraldina."

to make himself captive, and that instinct, as never before or since, served him well and prepared a great period of beatitude stretching from mid-October to Xmas. . . . For two months and more he lay stretched in the cup, sheltered from the winds and sheltered from the waters, knowing that his own velleities of radiation would never scale the high rim that he had contrived all around and about, that they would trickle back and replenish his rumination as marriage the earth and virginity paradise, that he could release the boomerangs of his fantasy on all sides unanxiously, that one by one they would return with the trophy of an echo. He lay lapped in a beatitude of indolence that was smoother than oil and softer than a pumpkin, dead to the dark pangs of the sons of Adam, asking nothing of the insubordinate mind. He moved with the shades of the dead and the dead-born and the unborn and the never-to-be-born, in a Limbo purged of desire.[6] They moved gravely, men and women and children, neither sad nor joyful. They were dark, and they gave a dawn light to the darker place where they moved. They were a silent rabble, a press of much that was and was not and was to be and was never to be, a pulsing and shifting as of a heart beating in sand, and they cast a dark light.

If that is what is meant by going back into one's heart, could anything be better, in this world or the next? The mind, dim and hushed like a sick-room, like a chapelle ardente, thronged with shades; the mind at last its own asylum, disinterested, indifferent, its miserable erethisms and discriminations and futile sallies suppressed; the mind suddenly reprieved, ceasing to be an annex of the restless body, the glare of understanding switched off. The lids of the hard aching mind close, there is suddenly gloom in the mind; not sleep, not yet, nor dream, with its sweats and terrors, but a waking ultra-cerebral obscurity, thronged with grey angels; there is nothing of him left but the umbra of grave and womb where it is fitting that the spirits of his dead and his unborn should come abroad.

He understood then, when he came out of the tunnel, that that was the real business, the Simon Pure of this frail life that has already been described as being all temptation and knighthood. . . . Torture by thought and trial by living, because it was

[6] The recurrent indictment of desire, need, and will demonstrates the affinity between the views of Schopenhauer and those of Beckett.

fake thought and false living, stayed outside the tunnel. But in the umbra, the tunnel, when the mind went wombtomb, then it was real thought and real living. . . . Live cerebration that drew no wages and emptied no slops. In the tunnel he was a grave paroxysm of gratuitous thoughts, his thoughts, free and unprofessional, non-salaried, living as only spirits are free to live. . . . He was in the gloom, the thicket, he was wholly a gloom of ghostly comfort, a Limbo from which the mistral of desire had been withdrawn.   (pp. 38-40)

To these images of a quiet zone above the sky, of the cup and the funnel and limbo, another passage joins the metaphor of purgatory: "the intact little cameo of a bird-face, so moving, and the gay zephyrs of Purgatory, slithering in across the blue tremolo of the ocean with a pinnace of souls, as good as saved, to the landing-stage, the reedy beach, bright and blue, merging into grass. . . . When she went away, [he dreamt] of the shining shore where underneath them the keel of their skiff would ground and grind and rasp and stay stuck for them, just the pair of them, to skip out on to the sand and gather reeds and bathe hands, faces and breasts and broach the foothills without any discussion, in the bright light with the keen music behind them . . ." (p. 101).[7] Somewhat later, the image of a marsh is added:

The third being [besides Phoebus and Narcissus] was the dark gulf, when the glare of the will and the hammer-strokes of the brain doomed outside to take flight from its quarry were expunged, the Limbo and the wombtomb alive with the unanxious spirits of quiet cerebration, where there was no conflict of flight and flow and Eros was as null as Anteros and Night had no daughters. He was bogged in indolence, without identity, impervious alike to its pull and goading. The cities and forest and beings were also without identity, they were shadows, they exerted neither pull nor goad. His third being was without axis or contour, its centre everywhere and periphery nowhere,[8] an unsurveyed marsh of sloth.   (pp. 107-108)

Considerably further on in "Dream," when Belacqua speaks of himself as a "dud mystic," he uses the image of an intermediate state

---

[7] Cf. Canto II of Dante's *Purgatorio*.

[8] An allusion to the *Confessions* of St. Augustine.

somewhere between earth and heaven: "John" he said "of the Crossroads, Mr. Beckett. A borderman" (p. 166). The line is significant, for a great number of the images used to describe the microcosm suggest an in-between state: limbo and purgatory, both conditions between the extremes of heaven and hell, and dusk, the time between day and night. Elsewhere we find figures of margins, edges, borders. In the poems and the early prose, beaches, between land and sea, are a frequent setting. Sleep (when it is not spoiled by dreams) is a similar state between life and death, as the longed-for womb is a place on the edge of life. In "Ding-Dong" the pause is a neutral, disengaged position between poles of activity and commitment. Belacqua is careful to distinguish his in-between state from the withdrawal of brooding: "My mind goes blank. It is no brooding, it is no reflecting. It is the abdication of the daily mind, it is the hush and gloom ousting the workaday glare . . ." ("Dream," p. 170). In "Yellow," when he tries before his operation to gain control of his mind, Belacqua is described by the narrator as "an indolent bourgeois poltroon, very talented up to a point, but not fitted for private life in the best and brightest sense, in the sense to which he referred when he bragged of how he furnished his mind and lived there, because it was the last ditch when all was said and done" (*MP*, p. 233). When Belacqua has died and looks back on his life in the unpublished short story "Echo's Bones," he uses two other images to describe his life: "In this world . . . which, as you know, is all temptation and commercial travelling, I contrived, notwithstanding my numerous wives and admirers, to pass the greater share of my time in the privy, papered in ultraviolet anguish, of my psyche, projecting diggings so deep that their intrigues should never be discovered . . ." (p. 21); and later: "scarcely had my cord been clumsily severed than I struggled to reintegrate the matrix, nor did I relax those newborn efforts until death came and undid me" (p. 25).

There is little doubt that the exploration of the microcosm, which will hold such a central place in Beckett's subsequent writing, has its origin in a solipsistic position that stems in turn from a deep sense of the individual's essential isolation, an awareness that the "profound antagonism latent in the neutral space . . . between beings victims of real needs is . . . irreducible" ("Dream," p. 170). Beckett compliments the Alba highly when he gives her credit for a restraint that instinctively respects the isolation of the other person:

327

"*Savoir ne pas faire* was a jewel of great price in man or woman: the delicacy, on the spiritual plane, that has a sense of distance . . ." ("Dream," p. 171). But he pays her a still greater tribute when he endows her with the Belacqua gift, which is as far beyond "surety of abstention, free nilling" as the latter beyond the grace of "elegant participation." These two postures are, after all, no more than highly prized social amenities. When she says *my soul has no use for an anchor*," she demonstrates her understanding ("as rare as heavenly bodies colliding") and her acceptance of the ultimate solitude of each individual ("Dream," p. 171).

The Artist of the Microcosm and His Art

1. Wordplay and Intellectualism

Beckett began his career far removed from the ascetic rejection of artifice and virtuosity that marks his mature position as a writer. In his earliest efforts he is fascinated with wordplay in itself and quite apart from any place it may have in the total economy of the poem or story. He is subverted by the interplay of verbal sound and taste and feel, by the mysterious and fugitive shades of emotion and meaning that emerge with the enticing promise of a mirage from the kaleidoscopic encounter of words. As to many a young writer, the world of words must have seemed an exciting liberation from the monotony of a routine existence. At Trinity College, before he knew Joyce, Beckett was manipulating language with gay abandon. In the pedantic daring of "Che Sciagura" (1929), signed "D.E.S.C." ("di essere senza coglioni," from Voltaire's piquant episode in Chapter XI of *Candide*) Beckett begins his discussion of the unavailability of contraceptives in Ireland as follows: —"Frequently."—"In this country?"—"Strictly speaking—never in this country."—"Permit me to protest against the double-barreled qualification. Am I to reduce the coefficient of spatial, or that of qualitative elasticity?" With exuberant vitality in a piece entitled "The Possessed," Beckett, one of the actors in a student parody of Corneille's *Le Cid* (entitled *Le Kid*), opens his defense of the production against hostile critics: "Ladies and Gentlemen! On my left, torturing his exquisite Pindaric brolly, the Divine Marquis of Stanfor (cries of "What?" "Whom?" "Never!"). On my right and slightly to my rere, ineffably manipullulating his celebrated tipstaff, his breastfallen augs sorrowfully scouring the arena for two snakes

328

in the grass, Professor Giovannino Allcon, direct from the Petites Maisons. . . ."[9] Beckett continued to write in this mode while he was at the Ecole Normale and in 1932 published two prose pieces no doubt influenced by Joyce but at the same time representative of his own talent as a "wordman": "Sedendo et Quiesciendo" and "Text." The first is taken from "Dream of Fair to Middling Women" (pp. 58-68) and begins,

> Down you get now and step around. Two hours menopause. Drag your coffin my lord. Half a day and I'll be with. HIER! The bright beer goes like water through the nearsighted Frankfort porter. In Perpignan exiled dream-Dantes screaming in the planetrees and freezing the sun with peacock feathers and at last at least a rudimentary black swan with the bloodbeak and HIC! for the bladderjerk of the little Catalan postman. Oh who can hold a fire in his hand by thinking on the frosty Caucasus. Here oh here oh art thou pale with weariness. I hope yes after a continental third-class insomnia among the reluctantly military philologists asleep and armed as to nasals and dentals. Laughter.[10]

It continues in this manner for over seven pages. Similar writing occurs at intervals throughout "Dream" and only relatively less frequently in *More Pricks Than Kicks*.

The prose fragment "Text," reproduced below, is taken from page 74 of "Dream." It makes use of Elizabethan language and the less than inhibited lustiness of the period.

> Come come and cull me bonny bony doublebed cony swiftly my springal and my thin Kerry twingle-twangler comfort my days of roses days of beauty week of redness with mad shame to my lips of shame to my shamehill for the newest news the shemost of she-news is I'm lust-be-lepered and unwell oh I'd rather be a sparrow for my puckfisted coxcomb bird to bird and branch or a coalcave with goldy veins for my wicked doty's potystick trimly to besom gone the hartshorn and the cowslip wine gone and the lettuce nibbled up nibbled up and gone nor the last beauty day of the red time opened its rose and struck with its thorn oh I'm all of a galimaufry or a salady salmagundi singly and single to bed she said I'll have no toadspit about this house and whose

[9] In *T.C.D.*, XXXVII, No. 648 (12 March 1931), 138.
[10] "Sedendo et Quiesciendo" was reprinted in *Transition*, No. 21 (March 1932), pp. 13-20.

quab was I I'd like to know that from my cheerfully cornuted Dublin landloper and whose foal hackney mare toeing the line like a Viennese Täubchen take my tip and clap a padlock on your Greek galligaskins before I'm quick and living in hope and glad to go snacks with my twingle-twangler and grow grow into the earth mother of whom clapdish and foreshop.[11]

Both *More Pricks Than Kicks* and "Dream" are essentially art as intellectual play. The author's fascination with verbal manipulation is everywhere evident. "Weib," he writes, "is a fat, flabby, pasty kind of a word, all breasts and buttocks, bubbubbubbub, bbbacio, bbboca, a hell of a fine word . . ." ("Dream," p. 89). Besides English, German, and Italian, French and Latin are called upon to contribute to the game: for example, Belacqua's phrase "Mens mea Lucia lucescit luce tua" (*MP*, p. 197). Not infrequently new words are created: "Capper Quin arrived on tiptire" (*MP*, p. 262). The poet invents comic advertising slogans: "Guinness for Thinness, stultifying stout" (*MP*, p. 267) and creates farcical paraphrases more for the joy of the linguistic construction than to avoid vulgarity: "in consideration of which he had pleasure in referring his wife and first-born to that portion of himself which he never desired any person to kick nor volunteered to kiss in another" (*MP*, p. 166). Delight with language is constant. Belacqua teases his low-vocabulary sweetheart with the distinction between the English "man" and the German *Mann* ("Dream," p. 83). Elsewhere, semantic ambiguity plays a part in the joke about "a lady member of the Lower House . . . of Dublin stock . . . [who] declared 'I would rather commit adultery than suffer one drop of intoxicating liquor to pass my lips.' To which a gross baker, returned in the Labour interest, retorted: 'Wouldn't we all rather do that, Maam?' " (*MP*, pp. 205-206).

The author plays with literature as well as language. The early prose is packed to overflowing with allusions and modifications of allusions. Varying Hamlet's remark, Belacqua advises: "Get thee to a stud" ("Dream," p. 90). In "Draff," the last story in *More Pricks Than Kicks*, a character called Hairy (one suspects the author of baptizing him thus in order to set up his final union with Smerry, a nickname for the Smeraldina) transmogrifies 1 Corinthi-

---

[11] "Text" (not to be confused with the poem of the same name) was reprinted in *The New Review*, II, No. 5 (April 1932), 57.

ans 15:55: "O Anthrax where is thy pustule?" (*MP*, p. 272). In "Love and Lethe," when Belacqua comments, "Oh yes the usual pale cast," the author comments, "Notice the literary man" (*MP*, p. 132). Intervention by the author, ironic or straight, occurs repeatedly in the early prose. Sometimes amusing, it more often irritates. Taking the reader into his confidence the author asks, for example: "Shall we consider then in the first instance that powerful vedette that we have been hearing so much about, the Smeraldina-Rima? Shall we? To begin with then . . ." ("Dream," p. 101). After the pages published as "Sedendo et Quiesciendo" the author comments: "All that sublimen of blatherskite just to give some idea of the state the poor fellow was in on arrival" (p. 66). On another occasion he patronizingly explains to the reader that "a rosiner is a drop of the hard." Elsewhere he comments in a footnote on his own false analogy (*MP*, p. 277), placed and left in the text for formal reasons and in complete disregard of semantic coherence. Similarly, repeating an image used in an earlier story, he indulges in one-upmanship by noting the fact himself in another footnote (*MP*, p. 151).

Beckett's mockery is more often turned, however, on himself than the reader. In the unpublished "Echo's Bones" the "womb-tomb" (p. 2) later becomes "womby-tomby," and in "Dream" he describes this creative enterprise in the following way: "would it not be idle on our part to temporise further and hold up the happy event with the gratuitous echolalia and claptrap rhapsodies that are palmed off as passion and lyricism and the high spots of creative ecstasy . . . and which, as a matter of fact, are nothing more or less, if any dear reader would care to come in on a good thing, than padding . . ." (pp. 149-150). He intervenes more subtly in an ironic self-advertisement when he attributes authorship of "Dream" to a character named Walter Draffin: "Walter . . . merely had to close his eyes to be back in Pisa. The powers of evocation of this Italianate Irishman were simply immense, and if his *Dream of Fair to Middling Women*, held up in the *limae labor* stage for the past ten or fifteen years, ever reaches the public, and Walter says it is bound to, we ought all be sure to get it and have a look at it anyway" (*MP*, p. 203). In a great many interventions we can see the intellect of the young author at war with his sensitivity. The reader often senses the writer's painful awareness of the ease with which words fall into predetermined and artificial patterns, how quickly they can betray the uniqueness of individual experience. Not only is he embarrassed by his own emotion, which he undercuts again and again with his irony, and ashamed at exposing his inner feelings, but at times he appears obsessed by a fear of the trite and conventional, which he will go to almost any lengths to avoid:

Not that the Silver Strand—looking back through our notes we are aghast to find that it was Jack's Hole; but we cannot use that, that would be quite out of place in what threatens to come down a love passage—not that it were (mood of Fall indispensable) by any manner of means definitely hostile as atmosphere and scape to the Olympian romance that may break over it now at any moment. For *oui, les premiers baisers, oui, les premiers serments* it was as nice a site as any in the country. The rock was there, crumbling beyond a shadow of doubt, into dust; the wind was on the job, exfoliating the wrack; the inconstance of the sky was incontestable. And, over and above all these conditions, the fickle sea and sand. Lying there to a casual eye so calm between its headlands this little beach, without being the Bride of the Adriatic or anything of that kind and in spite of its leaving a few trees to be desired, furnished as neat a natural comment on the ephemeral sophism as any to be had in the Free State. Which is saying the hell of a lot.   ("Dream," pp. 168-169)

At the same time, his own intellectual awareness of the inadequacy of his effort is a redeeming trait. The narrator assesses the Belacqua Beckett with an honest effort at objectivity through the intermediary of the Mandarin and the Alba. The former argues lucidly: "Your vocabulary of abuse . . . is arbitrary and literary and at times comes close to entertaining me. But it doesn't touch me. You cannot touch me. You simplify and dramatise the whole thing with your literary mathematics. I don't waste any words with the argument of experience, the inward decrystallisation of experience, because your type never accepts experience, nor the notion of experience" ("Dream," pp. 90-91). And the Alba is a true prophet when she says, "I read your poem . . . but you will do better than that. It is clever, too clever, it amused me, it pleased me, it is good, but you will get over all that" (p. 150). More than anything else, the early prose seems to be an attempt to exorcize the Beckett that was or might have been Belacqua. The "Pylades and Orestes" relationship ended because Belacqua "was not *serious*" (*MP*, pp. 44-46). The need to move his art out of the realm of

332

detached play and into a world taken to be more "real," more "serious," and hence of more value will determine much of Beckett's subsequent writing.

2. Between the Intellectual and the Organic

An intellectual art is not necessarily doomed to frivolity and mediocrity, and Beckett might well have followed the path of Swift, as his social satire, his gift for caricature, and his mordant irony demonstrate. The following scene between the Polar Bear and Chas will give some notion of Beckett in the role of satirical portraitist. In such passages his tendency to flamboyant and imaginative elaboration is relatively restrained:

The Polar Bear:
cursing, blaspheming, purple in the face with a terrible apprehension, he stampeded miserably through the vortex. He lurched up safe and sound on the sidewalk.
"God b—the bastards" he snarled, "merde and remerde for the bastards." He snatched off his huge old hat and his head shone high above the crowd. He was an enormous stout block of a man. "Merde" he snarled "merde, merde." Still it was a relief to be across at all. It was only the mercy of God that he was across at all with what little life was still in him. Now, what the hell had he got to get now? Oleum ricini for his ailing sister. Merde for his sister. Then there was some other bloody nonsense he had said he would get. What was that? Straining every nerve he suddenly got it: a two shilling chicken for his ailing family. Merde for his family. Though they really were darlings, they were pets, with all their little faults and shortcomings, and so good to him. He ground his teeth together, he gnashed them in the extremity of his affection for his ailing family. Hawking oleum ricini and two shilling pullets (they do not exist) all over the fornicating city.
He set his course now for where he knew he could pick up the oil on the cheap, he stumped along now, gasping and humped and enormous, ponderously in the middle of the sidewalk. He was gone in the legs. Hearing himself named he drew up, and on perceiving M. du Chas he raised the old hat courteously.
"If you like" he said in his distinguished voice, tinged with a lallation, "you can come along and help me buy a bottle of oleum ricini for my blasted sister."

333

They made ground together.

"Merde" said the Polar Bear agreeably "for my sister."

"Hoffentlich" said Chas.

That was a quip, so the P.B. loosed a great guffaw.

"You can carry my bag, you know" he said "if you like."

Chas took over the bag.

"It's full of bloody shockers" said the P.B. "for my ailing family."

"What ails it?" enquired Chas.

"That is why it is such a weight" said the P.B. "I am tired, truly I am tired out, hawking the bastard round. And you are young and I am old."

He turned now and stormed venomously through the flux of pedestrians and made irruption into the pharmacy where he was known.

"And so he fears" carried forward Chas "to be a . . ."

That was the worst of Chas, that was his weakness, the ham that his any foe at any time could slit and string, this abominable production of text, as well of a great number of original and spontaneous observations, to a mysterious terminus of fitness closing the line or the couplet or the quatrain or the phrase or the period, whatever the area to which he felt dimly closure should be applied, we don't presume to know how that point was established. Anal complex anyway. Many a time had Belacqua, responding to the obscure need to verbalise a wombtombing or such like, murmured a syllable or two of incantation: "La sua bocca . .", "qui vive la pietà . .", "Before morning you shall be here . .", "Ange plein . .", "Mais elle, viendra . ." "Du bist so . . ." "La belle, la . . .", only to have this filthy little hop-me-thumb Bartlett-in-the-box pop aloft with a hod of syllables, gash a glaring Caesarean in the nightfall of the ambiente, stitch and hemistich right left and centre the dying meditation, and drum the brain back into the counting-house. Then Belacqua loathed his dear friend. Not but what Chas was not a modest man, not but what it ever occurred to him, we feel sure, to preen himself however little on this infallible instinct of his for context. Twas as has been said, the alto of an inhibition, like the Platonic prancing and gallivanting before the Ginette seen through the glass rose-darkly, through the tissue of tears.

. . . .

"Where" the P.B., inexpressibly relieved now that he had the oil safe and sound in his pocket, would be interested to know "is it possible to acquire a chicken for the sum of two shillings? At the great poulterer's of D'Olier Street, at Brady's of Dawson Street, or in the Market?"

"You would need to keep vigil all night" said Chas "and go to the Halles with the first streaks of morning."

"Haffner's pork sausingers" the Polar Bear narrowed down the field of research "are prime, but their birds are dear. And if my family thinks" cocking the jaws "that I am going to burst myself sweating up Georges Street."

"Well sir" said Chas, tendering the gravid bag, "now I must fly. I have an A.P."

"Well" said the Polar Bear "I hope she is very nice."

"With Belacqua" said Chas, refusing to play, " 'aven't you seen him?"

The P.B. admitted gloomily to having seen him but the day before. He had found him very much—how would he say—changed.

"Not altered?" Chas hoped.

That was not for the Polar Bear to say.

"Other" was as far as he cared to go. "A lot of people have been asking after him tenderly."

"That so" said Chas, "well" advancing the bag "I must fly."

The Polar Bear raked his nose and swallowed it.

"Notably" he said "the Alba."

"Alba?"

"A girl" sighed the P.B. "wunnerful girl. Great friend or was of your friend and colleague Monsieur Liebert."

"Indeed . ."

"Well" the Polar Bear was tired of Chas "now I must fly." Suddenly he became aware of the bag. "Here!" he growled "don't run away with the bag. If I went home without the bag" he said slyly, when he had it safe in his grasp, "do you know what would happen?"

Chas had no idea.

"I'd be beaten" said the Polar Bear.

They flew apart.

He found the pullet, hard and taut and small, tant pis, but for the budgeted amount. That was a great satisfaction. Beat the thieving bastards down. Half-a-crown for a sabre-breasted hen! Merde. The Baby he could buy on his way home. The oil and the bird entered the bag.

"Now" he said, scraping his throat and swallowing it, launching a high red cacklebelch of duty done, "now." ("Dream," pp. 130-134)

When the young Beckett allows himself free rein, however, something like this rendering of the Frica results:

Now a most terrible and unexpected thing happens. Into the quiet pages of our cadenza bursts a nightmare harpy, Miss Dublin, a hellcat. In she lands singing Havelock Ellis in a deep voice, itching manifestly to work that which is not seemly. If only she could be bound and beaten and burnt, but not quick. Or, failing that, brayed gently in a mortar. Open upon her concave breast as on a lectern lies Portigliotti's *Penombre Claustrali* bound in tawed caul. In her talons earnestly she clutches Sade's *Hundred Days* and the *Anterotica* of Aliosha G. Brignole-Sale, unopened, bound in shagreened caul. A septic pudding hoodwinks her, a stodgy turban of pain it laps her horse-face. The eye-hole is clogged with the bulbus and the round pale globe goggles exposed. Solitary meditation has furnished her with nostrils of generous bore. The mouth champs an invisible bit, foam gathers at the bitter commissures. The crateriform brisket, lipped with sills of paunch, cowers ironically behind a maternity tunic. Key-holes have wrung the unfriendly withers, the osseous rump screams beneath the hobble-skirt. Wastes of woad worsted are gartered to the pasterns. Aïe! ("Dream," p. 160)

Often Beckett's satirical wit is turned against that sometime friend of his, Belacqua Shuah, and the facile side of Irish literature. The following words come to us from the Alba: " 'I hate Omar' she said 'and your fake penumbra. Haven't we had enough of that in this festering country. Haven't we had enough Deirdreeing of Hobson's weirds and Kawthleens in the gloaming hissing up petticoats of sor-rarrhoea? Haven't we had enough withered pontiffs of chiarino-scurissimo.' 'The mist' she sneered 'an it rollin' home UP the glen and the mist agin an' it rollin' home DOWN the glen.' Up, down, hans arown . . Merde. Give me noon. Give me Racine' " ("Dream," p. 176).

Such examples of satire and caricature are more than arid intellectualism masquerading as art. At their best they are both cognitive and affective responses to reality, amused, irritated, or sardonic reactions that are part of a more or less unpremeditated way of seeing. In Beckett's use of colors we have a similar marriage of sensibility and practical reason:

The sun had bleached it [the Smeraldina's beret] from green to a very poignant reseda[12] and it had always, from the very first moment he clapped eyes on it, affected him as being a most shabby, hopeless and moving article. It might have been a tuft of grass growing the way she ripped it off her little head and began to wave it with an idiotic clockwork movement of her arm, up and down, not to flutter it like a handkerchief, but grasping it in the middle to raise it and lower it with a stiff arm as though she were doing an exercise with a dumbbell. The least reference of his thought now to these valedictory jerks, the monstrous grief in the hand clutching the livid beret like a pestle and pounding up and down, so that every stroke of the stiff arm seemed to bray his heart and propel her out of his sight,[13] was enough to churn his mind into the requisite strom of misery.

("Dream," pp. 2-3)

As we have seen in the poems, various off-greens affect the author strongly, and we often find them associated in his work with disillusionment. Green being both a natural and traditional symbol of hope, such a response makes perfectly good intellectual sense, but that is not to deny immediate spontaneous reaction on the part of the poet. Both the color green and the color red (which Beckett says he must have around him, and which in "Dream" is usually linked to the Alba), whatever affective force they may have, are certainly connected to intellectual attitudes, as the following amusing passage featuring the Polar Bear shows:

"Can't the bloody thing be stopped?" he cried.
"Next stop the Green" said the conductor.
"Damn the Green" cried the P.B. "Damn you and your damn Green."
He drew his plump hand's glabrous crown across his raw mouth.

[12] In "Draff" Belacqua compares the Smeraldina's eyes to "shafts of reseda" and the narrator interjects: "his favorite color" (*MP*, p. 257).
[13] Cf. lines 25 through 28 in the poem "Cascando."

Three nouns, three adjectives.

"The Dublin United Tramways Bloody Company" he vociferated "seems to exist for the sole purpose of dragging its clients forcibly out of their way to Greens. Isn't there enough green in this merdific island? I get on to your accursed bolide at the risk of my life at the College Green and get fired out at the next of your verminous plaguespots whether I like it or not. If it's not the Steven's Green it's Green's bloody library. What we want" he screamed from the sidewalk "in this pestiferous country is red for a change and plenty of it." ("Dream," p. 140)

Depending on the circumstances red may suggest love, death, vitality; while white may evoke purity, coldness, death. The interplay of the Alba's colors is crucial in her two dreams, which are inserted as hors-d'oeuvres in the latter part of "Dream":

1. *Mild Form.*

I was all set in a long white silk gown that became me to marry a man in a bowler whom I had never seen and did not want to, for somehow he was not worth seeing. Suddenly I thought: My God, I can't be married in white, off with this bloody thing. Then I saw that it was not white silk, but rather écru. Still I thought: can't possibly be married in this bloody thing. So I tore it off in handfuls, I ripped it away in tufts, it seemed to be coming *up* rather than *off*, from my hips, breasts and shoulders. Grandmother was there and I regretted having to destroy the gown.

2. *Mild Form.*

My father must have been a butcher. I was coming home from some dance or ball or other, because I wore a superb evening gown that became me and satin shoes. I crossed the road and went into the house. It was a big bare room, in a lather of blood. Afraid of staining the gown I caught it up, like Nicolette in the dew, and tiptoed over to the foot of the stair. I was surprised how easily and gracefully I was able to avoid the red puddles. Upstairs just a bare skivvy's cell: wash-hand stand, dresser, stretcher, cracked mirror. Suddenly it seemed that everything, I, my body, my clothes, the party, the whole content of the evening, was a result of the blood I had come through on my way up.

(pp. 177-178)

In the novel the Alba is the intellectual, literary, detached, and self-possessed girl who wants to be the "belle of the ball" at the Frica's party, to which she wears a red dress. The lusty physical body of the Smeraldina wins out over the platonic promise of her cameo-like face. Her colors are green and black (*MP*, p. 258), green perhaps associated with Belacqua's platonic aspirations and black with his disappointment. Interpretation of Beckett's use of colors is a somewhat tricky business. Their values are not given once and for all but vary to some extent with the context. They cannot be reduced to a system of one-to-one correspondences. That much granted, it remains true that colors are never neutral in the early prose. The author's choices are always meaningful, as is evident in a passage like the following, taken from "A Wet Night":

> Bright and cheery above the strom of the Green, as though coached by the Star of Bethlehem, the Bovril sign danced and danced through its seven phases.
>
> The lemon of faith jaundiced, annunciating the series, was in a fungus of hopeless green reduced to shingles and abolished. Whereupon the light went out, in homage to the slain. A sly ooze of gules, carmine of solicitation, lifting the skirts of green that the prophecy might be fulfilled, shocking Gabriel into cherry, flooded the sign. But the long skirts came rattling down, darkness covered their shame, the cycle was at an end. *Da capo.*
>
> (*MP*, pp. 61-62)

3. Anti-intellectualism and the Artistic Imagination

Although the excesses of intellectualism, art as verbal frolic, are everywhere apparent in "Dream of Fair to Middling Women" and have by no means been eliminated from *More Pricks Than Kicks*, there is a strong undercurrent of anti-intellectualism in both works. If Beckett admits at one point in "Dream" that there was a time when he was "very strong on architectonics" (p. 159), it is only in order to excuse his present attacks on structure. He rails repeatedly against categories and causal organization. Introducing a conversation between the exuberant Polar Bear and a Jesuit with "little or no nonsense about him," the author describes the former's anti-Christian polemic as "tongue-play" (*MP*, p. 74) and seems to sympathize with the latter's (surely atypical) weary rejection of the frivolities of logic and reason: " 'Observe' he said, 'I desire to get

339

down. I pull this cord and the bus stops and lets me down. . . . In just such a Gehenna of links' said this remarkable man, with one foot on the pavement, 'I forged my vocation' " (*MP*, pp. 76-77). "Beauty . . . is beyond categories," says the narrator in "Dream" (p. 31), and he rejects deterministic systems à la Taine: "Milieux, race, family, structure, temperament, past and present and consequent and antecedent back to the first combination and the papas and mammas and paramours and cicisbei and the morals of Nanny and the nursery wallpapers and the third and fourth generation snuffles. . . . That tires us. . . . The background pushed up as a guarantee . . that tires us" (p. 10). Later, apropos of his denunciation of a certain type of novel, he castigates the "ardent young politico-social psycho-scientific sleuth" (p. 142). Perfectly aware that he himself indulges in the kind of writing he excoriates, Beckett defends his portrait of Belacqua:

Apollo, Narcissus and the inaccessible Limbese? Are they simple themselves? . . . Can we measure them once and for all and do sums with them like those impostors that they call mathematicians? We can not. We can state them as a succession of terms, but we can't sum them and we can't define them. They tail off vaguely at both ends and the intervals of their series are demented. We give you one term of Apollo. . . . And one term of Narcissus. . . . But we took very good care not to mention the shepherd or the charioteer or the healer or the mourner or the arquitenens or the lyrist or the butcher or the crow; and very good care not to mention the hunter or the mocker or the boy howling for his pals or in tears or in love or testing the Stygian speculum. ("Dream," p. 111)

Although the young author is a long way from having discovered his own novelistic mode, he is quite sure what kind of novel he does *not* want to write. Balzac is his whipping boy:

Much of what has been written concerning the reluctance of our refractory constituents to bind together and give us a synthesis is true equally of Belacqua. Their movement is based on a principle of repulsion, their property not to combine but, like heavenly bodies, to scatter and stampede, astral straws on a timestrom, grit in the mistral. And not only to shrink from all that is not they, from all that is without and in its turn shrinks from them, but also to strain away from themselves. They are no good from the builder's point of view, firstly because they will not suffer their systems to be absorbed in the cluster of a greater system, and then, and chiefly, because they themselves tend to disappear as systems. Their centres are wasting, the strain away from the centre is not to be gainsaid, a little more and they explode. Then, to complicate things further, they have odd periods of recueillement, a kind of centripetal backwash that checks the rot. The procédé that seems all falsity, that of Balzac, for example, and the divine Jane and many others, consists in dealing with the vicissitudes, or absence of vicissitudes, of character in this backwash, as though that were the whole story. Whereas, in reality, this is so little the story, this nervous recoil into composure, this has so little to do with the story, that one must be excessively concerned with a total precision to allude to it at all. To the item thus artifically immobilised in a backwash of composure precise value can be assigned. So all the novelist has to do is to bind this material in a spell, item after item, and juggle politely with irrefragable values, values that can assimilate other values like in kind and be assimilated by them, that can increase and decrease in virtue of an unreal permanence of quality. To read Balzac is to receive the impression of a chloroformed world. He is absolute master of his material, he can do what he likes with it, he can foresee and calculate its least vicissitude, he can write the end of his book before he has finished the first paragraph, because he has turned all his creatures into clockwork cabbages and can rely on their staying put wherever needed or staying going at whatever speed in whatever direction he chooses. The whole thing, from beginning to end, takes place in a spellbound backwash. We all love and lick up Balzac, we lap it up and say it is wonderful, but why call a distillation of Euclid and Perrault *Scenes from Life*? Why *human* comedy?

("Dream," pp. 105-107)

If success is one's aim, the formula never fails: "The public never spots the deception. The public is too busy admiring the seamless tights of the performer and listening to the patter of the parable. All that is necessary is to follow directions" ("Dream," p. 143).

Against facile and arbitrary intellectual constructions the young author opposes a belief and a promise that he will spend the next thirty-five years and more fulfilling: "The reality of the individual . . . is an incoherent reality and must be expressed incoherently" ("Dream," p. 91). Here Beckett states a position that raises a question important in contemporary discussions of literary theory and criticism. In a recent history of the subject the authors put it this way: "Drab realism may be at times merely neutral, but it has at least a tendency toward the formless and subrational, and hence toward producing the problem for criticism which one 20th-century American critic has sharply focussed in the phrase 'fallacy of imitative form.' If a fullness of imitative embodiment is what poetry must achieve and that through its form, can this form survive the imitation of negative or formless materials?"[14] While even in a recent novel like *Comment c'est* author and character are still distinguishable and form can still in some sense be said to order chaos, Beckett has gone very far toward achieving the task he set for himself in this early statement, toward undermining intellectual form and structure and allowing greater scope for the incoherent reality behind it, which he often figures as occupying the silences, the empty spaces, in the interstices of form: "The experience of my reader shall be between the phrases, in the silence, communicated by the intervals, not the terms, of the statement . . . his experience shall be the menace, the miracle, the memory of an unspeakable trajectory" ("Dream," p. 123). And Belacqua continues for two pages with terms like "implication lurking behind the pictorial pretext," "a disaggregating, a distintegrating," "corrosive ground-swell of Art," "pitted with dire stroms of silence." Beckett discusses the application of his "aesthetic of inaudibilities" ("Dream," p. 126) not only for the reader and the work of art but also for the author. In an extended metaphor he describes the functioning of the creative mind:

> The night firmament is abstract density of music, symphony without end, Illumination without end, yet emptier, more sparsely lit, than the most succinct constellations of genius. Now seen merely, a depthless lining of hemisphere, its crazy stippling of

[14] Cleanth Brooks and W. K. Wimsatt, *Literary Criticism: A Short History* (New York: Knopf, 1962), p. 202. They add—significantly for our present discussion—"On the other hand, of course, stands the question: can the fullness of this form, its quality of embodiment, survive the imitation of the highly rational, the scientific or metaphysical?" See also Ivor Winters, *In Defense of Reason* (New York: Alan Swallow, 1937 and 1947).

342

stars, it is the passional movements of the mind charted in light and darkness. The tense passional intelligence, when arithmetic abates, tunnels, skymole, surely and blindly (if we only thought so!) through the interstellar coalsacks of its firmament in genesis, it twists through the stars of its creation in a network of loci that shall never be co-ordinate. The inviolable criterion of poetry and music, the non-principle of their punctuation, is figured in the demented perforation of the night colander. The ecstatic mind, the mind achieving creation, take ours for example, rises to the shaft-heads of its statement, its recondite relations of emergal, from a labour and a weariness of deep castings that brook no schema. The mind suddenly entombed, then active in an anger and a rhapsody of energy, in a scurrying and plunging towards exitus, such is the ultimate mode and factor of the creative integrity, its proton, incommunicable; but there, insistent, invisible rat, fidgeting behind the astral incoherence of the art surface. That was the circular movement of the mind flowering up and up through darkness to an apex, dear to Dionysius the Areopagite, beside which all other modes, all the polite obliquities, are the clockwork of rond-de-cuirdom.   ("Dream," pp. 14-15)

Not only in the theorizing of the narrator but also in the thoughts and attitudes and actions of his principal character, Belacqua, we can discover the Beckett-to-be and his preference for the non-conceptual. Belacqua tends to assimilate reality to art. A smile suggests the Gioconda; the girl is a Madonna ("Dream," pp. 85-86). In "Ding-Dong" he refuses to fall into his interlocutor's logical traps and accepts his own incoherence. The narrator describes his "fairy-tale need" (*MP*, p. 163). Images taken from painting, literature, music are everywhere (*MP*, pp. 55, 120, 131, 132, etc.). Architectural details of the Dublin fire station project him into Renaissance Florence. Perhaps a typical example of this Belacqua-as-budding-poet is a passage found in *More Pricks Than Kicks*:

Now Belacqua began to worry lest the worst should come to the worst and the scarlet gown be backless after all. Not that he had any doubts as to the back thus bared being a sight for sore eyes. The omoplates would be well defined, they would have a fine free ball-and-socket motion. In repose they would be the blades of an anchor, the delicate furrow of the spine its stem. His mind pored over this back that inspired him with awe. He saw it as a flower-de-luce, a spatulate leaf with segments angled back, like the wings of a butterfly sucking a blossom, from their common hinge. Then, fetching from further afield, as an obelisk, a cross-potent, pain and death, still death, a bird crucified on a wall.

(pp. 69-70)

Perhaps the best guarantee against the dangers of photographic realism inherent in the notion of an imitation of the subrational is this highly developed imaginative faculty. If it is dangerous both to exclude intellect totally and to place art wholly under its control, then it may be that in a twilight zone between reason and unreason, in some preconscious faculty of imagination, may be found the realm where art is most at home. In any case the fictionality of the characters in "Dream of Fair to Middling Women" is given clear priority over their correspondence to real people on a number of occasions. Of the Syra-Cusa the young novelist writes, "[She] belongs to another story, a short one, a far far better one. . . . We could chain her up with the Smeraldina-Rima and the little Alba, our capital divas, and make it look like a sonata, with recurrence of themes, key signatures, plagal finale and all. . . . She might even, at a stretch, be persuaded to ravish Lucien. . . . She could be coaxed into most anything. Ca n'existe pas. Except to keep us in Paris for another couple of hundred words" ("Dream," p. 43). The same is true, asserts the author, of Belacqua: "There is no authority for supposing that this third person Belacqua is the real Belacqua. . . . There is no real Belacqua, it is to be hoped not indeed, there is no such person" ("Dream," p. 108). The dreamlike nature of the hero's various loves is often apparent but nowhere more so than on page 75 of "Dream": "Then the proud hellblond beauty receded or perhaps seemed only so to do as gravely with the indifferent movement of my succubus my Infanta defunct oh Schopenhauer stepped across her the hard breastless Greek slave or huntress the hard nautch-gal. . . ." And indeed the title "Dream of Fair to Middling Women" suggests the degree to which the characters are figments of the author's imagination. There is little doubt, in fact, at least at this stage of Beckett's development, that the danger of excessive intellectualism, unrestrained fancy, wordplay, and literary borrowing was greater than the threat of anything that might conceivably be called "realism."

More Pricks Than Kicks represents a considerable artistic

advance over "Dream of Fair to Middling Women." Much if not all of the verbal exuberance and undisciplined fantasy has been eliminated, along with a large number of passages in which the author intervenes as author to have an extended self-conscious chat with the reader. The very fact of reorganizing the novel into ten individual stories, each with something approaching organic unity, is already by comparison a triumph of control. In most of the stories a central concern dictates the nature of events and the tone, while more than once a relatively subtle metaphoric unity forecasts the mastery of the mature writer. The organization of "Dante and the Lobster" around the conflict between mercy and justice has already been discussed. In "Fingal" the title itself suggests the relationship between art and nature that forms the thematic core of the tale. Winnie and Belacqua are set side by side as archetypal expressions of physical nature and its demands as contrasted with the imaginative character of the poet, for whom nature is comprehensible only through art. Throughout *More Pricks Than Kicks*, woman—as represented by Winnie Coates, Ruby Tough, Lucy, Thelma bboggs, the Smeraldina, and to some extent even by Alba Perdue—and on the other side man, somewhat ambiguously represented by Belacqua, are pictured in general as the antithetical tendencies of body and mind, nature and art. Thus, within the macrocosm itself we find again the dualistic vision. As we have seen, "Ding-Dong" derives its unity from a confrontation between macrocosm and microcosm, developed principally through the images of directed versus directionless or circular movement, activity versus stasis, and engagement versus withdrawal. The two most flamboyant stories in the collection, "A Wet Night" and "What a Misfortune," provide Beckett with opportunity to indulge his bent for satire, caricature, and irony. In spite of the apparent lack of unity in these stories, they are both fundamentally concerned with a tension between the vacuity of social existence, where chatter is idle and laughter is the laughter of fools, and the sorrowful and suffering solitude of the inward-turning individual. "Love and Lethe" recounts a suicide pact between Belacqua and Ruby Tough. As the title indicates, it probes the nature of the relationship between love and death, a theme suggested perhaps by the last lines of the Ronsard sonnet alluded to in the story. The French poet, finding the two almost equally painful, proposed that "l'Amour et la Mort n'est qu'une mesme chose." Forms of suffering or forms of forgetfulness,

345

they sort themselves out into the same dualism described above. The romantic suicide pact is the notion of the art-obsessed Belacqua, and it is frustrated finally by the physical attractions of the "more-down-to-earth" girl.

The two opposed types in "Walking Out" are fundamentally no different. In this story the author works them out in terms of a "normal lusty physical love," which goes hand in hand with a conventionalism that is easily shocked, and on the other side the deviate sexuality of Belacqua, basically one more metaphor for contemplative withdrawal from excessive physicality. Thanks to Lucy's accident, which cripples her, Belacqua triumphs in this story, and his victory is the victory of the solitary, visionary self over Eros à deux. "The Smeraldina's Billet Doux" develops a similar opposition indirectly through the portraits of Belacqua and the Smeraldina that emerge from her letter to him. "Yellow" explores the abilities of a man of the microcosm (aided and comforted by the laughter of Democritus) to cope with his own mind and with the pressures of the macrocosm under conditions of danger, anxiety, and fear—as indicated by the title. In the last story in the collection, "Draff," the death of Belacqua has resolved the tension between mind and matter once and for all. Like unto like, Smerry gravitates to Hairy with the attraction of one body to another, while Belacqua finds what he had always sought and never for long succeeded in attaining through his various surrogate escapes: the solitude and peace of the grave.

Even this very brief analysis of the stories reveals that a thematic and even metaphoric unity binds them together and betrays their common origin in the unpublished novel "Dream of Fair to Middling Women." It is a tensional unity founded on a dualistic vision of reality. The author has exteriorized two fundamental tendencies in himself and in addition pitted his dominant inclination against its opposite as incarnated in a series of young ladies. Out of this dualism he has created ten short pieces of fiction that are a good deal more varied than would appear from the above account. The entire collection is unified in still another way, as indicated by its title, taken from the Bible, Acts 9:5 and 26:14. The Lord said to Paul on the road to Damascus: "it is hard for thee to kick against the pricks." Beckett, with Belacqua, would ruefully counter that there is more suffering than revolt in this earthly existence. The difficulty Belac-

346

qua has in making his way through life is an overriding theme common to all the stories.[15]

Along with the intellectual virtuosity of "Dream of Fair to Middling Women" and *More Pricks Than Kicks* there is anti-intellectualism and a latent organicism biding its time, just as there is a "realm of grey angels," a microcosm waiting to engulf the macrocosm. In a similar way, the frivolity of verbal aestheticism, present in some of the early poetry, yields to graveness. The inner world expands, pushing back the encroaching frontiers of social existence until finally it becomes a place to live and write in. The dim awareness that the future belongs to the microcosm grows little by little into conscious conviction and finally comes to unequivocal expression in two poems in the Addenda to the novel *Watt*. More clearly than any of the earlier poems they forecast the novels and plays of Beckett's artistic maturity.

[15] Something of the suggestion of resigned impotence in a world of erotic physicality inherent in the title is made explicit, curiously enough, in the novel *Watt* (pp. 169-170), where it combines with the theme of "too late" and the image of the tardy Irish sun: "Arthur said: Do not despair, Mr. Graves. Some day the clouds will roll away, and the sun, so long obnubilated, burst forth, for you, Mr. Graves, at last. Not a kick in me, Mr. Arter, said Mr. Graves. Oh Mr. Graves, said Arthur, do not say that. When I says a kick, said Mr. Graves, I means a ——. He made a gesture with his fork. Have you tried Bando, Mr. Graves, said Arthur."

347

ix. Watt
and the Last Poems

The Biographical Setting and Its Relation to the Novel

Beckett took part in the June 1940 exodus from Paris before the advance of the invading German army, and arrived in Vichy later that summer. It was there that he saw Joyce for the last time. The hotel in which he and the Joyce family were staying was, like most of the hotels, being evacuated and he had to "get on, clear out." Joyce and his family went to a little town near Vichy where Madame Jolas (of *Transition* fame) had a school. Joyce stayed there until December, when he obtained a permit to go to Switzerland. Beckett started south on foot from Vichy. On the way he managed to board a train that went as far as Toulouse. There he avoided the refugee center, slept out on benches and finally got a bus west as far as Cahors, where it was "all out" in the pouring rain. Famished, exhausted, he finally managed to find a spot on the floor of a shop dealing in religious articles, where he spent the night. Hiding in a truck the next day he succeeded in getting out of Cahors and traveling as far as Arcachon, where he was able to locate Mary Reynolds, an American he had known in Paris. She helped him find a place to stay, and he managed to obtain a little money sent under difficult conditions by his family in Ireland.

In October he returned to occupied Paris, his apartment, his books, and bread lines. In Paris he reestablished contact with Alfred Péron, a good friend whom he had first known in Dublin when Péron was an exchange student from the Ecole Normale to Trinity College. (This same reciprocal arrangement later sent Beckett from Trinity to the Ecole Normale as a *lecteur*.) It was through Alfred Péron that Beckett joined a Resistance network engaged in collecting information from various parts of France on German troop movements. Beckett classified the information, translated it into English, typed it, and in general prepared it for microphotography, after which it was sent into the free zone of France and then flown to London. In August 1942 a leader of the network was captured by the Gestapo and under torture revealed the names of its members. Péron was arrested in Anjou, sent to Drancy, and then deported to Germany. Péron's wife sent an open telegram to Beckett: "Alfred arrêté par Gestapo. Prière faire nécessaire pour corriger l'erreur." The telegram reached Beckett at 11 A.M. on August 15, 1942 and he was gone by 3 P.M. He was one of about thirty from a total membership of eighty that managed to escape. For some two months he moved in and around Paris from one apartment to another until he was able to get false papers and make contact with a *passeur*. In October the *passeur* led a group of ten refugees cross-country during the night into the unoccupied zone. Once again Beckett found himself in Vichy, then in Avignon, and finally in the tiny village of Roussillon near Apt in the Vaucluse, where through friends of friends he was able to find a place to stay. It was there that he worked for Bonelli (mentioned in *En attendant Godot*) and received wine in exchange for his labors. One triumph of this period was obtaining permission to glean in a field after the potato harvest. Under conditions prevailing in those days, finding a potato in the sea of mud was like finding a gold nugget. A man named Aude was kind to Beckett and others during this time, and once a week Beckett had a meal at his home. In return Beckett cut wood for Aude, helped him with the harvest, and did other odd jobs. It was in Roussillon, in the evenings, that Beckett wrote the novel *Watt*.

Something of the experience of the refugee tramping wearily along the roads of France, doing manual labor in the service of others in order to survive, living with a heightened sense of exile in the uncertainty and relative solitude that prevailed under such conditions in wartime France finds its way into *Watt*. Equally important, however, seems to have been the fact that these conditions obtained at a particular moment in the life of the author. Beckett wrote *Murphy* between 1933 and 1935 in London.[1] He

[1] A curiously autobiographical note occurs in *Watt* on page 212, where Beckett writes that sometimes in the early hours of the morning his protagonist "went to the window, to look at the stars, which he had once known familiarly by name, when dying in London. . . ." Since for Beckett man is always in the process of dying the phrase "dying in London" may be taken as roughly equivalent to "living in London." It was Samuel Beckett, of course, who was "living-dying" there during the years of misery following the death of his father. In the *Watt* passage the author speaks briefly not as narrator but as author. He testifies to the ambiguous relationship between creator and character, the same and yet distinct. Two notions are implicit in

wrote *Watt* approximately ten years later, between late 1942 and late 1944, when he was between thirty-six and thirty-eight years old, that is to say more or less at the traditional midpoint of life. No doubt the break in normal existence occasioned by the war served to accentuate this passage from youth to middle age.

A Novel of the Middle Years of Man

Belacqua is a young man. His experience of the "womb-tomb" where both the world and the self die is extremely limited. All in all he is a man of the macrocosm caught between Phoebus and Narcissus. Slightly older, Murphy makes a serious attempt to enter the "little world" which is unencumbered by self or others: "But it was not enough . . . it had never been enough and showed no signs of being enough. These dispositions and others ancillary, pressing every available means (e.g., the rocking-chair) into their service, could sway the issue in the desired direction, but not clinch it. It continued to divide him, as witness his deplorable suscepti-bility to Celia, ginger, and so on" (*Murphy*, p. 179). As with Belac-qua, Murphy's youth and the girls with whom he becomes involved, half in spite of himself, are largely responsible for his failure. In *Watt*, age is a powerful ally. Youth is a tension, a coming and a going. Middle age brings the hope of a staying. Near the beginning of *Watt* we find a prose version of the little poem "Dieppe" situated in this context:

> All the old ways led to this, all the old windings, the stairs with never a landing that you screw yourself up, clutching the rail, counting the steps, the fever of shortest ways under the long lids of sky, the wild country roads where your dead walk beside you,

---

his statement. First, the Proustian idea of the multiple self: Beckett-Murphy must die in order to make way for his successor, Beckett-Watt. Second, a view more characteristic of Beckett: On the one hand each self is fictional in the deepest sense of the word. Man knows his own being, if it exists, imper-fectly at best. His literary creations are phantoms of his imagination, without grounding in reality. Neither Murphy nor Watt is Beckett. On the other hand they resemble each other in too many ways to be thought of as wholly arbi-trary. If one, as the *Watt* passage suggests, can be thought of as the prolonga-tion of the other, it is because each bears some relationship to a mystery-shrouded but permanent core of being. The triology, and in particular *L'Innommable*, bears witness to the tension between such a despair and such a faith.

on the dark shingle the turning for the last time again to the lights of the little town, the appointments kept and the appointments broken, all the delights of urban and rural change of place, all the exitus and redditus, closed and ended. All led to this, to this gloaming where a middleaged man sits masturbating his snout, waiting for the first dawn to break." (p. 40)

Again, there are the words of Arsene, about to leave Knott's house for good, to the newly arrived Watt: "Not that I have told you all I know, for I have not, being now a good-natured man, and of good will what is more, and indulgent towards the dreams of middle age, which were my dreams, just as Vincent did not tell me all, nor Walter Erskine, nor the others the others, for here we all seem to end by being good-natured men, and of good will, and indulgent towards the dreams of middle age, which were our dreams . . ." (p. 62). It is in this context that Arsene uses an image strongly recalling Dante. He speaks of the servants in the house "eternally turning about Mr Knott in tireless love" (p. 62). Different as it is, *Watt* recalls the *Commedia* in more ways than one, and to begin with both are concerned with the stocktaking that may well occur "nel mezzo del cammin di nostra vita":

To think, when one is no longer young, when one is not yet old, that one is no longer young, that one is not yet old, that is perhaps something. To pause, towards the close of one's three hour day, and consider: the darkening ease, the brightening trouble; the pleasure pleasure because it was, the pain pain because it shall be; the glad acts grown proud, the proud acts growing stubborn; the panting the trembling towards a being gone, a being to come; and the true true no longer, and the false true not yet. And to decide not to smile after all, sitting in the shade, hearing the cicadas, wishing it were night, wishing it were morning, saying, No, it is not the heart, no, it is not the liver, no, it is not the prostate, no it is not the ovaries, no, it is muscular, it is nervous. Then the gnashing ends, or it goes on, and one is in the pit, in the hollow, the longing for longing gone, the horror of horror, and one is in the hollow, at the foot of all the hills at last, the ways down, the ways up, and free, free at last, for an instant free at last, nothing at last. (p. 202)

Watt takes Arsene's place, and when he in turn is on the point of leaving Knott's house, a successor arrives, as Watt had arrived, and

351

the successor also is at the beginning of the middle years: "Nor was Micks a little girl, or an innocent little choirboy, no, but a big placid man, who had seen something of the world, both at home, and abroad" (p. 220). When Watt leaves Knott's house, he enters old age. His bags are "three quarters empty" (p. 217). He is "an old rose now" (p. 253). Finally, on page 13 of *Watt* we find an analogy between the author, approaching forty, and Larry Nixon, who "will be forty years old next March." This is not the first time that in line 13 or on page 13 of a work of Beckett's we come upon an allusion to birth. Like Larry Nixon, Beckett was born in the spring (on April 13), and we recall that in *Murphy* (p. 180) Larry is short for Lazarus, "whose raising seemed to Murphy perhaps the one occasion on which the Messiah had overstepped the mark." The contexts of the two "Larry passages" are thematically very closely related. In both we discover again the notion, familiar to readers of the Good Friday poet, that man abandoned to postnatal suffering and solitude would be better off unborn.

The Renunciations of Watt

Very early in the novel, when we first encounter Watt, he is on his way to the railroad station to undertake a mysterious journey. After a brief conversation with Mr. Nixon, he continues on his way, and Mr. Nixon crosses the street to return to his wife and a hunchback named Mr. Hackett. Their ensuing conversation establishes the atmosphere of mystery that serves as setting for the principal theme of the novel: the need to know and the difficulty and indeed impossibility of knowing. "You cannot be in ignorance of all this," says Mr. Hackett. "Utter ignorance," replies Mr. Nixon. "I tell you nothing is known. . . . Nothing" (p. 21). As it turns out, a few meager morsels of information, mostly of a speculative or downright negative character, are available: "He has no fixed address that I know of," admits Mr. Nixon (p. 20).

If we put together this lack of information, lack of address, and the fact that Watt is leaving town, they lead us to the first moment in the inner development of the novel, the moment of renunciation. On the literal level it seems that Watt, "half hoping he may miss his train" and "too fearful to assume himself the onus of a decision," "refers it to the frigid machinery of a time-space relation" (p. 21). Metaphorically, the quest for meaning undertaken by Watt (the quasi-homophone of "what") is at least as much an involuntary drive as a conscious decision. It comes to most men at some point in their existence but to the greater part at the start of the middle years, when the needs of youth have subsided and "the true [is] true no longer" (p. 201). The quest implies an antecedent withdrawal, by things or from things. Certain realities have retreated or been pushed back. The passage that makes this first step explicit occurs about three-fifths of the way through the book. Translated from one of Watt's several variant forms of backward speech, it reads: "Abandoned my little to find him. My little to learn him forgot. My little rejected to have him. To love him my little reviled. This body homeless. This mind ignoring. These emptied hands. This emptied heart. To him I brought. To the temple. To the teacher. To the source. Of nought" (p. 166). Watt has given up the little he had: home, knowledge, possessions, attachments.[2] He brings with him (in Beckett's typically dualistic conception) a physical being (body, hands) and a spiritual being (mind, heart). His purpose is to find, to understand, to possess, and to love. He comes, as on a religious pilgrimage, to the temple, the teacher, the source—of nought. Before jumping to the conclusion that the journey ends in failure, it is well to recall the quotation from Democritus (*Murphy*, p. 246), for whom the void was filled with atomic particles: "Not the numb peace of their own suspension, but the positive peace that comes when the somethings give way, or perhaps simply add up, to the Nothing, than which in the guffaw of the Abderite naught is more real." "Naught" suggests "Knott" (homophonous in the Anglo-Irish pronunciation), whose house is Watt's destination and his abode for a considerable period of time (the middle years). The name Knott, besides evoking the microcosmic state of peace so desired by *Murphy*, also calls up the idea of a riddle (knot), and indeed Knott remains ultimately enigmatic.

To return to Watt's renunciations, a large part of the novel is taken up with their nature and variety. Many of the comic, satirical, and ironic aspects of the story are dedicated to the dismissal of these less real facets of human existence. Newspapers that relate indefatigably the meaningless trivia of life end up, after an exaggerated number of rereadings, in the "ladies' house of office" (p. 237). Official institutions that tend to lose their vitality and fade

---

[2] The parallel to Beckett's own renunciations when he left home, country, religion, profession is strikingly apparent.

into the shadows of routine come under fire, from the church, marriage, and the university through the shabby Irish aristocracy and railroad officialdom—and in general the unthinking and insensitive optimism that routine fosters. "All the same, said Mr. Gorman, life isn't such a bad old bugger" (p. 245). Superficial and exterior also and hence less real for the author, clothes and the bodies that wear them are viewed in comic terms. Physicality finds its most perfect example in the oversize buttocks which, once again, are the object of a vigorous satirical drubbing (p. 157). From Watt's contorted walk to Mr. Nackybal's learned scratching to sex in Ireland (among numerous examples is Sam, of the Lynch clan, who "committed adultery locally on a large scale, moving from place to place in his self-propelling invalid's chair" [p. 106]), the portrait of man's involvement with physical and intellectual surfaces is drawn with a mixture of amusement and revulsion. Watt has to a large extent been freed from the erotic possibilities that both attracted and repelled Belacqua and Murphy, but more through his greater age and lesser strength than by any act of his own will. In his liaison with the fish-woman, "Watt had not the strength and Mrs. Gorman had not the time . . ." (p. 141). Intercourse between human beings whether on the physical or spiritual plane is very partial and defective in *Watt*. The hero's departure from the community (of which apparently he had long since ceased to be an integrated member) into relative solitude finds its counterpart on the level of satire in the prolonged and hilarious pages on the nature of committees (pp. 174-197).

Watt's journey is preceded and made possible by an abandonment of all that has come to seem emptied of substance. But it is also a flight from anxiety and pain and a search for peace. As in earlier works, the presence of suffering in the world is the enigma of enigmas, and Beckett unleashes his most bitter irony and succumbs to his deepest sorrow in its presence. Thus marriage and unimpeded procreation appear as the worst of follies and cruelties, as they guarantee the unending propagation of pain. Near Knott's house in the Irish countryside, "immense impoverished families abounded for miles around in every conceivable direction." Of these the author describes the Lynch family at length, and his description is a catalogue of man's ills and a castigation of his optimistic blindness and acceptance. To take two of many examples, Kate Lynch is "covered all over with running sores of an unidentified nature but otherwise fit and well," while Sam Lynch (the adulterer) is "paralysed by a merciful providence from no higher than the knees down and from no lower than the waist up." In contrast to sex and religion, which are held responsible at least as immediate causes for enormous and unspeakable miseries, man's compassion is most often wholly ineffectual. Mrs. Nixon, "quivering with solicitude" ("Mr. Hackett thought she was going to pat him on the head, or at least stroke his hunch"), hardly compensates for the neglect of Hackett's mother, who left him alone to fall off the ladder and break his back while she went off to "the pub, or the chapel, or both" (pp. 10, 16). Watt escapes marriage and procreation. He avoids official religion, abstains from alcohol, and he is not given to futile movements of compassion. And in Watt's house he is less vulnerable to time, to the painful spectacle of natural beauty that in Beckett invariably evokes its own and man's decay and death.

We learn of Watt's separation from the world of surfaces not only through the author's irony, but also, more directly, through Watt's experience in Knott's house, where the ascesis continues and takes on a significance that goes far beyond social satire. Watt, we discover, has long since given up the search for any kind of profound inner meaning. Watt "had not seen a symbol, nor executed an interpretation, since the age of fourteen, or fifteen . . . [he] had lived, miserably it is true, among face values all his adult life. . . . And he had experienced literally nothing, since the age of fourteen or fifteen, of which in retrospect he was not content to say, That is what happened then." In Knott's house, however, each incident of note, as it repeats itself inside Watt's head, tends gradually to lose, "in the nice processes of its light, its sound, its impacts and its rhythm, all meaning, even the most literal" (p. 73). Pure form, in other words, takes over, and meaning evaporates. Again we recall Murphy's "accidentless One-and-Only, conveniently called Nothing," which results when the "somethings give way," and his flux of "forms becoming and crumbling into the fragments of a new becoming" (*Murphy*, pp. 246, 112). This "fragility of the outer meaning" has a bad effect on Watt, however. It leads him to seek "for some meaning of what had passed," not for the real meaning, "for to explain had always been to exorcize, for Watt" (pp. 73, 78). The trouble with Watt, we learn, is that he has great difficulty, until "towards the end of his stay in Mr Knott's house," in accepting the

355

fact that "with all the clarity and solidity of something. . . . nothing had happened, . . . a nothing had happened . . ." (pp. 76, 80).

Not only events but their components, things, lose their familiar identity in the little world of Knott's house, and Watt experiences something like the anguish of Proust's young protagonist trying to go to sleep in a strange bedroom among unfamiliar and therefore terrifying objects. Man's need to domesticate the world about him, to dispel mystery by assigning phenomena to tried and true categories is great, so great that the categories very often substitute themselves permanently for the ever-new, ever-mysterious things about him. The experience of the microcosm, which is preceded by loss of faith in the familiar groupings, or, more organically, by loss of the capacity to see things in terms of categories, was for Murphy, all in all, "so pleasant that pleasant was not the word" (*Murphy*, p. 113). But Watt, especially at the beginning of his stay in Knott's house, only rarely "envisaged this dereliction with something like satisfaction" (p. 84). For Proust's young protagonist the breeching of the protective fortress of habit is temporary and terror soon gives way to the relief of boredom. But eventually the workings of involuntary memory come to the rescue and restore the individual integrity of things not in the terror of unfamiliarity but in the paradisiac joy of the past resuscitated and made timeless. For Proust, then, the relationship between subject and object is never really lost completely. It is maintained, either in dullness at the level of the species or else in anxiety or ecstasy at the level of the mysterious individual. In Beckett the relationship itself is in question. Can the subject survive in unknowingness, out of contact with the objective world— including his own physical being? Such is the question at the core of *Watt*.

In the beginning the protagonist of the novel is perfectly content with categories, in fact very much in need of them. "Not that Watt desired information, for he did not. But he desired words to be applied to his situation. . . . [he] would have been glad to hear Erskine's voice, wrapping up safe in words the kitchen space, the extraordinary newel-lamp, [etc.] . . . And Watt's need of semantic succour was at times so great that he would set to trying names on things, and on himself, almost as a woman hats" (pp. 81-83). Unfortunately for Watt's peace of mind, things have become recalcitrant. "Watt now found himself in the midst of things which, if they consented to be named, did so as it were with reluctance. And the state in which Watt found himself resisted formulation in a way no state had ever done. . . . Looking at a pot, for example . . . it was in vain that Watt said, Pot, pot. . . . For it was not a pot, the more he looked, the more he reflected, the more he felt sure of that, that it was not a pot at all. It resembled a pot, it was almost a pot, but it was not a pot of which one could say, Pot, pot, and be comforted. . . . And it was just this hairbreadth departure from the nature of a true pot that so excruciated Watt." And yet "the pot remained a pot, Watt felt sure of that, for everyone but Watt. For Watt alone it was not a pot, any more." Watt turns for reassurance to himself, "who was not Mr Knott's, in the sense that the pot was, who had come from without and whom the without would take again." It is no use, for he makes "the distressing discovery that of himself too he could no longer affirm anything that did not seem as false as if he had affirmed it of a stone. . . . he could no longer call it a man, as he had used to do, with the intuition that he was perhaps not talking utter nonsense" (pp. 81-83). While Watt suffers from this situation and for a time hopes that it results simply from the difficulty with which his body adjusts to "an unfamiliar milieu," and that eventually things will "consent to be named, with the time-honoured names, and forgotten," there are times when he rather enjoys the prospect of "being so abandoned, by the last rats. . . . [even though] it would be lonely, to be sure, at first, and silent, after the gnawing, the scurrying, the little cries. Things and himself, they had gone with him now for so long in the foul weather, and in the less foul" (p. 84). And eventually, we learn, after Watt's world has become "unspeakable," he does indeed grow "used to his loss of species" (p. 85).

The Utopia of Mr. Knott's House

Arsene's parting words tell us a good deal about the situation in which a man like Watt, at a certain age, may find himself. As in poems discussed earlier, it is a situation defined in essentially negative terms. Watt's arrival means first of all an end to blind wandering: "The dark ways all behind. . . ." Movement does not cease altogether, but it is no longer a flight or a search or a social commitment. Instead it has become "a stirring beyond coming and going." Activity does not come to a halt, but there are no more questions, orders, explanations, for the sounds that come "demand nothing, ordain nothing, explain nothing" (p. 39). Even though the new arrival in Knott's house does not find, as he hoped he would, "a situation where to do nothing exclusively would be an act of the highest value, and significance," quite different from the "superficial loitering" and "disinterested endeavour" that tormented and horrified him, respectively, in the past, he is soon reconciled to a service of "unquestionable utility . . . [and] exceptional fruitfulness" (p. 41) that benefits him even more than his master. It is significant that the work done for Mr. Knott ("he peels the potato and empties the nightstool") is of a routine, manual nature, requiring no decisions and exempt from anxiety. Knott's servant goes about his tasks "calm and glad" (p. 42). Knott's home is a "refuge" (p. 39) and, as the etymology of the term implies, a retreat or flight back to the source. We are therefore hardly surprised to find figures of a return to the womb along with related images incorporating softness, warmth, darkness, or enclosure. Approaching Knott's house, Watt feels weak and rests by the side of the road, assuming the foetal position (p. 33). Earlier, a clearly positive value is attached to the "warm nest of books and periodicals" (p. 25) of the news agent who witnesses Watt's run-in with the porter in the railway station. At the end, in the insane asylum, Watt enjoys the "separate soundless unlit warmth" of his padded cell. On the level of irony, the conditions obtaining in the mind of Mr. Thomas Nackybal, the Visicelt brought back by Mr. Ernest Louit from western Ireland in support of his dissertation, "The Mathematical Intuitions of the Visicelts," compose a metaphorical correlative of the ideal state to be found in the womb. Apart from an almost instinctive "knowledge of how to extract, from the ancestral half-acre of moraine, the maximum of nourishment, for himself and his pig, with the minimum of labour," his mind is "an ecstasy of darkness, and of silence" (p. 175).

In the amusing hoax perpetrated by Mr. Louit, Beckett takes advantage of a variant form of the myth of the good savage to satirize academia and, indirectly, man's obsessive need to know. At the same time he suggests a link between what Murphy called the microcosm of the mind and the prenatal state. Under the proper conditions perhaps the former can approximate the latter, can become, that is, a place in which one can live. The utopia of Mr. Knott's house has much in common with the "little world" of Murphy's mind. Indeed, the author employs the identical term to describe it when he writes of "the little world of Mr Knott's establishment" (p. 85). Often enough, however, the focus narrows still further to the microcosm inside Watt's skull. There, when thought stops and the body is placated and quiet, Watt experiences, in auditory terms, something closely akin to Murphy's "pure forms of commotion" (*Murphy*, p. 112): "He lay on the seat, without thought or sensation, except for a slight feeling of chill in one foot. In his skull the voices whispering their canon were like a patter of mice, a flurry of little grey paws in the dust" (p. 232). Such an experience, the enjoyment of pure form, is conditional upon an absence of thought or meaning. It can arise spontaneously in the mind if circumstances are favorable, or it can come from the song or speech of Mr. Knott: "The words of [Mr. Knott's] songs were either without meaning or derived from an idiom with which Watt, a very fair linguist, had no acquaintance. . . . Mr Knott talked often to himself too, with great variety and vehemence of intonation and gesticulation, but this so softly that it came, a wild dim chatter, meaningless to Watt's ailing ears. This was a noise of which Watt grew exceedingly fond. . . . while it sounded he was gladdened, as by the rain on the bamboos . . ." (p. 209). The phrase "rain on the bamboos" recalls the poem "Alba" and by thematic association "Dortmunder" as well, and the state of contemplative ataraxy produced in both poems through the influence of music, i.e., nonreferential sound, pure form. As we shall shortly see, the ghost of Schopenhauer, invoked in "Dortmunder," is with us still in *Watt*.

A number of other images are used to describe the utopia of *Watt*, all of them in one way or another suggesting a negation. On several occasions life is rendered inanimate or scaled down from the human or animal to the vegetable level. Arsene imagines himself "longing to be turned into a stone pillar or a cromlech" (p. 49) and the fate of Daphne, metamorphosed into a laurel tree, is envisioned not with sadness but rather as an altogether happy way out of a disagreeable situation (p. 44). Images of freedom *from* and separation *from* are further indications of a continuing process of stripping away, not unrelated to Arsene's description of the three kinds of laughter as "successive excoriations of the understanding" (p. 48). Existence in the macrocosm is like existence on a ladder, a constant mounting and descending, an organized relation between one thing and another, between one step and another, a logical, practical, tiring business. Life in Knott's house, at least at times, is

359

equivalent to "existence off the ladder" (p. 44). In this context the joke "Do not come down the ladder, Ifor, I haf taken it away" (p. 44) suggests a utopian situation. Treadmill existence has been replaced by isolation, nonrelation, reduced mobility, and possibly a greater sense of enclosure—recalling the womb, Knott's house, and life in the mental microcosm. Much later in the novel we find a related passage with images that suggest Belacqua's cup or funnel: "one is in the pit, in the hollow . . . at the foot of all the hills at last, the ways down, the ways up, and free, free at last . . ." (p. 202). Arsene's sentiments were identical when he spoke of the "sites of a stirring beyond coming and going," of a being "light and free," of "the secret places where nobody ever comes" (p. 39).

The logical culmination of the tendency to reduce, negate, eliminate is *le néant*, and we do indeed find that images of nothingness, beginning with the house of Mr. Knott, are very frequent. When Beckett finishes describing Watt's aversions, little is left: "For if there were two things that Watt disliked, one was the moon, and the other was the sun" (p. 33). And very shortly thereafter, "And if there were two things that Watt loathed, one was the earth, and the other was the sky" (p. 36). Arsene speaks of a being that is "as the being of nothing" (p. 39). Much later we learn that "In empty, in airless gloom, Mr Knott abode. . . . And from it this ambience followed him forth, and when he moved, in the house, in the garden, with him moved, dimming all, dulling all, stilling all, numbing all, where he passed" (p. 200). The middle years, between the contrary yearnings of youth and the decay of old age, are like Mr. Knott's house, a kind of respite between torments where "the gnashing ends" and "one is . . . nothing at last" (p. 202). Belacqua had his "womb-tomb," his "limbo," as Murphy had his "little world," but they were occasional escapes; Mr. Knott's house, for a time at least, is Watt's world, and everything else is peripheral. When Arsene speaks of the transition from the outside world of youth to the inner world of middle age, his words describe a Belacqua, the "border man," becoming a Watt: "he will be in his midst at last, after so many tedious years spent clinging to the perimeter" (p. 41). A similar figure involving the circle occurs later on in the same context of alienation from and integration into one's proper context. The painting in Erskine's room, of a circle and a point, causes Watt to wonder "how long it would be before the point and circle entered together upon the same plane. . . . if they had sighted each other . . . [whether] the artist had intended to represent . . . a circle and its centre in search of each other, or . . . a circle and a centre not its centre in search of a centre and its circle respectively, in boundless space, in endless time . . . and at the thought that it was perhaps this . . . Watt's eyes filled with tears that he could not stem . . ." (p. 129).

All the externals that are stripped away are "other." Together they make up the illusory, insubstantial outside world. They distract. They clutter the context called Nothing, in which a man can be at home, perhaps discover the true nature of his own being. As Arsene explains, in Knott's abode the wanderer reaches his destination. Finally, for the first time, the alien, the misfit, is "the right man, at last" and "in the right place, at last" (p. 40). The theme of untimeliness that we found in the poetry recurs in *Watt*. It is a temporal form of the spatial out-of-placeness that Lucky evokes in *Godot* when he refers to "l'air la terre, faits pour les pierres" (and not, he implies, for man). Outside are "the languor and the fever of the going of the coming too late, the languor and the fever of the coming of the going too soon. But to Mr Knott, and with Mr Knott, and from Mr Knott, were a coming and a being and a going exempt from languor, exempt from fever, for Mr Knott was harbour . . ." (p. 135). Beckett's dualistic vision, in which the two halves exist in uneasy, inappropriate alliance, for once, even if briefly, gives way to a kind of mystical harmony between man and nature. Arsene describes the moment when one arrives at Mr. Knott's house and feels the "premonitions of harmony . . . , of imminent harmony, when all outside him will be he, the flowers . . . the sky . . . the earth . . . , and all sound his echo . . ." (pp. 40-41). Arsene would seem to accept his creator's adaptation of the insight of Democritus that nothing is more real than nothing (*Murphy*, p. 246), for in his opinion "it was not an allusion, as long as it lasted, that presence of what did not exist, that presence without, that presence within, that presence between . . ." (p. 45).

If Nothing is a state more real than the one in which man finds himself in the world beyond Mr. Knott's house and garden, it is nevertheless defined primarily in negative terms. And the principal precondition for the "presence of what did not exist," to which we now come, is the absence of desire, need, will. Once Arsene "was in the sun, and . . . was the sun . . . and the wall and the step, and the yard, and the time of year, and the time of day." His "personal

361

system was so distended . . . that the distinction between what was inside it and what was outside it was not at all easy to draw." Then "something slipped," and he finds himself back in the old dualistic fix, in an alien land as before, with the old needs, the old yearnings. The metamorphosis has been reversed: "The Laurel into Daphne" (pp. 42-44). Especially as it relates *Watt* to the central predicament of Belacqua, the invocation of the myth is of the utmost importance. Belacqua was torn between two desires, figured by Apollo and Narcissus or the need to go out to the other and the need to retreat into the self, pursuit of the girl (for youth, the emblem par excellence of desire) and flight from her. Limbo was the abolition of both needs. The laurel occupies the same place in *Watt*. Devoid of need, conscious need in any case, the tree is a part of nature and in harmony with it. There is no longer any distinction between subject and object. Turned back into Daphne, this being reenters a world of attractions and repulsions, loves and hates, comings and goings determined by needs positive and needs negative, desires for association and yearnings for solitude.

How much better would life be without *atra cura*, the "black want" of the poems. "And yet it is useless not to seek, not to want, for when you cease to seek you start to find. . . ." Satisfaction of needs merely gives rise to other needs. And fulfillment itself is considerably less desirable than the state of wanting: "when you cease to want, then life begins to ram her fish and chips down your gullet until you puke, and then the puke down your gullet until you puke the puke, and then the puked puke until you begin to like it." For Arsene, at least, the depressing fact is that the closest one can get to happiness is the state of unfulfilled desire, "to hunger, thirst, lust, every day afresh and every day in vain, after the old prog, the old booze, the old whores . . ." (p. 44). And yet Beckett, with Schopenhauer, makes it clear enough that the root of our misery is desire, that its ablation would be felicity. Influenced no doubt by the torments of Swann needing Odette, of the narrator wanting Gilberte, Beckett ends his introduction to *Proust* with a quote from Leopardi that gives away his own view of the dilemma: "non che la speme, il desiderio è spento."

Although Arsene rejects fulfillment as a way out, it seems to play some part in the ideal hypothetical solution that the author sets up. For Mr. Knott is perhaps above all the one who does *not* need. He provides the standard against which all other attempts to establish a utopian mode of existence must be measured. "For except, one, not to need, and, two, a witness to his not needing, Knott needed nothing, as far as Watt could see." Mr. Knott seems to maintain his happy state of indifference by doing things—even though he has no need to do them—that, were they left undone, might have the power to create needs in him. He wears many varieties of clothes, for example, clothes for all seasons and occasions, but indiscriminately, without regard to the season or occasion. So it is with his other activities. They are invariably explainable by his nature: that of a non-needing being. "If he ate and he ate well; if he drank, and he drank heartily; if he slept, and he slept sound; if he did other things, and he did other things regularly, it was not from need of food, or drink, or sleep, or other things, no, but from the need never to need, never never to need, food, and drink, and sleep, and other things" (p. 202).

Knott's mode of being has an effect on the surroundings. "This ataraxy covered the entire house-room, the pleasure-garden, the vegetable-garden and of course Arthur [Watt's successor on the ground floor]" (p. 208). In referring to the root condition of the utopia he calls "Nothing" Watt speaks of "the longing for longing gone, the horror of horror" (p. 202). Not only have attraction and repulsion, or positive and negative desire, vanished. The need for desire has also been abolished, and that is the crux of the matter. Man not only desires, he desires to desire—which is disastrous. He seems incapable under ordinary conditions of living in limbo. He seeks to want. His comings and goings are purposeful, and he is forever coming and going. Only Knott "seems to abide" (p. 58). And yet human progress is no progress at all, as Watt's vision after leaving Knott's house indicates. Since the flame of desire is eternally rekindled from its own ashes, all our comings and goings, which in *Watt* are figures of the needs that propel us, are futile. All motion is equivalent to stasis, since it brings us right back to the starting point: need. With Estragon and Vladimir, we move in place.

In the metaphoric structure of the novel, the sojourn in Knott's house is a time of staying and a time of nonwilling. It represents in general an end to the comings and goings that are outward manifestations of desire. The comings and goings in Knott's house are of a different nature. They are not determined by Watt. He is a servant who follows the rules of the establishment. He is not expected to

363

make decisions.[3] His status as an obedient servant is a principal prerequisite to the tranquility of indifference (p. 39), to the "will-lessness" that is the *summum bonum*. Watt enjoys Knott's "wild, dim chatter," but he is not sorry when it ceases nor glad when it begins again (p. 209). When he leaves Knott's house, he does so "with the utmost serenity." Only after he has left the premises does "he burst into tears" (p. 208). While in Mr. Knott's house he suffers "neither from the presence . . . nor from [the] absence" of his master (p. 207). And yet Watt is by no means always exempt from the common condition of need, even in Knott's house. The novel, then, appears to pose the following question: "Is there a place, like the house of Mr. Knott, in which the normal condition of need can be transcended?"

The Religious Dimension

Concern with the themes of freedom and will is traditional and of central importance in Christianity from "not my will, but thine, be done" (Luke 22:42) to the present. In the *Commedia*, a *livre de chevet* of Beckett, Dante's words "liberi soggiacete" (*Purg.* XVI, 80) and "E'n la sua voluntate e nostra pace" (*Par.* III, 85) express religious views that are very close to notions developed in *Watt*. Service, obedience, renunciation of personal will are liberating. They provide a way to "a being so light and free that it is as the being of nothing" (p. 39). The renunciations of Watt are couched in religious language that suggests the ascetic preliminaries to mystic experience. Mr. Knott and his premises are often described in terms that evoke the deity. All is mobility save Knott, who "abides . . . like an oak . . . and we nest a little while in his branches" (p. 57). His house is mystery and fixity. It is no easier to remain long in his presence than to be long out of it. "For there was no other place . . . whose mysteries, whose fixity . . . so thrust forth [yet] called back so soon, with such a call" (p. 199). Watt rejects certain speculations about the nature of Knott as "anthropomorphic insolence" (p. 202). The term "witness," so current in religious usage, occurs on a number of occasions. A minor rebellion by Watt goes, to his surprise, unavenged: "No punishment fell on Watt, no thunderbolt . . ." (p. 115). He reasons that perhaps his "transgression," sur-

---

[3] Cf. Belacqua in "Ding-Dong." Incapable of deciding which direction to take, he must wait for a sign.

rounded as it was "with such precautions, such delicacies," appeared no transgression at all, that his manner was "counted to him for grace" (p. 116). In language that recalls Dante's inscription over the gate of hell, the narrator speculates that Watt, while still on the ground floor, "little by little abandoned all hope, all fear, of ever seeing Mr Knott face to face" (p. 146). Arsene admits that the "dreams of middle age" were his dreams, in spite of occasional "blasphemous words and expressions." And what he knows toward the end of his stay with Mr. Knott "partakes," he asserts, "[of] the unutterable or ineffable" (p. 62).

Biblical allusions help to give a Christian tone to the vaguely religious atmosphere that permeates the novel. St. Paul comes to mind when Watt does catch glimpses of Mr. Knott, for they "are not clearly caught, but as it were in a glass, not a looking glass, a plain glass, an eastern window at morning, a western window at evening." Mr. Knott likes a small number of rather down-at-the-heels servants, "for to seediness and shabbiness and fewness in number he is greatly attached." Although the expression "give glory" is not used, we hear a faintly ironic echo of its meaning when Arsene states that the purpose of these servants is "to make much of him [Knott]" (p. 59). Through a footnote, we learn that both Arsene and Watt have an "eleventh hour vision, of what might have been" (p. 82). Mr. Knott rests on the seventh day (p. 86). Arsene must leave Mr. Knott's establishment "before the cock crows" and leaving he will perhaps long "to be turned into a stone pillar" (p. 49). Later the narrator, like Veronica,[4] has compassion on Watt and wipes his face with a cloth. And like Mary Magdalene he anoints his face and hands. The examinations committee leaves the university in reverse order "so that the first was last, and the last first" (p. 196), which is perhaps not without relation to the backward speech of Watt's post-Knott days. Occasionally a clear allusion to a well-known prayer reinforces the religious atmosphere. Thus "as it was in the beginning, is now, and ever shall be" turns up in the form: "as it was now, so it had been in the beginning, and so it would remain to the end" (p. 131).

In one especially crucial area, the analogy between Knott and the deity seems to hold. The satire of religion that we have already noted goes beyond an attack on institutions. Beckett suffers from the knowledge of the suffering of his fellows, and his pain emerges

[4] Cf. "Enueg II."

365

in the form of bitter irony that links the mystery of evil and the mystery of divinity. The news agent, "a man of more than usual acerbity" who seems "to suffer from unremitting mental, moral and perhaps even physical pain," is short and limps dreadfully. Once he gets started he moves rapidly, "in a series of aborted genuflexions" (pp. 25-26). The same implicit question, to serve or not to serve under such conditions, arises in connection with the "faithful emaciated dog" (p. 97), endowed with free will, which is supposed to eat Mr. Knott's leftovers—whenever there are any. The principal garbage men attached to the service of Mr. Knott, who "exploit" (p. 98) the dogs, are members of the malady-ridden Lynch clan, whose ailments seem to be an expansion of the case of Job, utilized by Beckett in the poem "Text." The metaphysical protest reaches paroxysmal proportions in the description of the later activities of Sam and Watt in the mental institution. They take delight in stoning birds, especially the confiding robins, which they destroy in great numbers. They grind the eggs of larks into fragments under their feet "with peculiar satisfaction." But their favorite friends are the rats, to which they feed frogs and baby thrushes, "or seizing suddenly a plump young rat, resting in [their] bosom after its repast, [they] would feed it to its mother, or its father, or its brother, or its sister, or to some less fortunate relative." It is on such occasions, they agree, that they come "nearest to God" (pp. 155-156). Close upon this ferocious, if theologically dubious, passage comes a double juxtaposition that associates "Knott, Christ, Gomorrha, Cork" (p. 156).

To identify Knott and the Divinity is as risky as equating Godot and God. For one thing, the asylum where Watt tells his story to Sam is *also* described in terms borrowed from the Bible (p. 151) and used there to describe heaven ("In my Father's house are many mansions" [John 14:2]). For another, many of Knott's actions have surely never been associated with the god of any known religion: his habits of dress and his gastronomic preferences, for example. Certain aspects of his nature also give pause. In the Addenda we learn that "Mr. Knott too was serial . . ." (p. 253). There was a time, then, when Mr. Knott, unlike God, did not yet exist.[5] How-

---

[5] In any consideration of the religious dimension of Watt it is essential to keep in mind Beckett's consistent separation of Christ, seen as man, the suffering servant, himself a victim, and the Divinity, enigmatic source of the mystery of evil. Arsene, describing himself as much as Watt, suggests the

ever, one prime characteristic, valued highly by Watt, is shared by Knott and the Divinity: an absence of need. Belacqua did spend over two months at one stretch in his "umbra" ("Dream," pp. 38-40), but he was never able to duplicate the feat again, let alone approach the all-time record of his namesake in purgatory. The consuming curiosity of Watt violates the indifference requisite to the limbo that he too would inhabit. Everything in Mr. Knott's little establishment, on the other hand, is organized with a view to eliminating all need—save the need "not to need" and "a witness to his not needing" (p. 202). Only this minimal link to the macrocosm intrudes on the self-sufficiency of his private world. If we turn now to Lucky's speech in *En attendant Godot*, we find a pertinent description (like the portrait of Mr. Knott, half-satirical and half-serious) of a deity who exists "hors du temps de l'étendue" in a state of "divine apathie . . . divine athambie . . . divine aphasie" (pp. 71-72). Characterized, like Murphy's microcosm and Belacqua's cup, by negative attributes, this timeless, spaceless condition is all but sealed off from the world of men. The triple qualification suggests the trinitarian God, but the absence of feeling or suffering, of brilliance ($\theta\alpha\mu\beta os$), and of speech would require stretching and a different sequence to work specifically against the power, wisdom, and love traditionally associated with the Father, Son, and Holy Spirit. The three terms describe accurately enough, however, the indifferent, darkly mysterious, and uncommunicative Almighty of Beckett's vision, and, curiously, they apply equally well to the desirable state sought in the sanctuary of mind by all Beckett's early protagonists, including the "I" of a number of poems—and to Mr. Knott. "Apathie" for Belacqua is "a beatitude of indolence . . . in a Limbo purged of desire" ("Dream," p. 38). "States of peace" describe the corresponding experience in *Murphy* (p. 112). "Dispassionate" Anteros is summoned to "choke . . . regret" in "Return to the Vestry" (35-39). The untroubled calm of "ataraxy" pervades the house and grounds of Mr. Knott, and only when he passes beyond the gate does Watt's total "serenity" give way to "tears" (p. 208). Similarly, "athambie" turns up as grayness, dimness, absence of sun and glare, gloom, half-light; while "aphasie" trans-

---

stigmata when he refers, in another context, to head, side, hands, and feet (p. 39). Later Sam likens Watt, and himself, to this same Christ (p. 159).

lates as hush, country of quiet, silence, softness of sound, dim meaningless chatter.

In the privileged and relatively rare experience of inner being Beckett finds his utopia, the beatific condition so prized by a succession of fictional surrogates. Its excellence can only be adequately described (as Proust's narrator describes the workings of involuntary memory) by recourse to religious imagery. In the negative Mr. Knott we have the postulate of a human mastery of this godlike mode of being, described as a very real Nothing in *Murphy*. Knott's characteristics and actions stem from this imaginative postulate. His achievement accounts for the supernatural aura that surrounds him. By comparison with Knott, Watt is indeed an apprentice— in some ways a singularly inept one. Because he is older, however, and relatively free of the erotic distractions that plagued his younger forerunners, he has some degree of success. Because his effort is serious and moving even while remaining comic, he emerges as a strangely impressive and haunting figure in the Beckett canon.

If Watt is middle-aged, Knott is an old man, as we learn from Arthur's encounter with Knott's contemporary in the garden (p. 252). Certain passages indicate that age is an important ally in the conquest of inwardness. Watt's reaction when Arthur relates his encounter is especially noteworthy: "There had been a time when [knowing] . . . that Mr. Knott too was serial . . . would have pleased him. . . ." (The knowledge of a reduced distance between apprentice and master might have raised Watt's expectations.) "But not now. For Watt was an old rose now, and indifferent to the gardener" (p. 253). The indifference of old age, antidote to the poison of curiosity that inhibits the imitation of Knott, resembles the deific "apathie" in *Godot*. It may be the open sesame to the asylum where he passes his declining years and where he comes to resemble Knott in more ways than one. His abode brings to mind the Magdalen Mental Mercyseat, where Murphy cultivates the "sanctuary" (p. 177) that he calls his "dungeon in Spain" in admiring imitation of patients successfully "immured in mind" (p. 180). No less compellingly, the situation of Sam and Watt recalls Belacqua's experience of limbo: "the mind at last its own asylum, disinterested, indifferent . . ." ("Dream," p. 39).

In *Watt* Beckett probes the microcosm more searchingly and more seriously—but seldom without the skeptical queries of irony and laughter. In "Dream" the Alba suspects Belacqua of being "inextricably Limbese" and promises to leave him to "rot away in his darling gloom" if she turns out to be right (p. 173). Even at the asylum, as he acquires dimensions lacking in Belacqua and Murphy, Watt does not cease to be a comical figure. The parallel between a microcosmic deity and microcosmic man (made in His image?), each cruel in his self-enclosed indifference, implies a radical criticism of inwardness. As certain passages in Part III appear to suggest, Watt's solitude at the end may be less beatitude and fulfillment than the anxiety of a continuing, if changed, need. Ultimately, religious metaphor takes on more than metaphoric value, and the vaunted inner existence seems more the calvary of an exile than a heaven of untroubled bliss.

The Fly in the Ointment of Microcosmos

In the motif of the serial and the nonserial we can see more clearly why Watt, better equipped in some ways than his precursors, is far from wholly successful in his undertaking. In a lamentation over the return of the days, the months, and the seasons (which includes biographical references to Beckett's early years at Cooldrinagh in Foxrock: "The larch turning green every year a week before the others," "the consumptive postman whistling *The Roses Are Blooming in Picardy*"), Arsene ends the year in April (when Beckett was born) with the words "and then the whole bloody business starting all over again." Later in the book Watt follows in his footsteps, attaching "great importance" to the question "Was the picture a fixed and stable member of the edifice . . . [or] a term in a series, like the series of Mr Knott's dogs, or the series of Mr Knott's men, or like the centuries that fall, from the pod of eternity?" (p. 131). Little by little Watt comes to the opinion that no "presence" ever changes in Mr. Knott's house; only appearances, surfaces change, but they are in a process of unending change. Although he has a will to know, he can learn little from the phantom forms of a world in eternal flux. Reluctantly, then, Watt, who has not attempted to get at underlying meaning since the age of fourteen or fifteen, who has lived "among face values all his adult life," feels impelled to seek some other meaning, to find reasons and causes, to penetrate—beneath the accidents—the mystery of being (p. 117). Watt's curiosity, however, does not lead him to pursue truth for its own sake. He works at the "ancient labour"

369

of trying to find out only in order to exorcise the demons of desire. The conceptions that Watt has no *need* for at the moment he puts aside like an umbrella in readiness for a rainy day. He tries to distinguish truth, "whatever that is," from falsehood, "whatever that means," but he feels that it is "greatly to be deplored" that he cares to do so (pp. 135-136, 226). Watt seeks, then, not knowledge itself but freedom from the epistemological craving that "disquiets" him.

Paradoxically, a very large part of the novel is given over to Watt's extraordinarily persistent attempts to know. With the oil of information he again and again momentarily dims the flames of curiosity only to see them burn again with a new intensity. Through his principal character Beckett explores a whole gamut of types of knowledge, ways of learning, and obstacles to understanding. The identity-card type of data that is wholly exterior reveals nothing of the essential being (p. 21). With Mr. Spiro (whose name suggests air, in this case of the hot variety) erudition is down the drain (p. 29). Intuition fares only slightly better, and any hope that primitive man, blessed with an underdeveloped cerebrum, might have access to nonrational sources of discernment is laughed out of court in the episode of Mr. Nackybal, the Visicelt (p. 198). In the same fell swoop academic research and group attempts to reach truth are ridiculed in Arthur's comical story of the examinations committee with its deaf recording secretary. Eye-witness evidence is invalidated by Watt's hallucination. Experience itself is like the "sterile pus" used in Watt's "course of injections" (p. 253). We can learn neither from the outer world nor from dreams (p. 232). The tools of logic and mathematics (and sometimes music) are of no avail. Religious faith is not enough (p. 192). The motives for human actions escape us (pp. 240, 245). Ultimately, man's intellect is ill-adapted to the task, his memory imperfect, his senses untrustworthy. Fatigue, desire, imagination, convention, time and circumstances of life are distorting lenses. But the receiving subject is no less flawed than the transmitter. And the mode of communication and the conditions under which the message is transmitted must share the blame. "Watt spoke also with scant regard for grammar, for syntax, for pronunciation, for enunciation . . . [in] a voice *at once* so rapid and so low . . . [that] much fell in vain on my [Sam's] imperfect hearing and understanding, and much by the rushing wind was carried away, and lost for ever" (p. 156). Arsene warns beforehand of the futility of the quest in his anecdote about one Mr. Ash, who had buttonholed him in a snowstorm on Westminster Bridge and who, unsolicited and at great inconvenience to himself, had dug out his grossly inaccurate watch to give him the time of day just a moment before Big Ben struck the hour. This bit of knowledge—painful to come by, undesired, wrong, and superfluous —is according to Arsene "the type of all information whatsoever" (p. 46). Watt, for whom knowledge is no more than a means by which he hopes to vanquish the "dis-ease" of the intellect and find asylum, might have spared himself the effort. The hunger to know is insatiable at a certain time of life, and as Beckett writes in *Proust*, "Wisdom . . . consists not in the satisfaction but in the ablation of desire" (p. 7).

Watt opens with a symbolic departure from the city. Its structure resembles a three-stage *rite de passage* (in this case a passing from maturity to old age): the hero goes out, spends a period of initiation in a privileged locus, and returns equipped with new power or wisdom. Like Arsene before him, Watt will acquire a certain wisdom in Knott's house, an inexpressible and "quite useless" (p. 62) wisdom. Arsene compares his sagacity to that of "Theseus kissing Ariadne, or Ariadne Theseus, towards the end, on the seashore . . ." (p. 63). Sagacity is the awareness of coming separation, living in the knowledge that we are given over to sorrow and loss. When Watt leaves the ground floor of Mr. Knott's house he is already well along the road to such sagacity:

> What had he learnt? Nothing.
> What did he know of Mr Knott? Nothing.
> Of his anxiety to improve, of his anxiety to understand, of his anxiety to get well, what remained? Nothing.
> But was not that something?
> He saw himself then, so little, so poor. And now, littler, poorer.
> Was not that something?
> So sick, so alone.
> And now.
> Sicker, aloner.
> Was not that something?   (p. 148)

The one thing we can know is our own want, our own lack and need. Since Mr. Knott needs nothing, he knows nothing of himself (p. 203). Were Watt himself to reach his goal, the nirvana of non-need, he too would cease to be conscious of his own being, since that being is unknowable except as need, and Beckett's paraphrase of Descartes would seem to be "I need, therefore I am." *Film* (1965) expresses anew this cornerstone concept in the edifice of Beckett's works through yet another attempt to escape the pain of awareness, inflicted either by the gaze of the other or the reflexive contemplation of the self, in a limbo of unselfconscious being.

The need to know destroys utopia. *Watt* is perhaps more than anything else a long development of the story of Eden. The fruit of the tree of knowledge is forbidden fruit, and the penalty for disobedience is banishment from the garden. From one point of view, Watt's departure from Mr. Knott's house and garden is indeed symbolic. For the most part he has never really lived there, and his leaving simply expresses his inability to be an unthinking, unneeding part of the innocent, peaceful "nothingness" of nature. Like Arsene he could not remain a laurel tree, one with the sun and the garden and the time of day and year. Leaving Eden, Adam and Eve saw their nakedness and were ashamed. Watt understands better than ever his own increasing indigence. Such wisdom is dearly paid for (p. 50). In his description of the varieties of laughter as "successive . . . excoriations of the understanding," Arsene comes finally to the deepest level of wisdom, to the mirthless laugh, "the *risus purus*" or "laugh laughing at the laugh" (p. 48). This is the moment of self-consciousness, when man discovers that his need to know has led ultimately only to the sure knowledge that he is a creature with a need to know—a need that has lost him Eden.

Arsene admits ruefully that "wiser [he] could hardly become without grave personal inconvenience" (p. 50). Perhaps the aging Watt too began to weigh inquisitiveness in the balance. By the time he moves from the ground floor to his new duties upstairs, he is too tired to revise a faulty hypothesis or seek a finished formulation. Even his need is no longer certain: translated, "Deen did tub? Ton sparp." (p. 166) comes out "But did need? Praps not." His experience in Mr. Knott's house is termed a "long dwindling supposition" (p. 131), and in his final indifference as he leaves the establishment we may see a reflection of Leopardi's lines, quoted by Beckett in *Proust* (p. 7): "In noi di cari inganni/non che la speme, il desiderio è spento." Watt in the asylum with Sam is certainly a changed person. His speech progresses from one form of inversion to another in a parodic mirror image of the logic of permutations and combinations he was wont to utilize. He even walks backwards. Like Dante's wrongheaded soothsayers, Watt pays for his attempts to "see." At the end he cannot even see where he is going. He has a peculiar and obscure way of talking; he progresses blindly; he has, in short, become an artist.

Watt as Artist and Art in *Watt*

The protagonist abandons reason at the end and gives up the attempt to know for the attempt to make. He becomes a storyteller, but one who by this time is so convinced of the inadequacy of ordinary language that he feels compelled to invent verbal structures that are more closely related to his experience. Beckett's metaphor of Watt's backward language is related to his own view of the creative process. In conversations in 1961 he spoke of writing as a "groping in the dark," an enterprise that required the writer to "see with his fingers." We find, then, at the heart of Beckett's artistic credo, a correspondence between the intellectual darkness in which man is doomed to live and the irrational organization of words imposed upon the serious artist who wants to say something valid about the conditions of human existence. We noted the symbolic darkness inside the egg in *Whoroscope* and its relation to the "starless inscrutable hour" denied to the fictional Descartes. Over thirty years later, the characters in *Comment c'est* live out their lives plunged in a similar obscurity.

Watt is not the only figure of the artist in the novel to which he gives his name. Since we might view the entire work as a development of the relationship between knowing and making, epistemology and art, it is not surprising that we find in it other artist-figures as well as a pervasive concern with questions vital to art. In the opening pages of the book Hackett reads a poem from the solicitor Grehan, who is serving a term in jail for having "slightly overstepped his prerogatives" (p. 10). "To Nelly" is the first tale within a tale. It is a parody that serves to illustrate by the contrast between its elevated, outdated style (use of the familiar second-person plural, archaic literary vocabulary, inversion, allusion, punning, onomatopoetic effects, etc.) and its realistically erotic content the notion that a gulf exists between language and life, art and reality. It begins,

To thee, sweet Nell, when shadows fall
Jug-jug! Jug-jug!
I here in thrall
My wanton thoughts do turn.
Walks she out yet with Byrne?
Moves Hyde his hand amid her skirts
As erst? I ask and Echo answers: Certes.

(p. 11)

Immediately thereafter, Tetty Nixon recounts at considerable length the birth of her son Larry. After that it is Mr. Hackett's turn at storytelling, and he relates briefly his early childhood and the traumatic origin of his deformity. All these preliminary accounts combine to establish narration—and curiosity—as important themes. They prepare the way for the dramatic entrance of Watt, the central question mark, and his story. As a good audience should, Mr. Hackett comes alive with interest:

Mr. Hackett did not know when he had been more intrigued, nay, he did not know when he had been so intrigued. He did not know either what it was that so intrigued him. What is it that so intrigues me, he said, whom even the extraordinary, even the supernatural, intrigue so seldom, and so little. Here there is nothing in the least unusual, that I can see, and yet I burn with curiosity, and with wonder. The sensation is not disagreeable, I must say, and yet I do not think I could bear it for more than twenty minutes, or half an hour.

The lady [Mrs. Nixon] was also an interested spectator.

(p. 17)

Along with the tale within the tale, the author supplies an inner audience, made up of characters who are themselves on occasion tellers of tales. In the above passage the triple repetition of "did not know," and the recurrence of "when" and especially "what," suggest man's need to know but this time in the special perspective of the work of art. The passage even has a word on the nature of spectator psychology. His need to know, or curiosity and wonder, motivates him in his role as audience. As the etymological meaning of the two terms suggests, his state is ambiguous. The Latin *cura,* which gives curiosity, can tend in the direction of anxiety, while wonder evokes not only curiosity but also a pleasurable admiration.

374

The *dulce* and *utile* of Horace, the French *plaire* and *instruire*, which point to the playful and the serious sides of art, find here a particular expression as wonder and curiosity. Mr. Hackett makes this explicit when he describes his feeling as "not disagreeable" yet close to unbearable. Art, of the present variety at least, has its pleasurable pain or its painful pleasure that corresponds to Beckett's particular vision of art and life and their relationship.

The next storyteller is the minor character Mr. Spiro, editor of a popular Catholic monthly, who harangues Watt in the train on the way to Mr. Knott's house. He is presumably the type of the bad artist, for he loses his audience. Watt hears nothing of his theological argumentation because he is listening to "other voices" (p. 29), voices within. Again we have the contrast between a rational and an intuitive approach to art, with the latter clearly preferred. Arsene's story is, next to Watt's, the most important in the novel, but we also have Arthur's long account of Louit, Mr. Nackybal, and the examinations committee. Through Arsene, Beckett suggests the role that art plays in passing on what little we know from one generation to the next; its part in awakening in us the desire to know, which leads to a consciousness of our nature, condition, and fate; its universality (p. 45); and its limitations:

> And I think I have said enough to light that fire in your mind that shall never be snuffed, or only with the utmost difficulty, just as Vincent did for me, and Walter for Erskine, and as you perhaps will do for another. . . . Not that I have told you all I know, for I have not, being now a good-natured man, and of good will what is more, and indulgent towards the dreams of middle age, which were my dreams . . . and perhaps also because what we know partakes in no small measure of the nature of . . . the unutterable. . . . (p. 62)

Through Arthur, Beckett tells us something of the psychology of at least one type of artist. While he tells his story, Arthur is "transported far from Mr Knott's premises, of which, of the mysteries of which, of the fixity of which, Arthur had sometimes more, than he could bear" (p. 198). Art is both a respite from curiosity and the refreshment of activity in the midst of meditation. But the escape is no more than temporary. Arthur falls silent in the middle of his story not from fatigue but from an overwhelming "desire to return . . . to Mr Knott's house, to its mysteries, to its fixity. For he had

375

been absent longer from them, than he could bear" (p. 199). The artist of the inner world shuttles between contemplation and creativity, filling quietude with sound, then returning to the depths of silence, overcome in turn by a need for words and a sense of their inadequacy, their lesser reality.

Watt is both the principal character in the work and its foremost artist-figure. The novel is his story, told in his style. If, however, we choose the perspective in which Watt is a character, then Sam becomes an author, or perhaps more accurately a scribe like Habbabuk in "Dortmunder." He is the author not as imaginative creator but as imperfect and relatively impersonal recorder. As author Watt too is chiefly a witness, but his testimony is more deeply affected by his particular nature, his needs and his limitations. Sam, as his name suggests, is partly, but only partly, Beckett. One implication of this device seems to be that the author is always to some degree and in some ways one with his characters, and at the same time he is other and relatively detached. Something of the romantic and something of the classical position obtains in every author-character relationship. A second purpose of this structure of receding planes (from Knott to Arsene to Watt to Sam to Beckett to the reader, for example) is, of course, to undermine the foundations of certain knowledge and suggest that we live in ignorance, surrounded by impenetrable mysteries. The substance of what we know is like the substance of dreams; and art, like the dreams of Calderón (quoted by Beckett in *Proust*) is the dream of a dream. And yet, because it partakes of the fictional, art may be a truer mirror of reality than science with its presumptuous etymology.

Among the numerous passages that show to what an unusual degree *Watt* is art about art, two are especially explicit. In the first, which incidentally shows the extent to which the preoccupations of *En attendant Godot* (indicated by my italics) are already present in Beckett's mind, the themes of sameness and *limae labor* (cf. "Serena I") come together in the context of artistic creation: "Other traits, other little ways, *little ways of passing the little days*, Watt remarked in Mr Knott, and could have told if he had wished, if he had not been tired, so very tired, by all he had told already, tired of adding, tired of subtracting to and from the same old things the same old things" (p. 212). In the second, Beckett links Watt's composition to a traditional literary form and goes on to destroy a pat literary cliché, in both cases pointing up the gap between literature and life, words and things: "As Watt told the beginning of his story, not first, but second, so not fourth, but third, now he told its end. Two, one, four, three, that was the order in which Watt told his story. Heroic quatrains are not otherwise elaborated. As Watt came, so he went, in the night, that covers all things with its cloak, especially when the weather is cloudy" (p. 215).

Even Mr. Knott is drawn into the reflexive mode of the novel, for he is associated not only with the theme of knowing but also with its counterpart, making. He is the successful artist who has created his own world and lives in it almost exempt from desire. His one need (besides not to need) is to be witnessed. He wants, in other words, an audience, as every artist finally does—not, as Beckett makes tellingly clear, so that he may know himself, "but that he may not cease" (p. 203). Watt too needs an audience, as Sam explains: "But he [Watt] could not bear that we should part, never to meet again (in this world), and I in ignorance of how Mr Knott put on his boots, or his shoes, or his slippers, [etc.]" (p. 212). It is often asserted of the artist that he is like the child in that he sees things in their pristine freshness and uniqueness. His is an Edenic view that has not replaced individual realities by categories of the mind. Mr. Knott meets this test also: "When [he] moved in the midst of his garden, he did so as one unacquainted with its beauties, looking at the trees, looking at the flowers, looking at the bushes, looking at the vegetables, as though they, or he, had been created in the course of the night" (p. 203).

Again, like an artist without a personal ego, who himself is *not*, but who lives many lives, imagines many selves, wears many guises in the world he creates, Mr. Knott is never the same. He is a master of metamorphosis (p. 211) who continually changes the arrangement of the furniture in his room, who wears clothes of all kinds without regard to the season, exhibiting a freedom of fantasy proper to the true artist, who can never be held within the limits of a narrow realism. Even his physical appearance changes from day to day in a radical way (p. 209). He sings, but his song, like all art that is validly original, is in an idiom that is not easily comprehensible. If all artists can be called animists in that they endow things with personalities, give the mysterious life of subjects to the objects about them, then Mr. Knott is surely a figure of the artist, for he sidles up to shoes with "an artless air" (*ars est celare artem*), pounces on them, and while putting one on holds the other tight, "lest it should escape" (p. 213). We have seen the link that Beckett makes between art and a microcosm that is above all a turning inward, an exclusion of the macrocosm with its distracting, unreal surfaces. Mr. Knott's house and grounds are one metaphor for this little world of art. With another image that evokes a further degree of inwardness, Watt describes the one and only characteristic gesture of Mr. Knott, "that which consisted in the simultaneous obturation of the facial cavities, the thumbs in the mouth, the forefingers in the ears, the little fingers in the nostrils, the third fingers in the eyes and the second fingers, free in a crisis to promote intellection, laid along the temples. "And this," he adds, "was less a gesture than an attitude, sustained by Mr Knott for long periods of time, without visible discomfort" (p. 212).[6]

The double analogy, between Knott and God and between Knott and the artist, suggests the venerable comparison between God and the artist, and it is natural enough for a maker-with-words to consider with more than casual interest the creative aspect of divinity. Beckett gives a particularly interesting twist to this ancient preoccupation when he stresses the inadequacy of the word, its failure to represent and its incomprehensibility. How, Beckett seems to ask, since we live in ignorance, can words, which are supposed to be meaningful, be used in a valid representation of reality? If the artist is in any way like the unknowable, uncommunicative divinity, if he is the first creator's metaphor of creativity, a god-figure in the tale of the original author, is he too not doomed to obscurity or even meaninglessness? On the level of words a disintegration of sense becomes evident very early in the novel. Labels are only with difficulty attached to things. Mr. Hackett calls Mr. Nixon Mr. Nesbit (p. 18) and later Mr. Nisbit (p. 24). The names Watt and Knott are symptomatic of a profound skepticism. Tags may be applied to mysteries, but mysteries they remain. Things are not stable: "the stairs . . . were never the same . . . even the number of

---

[6] It is interesting to note, apropos of his affinity for Schopenhauer or his interest in Chinese K'in music, the vaguely Oriental flavor of occasional images and ideas in Beckett. Lao-tzu (*The Simple Way*, No. 52) makes an association between curiosity and inwardness in language that reminds the reader of Mr. Knott's characteristic attitude and Watt's insatiable desire to know: "Keep your mouth shut, and close up the doors of sight and sound, and as long as you live you will have no vexation. But open your mouth, or become inquisitive, and you will be in trouble all your life long."

steps seemed to vary, from day to day, and from morning to night" (p. 83). We have seen the difficulty Watt has in accepting the term "pot." In Mr. Knott's house things begin to refuse their names, and eventually Watt's world becomes unspeakable (p. 85), so that he must try to find a new language to express the inexpressible. Syntactical questions, as well, bother Watt. "But was a dog the same thing as the dog?" (p. 96) he asks himself. Even before he develops his various forms of backward language, Watt employs unusual syntactical forms that violate normal conventions. The breakdown of language is only one form, though indeed a principal form, of what might be called in the broadest sense of the phrase the ironic dimension of the novel. Beckett uses language but has no faith in language. He adopts a novelistic structure and erodes it by intervening as author both in the text and in footnotes. He satirizes mores and institutions in Ireland and parodies traditional poetry. Above all, however, he turns his irony against reason and the quest for knowledge, against Watt himself. Finally, he calls into question the creative process, again primarily through the portrait of Watt, who when all is said and done is not a very good artist. Beckett's irony spares little, and certainly not himself. As intellectual and artist he is the original and foremost butt of his own joke. Almost as much as Emma Bovary was Flaubert, Watt is Beckett. If the irony is often mingled with commiseration, the aesthetic distance that lends objectivity is never so slight as to favor confusion between the author and his character. We never have self-pity, only sorrow for man and his condition.

Since the author's irony is directed chiefly against the search for an unobtainable or nonexistent meaning, it is not surprising that in terms of the linguistic and artistic enterprise the problem of form and content assumes major importance. Unexpectedly, at one point in his speculations about the disposition of the leftovers from Mr. Knott's meals Watt allows himself to abandon normal prose usage for the pleasure of rhyme, and he is not at all averse to poetic inversion and word deformation in order to achieve his end. Out of the blue comes this: "But might not even the most hardy . . . of messengers . . . have still some food got, in the old pot, when ten o'cluck strock, from the old clock . . ." (p. 96). His enjoyment of pure form leads him on another occasion to listen to the newly arrived Micks as one listens to music: "Watt listened for a time, for the voice was far from unmelodious. The fricatives in particular were pleasing. But as from the proscript an encountered nightsong, so it faded, the voice of Micks, the pleasant voice of poor Micks, and was lost, in the soundless tumult of the inner lamentation" (pp. 216-217). Many of the incidents that occur at Mr. Knott's house are, like the episode of the Galls, "of great formal brilliance and indeterminable purport" (p. 74). The loss of meaning leaves form isolated, which opens the way to aestheticism of a kind. One response to pure form is uncomplicated enjoyment, something perhaps on the order of Murphy's delight in his flux of forms. For someone as obsessed with knowing as Watt, however, it is difficult to accept for long the notion of unrelieved meaninglessness. Arsene, too, in his description of three kinds of "laughter," describes the progression from one to the other as a passage "from the outer to the inner . . . , from the matter to the form" (p. 48), and he speaks of the pure laugh that is linked to the deepest wisdom. In effect, a second response involves more than the mere enjoyment of meaningless form. It supposes a new alliance, a new quest. Watt, as the novel suggests, has not only a need to know but also a need to make verbal structures, to tell his story. If the first goes unfulfilled, the second does not. We do have the novel called *Watt*. Watt learns nothing. He experiences uncertainty, unfulfillment, solitude, deprivation, emptiness. He lives out a fruitless quest. As a maker he must discover or invent verbal forms to express this experience. Murphy succumbed during the enjoyment of meaningless form—and perhaps it would be fair to say that he succumbed to the temptation of meaningless form, to a variety of aestheticism enjoyed in a private world cut off from any other. Watt is not Murphy. He is not merely the audience of the inner spectacle, the hedonist enjoying his flux of meaningless forms. He is the artist in search of the form of meaninglessness, which is also, paradoxically, a kind of meaning. "What had he learnt? Nothing. . . . But was not that something?" (p. 148).[7]

Elsewhere in the novel we learn that Watt had great difficulty

[7] The distancing of Beckett the author from Watt through the device of Sam, the scribe, and the abandoning of the omniscient-author point of view used in *Murphy* can be explained not only as structural metaphors related to the theme of knowing (in the first case information is lost and distortion is introduced through transmission via several narrators, and in the second case omniscience would contradict uncertainty, mystery, and ignorance) but also as corollaries to the role of the two protagonists, Watt as artist in his own right and Murphy as spectator.

accepting the fact that "nothing had happened, that a thing that was nothing had happened, with the utmost formal distinctness" (p. 76). The question of the relationship between a content that is "nothing" and a form is central in the novel. Following the passage (p. 47) on living one's life again and the related development of the theme of sameness[8] ("the whole bloody business all over again . . . the result would be the same"), Arsene recites a significant little poem to Watt, significant because it is one of the first small-scale attempts to put form and content back together again, to find a style for sameness—which is already an approach to nothingness. Unlike the poem "elles viennent," this short piece is ironic in intent. The principal stylistic device, syntactical rearrangement of an identical content, is too mechanical and too obvious, and it fails to incarnate adequately the true experience of sameness, which involves real diversity, if only on the surface level.

> We shall be here all night,
> Be here all night shall we,
> All night we shall be here,
> Here all night we shall be.
> One dark, one still, one breath,
> Night here, here we, we night,
> One fleeing, fleeing to rest,
> One resting on the flight.

Arsene "laughs" ("Haw!") and comments, "You heard that one? A beauty. Haw! Hell!" (p. 48) and then continues with the discourse on the three laughs that are really modes of ululation. Even in this "bad" poem the incantatory values of repetition and variation are evident, and playing with word order does produce the pigeon-English profundity "we night" and the fairly good concluding lines with their evocation of immobility within movement (cf. *Godot*), the downward trajectory of man's life, the passage of time, and the brevity of existence. Beckett once called *Watt* "a joke," an exercise enabling him to "keep [his] hand in" during an otherwise unintellectual and unartistic existence in southern France during the war. In spite of its significance and its partial success, the above poem is a "joke" in the same sense. The element of play is uppermost. The ironical, the comical, the playful take general

---

[8] Descartes in *Whoroscope* gives expression to analogous sentiments when he asks Weulles to grant him a "second/ starless inscrutable hour."

precedence, both in this exercise and in *Watt*, even though the serious in its various forms is close to the surface.

Arsene's three types of ululation involve both faces of art, but perhaps the passage on the danger of dogs and other beasts is a more typical example of the weighted balance.

> Watt, reflecting on this, heard a little voice say, Mr Knott, having once known a man who was bitten by a dog, in the leg, and having once known another man who was scratched by a cat, in the nose, and having once known a fine healthy woman who was butted by a goat, in the loins, and having once known another man who was disembowelled by a bull, in the bowels, and having once frequented a canon who was kicked by a horse, in the crotch, is shy of dogs, and other four-footed friends, about the place, and of his inarticulate bipedal brothers and sisters in God hardly less so, for he once knew a missionary who was trampled to death by an ostrich, in the stomach, and he once knew a priest who, on leaving with a sigh of relief the chapel where he had served mass, with his own hands, to more than a hundred persons, was shat on, from above, by a dove, in the eye.
>
> Watt never knew quite what to make of this particular little voice, whether it was joking, or whether it was serious.   (p. 91)

Here, even though the themes of suffering, the mystery of God's ways, and something approaching metaphysical revolt are clearly present, the passage is in a comic key. The play of form for its own sake dominates, and the "message" is softened. "In the stomach" is no longer appropriate, but the formal momentum is irresistible and wins out over logic. The poet gives in to the temptation of pure sound, and we get "disembowelled . . . bull . . . bowels" and "above . . . dove." As Watt admits on another occasion, art can bring "comparative peace of mind" by turning "a disturbance into words," by making "a pillow of old words, for a head." It is not necessary, in order for art to fulfill this half of its task, to penetrate "the forces at play" or obtain "the least useful information" concerning oneself or others (p. 117). The useful, the instructive, meaningful content, the serious aspect of art may be muted in favor of the amusing, the pleasing, simple symmetries and asymmetries of form. Art may be distraction. Watt himself tends to evaluate language in terms of its aesthetic appeal. His own statement, "Obscure keys may open simple locks, but simple keys obscure locks never," soon causes him displeasure, but his displeasure diminishes until the words, "plain and modest . . . of a meaning so evident, and a form so inoffensive" and the sounds, "so gentle, so cajoling, in his skull," please him again. A little later, however, he suffers acute remorse at having uttered them, and ends up not knowing "what to think of them . . . whether to think poorly of them, or highly of them, or with indifference" (pp. 124-125).[9]

The predominance of play in Watt means above all that two serious undertakings, seeking to know and trying to make, that is, to discover forms for his experience of nothingness, are both failures. Watt is a comic character—to the extent that he *is* a comic character—partly because he attempts what he should know is impossible, partly because, as his name suggests, his attempt becomes a mania, and partly because he is so ill-qualified for the task. The author's opinion of Watt is perhaps best summed up in the lines "Watt could not easily imagine Arsene ever behaving in such a way, nor himself either for that matter. But there were many things that Watt could not easily imagine" (p. 120). An artist lacking in imagination is seriously handicapped, and Watt is, finally, a bad artist, even though he is aware of the double nature and the unity of art and the problem that faces him as a painter of emptiness. Like his thinking, Watt's making is too systematized, too mechanical, too rigidly inflexible. His stylistic obscurity may mirror the experiential darkness he has known, but once the key is discovered it can be deciphered like a code, which is not true of his experience. A style and a code differ. Style incorporates in verbal form the quality of experience. A code establishes one-to-one equations; for facts and events it substitutes impersonal counters that are incapable of evoking feeling.[10] Watt's various backward styles are merely an inversion of his previous mathematical mode of thinking. First he inverts only the order of the words in the sentences, then

[9] The episode of the Galls, too long to quote here, is crucial to an understanding of the relationship between form and content, pleasure and knowledge in the development of Watt as maker and thinker. We recall simply that the episode was characteristic "in the vigour with which it developed a purely plastic content, and gradually lost, in the nice processes of its light, its sound, its impacts and its rhythm, all meaning, even the most literal" (pp. 72-73).

[10] When Beckett writes in the Addenda "no symbols where none intended" (p. 254), it is quite probable that he refers to something resembling the mathematical symbol, which is an arbitrary construct of the intellect that bears just such a one-to-one relationship to the thing it represents.

only the order of the letters in the words, then only the order of the sentences in the periods. Then, as the reader foresees, he continues until he has exhausted all the possible combinations of inversion, first one at a time, then one after another in the same conversation. Watt's backward manner is suggestive. On his way to Mr. Knott's house, early in the story, he sits with his back to the engine, and the narrator comments, "Already Watt preferred to have his back to his destination" (p. 26). Like Arsene he has perhaps already acquired enough wisdom to suffer from it. He would rather not see where he is headed. Thus his backward mode of locomotion and speech develops in part from his nature as a thinking being. It also grows out of his shift from thinking to making, for the artist is one who looks back into his own past.

More than anything else, however, Watt's backward style is Beckett's irony. It suggests that Watt's mechanical mode of thought, his rigid rationalism, is itself "backwards," even before it becomes literally so. Reason and mathematics will lead neither to knowledge nor creativity. Mr. Knott's language, by contrast, cannot be deciphered and this it shares, Beckett appears to be saying, with the language of the Divinity. His meaningless chatter, like the voices of nature to which it is compared, may give pleasure in the same way that the pure forms of art do. Presumably, however, the strictly human artist should be like neither Watt nor Mr. Knott, neither decipherable like a code nor incomprehensible. If "the same things happen to us all," and if the artist can discover the forms of these things (in this case the forms of the thing that is Nothing), his art should be understandable (but not translatable)—intuitively, obscurely knowable—"if only we [choose] to know it" (p. 45).

The Art of *Watt* and the Novels to Come

Of course it does not follow that Beckett is a bad artist because Watt is. Watt, as artist, develops an inadequate style, but Watt's story is translated by Sam into a language that has its own style, a style that reveals Watt at earlier stages in his development. The fact that the narrator is named Sam suggests, in addition, that Sam Beckett may be willing to take a greater responsibility for the earlier Watt. Through the introduction of this third level of narration, intermediary between Watt and Beckett, ironic distance is reduced and sympathy becomes possible. In effect, stylistically as well, the novel faces in two directions. There is a comic style that portrays Watt's methods of investigation and the minimal results he achieves through his enormously disproportionate expenditure of effort. But there is another style that evokes emptiness and need. It often arouses our pity at the spectacle of Watt's persistent, meticulous, fruitless attempts to bring thought and things into some kind of not too inadequate relationship. Frequently the two styles go hand in hand, as in the following passage where motif and form suggest life's monotonous alternation.

> . . . in the morning . . . Mary . . . settled herself firmly in a comfortable semi-upright posture before the task to be performed and remained there quietly eating onions and peppermints turn and turn about, I mean first an onion, then a peppermint, then another onion, then another peppermint, then another onion, then another peppermint, then another onion, then another peppermint . . . [and so on ten more times], while little by little the reason for her presence in that place faded from her mind, as with the dawn the figments of the id, and the duster, whose burden up till now she had so bravely borne, fell from her fingers, to the dust, where having at once assumed the colour (grey) of its surroundings it disappeared until the following Spring.
>
> (p. 51)

We recognize the theme of the sameness that gradually swallows up individual things and events until only a monochrome absence remains. In this case, the author lets us take the final step[11] that associates Mary, the house and parlor maid, with the duster and returns her as well to the uniform grayness (*quia pulvis es . . .*). Not only the veiled allusion to the Lord's words to Adam before his expulsion from Eden (Genesis 3:19) but also the implicit comparison of life to a dream that fades into oblivion, the emotive value of "burden . . . bravely borne," and even the ruefully ironic suggestion of a resurrection for dusters (helped along by the capitalization of "Spring") are part of a style of sorrow. At the same time, the amusing choice of the onion-peppermint combination; the imitation of monotony through a comically prolonged series of repetitions (one of many methods used in the ludicrously ineffectual

---

[11] He takes it himself in recounting the episode of the Galls. "The piano is doomed, in my opinion, said the younger. The piano-tuner also, said the elder. The pianist also, said the younger" (p. 72).

attempt to bring language and reality into closer correspondence);
and the blend of hyperbole and pseudo-precision in the sentence
that continues the passage quoted ("An average of anything from
twenty-six to twenty-seven splendid woollen dusters per mensem
were lost in this way by our Mary during her last year of service in
this unfortunate house")—all contribute to the style that is man
as intellectual seeking to know.

The quest for knowledge determines many other stylistic characteristics of the novel. When he makes a generalization, the narrator
is seldom able to resist enumerating in an exhaustive way all the
cases it covers. Then, often, when the unexceptionable nature of the
thesis seems firmly established, an exception appears and vitiates it.
On the subject of eating we have the following: "Let him be a small
eater, a moderate eater, a heavy eater, a vegetarian, a naturist, a
cannibal, a coprophile, let him look forward to his eating with
pleasure or back on it with regret or both, let him eliminate well or
let him eliminate ill, let him eructate, vomit, break wind or in other
ways fail or scorn to contain himself as a result of an ill-adapted
diet, congenital affliction or faulty training during the impression-
able years [and so on] . . . the fact remains, and can hardly be
denied, that he proceeds by what we call meals." Mary, the maid,
however, "ate all day long, that is to say from early dawn . . . to
late at night . . ." (p. 53). The utopian hope of encompassing all
phenomena takes other forms as well. It expands to hyperbolic
length in the description of the congenital miseries of the Lynch
family, controls and orders itself in enumerations (pp. 89-90) and
tabular expositions (pp. 97-98, 137-138), and reaches a kind of
ne plus ultra of brevity in the mathematical formula. In a related
desire for precision, Mr. Hackett corrects Mr. Nixon meticulously.
Grehan is a solicitor, not a poisoner, and he got seven, not six, years
in prison (p. 10). Often a phrase hastily said is corrected in order
to achieve greater accuracy: "Mr. Hackett did not know when he
had been more intrigued, nay, he did not know when he had been
so intrigued" (p. 17). Sam takes notes as Watt "spins his yarn,"
and he scrupulously refuses to interpolate later when he finds certain passages illegible. In the novel, as a result, we come periodically
to question marks indicating lacunae in the text. To rule out any
possibility of misinterpretation, syntactical redundancy is often
introduced. Instead of: "the movements of the legs could be
accounted for, in a number of ways. And as she reflected on some

386

of the ways, she recalled the old story . . . ," we get: "the movements of the legs could be accounted for, in a number of ways.
And as she reflected on some of the ways, in which the movements
of the legs could be accounted for, she recalled the old story . . ."
(p. 31). In order to avoid even a remote possibility of ambiguity,
Sam eschews the normal "Watt's side of his fence" in favor of "Watt's
side of Watt's fence." Then, perhaps for the sake of the parallelism
or of concision, he avoids "from my side of mine" for the startling
"from mine of mine" (p. 161). On occasion the narrator, as though
beset by doubt, appears to desire confirmation: "This was indeed
a merciful coincidence, was it not, that at that moment . . ." (p.
113). Earlier this device seems to parody the French *n'est-ce pas*:
"Sorrow is a thing you can keep on adding to all your life long, is
it not, like a stamp or egg collection, without feeling very much
the worse for it, is it not" (p. 50). One of the most striking features
of this style is the ubiquity of the comma. It sets off phrases that
would never normally be set off. A vast number of sentences are
thus divided into neat compartments, each containing a bit of
information that is like the answer to a question: "Watt saw, in the
grate, of the range, the ashes grey.[12] But they turned pale red, when
he covered the lamp, with his hat. . . . A handful of dry chips and
the flames would spring, merry in appearance,[13] up the chimney,
with an organ note" (p. 37).

The quest for accurate information naturally leads to the refinement of the *distinguo*. Watt is forever contrasting what he means
to say with a closely related notion that is *not* what he intends to
convey. Stylistically, these distinctions tend to assume a fixed pattern. Again and again we come across the revealing formula "not
that it would have . . . for it would not. But . . . ," or "Now this is
not to say that he . . . for he did, but only that. . . ." Indeed, the
conjunction "but" is a key to the style of *Watt*. Once a hypothesis
is set forth, "but" introduces the objections to it. Thus on pages 94
through 97 four hypotheses are listed. The paragraphs following
the statement of the hypotheses begin as follows: "But the chances
of"; "But the likelihood of"; "But then one of Mr Knott's men
would have had to"; "But was there any guarantee of"; "But was
there any guarantee, supposing"; "But was there any guarantee

[12] We cannot be sure the ashes *were* gray, but that is how Watt saw them.
[13] Again, there is no reason to believe the flames (or people) really *are*
merry.

that"; "But what would happen if"; "But might not even"; "But was a dog the same thing as"; "But was it likely that"; "But was it likely, if he did, that"; "But if he did, and he were found, might he not"; "But might not Erskine"; "But would not this."[14] Syntactical connectives in general are of decisive importance in *Watt*. "But" is one of the most important; "for" is another. Watt is a collector of observations and a tester of explanations. The discrete nature of these observations and explanations is often quite apparent, and the major stylistic role of connectives reflects Watt's attempts to relate and organize his disparate information. As already noted, the abundant commas chop grammatical units into series of more or less discontinuous pieces, into the "tins" Watt opens with his "blowlamp" (p. 136). He is "not easy," we learn, until he puts his speculations into "short and isolated phrases, or fragments of phrases, separated by considerable periods of time from one another" (p. 119). These fragments Watt tries to tie together. On one occasion the narrator piles up a series of six italicized causal links ("But Tom's two years on the first floor are not *because of* Dick's two years on the ground floor, or of Harry's coming then, and Dick's two years on the ground floor are not *because of* Tom's two years on the first floor" and so on until finally he explodes, "tired of underlining this cursed preposition" (p. 134). On other occasions an awkward link alerts the reader to the special role of conjunctions. "But one thought of him as the man who, among other things, never left off his cap, a plain blue cloth cap, with a peak and knob. For he never left off his bicycle-clips either" (p. 26). Here, instead of referring back to the verb "thought," "for" sets up an unexpected relationship with the subordinate verb "left off," which moreover is separated from it by an object, an appositional phrase, and a modifying adjectival phrase. The fact that the stylistic device so clearly calls attention to itself is an index of its ironic nature. Watt's excessive yet ineffectual efforts to organize his information show through in his linguistic ineptitude, in the gross way in which he disrupts the conventions of the language, not so gross, of course, as the inversions he comes to practice.

---

[14] Reservations and distinctions are not introduced solely by "but," of course. Take this example: "But what I could say, or at least in part, and I trust not the least diverting, I think I have said, and as far as it lay in my power to take you, under the circumstances, I think I have taken you, all things considered" (p. 63).

Beckett's note on Watt's "Davus complex" or morbid dread of sphinxes (p. 251) suggests a comparison between the sphinx of Thebes, which asks you a riddle and kills you if you fail to solve it, and life, that insoluble enigma that leads to the grave. Watt is he who does not know. Desperately he questions, as though his life depended on finding the answer before the dreaded question is asked. But Watt's happiness hinges, as did Adam's, on not seeking to know. The seeker earns emptiness and learns the loss of the garden and the presence it holds.[15] This want finds its expression in the second style of *Watt*—and is figured by the silences between the "isolated phrases" often used by the protagonist.

As we have seen in his other writings, Beckett attaches psychological and existential significance to colors. In *Watt,* as in the poetry and early prose, he shows a marked tendency to call attention to unusual hues. The moon, for example, is not simply yellow. It is "an unpleasant yellow colour"—and, at the same time, it is "long past the full" (p. 30). At the beginning of the story we find a similar association between color and time. As from the shadows Mr. Hackett watches the "last trams pass, oh not the last, but almost," he observes in the sky and still canal "the long greens and yellows of the summer evening" (p. 9). Given the context, "long" has more a temporal than a spatial value. The summer days are long, but the shadows do come, darkening the tinted light. The ending day and the ending tram service heighten our sense of the passage of time and the associated metamorphosis of color. Later Watt stands on the red floor of Mr. Knott's house, takes off his hat, exposing his red-grey tufts of hair, and alternately shading and uncovering the lamp watches the dying ashes in the grate "greyen, redden, greyen, redden" (p. 38). Watt too is dying, but it will take more to restore the pristine color to his remaining hair, to give it again the unadulterated hue of the "beautiful red floor," than is

---

[15] In his 1938 essay "Denis Devlin" (*Transition*, No. 27 [April-May 1938], p. 290) Beckett associates the Davus complex with practical life in society, which aims above all to fulfill needs and is opposed to art, which is pure interrogation and answers no questions. The name Knott, while it implies both the knot of a riddle and the not that negates the possibility of solution, is also a composite word. Like Godot and Mag (*Molloy*, p. 27), where *ot* diminishes God and *g* "abolishes" Ma, Knott's two *t*'s nullify Kno(w). Knott is the one who is not known—and, as a figure of the unselfconscious artist happy in his private world, does not know, either himself or the need to know.

required to revivify the fire in the stove. The painting in Erskine's room, which manages to create the illusion of movement in time as well as space, contains a point or dot and a circle, breached at the bottom. "It is by the nadir that we come, said Watt, and it is by the nadir that we go. . . ." The circle seems to be "receding." It is black. The dot appears "in the eastern background." It is "blue, but blue!" (pp. 128-130). Even in this radically abbreviated version of the account, the human significance Watt attaches to the painting is apparent, and we may note again that purity of color is associated with an early moment in a temporal span (beginnings are in the East), while darkness is the destiny that overtakes us as well as colors. The yew is "dark green, almost black" when Erskine leaves, the morning is "white," and the earth seems "dressed for the grave." Curiously, both black and white are associated with decline and death in *Watt*. An explanation can probably be found not only in such natural associations as night and winter snow, but also in the fact that both black and white, the former because of its complete absorption of light rays, the latter because of its reflection of all the rays that produce color, may be thought of as destroyers of color. In the Addenda Beckett describes Watt's "soul-landscape" as a color so dark it cannot be identified with certainty. "Sometimes it seemed a dark absence of colour, a dark mixture of all colours, a dark white" (p. 249). The real key, however, to Beckett's treatment of color comes in a passage that links it to time and change and the style of diminution and cessation:

> It was to be observed that the colours, on the one hand of this coat, on the other of this hat, drew closer and closer, the one to the other, with every passing lustre. Yet how different had been their beginnings! The one green! The other yellow! So it is with time, that lightens what is dark, that darkens what is light.
>
> It was to be expected that, once met, they would not stay, no, but continue, each as it must, to age, until the hat was green, the coat yellow, and then through the last circles paling, deepening, swooning cease, the hat to be a hat, the coat to be a coat. For so it is with time.   (p. 218)

If Beckett has a romantic side, it surely appears most clearly in the melancholy that accompanies the numerous manifestations of nothingness and the approaches to nothingness. Life is a brief moment between two voids, a hesitant, painful rise into the light followed by accelerating deprivation and final oblivion. Watt is an object of irony because he seeks intellectual increase, when the law is decrease. The lesson of his maturity, of the middle years that precede old age, comes in the house of "not." There he learns his future, or as much of it as he can bear. When he leaves, he weeps. His departure is one more in the series of "surrogate goodbyes" ("Da Tagte Es"). We say farewell to childhood, youth, manhood and finally to the little that is left of life itself. In the Addenda Beckett borrows lines from James Thomson (1700-1748) to express his vision:

> Bid us sigh on from day to day,
> And wish and wish the soul away,
> Till youth and genial years are flown,
> And all the life of life is gone.
>
> (p. 248)

The romantic focus on the ancient theme of *tempus fugit* in a spirit of what has been called morbid fascination by some and sorrowful resignation by others finds many an echo in Beckett. From one point of view he is in a tradition as ancient as literature and as universal as human nature. In *Watt* we have "failing light" in the first sentence. The day is forever "dying"; the dew "expires" (p. 245); the flowers are "engulfed" (p. 22); piano, tuner, and player are "doomed" (p. 72); time, "as time will," draws on (p. 146). The contextual setting often puts new life into such literary stereotypes, and on other occasions they are part of a parody of the romantic attitude. If Beckett is in part a traditionalist, he is not artistically naïve. Every artist works with givens that are timeless. His novelty appears in choices, stresses, the infinitely variable matrix.

In the case of Beckett, one is tempted to speak not only of tradition and originality but of "evocative density," which involves both value and generic distinction. A number of critics have noted the poetic quality of Beckett's prose. To an extraordinary degree, he has the talent for giving to commonplace (and to not so commonplace) situations overtones that evoke man's condition and destiny. Or to put it in terms of vision rather than making, he is able to see in nature, in people, in situations and events the signs of a single destiny. Such is the poet's gift. To a very considerable extent the excellence of Beckett's writing can be correlated with the genial level this capacity reaches in him. During a casual conversation by

391

a tram stop Mrs. Nixon, becoming slightly annoyed by Mr. Hackett's curiosity, protests, "What does it matter who he is? . . . Or what he does. . . . Or how he lives. Or where he comes from. Or where he is going to. Or what he looks like. What can it possibly matter, to us?" "I ask myself the same question," replies Mr. Hackett. No one can miss the serious implications imbedded in the casual realism of Mrs. Nixon's mild annoyance. Beckett chooses a physical, geographical, or social "come and go," and of this routine activity to which no transcendent significance is normally attached he makes a metaphysical motif that recurs from one end of the novel to the other, gaining poetic power with each new appearance. Eventually, when Arsene develops it—"for the coming is in the shadow of the going and the going is in the shadow of the coming" (p. 57)—it easily carries the arrival and departure of servants to a house far beyond the literal level. The song Watt hears in the ditch joins the related motif of "blooming and withering" to "come and go" and links "done," "gone," "home," and "oblivion" (p. 35). By the time the reader reaches the Addenda, the part that "come and go" plays in the poetry of nothingness is evident enough, yet several of the most beautiful verbal correlatives of human existence as Beckett sees it in these terms occur there, this one among others: "dead calm, then a murmur, a name, a murmured name, in doubt, in fear, in love, in fear, in doubt, wind of winter in the black boughs, cold calm sea whitening whispering to the shore, stealing, hastening, swelling, passing, dying, from naught come to naught gone" (p. 248). The brief crescendo and decrescendo are part of the imagery of rising and falling (with the emphasis of course on the latter) that contributes to the style of deprivation.

It is on this note that Beckett chooses to end *Watt*: "Mr. Gorman looking straight before him, at nothing in particular, though the sky falling to the hills, and the hills falling to the plain, made as pretty a picture, in the early morning light, as a man could hope to meet with, in a day's march" (p. 246). Related to falling, the imagery of endings recalls the "last/ even of last times" in the poem "Cascando": "Red, bluer, yellowist, that old dream was ended, half ended, ended. Again" (p. 148). Even in the comparison of adjectives, the order of increase is an illusion. Colors, too, fade, become less, least, and nothing. A number of the most moving passages incorporate images taken from nature, sometimes in combination with figures of movement (related to coming and going) and its cessation.[16] The metaphoric application to man in some of the best of these passages is all the more effective for remaining implicit. Lying in the ditch Watt listens to the night sounds, "the leaves that are never still, until they lie rotting in a wintry heap, and the breath that is never quiet." As the moon rises it pours its "whitening rays" upon Watt "as though he were not there" (p. 33). He dislikes the moon that like him becomes white as it grows older and seems in its indifference to forecast his own eventual absence. It will outlast him. As the whiskey bears a grudge against the decanter because of its relative immortality, Watt loathes sun and moon and earth and sky that contain his diminishing existence. *Tempus edax, tempus sitiens.* Sam, referring to Watt's speech when he tells his tale, notes that "of this impetuous murmur much fell in vain on my imperfect hearing and understanding, and much by the rushing wind was carried away, and lost forever" (p. 156). The nature imagery includes a number of comparisons between man and animals, which we might expect as one more means of impoverishment. The horse Joss in the print Watt sees on the wall of the railroad station waiting room has "its head sunk" and seems "to consider, without appetite, the grass." The light in the print is "that of approaching night, or impending storm, or both." The grass is "sparse, sere, and overrun with what Watt [takes] to be a species of cockle." The horse seems "hardly able to stand, let alone run" (p. 236). In the same waiting room the flies, "of skeleton thinness, excited to new efforts by yet another dawn" fly toward the window, where, "pressed against the impenetrable panes," they will enjoy "the light, and warmth, of the long summer's day" (pp. 236-237). Beckett uses other art images besides the print of the horse Joss. They are convenient metaphors of life; they speak, as it does, of the emptiness to which all men sooner or later must come. The painting of a circle and a point brings to mind the void of outer space in a cosmic corollary of the existential void through the recurring motif "in boundless space, in endless time" (p. 129).

The notion, destined to become so important in *Godot, Endgame,* and *Happy Days,* that art is above all a way to fill the vacant hours, to make the time go by while we wait for the end, is foreshadowed when Watt first arrives in Mr. Knott's house and busies himself covering and uncovering the lamp and watching the ashes

---

[16] Immobility becomes a characteristic form of deprivation in later works like *Endgame* and *Happy Days.*

"greyen, redden." This pastime so absorbs him that he fails to notice Arsene come in. "So his surprise was extreme, when he looked up from his little game. For it was no more than that, an innocent little game, to while away the time" (p. 38). The emptiness of life is increased by the occasional absence of others, and, as we grow older, by their definitive disappearance. At first Erskine will walk at Watt's side and guide him. Then for the rest Watt "will travel alone, or with only shades" to keep him company (p. 63). Each parting forecasts one's own departure. The separation of Watt and Sam, one of the most poignant episodes in the novel, gives some idea of the value placed on comradeship in Beckett's work and of the desolation that the loss of a friend leaves in its wake.

> Continuing then, when he had told me this, then he loosed my hands from his shoulders, and backwards through the hole went back, to his garden, and left me alone, alone with only my poor eyes to follow him, the last of many times to follow him, over the deep threshing shadows backwards stumbling, towards his habitation . . . until I saw him no more, but only the aspens. And from the hidden pavilions, his and mine, where by this time dinner was preparing, the issuing smokes by the wind were blown, now far apart, but now together, mingled to vanish. (p. 213)

As in the phrase "by the wind were blown," a variation in normal syntactical order can be used for poetic effect. Beckett takes discreet advantage of this ancient procedure fairly often in *Watt*. Another technique he employs to good effect might be termed the device of the displaced modifier. It is one variation on what is no doubt the principal syntactical invention—or better, stylistic discovery—of the entire novel. We have already discussed the unusual role played by the comma in the epistemological style of *Watt*. It is at least as important in the privative style of the novel. Like man disinherited, isolated in an alien environment, the individual phrase maintains for the most part only the most tenuous relationship to its syntactical milieu. The introduction of commas on the slightest pretext weakens linkage and logic. In the long run, and in spite of a counterattack of connectives, it amounts to an invasion. That Beckett is well aware of what he is doing is too evident to need demonstration. It is fascinating, nonetheless, that on one occasion Sam interrupts himself in exasperation halfway through a long narration punctuated by commas that subdivide sections set off by semicolons

394

to growl in disgust, "How hideous is the semi-colon" (p. 158). Hideous because it is part of the false logic of grammatical architecture, but more vitally because it mirrors the existential misery of false endings and everlasting recommencings ("the whole bloody business starting all over again" [p. 47]). Ambiguous, the semicolon neither frankly pauses momentarily within an overriding continuity nor ends at least one concern in a definitive way. It promises and withholds. As life is forever doing, it requires a new beginning. In a later work like *Comment c'est* Beckett will shift his stylistic stress from the brief halt of the comma to the full stop of the period. He will go on to find other ways to expand the silence between words and phrases. For the present, however, he contents himself with the pause provided by the comma, perhaps because *Watt* is a novel about the middle years, which see no more than the beginnings of the stasis and accompanying silence that the advancing years will augment.

The displaced modifier occurs in several forms. In one case an adverbial phrase is separated from the verb it modifies by a series of objects and a parenthetical expression. When it does occur finally, the reader is brought to a halt. Confronted as he is by a seemingly isolated phrase, he is forced to consider it in itself with special attention, then to relate it to its verb. Beckett takes full advantage of this double necessity to focus the reader's thoughts on essential manifestations of privation:

> For not only was a wife, a mother, a mother-in-law, an aunt, a sister [etc.] snatched from her grandfather-in-law, her father-in-law, her uncles-in-law, her aunt, her aunts-in-law [etc.] (who however exhibited no sign of emotion other than that of curiosity, being too young no doubt to realize the dreadful thing that had happened, for their total age amounted to no more than sixteen years), never to return, but the Lynch millennium was retarded by almost one year and a half. . . .   (p. 105)

Not only is "never to return" placed in the limelight but "snatched" is also accentuated. In another case, an intervening antecedent creates an intentional ambiguity of reference:

> . . . leaves falling through the dark from various altitudes, never two coming to earth at the same time, then bowling red and brown and yellow and grey briskly for an instant, yes, through

the dark, for an instant, then running together in heaps, here a heap, and there a heap, to be paddled in by happy boys and girls on their way home from school looking forward to Hallow's E'en and Guy Fawkes and Christmas and the New Year, haw! yes, happy girls and boys looking forward to the happy New Year, and then perhaps carted off in old barrows and used as dung the following spring by the poor. . . .   (p. 57)

The leaves, not the boys and girls, are the antecedent of "carted off," but the juxtaposition makes the point that people go the way of leaves. The terrain is prepared for the syntactical ambiguity by hints, scattered throughout the passage, that build an analogy between leaves and men: existence in the dark, the out-of-phase coming to earth, four colors (the white race gray with age; gray leaves are less improbable than white), brevity of life, return to earthy origins. Direct address, repetition, and irony help establish the extraliteral meaning, and the theme of sameness ("New Year, haw!") links man and nature in the seasonal cycle.

While we can make no attempt here at an exhaustive analysis of the style, or styles, of *Watt*, we should mention briefly in closing one more prominent and rather daring syntactical innovation that the author uses in achieving his aesthetic ends—daring because he uses it both ironically and seriously and runs the risk of interference of one mode with the other, daring because of its very obviousness and elemental simplicity, which together with its not infrequent use tend to give it a kind of naïve, mechanical earnestness that can as easily turn in the direction of laughter as sorrow. When Watt finds himself free of Mr. Spiro and headed on foot for Mr. Knott's house, the moon is up, "not far up, but . . . up." It is "of an unpleasant yellow colour. Long past the full, it [is] waning, waning" (p. 30). The serious impact of the repetition is attenuated, because this brief sketch of the natural setting occurs between two passages in which the comic element is strong. Toward the end of the book parody takes the device into its arsenal: "Of Watt's coat and waistcoat, of his shirt his vest and his drawers, much might be written, of great interest and significance. The drawers, in particular, were remarkable, from more than one point of view. But they were hidden, coat and waistcoat, shirt and underclothes, all hidden, from the eye" (p. 219). Man's ability to know is limited in more than the metaphysical realm. A few pages later Watt speculates about the sex of a figure he sees in the distance, a figure that seems of unusual size for a woman or a nun. "But Watt knew too well, too too well, of what dimensions certain women, and certain nuns, were capable ..." (p. 225). For the most part, however, the repeated, intensifying qualifier is part of the style of privation. Had Lady McCann aimed the stone she hurled at Watt more accurately, "a wound had perhaps been opened, never again to close, never, never again to close" (p. 32). For Beckett, of course, life is the wound that can never be healed. We find that more often than not "never" is the term stressed by the repetition, whatever the theme may be: *knowing*: Watt "was never to know, never, never to know, how the backdoor came to be opened ..." (p. 37); *surfaces*: "Some see the flesh before the bones, and some see the bones before the flesh, and some never see the bones at all, and some never see the flesh at all, never never see the flesh at all" (p. 73). Sometimes an equivalent or closely related negation replaces "never": *art*: any attempt to express the wisdom acquired during middle age "is doomed to fail, doomed, doomed to fail" (p. 62); *religion*: "It is so easy to accept, so easy to refuse, when the call is heard, so easy, so easy. But to us, in our windowlessness ... what call could come ... but a call so faint as to mock acceptance, mock refusal" (p. 152). It is noteworthy that an outstanding exception to the general stress on negation comes with the theme of comradeship: "To be together again, after so long, who love the sunny wind, the windy sun, in the sun, in the wind, that is perhaps something, perhaps something" (p. 163). Repetition in Beckett goes beyond intensification. Here already, in a stylistic device, we can catch a glimpse of the meaning of a two-act structure in the later plays. Two are needed to affirm or deny change. The downward curve of our days becomes the decline of yesterday and today. The two merge into the sameness of one except that now we are "littler, poorer ... sicker, aloner."

Two Poems and a Project

Partly at least through the device of the multiple narrator Beckett succeeds in *Watt* in transforming his love of verbal manipulation from what was on occasion gratuitous and self-conscious exhibitionism into something that might be called "serious play." The distance he maintains between author and principal character objectivizes the style and tends to make it functional. The character's fictionality confirmed, language becomes a means of characterization and no longer simply a sign of youthful talent and exuberance. The style of permutations and combinations and Watt's backward speech may still point to the author but they also play a role in the definition of Watt. In the two prophetic poems he places in the Addenda at the end of his novel Beckett says his farewell to even this last vestige of lighthearted apprenticeship and defines his artistic future in terms that are wholly serious and responsible. The longer of the two poems states the project in terms of the present enterprise:

> Watt will not
> abate one jot
> but of what
>
> of the coming to
> of the being at
> of the going from
> Knott's habitat
>
> of the long way
> of the short stay
> of the going back home
> the way he had come
>
> of the empty heart
> of the empty hands
> of the dim mind wayfaring
> through barren lands
>
> of a flame with dark winds
> hedged about
> going out
> gone out
>
> of the empty heart
> of the empty hands
> of the dark mind stumbling
> through barren lands
>
> that is of what
> Watt will not
> abate one tot
>
> (pp. 249-250)

Appropriately, the poem takes the form of a question and an answer: the first stanza makes the query and the last sums up the reply that is given in the five intervening stanzas. The frame provided by the structure is emphasized formally by the fact that the beginning and ending stanzas have three and the remaining stanzas four lines each. Watt (and of course Beckett) will go on doing what he has been doing, i.e., questioning the void, making the inward journey to the abode of the mystery that is Nothing, to the habitat of Knott. In a conversation Beckett once admitted that as a young man he was incapable of remaining in solitude for more than a week at a time. In his later journeys from Paris to the isolation of the Marne Valley, where he does his writing, and back again to Paris, he acquired this ability, a gift perhaps of the advancing years. In the poem the theme of "come and stay and go," which is not only a constantly recurring motif in *Watt* but forms as well the core of its overall structure, provides the answer to the initial question. Since "come and stay and go" sums up life itself, Watt answers in effect, "I shall go on living." The circular structure of the poem, seen in its entirety and reflected in individual stanzas in the "come and stay and go" theme, evokes that sameness we have seen so often in the early writing, the sameness of the circle that returns always to the identical point or life that returns from the darkness of the womb to the darkness of the grave—from nothingness to nothingness via nothingness. The affinity between Knott's abode and the mysterious void of the beginning and the end doubtless accounts for much of the fascination the house exerts. The third stanza repeats the circular pattern of the first, stressing the brevity of the stay and recalling other related images, notably the fusion of obstetrician and gravedigger in *Godot*. The next three stanzas expand the triune pattern, allotting four lines each to the going, the staying, and the returning. Just as the difference between stanza one and stanza seven is minimal (except for changes due to the shift from interrogative to declarative the only novelty is the substitution of "tot" for "jot") and as the difference between stanzas two and three is minimal, so the variation from stanza four (the coming) to stanza six (the going), which is determined by what happens in stanza five (the staying), is very slight. It is approximately the change indicated by the comparative "little-littler." Watt arrives and leaves with empty heart and hands, but the dim mind has become dark and the wayfaring has become stumbling. During the

399

stay in Knott's habitat the flame (among other things Watt's burning desire to know) has been extinguished. Both in *forme* and *fond*
the poem expresses Beckett's vision: life is a monotony varied only
by the unavoidable phenomenon of diminution. The road going is
the same as the road coming (stanza three), and the emptiness of
heart, hands, and mind is matched by the emptiness of the landscape (stanzas four, six) and the emptiness in Knott's abode.

The shorter poem is an even more explicit statement of Beckett's
plans as a writer:

> who may tell the tale
> of the old man?
> weigh absence in a scale?
> mete want with a span?
> the sum assess
> of the world's woes?
> nothingness
> in words enclose?
>
> (p. 247)

After the middle years that are an apprenticeship—Watt becomes
acquainted with deprivation and tries his hand at putting his experience of this nothing that is a something into words—comes old age,
when decline, loss, and solitude are the overriding factors in a man's
existence. Most art deals with the somethings; most art links subject and object; most art is a triumph over chaos through the creation of a verbal coherence, and in that sense it provides an answer.
"Who," Beckett asks, "will create an art that acknowledges the
inaccessibility of the object, that admits chaos and in so doing 'fails,'
that grants the unavailability of ultimate answers? Who will take
woe, want, absence, nothingness for his subject?" Relentlessly his
life, his nature, and the evolution of his writing, as we have tried
to show, seem to have prepared Beckett to be that person. All his
post-*Watt* works are attempts to meet the challenge spelled out in
the short poem quoted above. To just what extent he was aware of
the aesthetic implications of his plan, its excitement and revolu-
tionary promise as well as the dilemma it creates, is clear in his critical and theoretical writings. An analysis of these writings is the
subject of the concluding chapter of this book.

x. The Critical & Theoretical Writings

Beckett evolves toward spareness according to the Schopenhauer prescription. The inevitable physical asceticism of aging may be thought of as metaphoric, for it parallels a progressive spiritual disengagement. The early poetry and fiction is "impure" in the sense that its heroes are caught up in the struggles of will and practical reason. Murphy needs Celia; Belacqua, now Phoebus, now Narcissus, only rarely lives up to the promise of his eponym; the narrator in the poems betrays a lack of detachment in matters of the heart and mind that leads him on occasion to something at least approaching metaphysical and even social revolt. Beckett's early style, as well, is "impure," for the author sometimes fails to repress his weakness for gratuitous wordplay and erudite allusions. Even while he condemns technique and structure as artistic heresy perpetrated by intellect, the intellectualism of the young artist is everywhere apparent. Each story and each poem is at once an exorcism and an expression of an ego that must die if disinterested contemplation by a will-less subject is to be achieved and is to flower into true art. It does not always die easily. Watt's trajectory from society to the house of Mr. Knott to the asylum—from action to inquiry to recollection, from will to intellect to apperceptive meditation—is a figure of the evolution not only from young man to old but from citizen of the macrocosm to poet of the microcosm, an evolution that in the case of Murphy and Belacqua was incomplete. Beckett's writing taken as a whole is the image of such an evolution and in this sense the story of his life, a story that might be entitled "The Making of an Artist."

Beckett on Joyce and Proust

Beckett knew his own kind before he became aware that creative writing would be his destiny as well as theirs. Planning an academic career, he launched into literary criticism, but his early writings reveal affinities and a frame of reference that make this occupation a paradox and, at least in retrospect, cause his subsequent development to seem almost a foregone conclusion. In 1929 Beckett published an essay entitled "Dante. . . Bruno. Vico. .

401

Joyce," in which he outlines attitudes and procedures common to Joyce and the three Italian writers and defends the former against his detractors.[1] Beckett's central concern is to explain by means of a dualistic theory that forecasts Murphy's division of the universe into macrocosm and microcosm the reason for the modern reader's difficulty with what was to become *Finnegans Wake*. The essay opens with the statement "The danger is in the neatness of identifications," and goes on to object to "pigeon-hole[s]," "the stiff interexclusiveness . . . in neat construction[s]," words used as "mere polite symbols." He accuses the hypothetical reader of being interested only in ideas, content, abstractions and of lacking sensitivity to the particular and the concrete: "And if you don't understand it, Ladies and Gentlemen, it is because you are too decadent to receive it. You are not satisfied unless form is so strictly divorced from content that you can comprehend the one almost without bothering to read the other. . . . The wind in the trees means as little to you as the evening prospect from the Piazzale Michelangiolo." The youthful critic justifies this aggression by a prior exposition of Vico's theory of the three ages of man—Theocratic, Heroic, Human (civilized)—and corresponding stages of language —Hieroglyphic (sacred), Metaphorical (poetic), Philosophical (capable of abstraction and generalization):

> Poetry was the first operation of the human mind, and without it thought could not exist. Barbarians, incapable of analysis and abstraction, must use their fantasy to explain what their reason cannot comprehend. Before articulation comes song; before abstract terms, metaphors. . . . Poetry is essentially the antithesis of Metaphysics: Metaphysics purge the mind of the senses and cultivate the disembodiment of the spiritual; Poetry is all passion and feeling and animates the inanimate; Metaphysics are most perfect when most concerned with universals; Poetry when most concerned with particulars.

Language itself undergoes a similar evolution from the concrete particular to the abstract and general, while myth moves from literal representation to the intellectualized allegory of modern civilization. The trouble arises, then, because Joyce is engaged in the enterprise of "desophisticating" a language that has been

---

[1] In *Our Exagmination* . . . , pp. 3-22.

"abstracted to death." (Beckett opposes the "sensuous suggestion of hesitancy" in the German *Zweifel* to the transparent English counter, "doubt," replaced in Joyce by the phrase "in twosome twiminds.") "Here form *is* content, content *is* form. You complain that this stuff is not written in English. It is not written at all. It is not to be read—or rather it is not only to be read. It is to be looked at and listened to. His writing is not *about* something; *it is that something itself.* . . . When the sense is sleep, the words go to sleep. . . . When the sense is dancing, the words dance." Reinforcements are brought up in the evocation of Dante. Both he and Joyce "saw how worn out and threadbare was the conventional language of cunning literary artificers, both rejected an approximation to a universal language." Dante chose the " 'barbarous' directness" of the vulgar tongue in preference to the "suave elegance" of a sophisticated but less immediate and vivid Latin. Both he and Joyce, Beckett argues, composed a synthetic language from diverse linguistic elements in the interests of particularity and concreteness.

While Beckett develops his case in other ways (e.g., by an analysis of Bruno's union of contraries as a source of Vico's notion of a "providence" both immanent and transcendent but wholly human and by a discussion of the cyclical and purgatorial self-containment of the Joycean universe), the core of his argument is a distinction between the realm of ideas and the realm of poetry as the two find expression in language. It may seem a long way from the sensuous and particular to the poetry of nothingness, but at the beginning Beckett was concerned above all to proscribe intellect in all its manifestations. Other purifications followed in good time.

Proust, Beckett's principal contribution to literary criticism, was published two years later, in 1931. In it we discover again the radical cleavage between an intuitive, discontinuous, sensuous, and emotional evocation of reality and the abstract, logical continua constructed laboriously by conceptual reason. Proust and Beckett combine to drive apart the two ways of knowing, artistic and scientific, assigning worth to the former and devaluating the latter. A brief discussion of the main motifs in *Proust* will give a good idea of the ramifications of this dualistic vision and suggest perhaps that Proust was as important a force as Descartes in the intellectual formation of the young writer.

1. Macrocosm and Microcosm

In the epigraph to *Proust*, Beckett borrows a line from Leopardi's poem "A se stesso" in order to suggest the illusory nature of life in the world, the "infinita vanità del tutto," as Leopardi described the experience of nothingness. "E fango è il mondo," which stands as Beckett's first—and perhaps last—word on Proust's novel, evokes the world of Bom and Pim in *Comment c'est*, a world in which the ubiquitous mud, like sand elsewhere in Beckett's writing, translates in uniformity the absence of the accidental. The notion of surface and depth recurs throughout *Proust*. Our physical being that inhabits the outer world is termed a "carapace of paste and pewter" (p. 19), but hidden deep within this exterior shell, in what Proust calls the "gouffre interdit à nos sondes," is the pearl that represents the essence of our many selves. The narrator's second visit to Balbec completes the transformation of his deceased grandmother from "a creature of surface into a creature of depth—unfathomable . . ." (p. 35). Communication with another being, on the surface or in depth, is not possible. All save the "cosa mentale" is impenetrable. Friendship, a phenomenon of the surface world, a social expedient, is "like the madness that holds a conversation with the furniture." "The artist, who does not deal in surfaces," who realizes that "there is no communication because there are no vehicles of communication," knows that "art is the apotheosis of solitude." For him "the only possible spiritual development is in the sense of depth. . . . The only fertile research is excavatory, immersive, a contraction of the spirit, a descent. The artist is active, but negatively, shrinking from the nullity of extracircumferential phenomena, drawn in to the core of the eddy" (pp. 46-48). Elsewhere the images Beckett chooses are "the heart of the cauliflower [and] . . . the ideal core of the onion" (p. 16). Getting there, when it is not "poetical excavation" (p. 17) is "extract[ing] the total essence" (p. 63). When Beckett refers to Proust's "contempt for the literature that 'describes,' for the realists and naturalists worshiping the offal of experience [cf. "The Vulture," the opening of *Echo's Bones*], prostrate before the epidermis and the swift epilepsy, and content to describe the surface, the façade, behind which the Idea is prisoner," he clearly speaks for himself as well. For Beckett and for Proust the artist is like "Apollo flaying Marsyas and capturing without sentiment the essence, the Phrygian waters." To do this

404

he must, like Murphy and Watt, prefer the microcosm to the macrocosm. "Chi non ha la forza di uccidere la realtà," Beckett concludes with De Sanctis, "non ha la forza di crearla" (pp. 59-60).

2. Time and Habit

In the Proustian analysis man is a creature of habit immersed in time and space. Life is a succession of treaties between this subject and the objective world. The treaties, or patterns of habit, stabilize relationships and make living an endurable, if dull, affair. But a change in the spatial environment or the passing of time, which changes both subject and object (and according to no system of synchronization), inevitably disrupts the status quo and puts the subject in painful, though possibly also joyful and fruitful, contact with authentic being. The habitual or surface self dies again and again in the course of a lifetime to give rise, after each painful period of transition, to a new self, reassured and comfortable in its newly arranged and now familiar setting. In each case the subject's "total consciousness [is] organized to avert the disaster, to create the new habit that will empty the mystery of its threat—and also of its beauty" (pp. 10-11). In this tension between time and stasis, being and habit, it is not difficult to discover again the dualism that divides reality into microcosm and macrocosm, depth and surfaces—the latter under the sign of conceptual reason.

3. The Intellect and All Its Pomps

Practical reason, that workaday companion that eliminates all that is not crucial to the affair at hand, that throws out the baby along with the bath water, is the real villain. It erects the structures of habit well above the subterranean perils and enchantments. It chloroforms the butterfly and fixes it on a pin, shuts it up in a box among its immediate kin and files it away in the dusty museum of memory. Practical reason replaces the unique with the species, the species with the genus, the genus with the family, and so on, until reality has been wholly emptied out and only the transparent abstraction remains. To illustrate, Beckett describes the tourist "whose aesthetic experience consists in a series of identifications and for whom Baedeker is the end rather than the means. Deprived by nature of the faculty of cognition and by upbringing of any acquaintance with the laws of dynamics, a brief inscription immortalises his emotion. The creature of habit turns aside from the object

405

that cannot be made to correspond with one or other of his intellectual prejudices, that resists the propositions of his team of syntheses,
organized by Habit on labour-saving principles" (pp. 11-12).
Curiosity (characteristic of Watt) is the servant of practical reason,
the scout that reconnoiters the terrain ahead to facilitate annexa-
tion by the forces of intellect. Its aim is to reduce the unknown to
the known. Beckett describes it as a defense mechanism of strictly
utilitarian nature: "the hair of our habit tending to stand on end"
(p. 18). Voluntary memory, too, is an adjunct of the practical
reason that rules the macrocosm, no more than "the application of
a concordance to the Old Testament of the individual." Its power
to reproduce the past is limited to those former impressions "consciously and intelligently formed." Its monochrome presentation is
as arbitrary as the version offered by the imagination, and "equally
remote from reality" (p. 19). Voluntary memory is "uniform, a
creature of routine, at once a condition and function of . . . habit,
an instrument of reference instead of an instrument of discovery"
(p. 17).

Opposed to the scaffoldings of intellect and its workmen is the
oeuvre d'art. The greatest tribute that Beckett can pay to Proust,
the authentic artist, is to point out the extent to which his work is
nonrational. He does this in three principal ways. First, he analyzes
the mechanism of the Proustian dualism that devaluates practical
reason (summarized very briefly above). Second, he discusses the
nature of the experience of involuntary memory, which is a precondition to artistic creation. Beckett lists the occasions of its
recurrence in *A la recherche du temps perdu*, analyzes one of them
in detail (*Les Intermittences du coeur*, which he calls "perhaps the
greatest passage Proust ever wrote"), and finally shows how the
Proustian vision of two worlds finds its epiphany in the heart of
his novel, the Albertine tragedy.[2] Third, he points out how Proust's
position in relation to other artists, to other artistic schools and
movements, and to other arts, especially music, is a solidly aesthetic
one (that is to say, nonintellectual, even anti-intellectual). He ends
by demonstrating the nonrational nature of Proust's style, imagery,
structure, and characterization. The second of Beckett's three

[2] Beckett terms this central section of the novel "the Proustian *Discours
de la Méthode*," which recalls the capital fact that three major deities pre-
sided, Janus-like, at the birth of Beckett the artist: Joyce, Descartes, and
Proust.

approaches—which takes up the long central part of his exposition in *Proust* and deals with the positive experience leading to creation—is the crux of the matter. Before turning to it, let us briefly dispose of the third way, which concludes the book as it began, by focusing on the aesthetically negative forces that control the macrocosm.

Beckett makes a distinction between the "intellectual symbolism of a Baudelaire, abstract and discursive . . . determined by a concept, therefore strictly limited and exhausted by its own definition," and the nonconceptual "Idea, the concrete . . . the object [that is] a living symbol, but a symbol of itself," which is pursued by Proust. Beckett emphatically rejects the conceptual in art and condemns allegory and symbolism because their "significance is purely conventional and extrinsic" (p. 60). But he skirts Charybdis as well as Scylla, claiming that Proust retreats from a possible point of departure in Symbolism back toward Hugo and romanticism, eschewing the "notes d'après nature" of Daudet and the Goncourts and the naturalism of the Parnassians: "He solicits no facts, and he chisels no Cellinesque pommels."[3] Proust is a romantic "in his substitution of affectivity for intelligence, in his opposition of the particular affective evidential state to all the subtleties of rational cross-reference . . . in his skepticism before causality" (p. 61). Beckett goes on to speak of Proust's "relativism and impressionism" as "adjuncts of this same anti-intellectual attitude" (p. 65). He is relativistic in that he does not force beings evolving in time into intellectual pigeonholes but grants a lack of coherence due to their temporal evolution. By Proust's "impressionism" Beckett explains that he means "his non-logical statement of phenomena in the order and exactitude of their perception, before they have been distorted into intelligibility in order to be forced into a chain of cause and effect," and—very important for the understanding of Beckett's own work—he adds: "And we are reminded of Schopenhauer's definition of the artistic procedure as 'the contemplation of the world independently of the principle of reason'" (p. 66).

[3] Such a defense of art against intellectualism on the one hand and "materialism" on the other recalls inevitably Chapter I of Croce's *Aesthetic* (New York: Noonday Press, 1960): "Having thus freed intuitive knowledge from any suggestion of intellectualism and from every later and external addition, we must now explain it and determine its limits from another side and defend it from a different kind of invasion and confusion. On the hither side of the lower limit is sensation . . ." (p. 5).

407

Moving on to a discussion of style, structure, characterization, and imagery in the novel, Beckett attacks the intellectualistic view that reduces literature to ideas wrapped in a form manufactured a posteriori. Like Croce, he rejects anything that smacks of rhetoric and/or utilitarianism. "For Proust, as for the painter, style is more a question of vision than of technique. Proust does not share the superstition that form is nothing and content everything. . . . Indeed he makes no attempt to dissociate form from content. The one is a concretion of the other, the revelation of a world" (p. 67). Unlike the classical artist who "assumes omniscience and omnipotence . . . , raises himself artificially out of Time in order to give relief to his chronology and causality to his development," Proust accepts a more immediate, that is to say nonrational, structure. "Proust's chronology is extremely difficult to follow, the succession of events spasmodic, and his characters and themes, although they seem to obey an almost *insane* inward necessity [italics mine], are presented and developed with a fine Dostoievskian contempt for the vulgarity of a plausible concatenation" (p. 62). Faced with the apparently intellectual, analytical approach adopted by Proust toward his characters, Beckett observes cogently that although Proust is forever "explaining" his characters, "his explanations are experimental and not demonstrative. He explains them in order that they may appear as they are—inexplicable. He explains them away" (p. 67). Proust's apparent intellectualism is in reality a profound skepticism regarding man's ability to know through rational means. "Thus his purely logical—as opposed to his intuitive—explanations of a certain effect invariably bristle with alternatives" (p. 61). With fine insight Beckett notes that the majority of Proust's images are botanical. "He assimilates the human to the vegetal." This tendency Beckett explains as a natural accompaniment to Proust's "complete indifference to moral values and human justices." Like plants, the men and women in the Proustian world are "victims of their volition." Their will is "blind and hard," for will is "utilitarian, a servant of intelligence and habit" (pp. 68-69).

4. *The Miracle of Involuntary Memory*

In a revealing passage Beckett provides a key to the meaning of the Magdalen Mental Mercyseat in *Murphy* and the asylum in *Watt*. Referring to our truer self, that "smothered divinity whose whispered 'disfazione' is drowned in the healthy bawling of an all-embracing appetite," he suggests that we *may* recover this being that is lost in the "gouffre interdit à nos sondes." (It was, after all, "from this deep source [that] Proust hoisted his world.") But this is possible only "when we escape into the spacious annexe of mental alienation, in sleep or the rare dispensation of waking madness" (pp. 18-19). In these lines Beckett makes quite clear his view of the association between appetite (elsewhere desire, need, will), intellect, and the everyday world of the macrocosm. The artist must thwart these kidnappers if he is to make contact with being, in the depths of the microcosm. He must find his way to an asylum, a refuge, accept the status of alien, live as a "madman" (p. 19).

Early in his book Beckett states the dilemma of the subject-object relationship and soon after outlines the solution Proust proposes in *A la recherche du temps perdu*:

> The aspirations of yesterday were valid for yesterday's ego, but not for today's. We are disappointed at the nullity of what we are pleased to call attainment. But what is attainment? The identification of the subject with the object of his desire. The subject has died—and perhaps many times—on the way. For subject B to be disappointed by the banality of an object chosen by subject A is as illogical as to expect one's hunger to be dissipated by the spectacle of Uncle eating his dinner.   (p. 3)

Luckily, involuntary memory can, in its own time and place, unite subject and object in a timeless union by restoring the past in all its sensuous and emotive totality. Both the former self with its need and the object with all its desirability are resuscitated, but now need and possession coexist. The substance of the past is recaptured and at the same time freed from the dynamism of flux that held and changed it, so that the self that wants and the self that has are unalterably one. Beckett puts it in these terms:

> . . . the total past sensation, not its echo nor its copy, but the sensation itself, annihilating every spatial and temporal restriction, comes in a rush to engulf the subject in all the beauty of its infallible proportion. . . .

> The identification of immediate with past experience, the recurrence of past action or reaction in the present, amounts to a participation between the ideal and the real, imagination and direct apprehension, symbol and substance. Such participation

409

frees the essential reality that is denied to the contemplative as to the active life. What is common to present and past is more essential than either taken separately. Reality, whether approached imaginatively or empirically, remains a surface, hermetic. Imagination, applied—a priori—to what is absent, is exercized in vacuo and cannot tolerate the limits of the real. Nor is any direct and purely experimental contact possible between subject and object, because they are automatically separated by the subject's consciousness of perception, and the object loses its purity and becomes a mere intellectual pretext or motive. But thanks to this reduplication, the experience is at once imaginative and empirical, at once an evocation and a direct perception, real without being merely actual, ideal without being merely abstract, the ideal real, the essential, the extratemporal.

(pp. 54-56)

Such is the Proustian solution to the central predicament of human existence: need. On the first page of his essay Beckett suggests that Proust's essential subject is "the luminous projection of subject desire." In life this desire can never be fulfilled. Because two human beings are "two separate and immanent dynamisms related by no system of synchronisation" (cf. the theme of untimeliness, "too soon" and "too late," in Beckett's poetry), "our thirst for possession is, by definition, insatiable. . . . The tragedy of the Marcel-Albertine liaison is the type-tragedy of the human relationship whose failure is preordained. "One only loves that which is not possessed, one only loves that in which one pursues the inaccessible. . . . Love . . . can only coexist with a state of dissatisfaction, whether born of jealousy or its predecessor—desire. . . . Its inception and its continuance imply the consciousness that something is lacking" (pp. 35, 39). Quoting Proust, Beckett goes on to specify: "We imagine that the object of our desire is a being that can be laid down before us, enclosed within a body. Alas! It is the extension of that being to all the points of space and time that it has occupied and will occupy. If we do not possess contact with such a place and with such an hour we do not possess that being. But we cannot touch all these points." Hence Proust's definition of love as "Time and Space made perceptible to the heart" (pp. 41, 42). In life the only solution, the only wisdom, consists in the "ablation of desire" (p. 7). Since the definition of suffering is desire, only

410

by obliterating the latter can we eliminate the former. Schopen-hauer joins Leopardi and Brahma and "all the sages" in agreement (pp. 7, 8). But, as we have seen, not only the sages seek to avoid suffering. Intellect and its accomplices, habit and voluntary memory, can and usually do install the subject in a world of surfaces where the suffering of being is replaced by the boredom of living (p. 8). What sets the artist apart from other men is his willingness—more, his need—to replace the boredom of living by the suffering *and enchantments* (p. 11) of being. "The pendulum oscillates between these two terms: "Suffering—that opens a win-dow on the real and is the main condition of the artistic experi-ence, and Boredom—with its host of top-hatted and hygienic ministers, Boredom that must be considered as the most tolerable because the most durable of human evils" (p. 16).

The profound significance of the experience of involuntary memory that brings surcease of suffering is revealed in the pattern of imagery used by both Proust and Beckett to describe it. The latter writes that "if this mystical experience communicates an extratemporal essence, it follows that the communicant is for the moment an extratemporal being. Consequently the Proustian solu-tion consists . . . in the negation of Time and Death, the negation of Death because the negation of Time. Death is dead because Time is dead" (p. 56). Involuntary memory "restores, not merely the past object, but the Lazarus that it charmed or tortured . . ." (p. 20). It is a short step from imagery evoking a religious experience of communion with God, victory over death, and the miracle of resurrection to another metaphor, which is perhaps something more than a metaphor, that recurs in *Proust*. When the "imprisoned microcosm" is freed, "we breathe the true air of Paradise, of the only Paradise that is not the dream of a madman, the Paradise that has been lost" (p. 55).[4] The notion of an Eden to be recaptured

---

[4] See also, among other examples: "[Habit] disappears—with a wailing and gnashing of teeth" (p. 10); "the narrator's via dolorosa" (p. 12); "this inferno of unfamilar objects" (p. 12); "our life is a succession of Paradises successively denied" (p. 14); "The source and point of departure of this 'sacred action,' the elements of communion" (p. 23); "The last five visita-tions . . . may be considered as forming a single annunciation" (p. 24); "the Calvary of pity and remorse . . . flagellation" (p. 29); "the host of her lips" (p. 35); "the Goddess who requires this sacrifice . . . into whose faith and worship all mankind is born, is the Goddess of Time" (p. 41); "no anachro-nism can put apart what Time has coupled" (p. 43); "receive the oracle . . .

through the experience of involuntary memory completes what was begun at birth. That catastrophic event catches man up in flux, thrusts him onto the racetrack like a greyhound in everlasting pursuit of an ever-receding prey. "Tragedy is not concerned with human justice. Tragedy is the statement of an expiation, but not the miserable expiation of a codified breach of a local arrangement, organized by the knaves for the fools. The tragic figure represents the expiation of original sin, of the original and eternal sin of him and all his 'soci malorum,' the sin of having been born," and Beckett goes on to quote Calderón, " 'Pues el delito mayor/ Del hombre es haber nacido' " (p. 49). Birth is the birth of need. In Eden the desire to know lost man his paradise. Ever since, he has sought to know the unknowable "other" and, like Eve (or Watt), loses a paradise in the attempt. The metaphorical structure of *Proust* is firmly grounded in the Christian analysis even though the paradise regained is an earthly one, at least for the author of *A la recherche du temps perdu*. No one, not Beckett himself, can presume to assay the nature of his relationship to the God who is absent yet everywhere present in his writing. Perhaps no metaphor can be chosen with impunity. The two terms interpenetrate; one is irremediably affected by the other. Like the God for whom every "other" may be a surrogate and whose shadowy presence heightens the sense of His absence, Beckett's religious metaphors set up an uncertain oscillation between the something and the nothing, tantalize, and end by exacerbating the reader's experience of need. Beckett uses the metaphor for the sake of the metaphor, for its "metaphoricalness," that "twoness" composed of substance that may be shadow and shadow that may be substance.

The Proustian solution is aesthetic. Art is a remedy for the disease of life. Salvation lies in the *oeuvre*: "So now in the exaltation of his brief eternity, having emerged from the darkness of time and habit and passion and intelligence, he understands the necessity of art. For in the brightness of art alone can be deciphered the baffled ecstasy that he had known before the inscrutable superficies of a cloud, a triangle, a spire, a flower, a pebble, when the mystery, the essence, the Idea, imprisoned in matter, had solicited

---

and suffer a religious experience in the only intelligible sense of that epithet, at once an assumption and an annunciation" (p. 51); "Time made flesh" (p. 57); etc.

the bounty of a subject passing by within the shell of his impurity. . . ." To a certain extent Beckett will define himself by contrast with this apotheosis of an art that overcomes need in the "adequate union of subject and object" (p. 57). Already in *Proust* he underlines the precarious and ephemeral nature of the aesthetic paradise. Involuntary memory is an "unruly magician and will not be importuned" (p. 20). It performs that rare act, "a miracle," only "*by accident*" (Beckett's italics) and "given favorable circumstances" (pp. 21, 54). Its eternity is "brief" (p. 57). At the same time, Beckett stresses the otherness of the object. Can it indeed be *known* even in the union brought about when the idea is released from its prison of matter, when the masks fall? "When the object is perceived as particular and unique and not merely the member of a family, when it appears independent of any general notion and detached from the sanity of a cause, isolated and *inexplicable* in the light of *ignorance*, then and then only may it be a source of enchantment" (p. 11). But what if we, like Watt, are incapable of accepting its inexplicability and our own ignorance? Is the ablation of our desire to know possible? Can we, remaining mortal men, immersed in time, be satisfied with enchantment? Can we indeed recapture our lost Eden, or are solitude and need not our incurable condition on earth? "We are alone," writes Beckett. "We cannot know and we cannot be known." He subscribes wholly to Proust's assertion that " 'Man is the creature that cannot come forth from himself, who knows others only in himself, and who, if he asserts the contrary, lies' " (p. 49). Eventually the narrator in *A la recherche du temps perdu* comes to "understand the promise of Bergotte and the achievement of Elstir and the message of Vinteuil from his paradise and the dolorous and necessary course of his own life and the infinite futility—for the artist—of all that is not art" (p. 51). Still we may ask, "Can the artist be only an artist? Can he cease to be a man?" When Beckett shuttles between the macrocosm of Paris and the microcosm of his Marne Valley retreat, he makes a symbolic journey between "life" and art. Vladimir and Estragon in *Godot* alternate between their "distractions" and the void of waiting. We return to the project proposed in the little poem added at the end of *Watt*. Beckett will be the poet of absence, want, woe. His will be the tale not of resurrection, paradise regained, fulfillment but of the old man. His effort will be not to resuscitate the lost past in all its sensuous and emotive totality

413

but through words, through art, to recount man, his irredeemable need, his need to need, his exile, the nothingness to which he must come.

Beckett as Literary Journalist and Social Critic

In the early and mid-thirties Beckett tried his hand at literary journalism, while writing *Echo's Bones* and *Murphy* at the same time.[5] He published book reviews dealing with the work of Rilke, O'Casey, McGreevy, Pound, and Jack Yeats and with an essay by Giovanni Papini on Dante. In an unpublished piece of the same period, Beckett treated the question of censorship and birth control in Ireland. Besides illuminating the work of the authors reviewed, these discussions provide more than an occasional insight into the *Weltanschauung* of the reviewer. Beckett sees in terms of a consistent personal position that is becoming more complex. He reaches out to annex or reject, to relate and refine. In comparing Jack Yeats and Swift, he thinks in terms of two worlds, the public and the private, and takes his stand. As far as he is concerned the two should be driven as far apart as possible, not joined and interrelated. Art is not a *va-et-vient* between microcosm and macrocosm but an immersion in an imaginative "other." Hence symbolism and satire,

[5] Between 1933 and 1936 he published the following reviews and essays:

1. A review of Rainer Maria Rilke, *Poems*, trans. J. B. Leishmann (London: Hogarth Press, 1934). In *The Criterion*, XIII (1933-1934), 705-707.

2. "Papini's Dante," *The Bookman*, LXXXVII (Christmas 1934), 14. (A review of Giovanni Papini, *Dante Vivo*, trans. Eleanor Hammond Broadus and Anna Benedetti [London: Lovat Dickson, 1934].)

3. "The Essential and the Incidental," *The Bookman*, LXXXVII (Christmas 1934), 111. (A review of Sean O'Casey, *Windfalls* [New York: Macmillan, 1934].)

4. "Humanistic Quietism," *Dublin Magazine*, IX, No. 3 (July-Sept. 1934), 79-80. (A review of Thomas McGreevy, *Poems* [London: Heineman, 1934].)

5. "Ex Cathezra," *The Bookman*, LXXXVII (Christmas 1934), 10. (A review of Ezra Pound, *Make It New* [London: Faber and Faber, 1934].)

6. "An Imaginative Work!" *Dublin Magazine*, XI, No. 3 (July-Sept. 1936), 80-81. (A review of Jack B. Yeats, *The Amaranthers* [London: Heineman, 1936].)

Beckett also wrote an essay entitled "Censorship in the Saorstat," a manuscript probably completed during 1936 and to the best of my knowledge unpublished.

414

which point outward toward the big world, are disparaged in favor of internal connections. Parts of the work mirror each other. The *oeuvre d'art* is a closed world: "There is no symbol. The cream horse that carries Gilfoyle and the cream coach that carries Gilfoyle are related, not by rule of three, as two values to a third, but directly, as stages of an image. There is no satire. Believers and make-believers, not Gullivers and Lilliputians; horses and men, not Houyhnhnms and Yahoos. . . ." In "Censorship in the Saorstat"[6] Beckett refers to "the painful tension between life and thought" and characterizes thus an Ireland that practices censorship of literature and forbids control of the birth rate: "Sterilization of the mind and apotheosis of the litter suit well together, Paradise peopled with virgins and the earth with decorticated multiparas." In similar accents Belacqua lamented the physicality of the Smeraldina and retreated into the refuge of his inner limbo; thus did Murphy deplore his need for Celia and yearn for his microcosm of the mind.

In summing up the essential O'Casey, Beckett uses terms that are reminiscent of his own attacks on the macrocosmic surfaces and prefigure the disintegrations and dissolutions in his own later works. The artist must be capable of destroying if he is to have the power to create. O'Casey, writes Beckett, "discerns the principle of disintegration in even the most complacent solidities, and activates it to their explosion. . . . Mind and world come asunder in irreparable dissociation." He speaks of an "entire set [that] comes to pieces," of one character in "a final spasm of dislocation" and of another's "dissolution," and describes "Messrs. Darry Berrill and Barry Derril supine on the stage, 'expediting matters' in an agony of calisthenics, surrounded by the doomed furniture." All of this he attributes to the "disruptive intelligence, exacting the tumult from unity." Nevertheless, in these early writings Beckett has not yet fully developed his own views and program. For those who think of him as the very type of the antihumanist who takes a kind of unholy, sadistic delight in degrading man, it should be instructive to read the early essay on Rilke. There is no doubt that Beckett saves his sharpest barbs for that Promethean illusion that "provides for the interchangeability of Rilke and God," but he also castigates the childish "self-deception and naif discontent" that scorns one's fellow beings as

---

[6] Here as in the poem "Hell Crane to Starling" the Biblical allusion (the spelling is Tsoar in the poem) suggests inebriation, dubious sexual activity, and fraudulent procreation.

"human vegetables." In the essay on Thomas McGreevy's poetry, Beckett reveals the religious affiliation, for him, of the thesis that claims two extremes in art, Promethean humanism and misanthropic quietism, when he describes the former as the "pharisee poems (Goethe's *Prometheus*, Carducci's *Satan*)" and the latter as the "publican poems (*Vita Nuova, Astrophel and Stella, On the Death of Laura*, etc.)." A mean between the extremes of the "pharisee's taratantara" and the "publican's whinge," McGreevy's poetry comes off well as "humanistic quietism."

If Beckett is aware that a world must be destroyed before creation can take place, he is also alive to the crucial importance for creative activity of solitude, that nothingness out of which something may come. One trouble with Rilke, he writes, is that he "cannot make [solitude] his element . . . [but is] always popping up for the gulp of disgust that will rehabilitate the *Ichgott*, recruit him for the privacies of that divinity—until the next time." If art is a two-stage affair, the first is merely clearing the ground for inaction. Only the satirist, who is no more than half an artist, turns means into end, takes the preliminary for the essential. The paragraph that ends Beckett's review of McGreevy's poetry points to the relationship between solitude, the self, values, and art: "To know so well what one values is, what one's value is, as not to neglect those occasions (they are few) on which it may be doubled,[7] is not a common faculty; to retain in the acknowledgement of such enrichment the light, calm and finality that composed it is an extremely rare one."

The dualities of surface and depth, macrocosm and microcosm, society and the self, destruction and creation correspond to another pair: criticism and art, the first associated with the intellect and the second with imaginative experience. Running true to form, Beckett excoriates the former. In "Papini's Dante" he exposes the confusion that results from identifying Dante the citizen with Dante the artist. The fact that Signor Papini happens to be Florentine, a Catholic, and a poet of sorts most emphatically does *not* make him especially qualified to understand Dante. After an analysis of Signor Papini's self-contradictions, Beckett concludes that the Italian critic's purpose is "the reduction of Dante to lovable proportions." "But," replies Beckett with amusing cogency, "who wants to love Dante? We want to READ Dante—for example, his imperishable reference (Paolo-Francesca episode) to the incompatibility of the

---

[7] Art captures, re-creates, "doubles" the experiential value.

two operations." At this stage at least, Beckett argues consistently for an aestheticism that isolates the work of art from all extrinsic considerations. As the ironic title of his essay on Pound's *Make It New* ("Ex Cathezra") suggests, he rejects official pronunciamentos that evaluate art in terms of intellectual categories that are foreign to its very nature. To test literature in terms of "the two great [critical] modes of prognosis and excernment," i.e., knowing ahead of time what a work of art ought to be like and selecting *out* those works or parts of works that fail to measure up to the predetermined standards, is as bad as judging the effectiveness of a submarine by how well it can fly. Beckett's review of Jack Yeats's *The Amaranthers* is entitled "An Imaginative Work!" The exclamation point means approximately "it is *not* a work of the intellect." The review opens with a distinction between critic and artist: "The chartered recountants take the thing to pieces and put it together again. They enjoy it. The artist takes it to pieces and makes a new thing, new things. He must." It ends on a closely related quotation from Yeats. Thinking and imagining, to put it baldly, are incompatible: " 'You begin to stop emptying your heads, every time they begin to fill with thoughts, and then you will begin to think, and then you will stop thinking and begin to talk. . . . And then you will stop talking and begin to fancy, and then you will stop fancying and begin to imagine.' " Since the audience of a work of art may well be part of this outer world where practical reason reigns, the author cannot be shackled by the judgment of his readers. This further severance is implied in a line from "Censorship in the Saorstat": "This [the notion that the common-sense point of view is the appropriate measure of a work of art] is getting dangerously close to the opinion of Miss Robey, that for the artist as for the restaurateur the customer is always right."

In these earlier essays Beckett writes more about what art is not than about what it is. As in *Proust*, where he opposes the "pathological power and sobriety" of that author's writing to the romantic artist's inclination "to sensationalize" (p. 62), so in his review of *Poems* he complains of Rilke's "overstatement" and inability to "hold his emotion." By contrast, he defers to that artist capable of retaining in his creation "the light, calm and finality" that characterized the intuition preceding it. Aesthetic distance is a requisite. Emotion is an immediate organic response that is part of the process of living, not of making. Art follows upon vision, emotion contemplated. In neither the thin air of intellect nor the jungle of sensation and emotion can the *oeuvre* come to fruition. When Beckett implies in the McGreevy review that the ability to recognize and seize for art the moment of intuition may just possibly be an acquired ability but that a valid creative act (which he seems to conceive of in terms of fidelity to the intuition, itself a privileged experience purified of the macrocosmic dross of thought, feeling, and sensation) can be accomplished only by him to whom it is given to accomplish it, he appears to be saying that the artist is for the most part born, not made. The action of involuntary memory is not without analogy to the notion of "inspiration," and craft or *métier* as mere technique he rejects. Style and vision are one. His artistic sympathies, for this reason and others mentioned earlier, seem to be more with the romantic than the classical position. While he favors the restraint of classicism, he is impatient with its intellectualism and opposes the "omniscience and omnipotence" assumed by the classical artist, who "raises himself artifically out of Time" in order to organize his work in terms of chronology and causality (*Proust*, pp. 61-62).

In the essay on Jack Yeats, Beckett stresses the "autonomy of the imagined." He calls it "a world," implying its self-sufficiency and its independence from that other world we sometimes think of as the "real" one. Yeats's "landscape is superb, radiant and alive, with its own life. . . ." In the work of art the relationships are centripetal, not centrifugal. They do not invite the reader to make comparisons with aspects of the big world outside. In his attack on the second part of the 1929 Irish Censorship Act (dealing "with the constitution of and procedure to be adopted by the Censorship of Publications Board, the genesis of prohibition orders, the preparation of a register of prohibited publications and the issuing of search warrants in respect of prohibited publications"), Beckett deplores an assertion made by Deputy J. J. Byrne[8] to the effect that "it is not necessary for any sensible individual to read the whole of a book before coming to the conclusion whether the book is good, bad or indifferent." Such a claim violates outrageously the wholeness and autonomy of the work of art. The censor by the very nature of his position must conceive of the work as a system of referential links to social, political, ethical, and religious realities—and of the

---

[8] The name Byrne (not Jekyll) appears along with Hyde (and Jug-jug) in the poem "To Nelly" (*Watt*, p. 11), discussed in the preceding chapter. The *revers* of the puritan *médaille*.

418

artist as a potentially subversive agent of a peculiarly clever and unreasonably immune fifth column. While it would no doubt be going too far to think of Beckett as an early exponent of New Criticism, his aestheticism sometimes appears as a defensive reaction against incursions from realms that may be related to literature but may also, from ignorance or hostility, misunderstand and misuse it. A possible reaction to the inquisitional aspects of social organization in Ireland at the time was to build walls around the works and worlds of art.

Beckett published two other reviews (bracketing the time when *Watt* was written), one in 1938 on the poetry of Denis Devlin and one in 1945 on McGreevy's book on Jack Yeats. These two important pieces together with a very short *hommage* to Yeats provide us with a measure of the distance traversed since the earlier essays.[9] Not that Beckett abandons previously held positions. He does not. Rather, he develops them inexorably toward their ultimate consequences. The villain is still the macrocosmic mind. Art depends "on a minimum of rational interference." It has "nothing to do with clarity" but is born as a "totality" with "directness and concreteness." Given the need to avoid the rational, "it is naturally in the image that this profound and abstruse self-consciousness first emerges with the least loss of integrity." The best that Beckett has to say for mind is "that it can dispel mind." Once again, but more clearly and insistently than ever, we are told that art is a destruction of surfaces, an unveiling. To what purpose? To bring "light . . . to the issueless predicament of existence." The great artist "reduces the dark where there might have been, mathematically at least, a door."

The phrase "issueless predicament" introduces a new note. Scarcely heard in the preceding essays, it sounds strong and clear in these last three. The predicament is man's need, which can never

---

[9] "Denis Devlin," *Transition*, No. 27 (April-May 1938), pp. 289-294. (A review of Denis Devlin, *Intercessions* [London: Europa Press, 1937].)

"McGreevy on Yeats," *Irish Times*, ca. 1945. (Review of Thomas McGreevy, *Jack B. Yeats: An Appreciation and an Interpretation* [Dublin: Victor Waddington Publications, 1945].)

"Hommage à Jack B. Yeats," *Les Lettres nouvelles*, No. 14 (April 1954), pp. 619-620.

(Unless indicated otherwise, all quotations in this section are from these three short essays.)

be abolished. He is a creature of voids that ache to be filled, of nothingness that yearns to be something. Society, life in the big world, is organized to satisfy wants. Ephemeral and illusory as these satisfactions may be, they are nonetheless satisfactions. For the artist, however, they are no more than veils that obscure the painful reality of man's dilemma.

As between these two, the need that in its haste to be abolished cannot pause to be stated and the need that is the absolute predicament of particular human identity, one does not of course presume to suggest a relation of worth. Yet the distinction is perhaps not idle, for it is from the failure to make it that proceeds the common rejection as "obscure" of most that is significant in modern music, painting and literature. On the one hand . . . the need to need ("aimant l'amour"), the art that condenses as inverted spiral of need. . . . And on the other the go-getters, the gerrymandlers, Davus and the morbid dread of sphinxes, solution clapped on problem like a snuffer on a candle, the great crossword public on all its planes: "He roasteth roast and is satisfied. Yea, he warmeth himself and saith, Aha, I am warm."

As figure of the predicament Beckett chooses "the Dives-Lazarus symbiosis, as intimate as that of fungoid and algoid in lichen. . . . Here scabs, lucre, etc., there torment, bosom, etc., but both here and there *gulf*. The absurdity, here or there, of either without the other, the inaccessible other."

From the nature of being as need stems the nature of art, which is an "approximately adequate and absolutely non-final formulation . . . pure interrogation, rhetorical question less the rhetoric. . . ." In effect art brings man face to face with his irreducible need, no more, no less. Hence the futility of explaining art in terms of a society that does precisely the opposite, that rushes to deny, fulfill, gloss over, eliminate need. Art cannot be explained by "the local accident, or the local substance." "The national aspects of Mr. Yeats's genius," writes Beckett, "have I think been overstated, and for motives not always remarkable for their aesthetic purity. To admire painting on other than aesthetic grounds, or a painter, qua painter, for any other reason than that he is a good painter, may seem to some [Beckett, for one] uncalled for." Poetry must be "free to be derided (or not) in its own terms and not in those of the politicians, antiquaries (*Geleerte*) and zealots." In the case of literature, problems arise; for language, because of its practical functions in the big world and because of at least that part of its nature that is abstract and arbitrary representation, is ill-suited to be a medium of artistic expression. Thus we find Beckett fretting at the fact that "even the most competent linkwriting is bound to sag" and admiring a poem "for the extraordinary evocation of the unsaid by the said." From the foregoing it is clear that Beckett has by no means abandoned his aestheticism. It is also clear, however, that his aestheticism is no mere formalistic game. If it rejects the macrocosmic "realities" it is simply because they are seen as unrealities, less-than-realities, obfuscations of reality. Beckett's art will not cut him off from life but help him to reestablish contact with it in himself. If the *oeuvre* is a closed world, it is because the individual is a closed world. The subject can establish no meaningful communication with the unknowable object, the "other." The only fruitful art is "excavatory," a descent into the microcosm. "With himself on behalf of himself. With his selves on behalf of his selves. Tour d'ébène," writes Beckett of Denis Devlin. And of Jack Yeats, "Ce qu'a d'incomparable cette grande oeuvre solitaire est son insistance à renvoyer au plus secret de l'esprit qui la soulève et à ne se laisser éclairer qu'au jour de celui-ci. . . . Quoi de moins féerique que cette prestigieuse facture comme soufflée par la chose à faire, et par son urgence propre?" In the light of such unequivocal statements on the closed world of the solitary self and the *oeuvre* that probes it, we can have little difficulty in understanding and feeling the reality of the ash cans in *Endgame*, Winnie's mound of earth in *Happy Days*, the urns in *Play*, and the locked room and the eye of the objectivized self in *Film*.

Is there any place at all left for literary criticism? Anything that even resembles causal explanation of the work in terms extrinsic to itself seems ruled out. Source criticism is a gratuitous act of the imagination. "L'artiste qui joue son être est de nulle part. Et il n'a pas de frères." By the same token, impressionistic criticism is wholly arbitrary. "Broder alors? Sur ces images éperdument immédiates. . . . Sur cette violence de besoin. . . . sur cette suprême maîtrise qui se soumet à l'immaîtrisable . . . ," asks Beckett, and he replies with a categorical "non." "Il n'y a ni place, ni temps, pour les exploits rassurants. . . . S'incliner simplement, émerveillé." Still, in a review entitled "Hommage" we should perhaps expect *chapeau bas* and not criticism. Elsewhere Beckett is less peremptory. In the Devlin review

421

he at least hints at a role for the critic: "The only suggestions there-fore that the reviewer may venture without impertinence are such as have reference to this fundamental [need]. Thus he may suggest the type of need (Braque's is not Munch's, neither is Klee's, etc.), its energy, scope, adequacy of expression, etc."[10] When he comes to discuss McGreevy on Yeats he is still less hostile: "It is difficult to formulate what it is one likes in Mr. Yeats's painting, or indeed what it is one likes in anything, but it is a labour not easily lost, and a relationship once stated not likely to fail, between such a knower and such an unknown. There is at least this to be said for . . . art-criticism, that it can lift from the eyes, before *rigor vitae* sets in, some of the weight of congenital prejudice." Such a statement, if it does nothing else, opens the way to a view of the critic as someone with a public function. He can be useful in remov-ing barriers to appreciation. His position would seem to lie some-where between that of a popularizer and John the Baptist preparing the way.

If Beckett in these essays is still more interested in defending art from its enemies, among whom we generally find the intellectual, evaluative, often antagonistic rather than sympathetic critic, he is extremely helpful to the latter-day student of his own works, for in one precious passage in "McGreevy on Yeats" he provides what amounts to a white paper listing experiences he feels to be the proper concern of art and a black list that excludes certain areas and topics from the aesthetic realm:

> Mr. Yeats's importance is elsewhere to be sought than in a sym-pathetic treatment (how sympathetic?) of the local accident, or the local substance. He is with the great of our time . . . because he brings light, as only the great dare to bring light, to the issue-less predicament of existence, reduces the dark where there might have been, mathematically at least, a door. The being in the street when it happens in the room, the being in the room when it happens in the street, the turning to gaze from land to sea, from sea to land, the backs to one another and the eyes abandoning, the man alone trudging in sand, the man alone

[10] It is important to note that Beckett often uses the term "critic" in the sense of judge, one who evaluates. He is somewhat less severe toward the "reviewer," whose task is more simply descriptive. Thus the passage quoted ends, "There seems no other way in which this miserable functionary [the reviewer] can hope to achieve innocuity. Unless of course he is a critic."

thinking (thinking?) in his box—these are characteristic notations having reference, I imagine, to processes less simple, and less delicious, than those to which the plastic *vis* is commonly reduced, and to a world where Tir-na-nogue makes no more sense than Bachelor's Walk, nor Helen than the apple-woman, nor asses than men, nor Abel's blood than Useful's, nor morning than night, nor the inward than the outward search.

A careful examination of this passage makes it quite evident that Beckett excludes (in the last lines above) national or more generally public matters; the love of women and perhaps inspiration stemming from the literary tradition (allusions are either drastically reduced or used in a new, more closely integrated way as part of the very fabric of the work in his later writings—in *Happy Days*, for example); social causes; the problem of evil and suffering innocence (the religious torment that played such a part in "Ooftish," "Text," and elsewhere); questions of sexuality and sterility (the need of Belacqua and Murphy, the satire in the description of the Lynch family, for instance); other human beings (a psychological or sociological literature is out); the things of time (art has nothing to do with a realism of changing surfaces, as we learned in *Proust*. "Nature poetry" is uninteresting. Beneath the epidermis we find identity, which recalls the theme of sameness in poems like "elles viennent"); and finally the search (which we remember as a principal theme of *Echo's Bones*. Art is linked to the abolition of will, as Schopenhauer knew. Need must be accepted and hope of fulfillment abandoned).

In the first part of the passage we come upon the themes of "no exit" and untimeliness, or "too soon" and "too late." (The first, man in his box, was touched on above. The second, as we saw, occurs in a number of the early poems, among them "Ascension.") Art "reduces the dark," lifts veils, destroys illusions. It deals with solitude, man alone, man as alien, out of touch with the "other." Exiled, he is, like Belacqua, a "border man" between sea and land, an inhabitant of the periphery who knows the meaning of loss, indifference, leave-taking. Beckett's man knows the sameness of sand, yet understands he must "keep on the move" ("Serena III"). But he knows not only "trudging" but also "waiting" in the microcosm of his box. Like Lucky, he has given up "thinking," learning, as it were, from the experience of Watt.

Such attitudes and intuitions, by now familiar, are incorporated into Beckett's studies on the painting of the Van Velde brothers. These essays constitute the definitive elaboration of his views on the nature of art and its relationship to life and thought. They are essential to an understanding in depth of the masterpieces of fiction and drama that are the product of his artistic maturity.

The Aesthetics of Samuel Beckett

1. Some Consequences of Philosophical Dualism

Le Client: Dieu a fait le monde en six jours, et vous, vous n'êtes pas foutu de me faire un pantalon en six mois.
Le Tailleur: Mais Monsieur, regardez le monde, et regardez votre pantalon.

Thus begins the first of several attempts—ranging from a lengthy essay written in 1945 to an epigraph introducing the 1962 Le Prat edition of Abraham (Bram) van Velde's painting—on the part of Samuel Beckett to deal more or less discursively with the enigmatic Dutch painter (and his brother, Geer van Velde), and at the same time to set forth his own aesthetic position. These attempts had mixed origins—friendship certainly, some editorial coercion no doubt, a desire to crusade against the philistines in part, deep skepticism about the mode and very possibility of communication especially: "Avec les mots on ne fait que se raconter. Eux-mêmes les lexicographes se déboutonnent. Et jusque dans le confessional on se trahit."[11] On the second try (in 1947), Beckett starts out belligerently, but at the same time under an umbrella of protective irony, "J'ai dit tout ce que j'avais à dire sur la peinture des frères van Velde. . . . Je n'ai rien à ajouter à ce que j'ai dit. . . . Heureusement il ne s'agit pas de dire ce qui n'a pas encore été dit, mais de redire, le plus souvent possible dans l'espace le plus réduit, ce qui a été dit déjà. Sinon on trouble les amateurs."[12] A case has already been made for a measure of development in the author's thinking from the late twenties to the early forties. In the essays on the Van

[11] "La Peinture des van Velde ou le monde et le pantalon," *Les Cahiers d'art* (1945-1946), pp. 349-356. Whenever there is no indication of another source, quotations will come from this first and most important of Beckett's essays on the Van Velde brothers.

[12] "Peintres de l'empêchement," *Derrière le miroir*, Nos. 11 and 12 (June 1948), pp. 3-7.

424

Veldes, ranging from 1945 to 1962, however, the unity of the views expressed is indeed indisputable. It is this unity (in its considerable multiplicity) that the following analysis attempts to outline.

"Le Monde et le pantalon" is a subtitle that points to the core of the first essay, "La Peinture des van Velde." The obvious but significant dualism of the title sets a botched world against the painstaking, if less ambitious, product of man's craft. It draws a parallel between God and the artist and compares the macrocosm to the little world of the work of art. Beckett's preference is clear. He, like Murphy, is of the microcosm of the mind, and for its artistic issue.

> Mais il était peut-être temps que l'objet se retirât, par ci par là, du monde dit visible.
>
> Le 'réaliste', suant devant sa cascade et pestant contre les nuages, n'a pas cessé de nous enchanter. Mais qu'il ne vienne plus nous emmerder avec ses histoires d'objectivité et de choses vues. De toutes les choses que personne n'a jamais vues, ses cascades sont assurément les plus énormes. . . .
>
> La peinture de A. van Velde serait donc premièrement une peinture de la chose en suspens, je dirais volontiers de la chose morte. . . . C'est la chose seule, isolée par le besoin de la voir, par le besoin de voir. La chose immobile dans le vide, voilà enfin la chose visible, l'objet pur. Je n'en vois pas d'autre.
>
> La boîte cranienne a le monopole de cet article.

Unreality, or better unavailability, of things in the world outside; things hidden by surfaces, immersed in flux, subject to the conditions of space. In "Peintres de l'empêchement" Beckett writes that there are two kinds of artist, and two kinds of obstacle: "l'empêchement-objet et l'empêchement-oeil." One artist will say, "Je ne peux voir l'objet, pour le représenter, parce qu'il est ce qu'il est," the other, "Je ne peux voir l'objet, pour le représenter, parce que je suis ce que je suis." Both face the predicament of a sundered world that isolates man irreparably from his surroundings. Hence the painting of Bram van Velde, "cette peinture solitaire, solitaire de la solitude qui se couvre la tête, de la solitude qui tend les bras." Our isolation is not only from things but from other men as well. Ours is a world in which communication is precarious and perhaps impossible short of gross distortion. Cut off from the outside, man finds himself in a state of ignorance. He is disenchanted with surfaces, no longer the dupe of the phantom accident, but substance

425

still escapes him. And the new void spawns a new need: to know. "Les oiseaux sont tombés, Mante se tait. Tirésias ignore./ Ignorance, silence et l'azur immobile, voilà la solution de la devinette, la toute dernière solution./ Pour d'aucuns." Despair and persistence meet in unequal yet unending struggle.

When man turns in his search from the macrocosm of the world to the microcosm of the mind, he finds similar obstacles. The mind too has its surfaces. In one description of the painting of Bram van Velde, Beckett writes, "Un dévoilement sans fin, voile derrière voile, plan sur plan de transparences imparfaites, un dévoilement vers l'indévoilable, le rien, la chose à nouveau" ("Peintres de l'empêchement"). The influence of the Cartesian experience is evident in this latter-day unveiling. Surfaces come away in an effort to uncover the something or nothing beneath, to get at the bases of being. But Descartes was a philosopher and scientist; Beckett is a poet. What is essential, then, is to set forth the implications for art of this frankly dualistic, openly skeptical view of man and nature.

2. Implications for Art

THE ENEMIES OF ART

Two things from the world of surfaces are peculiarly inimical to art. One is the intellect in all its many forms, which all too often include language. Words can be a "défiguration verbale, voire un assassinat verbal." Emotions often leave no more than a "risible empreinte cérébrale," which language, abstraction of an abstraction, translates. Art is concerned with the unique and the elementary, and the intellect attempts the impossible when it tries to "raisonner sur l'unique" or to "mettre de l'ordre dans l'élémentaire."

The other is social existence. Life in the "normal" sense is a series of "processions vers un bonheur de mouton sacré." Truth in this world is "le pet du plus grand nombre." To the solitary nature of an art that strives to "see," Beckett opposes the blindness of the "foire" that is society. From such an art he warns the "amateurs de natron" to abstain.[13] Natron, a substance used in embalming, evokes an image of the living dead, as does the figure of a "plante à la croisée, . . . choux pensant et même bien pensant" that he uses elsewhere to express the same theme.[14]

[13] In the epigraph to *Bram van Velde* (Paris: Le Prat, 1962).

[14] In the undated and unpublished manuscript of an essay entitled "Les Deux Besoins."

426

THE ORIGIN OF ART: MAN'S TEMPORAL CONDITION

Painting—and, with some reservations, literature as well—has its origin in man's temporal condition: "A quoi les arts représentatifs se sont-ils acharnés, depuis toujours? A vouloir arrêter le temps, en le représentant./ Que de vols, de courses, de fleuves, de flèches. Que de chutes et d'ascensions. Que de fumée." Grateful for it, but not without a passing reference to the "tourbillons de viande jamais morte," Beckett suggests that such painting has had its day. It is time to move from traditional representations of the exterior world to the metamorphosed objects of the mind. It is inside the skull that "parfois le temps s'assoupit, comme la roue du compteur quand la dernière ampoule s'éteint." There "on commence enfin à voir, dans le noir. Dans le noir qui est aube et midi et soir et nuit d'un ciel vide, d'une terre fixe." Paradoxically, the daylight world is a realm of blindness where the myriad masks of temporal succession hide the permanent reality (if it exists) of the essential object. Concealed beneath the veil of its accidental surfaces, caught up in becoming, ultimate being escapes man. Space and time conceal—from a being whose deepest need is to see. It is the older brother, Bram van Velde, who abandons this daylight world for an art of the microcosm, whose artistic achievement and indeed whole life are grounded in the struggle of the mind to know itself. "Nous avons affaire chez Abraham van Velde à un effort d'aperception . . . exclusivement et farouchement pictural. . . ." Beckett realizes, of course, that to write "aperception purement visuelle" seems to make little sense, but he insists that our concern here is not with a "prise de conscience" but with a "prise de vision . . . au champ intérieur."

There is another way to deal untraditionally with time and space, that of the younger brother, Geer van Velde, painter of the macrocosm. While Bram immobilizes external space by idealizing it and giving it a "sens interne," Geer, turned toward the outer world, paints time, in the sense that he shows "le macrocosme secoué par les frissons du temps." In this "drôle de *memento mori*" he reveals man's most unshakable certainty: that neither present time nor immobility exist. "Chez G. van Velde le temps galope, il l'éperonne avec une sorte de frénésie de Faust à rebours." Beckett stresses the difference between the time-honoured "stop-watch" painting, which hardly succeeds in blocking terrestrial rotation, and the reverse process of the younger Van Velde.

427

Each painter, caught in the central dilemma of a spatial art that tries to represent change, reacts in his own way. Both start by recognizing the impossibility of the task. They diverge when one abstracts the object from time and the other submits it to temporal acceleration. Geer paints successive states "en imposant à ceux-ci un glissement si rapide qu'ils finissent par se fondre, je dirais presque par se stabiliser, dans l'image de la succession même." He succeeds, according to Beckett, in forcing "l'invisibilité foncière des choses extérieures jusqu'à ce que cette invisibilité elle-même devienne chose, non pas simple conscience de limite, mais une chose qu'on peut voir et faire voir. . . ." Thus both brothers, by opposed means, seek to know the unknowable, to see the unseeable, to nullify the root condition of human existence, man's privation, his loss of contact with ultimate reality. Both seek to fathom the mystery of substance with eyes and minds attuned to the accidental. And, of course, so does the poet, novelist, and playwright named Samuel Beckett.

It is not as though the end of the quest were joy and fulfillment. On the contrary. Beckett writes of the unknown in ambiguous terms. He calls it "cette chose adorable et effrayante." But the only alternative is to abandon the search, to "rentrer dans le temps, dans la cécité," to put on the boredom of the vegetative mode of existing. In the essay "Les Deux Besoins" the same dilemma is expressed in another way and its relation to the work of art becomes clear. "Les deux besoins, les deux essences, l'être qui est besoin et la nécessité où il est de l'être, enfer d'irraison d'où s'élève le cri à blanc, la série de questions pures, l'oeuvre." Man is condemned to dissatisfaction. His imperious need to know can never really be fulfilled short of the destruction of his essential nature. He is by definition a creature deprived, doomed to the eternal pursuit of an ever-receding goal. Out of this need to know once and for all and the impossibility of doing so arises the work of art, an anguishing oscillation between painfully inadequate alternatives.

THE NATURE AND FUNCTION OF ART

There would seem to be other paths to knowing, but Beckett rejects them. He speaks of the "pétitions de principe" of a science that assumes as its starting point the real existence of what has to be proved. Theology, another pseudoscientific conceptualism, indulges in "logoi croisés." Together they produce "les tempêtes de

428

pets affirmatifs et négatifs d'où sont sortis et sortent toujours ces foireux aposterioris de l'Esprit et de la Matière. . . ." For Beckett, art is a better link to the ultimate. Not that it provides answers. "L'artiste se met à la question, se met en question, se résout en questions, en questions rhétoriques sans fonction oratoire. . . . Car aux enthymèmes de l'art ce sont les conclusions qui manquent et non les prémisses" ("Les Deux Besoins"). What it does do is to maintain man in a state of awareness of his deepest nature, from which the *divertissements* (in the Pascalian sense) of the surface world, macrocosm or microcosm, turn him away. Beckett's man is at bottom not the *homo sapiens* of science and theology, nor even *homo faber*, the artist, in any triumphant sense. He does not bring reason and order out of unreason and chaos. He is closer to *homo indigens* in the double sense of lack and desire (*homo egens et cupiens*), but only if we understand that neither term may be modified or canceled by the other. For Beckett, man needs to be in a state of need or privation as much as he needs to be out of it. Such a position follows in part from Beckett's relinquishment of any transcendental point of view (and with it any consideration of either original or posthumous fulfillment), in part from a quasi-religious sense of "fulfillment" through privation, and in part from the philosophical idealist's feeling for the unreality of the world of the senses.

ART AND THE ARTIST

Not every man is an artist and few understand art. In a profound tribute to the brothers Van Velde and the lonely courage of their lives, Beckett writes of the two *oeuvres* (and the two kinds of art):

> Elles s'écartent de plus en plus, l'une de l'autre. Elles s'écarteront de plus en plus, l'une de l'autre. Comme deux hommes qui, partis de la Porte de Châtillon, s'achemineraient, sans trop bien connaître le chemin, et avec de fréquents arrêts pour se donner du courage, l'un vers la Rue Champ de l'Alouette, l'autre vers l'Ile des Cygnes.
> Il importe ensuite d'en bien saisir les rapports. Qu'ils se ressemblent, deux hommes qui marchent vers le même horizon, au milieu de tant de couchés, d'assis et de transportés en commun.

Symbolism of the starting point, the two directions of art, the solitary, difficult life of the artist, the two destinations (street or island,

429

lark or swan); then the figure, rich in overtones, of the artist among men, among those who have abandoned the quest, those whose voyage is not really their own, those supported by the society of their fellows. And the overall unity of all art in the quest, the uncertain, hesitating movement toward a common end or horizon. In "Les Deux Besoins" Beckett asserts that only the artist can "finir par voir . . . la monotone centralité de ce qu'un chacun veut, pense, fait et souffre, de ce qu'un chacun est." He devotes himself to this even when seeing nothing—but before accepting his blindness. Thus, if worst comes to worst (since "seeing" is by no means a joyous thing), he may end in lucidity.

Why is one man so driven and not another? A question of "obscures tensions internes." Why (since he is more than a seer) is he moved to make things? "Absurdes et mystérieuses poussées vers l'image." Evidently, we are in the realm of irreducibles. Something of *homo faber* does after all exist. But if the artist is privileged (or cursed) with a vision of the human condition, he is not always so perceptive concerning his craft. As to the correspondence between vision and image, "lui-même n'en sait rien la plupart du temps." Beckett remains very anxious to make a clear distinction between the artist and the intellectual. However, he does qualify his description in a later passage of the same essay: "Entendons-nous. Il sait chaque fois que ça y est, à la façon d'un poisson de haute mer qui s'arrête à la bonne profondeur, mais les raisons lui en sont épargnées." The same distinction between the rational and the organic or intuitive comes up again in the anecdote about Cervantes' painter, who, when asked what he is painting, replies, "Whatever comes from my brush."

ART AND THE AUDIENCE

Both the isolation of the artist and his unintellectual pursuit militate against "communication" with his audience. As we have seen, his motives in creating the work are mysterious, even absurd. He is compelled toward making (the term in another passage is "obsessed"), more in order to relieve inner tensions than to express himself. The need to communicate with his fellow man is at the very most a secondary, peripheral concern. For Bram van Velde, at least, not even practical considerations such as earning money with which to buy food in order to eat so that he might continue painting played any part. Has art then no public *raison d'être*? It does—for the "inoffensif loufoque qui court, comme d'autres au cinéma, dans les galeries, au musée et jusque dans les églises avec l'espoir—tenez-vous bien—de jouir." This gentleman, "au visage creusé par les enthousiasmes sans garantie," is concerned neither with learning something nor with becoming a better person. "Il ne pense qu'à son plaisir." In the time-honored trilogy, Beckett effects a fairly decisive cleavage, rejecting the true and the good and situating art exclusively in the realm of the beautiful. Or (if one prefers polarities), *plaire* in his view takes radical precedence over *instruire* for this ideal spectator who alone can justify "l'existence de la peinture en tant que chose publique." Before assuming an extreme aestheticism, however, we must take into account a line from "Les Deux Besoins," where Beckett grants, reluctantly it is true, that the artist can "si l'on veut, [finir] par faire voir aux quelques-uns pour qui il existe." Again, he admits that his amateur might conceivably discover *why* he loves a painting, but asserts that the chances are against it. Pleasure accompanied in privileged cases by insight? Surface pleasure distinct from the painful vision of man's nature and condition? Or pleasure in seeing, even though what is seen is frightening? No clear answer is forthcoming in these essays, but one is tempted, in view of a 1937 letter to a German friend in which Beckett speaks of the small and mass audience, to favor the first option. In any case, the three possibilities are not always mutually exclusive. After all is said and done, however, the emphasis is clear. The audience of the work of art is not an essential concern. Its reaction to art, writes Beckett in the above letter, "becomes more and more mysterious to me, and, what is worse, less and less important. For I cannot escape from the naive antithesis, at least in what concerns literature, that a thing is worthwhile or it is not worthwhile." And in "La Peinture des van Velde" he laments the fact that a work considered as "création pure, et dont la fonction s'arrête avec la genèse, est vouée au néant." Since the genesis is mysterious and absurd, and the end or function almost irrelevant, what can be the nature of this image or form that begins in unreason and ends in futility, save for rare instances when it may be an occasion of pleasure or insight?

THE WORK OF ART

As we might expect, the work of art is first of all a private object, intellectually inaccessible and inexplicable—nonrational.

431

"Achevé, tout neuf, le tableau est là, un non-sens. Car ce n'est encore qu'un tableau, il ne vit que de la vie des lignes et des couleurs, ne s'est offert qu'à son auteur." Moving out from this starting point, Beckett can write that there is no painting but only individual paintings. There is, however, a history of intellectualizations supposedly referring to painting (which nevertheless remains wholly enigmatic). To such a history of subjective formulations, Beckett, with self-deprecating irony, intends to contribute the present essays on the brothers Van Velde. In his sketch of the historical development of painting in general, he outlines several stages in the basic relationship between the artist and his occasion, between subject and object. The first brings the painter to a technical mastery in the representation of surfaces; he paints an ever-increasing range of objects in their accidental existence. In the next stage (generally, but not necessarily always, in chronological order), he moves toward a painting in depth, toward the representation of the object as substance, "vers la chose que cache la chose. . . . la choseté" or quiddity. The great effort of modern painting is to express "en quoi un clown, une pomme et un carré de rouge ne font qu'un" ("Peintres de l'empêchement"). Before the difficulty of such a task, a third stage comes into being, a new reflexive painting, an art that is critical of its means and doubtful of the very existence of the subject-object relationship. Many of the best modern paintings, writes Beckett, "ressemblent à des méditations plastiques sur les moyens mis en oeuvre." The originality of the brothers Van Velde, initiators of the fourth stage, is to have accepted as starting point the absence of relationship, the unavailability of the object. Thence they have moved to the representation of the conditions that mask the object, to space-internalized, immobilized by Bram, and to time-accelerated, made visible by Geer.

At this point, we come up against an apparent contradiction that brings us close to the center of these essays and that helps us understand not only the painting of the Van Veldes but Beckett's novels and plays as well—contradiction involving the triune nature of the artist as one who needs privation, who needs fulfillment, who needs to make. In accepting the unavailability of the object (i.e., the impossibility of fulfillment, of seeing), the new painting would seem to violate the second of the three axiomatic conditions, to end the need for fulfillment. And yet the very attack on time and space would have little justification were it not an attempt to reveal the ultimate, which they conceal. The ambivalence suggests the presence of a delicate balance between the need for privation and the need for fulfillment; and the synthesis of thesis and antithesis comes in the third condition, the need to make. Seeing is denied (in accordance with the first condition), but the need to see (the second condition) remains, and both are evidenced in the making (the third condition). This last reveals nothing in absolute terms, but first, it does testify, by its very existence, to the need for fulfillment, and second, by the lack of motive with which it is undertaken, it manifests the need for privation. Art, in such a view, becomes both more arbitrary and more serious than "play." It points to man's deepest nature, but in itself it is wholly meaningless and futile.

It is in the later essays that Beckett explores some of the implications for the work of art of such a view of the nature of man and the aesthetic. However, a key phrase in "La Peinture des van Velde," "la malfaçon créatrice voulue," shows that he was well aware in 1945 of the direction in which he was moving. Already in 1937, in fact, in the (unpublished) letter to his German friend Axel Kaun referred to above, he mentions a "literature of the un-word." Later he speaks of his "dream of an art unresentful of its insuperable indigence . . . an impoverished painting, authentically fruitless, incapable of any image whatsoever."[15] Such a paradoxical view becomes comprehensible only if we remember that Beckett had demanded no less of art than the expression of the ineffable. Art was to do what science, theology, intellect in whatever form had failed to do. In his own metaphysical longing, in his idealistic dedication to art as the one salvation, he had torn down the prudently erected "barrier" between art and life, between the aesthetic realm and the realm of being. Some, at least, have come to believe, after various attempts in both directions, that neither total autonomy nor total fusion is possible. In this case fusion, in theory if not in practice, may well have worked to the ultimate detriment of art. Traditionally, the artist's activity has usually been considered more or less positive. His attitude ranged from the relative humility of discovering order or taking accurate dictation from one muse or another to the pride of the triumphant humanist in his godlike sec-

---

[15] "Three Dialogues" [Samuel Beckett and Georges Duthuit on Tal Coat, Masson, and Bram van Velde], *Transition Forty-Nine*, No. 5 (Dec. 1949), pp. 97-103.

433

ond or even first creation. For Beckett (or Bram van Velde), "to be an artist is to fail, as no other dare fail. . . ." Failure is the artist's world "and to shrink from it desertion, art and craft, good housekeeping, living" ("Three Dialogues"). Art has been moved out of the "domain of the feasible" where expression, more or less adequate, was possible. Bram van Velde's "situation is that of him who is helpless, cannot act, in the event cannot paint, since he is obliged to paint. The act is of him who, helpless, unable to act, acts, in the event, paints, since he is obliged to paint" ("Three Dialogues"). The nature of *homo faber* remains, but his potential for expression has disappeared.

The form of the work of art, in any traditional sense of the word "form," is obviously in jeopardy in such an aesthetic. In his first essay on the van Veldes, Beckett writes that in the economy of art what is not said is the light of what is said, and every presence absence. He complains that every time one tries to make words express something other than themselves "ils s'alignent de façon à s'annuler mutuellement." Language belongs to the practical world of surfaces, to the domain of intellect. It is an instrument poorly adapted to the exigencies of art. Probably the most enlightening passages Beckett has written on language occur in the letter to Axel Kaun. He describes his own language as a veil which must be torn asunder in order to get at the things (or the nothing) lying behind. "Grammar and Style!" he writes scornfully. "They appear to me to have become just as obsolete as a Biedermeier bathing suit or the imperturbability of a gentleman. A mask." He hopes for the time when language will be best used where it is most zealously misused, and he outlines a program designed to bring it into disrepute (since it cannot be obliterated or excluded all at once), to erode it "until that which lurks behind it . . . begins to trickle through." He can imagine no higher goal for the modern writer. Shall literature remain so far behind the other arts? Is there something paralyzingly sacred in the unnaturalness of the word? "Is there any reason why that terribly arbitrary materiality of the word's surface should not be dissolved, as, for example, the tonal surface, eaten into by large black pauses, in Beethoven's Seventh Symphony, so that for pages at a time we cannot perceive it other than, let us say, as a vertiginous path of sounds connecting unfathomable abysses of silence."[16]

[16] It is interesting to find in "Dream of Fair to Middling Women" the fol-

Both form and content, then, at least in any usual sense, are to be eliminated; words can neither create meaningful order nor mirror experience. In "Three Dialogues" Beckett puts it this way: "The expression that there is nothing to express, nothing with which to express, nothing from which to express, no power to express, no desire to express, together with the obligation to express." Art, traditionally "possessive," triumphant, is in irreconcilable conflict with being, which is weakness, chaos. Failure to see has led to inability to express. Rejection of intellect has led to rejection of the instrument of intellect, words. Yet the need to make remains—and with it the obscure sense that somehow, somewhere is being. *Fonctionnement à vide* of the artistic reflex that testifies both to the sterility and the persistence of human effort. "Testifies to," not "expresses." The use of art to express the inability to express is the third stage in Beckett's history of painting. In the new "art," purposiveness is ruled out. We return again to our account (Chapter V) of conversations in 1962, when Beckett spoke of the special difficulty experienced by one who is given to making with words (rather than sounds or colors); of the need for a "syntax of weakness." He felt that "Being is constantly putting form in danger," and conversely that he knew of no form that didn't violate the nature of being "in the most unbearable manner." Referring to the snowman that the child builds, he remarked, "Well, this is like trying to build a dustman." His predicament he described as that of "one on his knees, head against a wall—more like a cliff—with someone saying 'go on.' " Later he said, "Well, the wall will have to move a little, that's all." On another occasion he put it differently. Art until now had sought forms and excluded all aspects of being that there were no forms to fit. "If anything new and exciting is going on today, it is the attempt to let Being into art." He spoke of depths where all is mystery and enigma. "We don't know what our own personality is." It certainly has little to do with the surface self, with that "existence by proxy" in the macrocosm. Somewhere, perhaps, Beckett believes, is an "abortive self," a being somehow

---

lowing words spoken by Belacqua: "the incoherent continuum as expressed by, say, Rimbaud and Beethoven. . . . The terms of whose statements serve merely to delimit the reality of insane areas of silence, whose audibilities are no more than punctuation in a statement of silences. How do they get from point to point. That is what I meant by the incoherent reality . . ." (p. 91).

435

stunted, undeveloped, but more real, more authentic than the public man, who seems closer to the second or third person than to the first.

3. *The Place of Criticism*

RISKS AND PERILS

In his essays on the Van Velde brothers, Beckett has a good deal to say about art criticism. He is after all indulging in it, but, as he knows full well, this in itself needs justification, given his own views and the nature of the painting he is discussing. He does indeed hit hard against traditional scholarship and criticism. Most of the work that considers art primarily as a product and seeks to explain it in terms of its origins he rejects. We can understand why. From a point of view that divides the world of consciousness into an upper zone of light where forms correspond to those in the physical world outside and a lower zone of darkness without such correspondence (*Murphy*, Chapter 6), and that links the new art to this zone of darkness—from such a point of view, explaining the new art either in terms of the upper zone of intellect or its macrocosmic correlatives makes no sense at all. It is like explaining the nature of a water lily by studying the composition of the desert soil out of which it does not grow. Biography of the author, then, receives almost no attention in these essays. Beckett does write, "J'allais oublier le plus important. A. van Velde est né à La Haye en Octobre 1895. Ce fut l'instant des brumes. G. van Velde est né près de Leyde, en Avril 1897. Ce fut l'instant des tulipes," but this "explanation" of the inward and outward turning of their work is symbolic, not deterministic. Psychological analysis of the author is likewise rejected as a form of criticism. The obscure inner tensions that give rise to a work of art are unavailable, because the critic is not "dans la peau du tendu." Apparently ruled out as well is any form of genetic criticism. The instinct of *homo faber* is an absurd and mysterious compulsion about which he himself most often knows nothing. The irrational urge of the artist and the intellectual activity of the critic are incommensurable. A similar gap separates the work from its social context, since an activist, superficial society hides from itself the eternal conditions of human existence with which art is concerned. Neither race, moment, nor milieu has any essential effect on the nature of true art. The dates, periods, schools, and influences of literary history are so many intellectual constructions usually without direct reference to individual works of art. Literary history itself would seem to be a "ligne préétablie" drawn by a small group of the initiated according to criteria known only to themselves and for the purpose of excluding. Beckett is severe toward such prescriptive criticism and vigorously defends the absolute freedom of the artist.

It follows from this and from what has been said earlier about the audience of the work of art, that concern with the uses to which art may be put has little more pertinence for Beckett than the study of its origins. The particular needs, dispositions, points of view of a given audience do not merit attention, since they do not affect the genesis of the work and since the latter is concerned with the human condition in its more universal aspects. Art is not useful in the sense that it imparts concepts or makes a person better, so history of ideas (those found in literature) and ethical criticism are beside the point. Beckett is especially antagonistic to art that is socially *engagé*. The final passage of "La Peinture des van Velde" is a tirade against the contemporary pressure toward humane art, that is, art put to the service of social progress: "Le peintre qui dit: Tous les hommes sont frères. Allons, un petit cadavre. . . . Ils sont capables de nous démolir la poésie, la musique, la peinture et la pensée pendant 50 ans." In a violent attack on the bourgeois blindness and complacency that stifles goodness and perverts truth ("le pet du plus grand nombre") and beauty ("l'homme réuni"), he warns that a society dedicated to materialistic togetherness is likely to stone an art that is both solitary and productive of painful visions.

When he comes to criticism of a more directly aesthetic nature, Beckett is somewhat less ferocious, but he is still very much the artist vitally concerned with defending art as a valid and autonomous domain of human activity for which no substitute exists. And more specifically, he is determined to point out the peril of interposing between the spectator and the work considerations alien to the nature of art and likely to prevent immediate contact. General aesthetics is a "jeu charmant" but far removed from the individual work. Bad criticism replaces the painting with a grotesque parody of itself. For its authentic life of line and color, viewers over the centuries will substitute another life. "Ils vont le charger, le noircir, de la seule vie qui compte, celle des bipèdes sans plumes. Il finira par en crever. Peu importe. On le rafistolera. On le rabibochera. On lui cachera le sexe et on lui soutiendra la gorge. On lui foutra un gigot à la place de la fesse. . . ." The best of criticism ("hystérec-

tomies à la truelle") is a gross operation that kills the capacity of
the work to radiate its magic, to give birth to its offspring pleasure
for those few who are its lovers. The mania for evaluation is one of
the most dangerous aberrations of criticism. Paintings, since they
are not sausages, are neither good nor bad, but the categorizers
insist on fitting them into pigeonholes labeled "chefs-d'oeuvre,"
"navets," and "oeuvres de mérite." " 'Dali, c'est du pompier. Il ne
saurait faire autre chose.' Voilà ce qui s'appelle ne rien laisser au
hasard. On étrangle d'abord, puis on éventre." The ultimate effect
of such obsessive judging is to destroy the experience of the individual work. "L'impossible est fait . . . pour qu'il [l'amateur]
accepte à priori, pour qu'il rejette à priori, pour qu'il cesse de
regarder, pour qu'il cesse d'exister, devant une chose qu'il aurait
pu simplement aimer, ou trouver moche, sans savoir pourquoi."
While all true art lays bare the human condition, each work is
unique, and we cannot reason about the unique. The amateur, if
he allows himself to be subverted by the intellectuals, will end up
one day saying to himself after a visit to the Louvre, "Suis resté
trois minutes devant le sourire du Professeur Pater, à le regarder."
The *Mona Lisa* will have vanished behind a verbal veil, and all
direct knowledge of it will have become impossible.

CRITICAL PERSPECTIVES

The field of criticism has been narrowed, to say the least. In
his skepticism about the existence of any common denominator
between being and intellect, between art (of the new unintellectual
kind) and criticism, in his resolve to protect the domain of art from
the incursions of foreign forces that threaten to annex and disfigure
it, this poet (himself an intellectual) seems to leave little room for
more than the pleasurable insight deriving from the experience of
art. He terms his own essay a "bavardage désagréable et confus,"
the main effect of which is to ruin the pleasure of the artistic experience that was its occasion: "Car il suffit que je réfléchisse à tous
les plaisirs que me donnaient, à tous les plaisirs que me donnent,
les tableaux d'A. van Velde . . . pour que je les sente m'échapper
dans un éboulement innombrable." He is quite aware that his criticism must seem arbitrary, schematic, twice removed from the mental images at the source of the painting, and he retreats to the cover
of a radical subjectivism: "Il n'a d'ailleurs été question à aucun
moment de ce que font ces peintres, ou croient faire, ou veulent

faire, mais uniquement de ce que je les vois faire"—not, however, without at least a gesture in the direction of a rapprochement. With added reservations and further shadings, it would no doubt be possible, he admits, though hardly worthwhile, to give his remarks a more persuasive appearance. Other similar statements in the essay open up critical perspectives. Images are more or less adequate with regard to the internal tensions they translate. How adequate not even the author always knows, which of course implies that sometimes he may know. The "amateur (éclairé)" can know not only how much he loves a work of art but sometimes why he loves it. Both possibilities suggest the hope of some productive link between interior vision, artistic image, and discursive writing. The authentic experience of a work of art is an absolute prerequisite, and to have it, the amateur must stop listening to the intellectuals and forget what he has read about art; and there is no guarantee at all that his vision is identical or even similar to the author's. The criticism that can thrive under such conditions obviously can lay no claim to universal validity or to scientific objectivity. It can, however, encompass both the subjective response and its stylistic occasion— as well as their interrelation.

Once he has cleared away the obstacles and apologized for the inadequacy of criticism, once he comes to discuss the paintings themselves, Beckett's remarks often reveal a nice blend of these two elements. The following is a good sample of a passage weighted on the impressionistic side.

> Que dire de ces plans qui glissent, ces contours qui vibrent, ces corps comme taillés dans la brume, ces équilibres qu'un rien doit rompre, qui se rompent et se reforment à mesure qu'on regarde? Comment parler de ces couleurs qui respirent, qui halètent? De cette stase grouillante? De ce monde sans poids, sans force, sans ombre?
>
> Ici tout bouge, nage, fuit, revient, se défait, se refait. Tout cesse, sans cesse. On dirait l'insurrection des molécules, l'intérieur d'une pierre un millième de seconde avant qu'elle ne se désagrège.

Typically, he undercuts it all with the ironic sally: "C'est ça, la littérature." Still, the lines are a masterful rendering of the impression of a chaotic flux of becoming and disintegration that is conveyed to the spectator, a rendering that is more an evocation through

439

images than an analytical description. The need to impart one's living impression without resorting to the cerebral dissection that kills, a need which for Beckett is imperious, leads to criticism that is re-creation. It is not at all surprising that such a critic should have moved on from re-creation to creation. The image is the mark of such criticism, and Beckett is a powerful maker of images in these essays: the line of literary tradition is not foreordained but unrolls "au fur et à mesure comme la bave de la limace"; the outside world may be painful, but the mind can be a refuge, as in the anecdote of the man "qui passait sa journée dans le Sacré Coeur pour ne plus avoir à le voir"; the symbol *par excellence* of the flight of time is the "jet d'urine"; intellectual painting "s'achève dans des tortillements d'enthymème"; natural space (as opposed to inner space) is defined as "celle qui tourne comme une toupie sous le fouet du soleil," for the macrocosm is "secoué par les frissons du temps." The examples could be multiplied many times over.

On occasion the writing becomes somewhat more analytical. Beckett explains the importance of the general divergence of style in the work of the two painters by arguing that for his task of translating the urgency and primacy of the interior vision, of portraying the thing in itself "coupée de ses amarres avec tout ce qui en faisait un simple échantillon de perdition, on dirait coupée de ses amarres avec elle-même," Bram van Velde needs a kind of "négligence catégorique" or "hautaine incurie," an "usage méprisant de moyens souverains," a mixture of "maîtrise" and "ennui." Such a style would be an irreparable mistake for Geer van Velde, who is concerned with complex objects caught up in becoming and must accelerate the process until the invisibility of objects becomes itself a visible object. "Voilà un travail d'une complexité diabolique et qui requiert un métier d'une souplesse et d'une légèreté extrêmes, un métier qui insinue plus qu'il n'affirme, qui ne soit positif qu'avec l'évidence fugace et accessoire du grand positif, du seul positif, du temps qui charrie."

Beckett understands style as a correlative of vision, not as its consequence or effect. Both arise spontaneously from the same occasion. Thus Bram van Velde's originality lies in his "objectivité prodigieuse," of which his style, "irraisonné . . . ingénu . . . noncombiné . . . mal-léché," is part. In the work of art, form and content are one; as they approach the representation of being (something or nothing?) they begin to disintegrate into formless-

440

ness and meaninglessness. When it comes to more detailed stylistic analysis, Beckett the critic and Beckett the *amateur d'art* (in the literal sense) part company. Analysis spoils appreciation, and for him the direct experience of art counts most. "La peinture des van Velde a d'autres secrets, qu'il serait facile de réduire (à l'impuissance) au moyen de ce qui précède. Mais je n'entends pas tout perdre." While admitting the possibility of a criticism that elucidates the correlation between image and response, between art and vision, he (and the Van Veldes) stress the second term and are reluctant to focus long on the first. Bram's artistic means, he writes, "ont la specificité d'un speculum, n'existent que par rapport à leur fonction. Il [Bram] ne s'y intéresse pas suffisamment pour en douter. Il ne s'intéresse qu'à ce qu'ils reflètent." The same is true for Geer. "C'est qu'au fond la peinture ne les intéresse pas. Ce qui les intéresse, c'est la condition humaine."

We come full circle, back to the starting point in the predicament of man, a creature blind, impotent, shaken back and forth by a terrier destiny, emitting the squeaks of an ineffectual art. To wonder about this unpleasant situation is only relatively less absurd than to question the nature, function, and quality of the squeaks. At the heart of all is being. The further from it we move the less authentically human we become. Art is closest (after seeing), especially the new art that is a sign of weakness, inadequacy, failure. "Perhaps the most perfect expression of Being," Beckett once said, "would be an ejaculation." Criticism, a form of the cerebral, is at a greater distance. Useful in its intellectual attacks on the products of intellect, in preparing the ground for in-tuition, in-sight, useful too in elucidating the nature, varieties, and goals of art, it can even illuminate artistic procedures, but it does so at a certain risk. It gains in value as it approaches the nature of art itself. For Beckett, as for Proust, "The artist is active, but negatively, shrinking from the nullity of extracircumferential phenomena, drawn in to the core of the eddy." In his pursuit of authentic self, he must plumb the " 'gouffre interdit à nos sondes.' " His inward, downward trajectory may uncover either this "pearl" that will "give the lie to our carapace of paste and pewter"[17]—or end in nothingness.

[17] *Proust*, pp. 48, 18, 19.

INDEX

This first study of Samuel Beckett's earliest writings, his poems and criticism from about 1929 to 1949, provides the opening chapter in the story of the unfolding of a formidable talent. Although not so well known as his plays, the poems are both powerful in their own right and, in their spontaneity and relative unguardedness, extremely revealing in the context of the mature work. Together with the criticism and other early prose they show the emergence of certain fundamental themes and aesthetic convictions and prefigure the spare asceticism of the novels and plays to come.

Professor Harvey introduces us not only to Beckett's poetry but to Beckett the poet. He combines detailed analysis of the poems with insights into the intellectual and physical world of the young Beckett, drawing on conversations with Beckett himself, on unpublished manuscripts, and on research in Ireland, England, and France. Along with these new biographical materials the author makes available for the first time the entire known corpus of Beckett's poetry, some of it previously inaccessible, as well as extensive excerpts from the early unpublished prose.

Here is convincing evidence that Beckett the explorer of inner space was already at work in these years